The Religion of Fools?

Superstition Past and Present

D1355003

OXFORD JOURNALS
OXFORD UNIVERSITY PRESS

OXFORD
UNIVERSITY PRESS

1 Great Clarendon Street, Oxford OX2 6DP

Oxford University Press is a department of the University of Oxford.
It furthers the University's objective of excellence in research, scholarship,
and education by publishing worldwide in

Oxford New York

Athens Auckland Bangkok Bogotá Buenos Aires Cape Town
Chennai Dar es Salaam Delhi Florence Hong Kong Istanbul Karachi
Kolkata Kuala Lumpur Madrid Melbourne Mexico City Mumbai Nairobi
Paris São Paulo Shanghai Singapore Taipei Tokyo Toronto Warsaw

with associated companies in Berlin Ibadan

Oxford is a registered trade mark of Oxford University Press
in the UK and in certain other countries

Published in the United Kingdom
by Oxford University Press Inc., New York

A catalogue for this book is available from the British Library

Library of Congress Cataloguing in Publication
Data (data available)

ISBN 0-19-956137-7
ISBN 978-0-19-956137-7

Subscription information for Past & Present is available
from:jnls.cust.serv@oxfordjournals.org

Typeset by Cepha Imaging Pvt Ltd, Bangalore, India
Printed by Bell and Bain Ltd, Glasgow, UK

Past and Present Supplements

Supplement 3, 2008

The Religion of Fools?
Superstition Past and Present
Edited by S. A. Smith and Alan Knight

The Religion of Fools?
Superstition Past and Present

CONTENTS

Contributions and Communications (two copies), editorial correspondence, etc., should be addressed to The Editors, *Past and Present*, 175 Banbury Road, Oxford OX2 7AW, UK. Tel: +44 (0)1865 512318; Fax: +44 (0)1865 310080; E-mail: editors@pastandpresent. org.uk. Intending contributors should write for a copy of 'Notes for Contributors'.

Introduction

S. A. Smith

In 'Science as a Vocation' (1918–19), Max Weber described modernity as a world 'robbed of gods'. 'The fate of our times', he wrote, 'is characterized by rationalization and intellectualization and, above all, by the "disenchantment of the world"'. This, he suggested, 'means that one can, in principle, master all things by calculation... One need no longer have recourse to magical means in order to master or implore the spirits, as did the savage, for whom such mysterious powers existed. Technical means and calculations perform that service.'[1] Weber's use of the term 'disenchantment' (*Entzauberung*) is significant, for it suggests he had in mind subjective experience as well as forms of social organization. 'The bearing of man', he writes, 'has been disenchanted and denuded of its mystical but inwardly genuine plasticity'. From the vantage point of the twenty-first century, one can only conclude that if a process of disenchantment was under way during the twentieth century, it was hugely uneven. As Wolfgang Behringer has recently observed, it is probable that a majority of the world's population today believes in witchcraft, which would mean, in absolute terms, that there are vastly more believers than there were in 1600.[2]

It was as a historian of the twentieth century that I was drawn to the problem of disenchantment and the apparent persistence of 'superstition' in the modern world. The Communist societies on which I work—the Soviet Union in the 1920s and 1930s and the People's Republic of China from 1949 to 1976—vigorously promoted 'disenchantment' of the world through state-coordinated efforts to root out what they called, in the Soviet case, 'religion and superstition' and in the Chinese case, 'feudal superstition'. Their aim was nothing less than to recast social life and popular culture along lines of science, rationality, and philosophical materialism through a combination of education, propaganda, physical destruction of religious institutions,

---

[1] From H. H. Gerth and C. Wright Mills (eds), *Max Weber: Essays in Sociology* (London, 1970), 155, 139.

[2] Wolfgang Behringer, *Witches and Witch-Hunts* (Cambridge, 2004), 7.

and the prosecution of religious and magical specialists. Yet the extent to which they failed—and the failure was a relative rather than an absolute one—is today glaringly evident. Following the fall of the Soviet Union in 1991, a rash of catchpenny books on fortune-telling and dream interpretation was published, faith healers (*extrasens*) appeared regularly on television, experts in astrology, apocalyptic prophecy and witchcraft were quick to advertise their services. That such interest is relatively 'respectable' is evident from the fact that in 2004 some parliamentarians hired Toizin Bergenov, a Siberian shaman, to purge the Russian duma of evil spirits that had been attracted by the negative energy of angry debates.[3] This resurgence of what had formerly been condemned as obscurantism was as nothing, compared with the explosion of once vilified religious practices that took place in China, as it beat a hasty retreat from Maoism in the 1980s. The era of economic reform saw a dizzying rush to rebuild temples and ancestral halls, a resurgence of spirit mediums and exorcists, and widespread enthusiasm for divination and feng shui. 'Jade emperors descended from heaven' emerged to lead some popular protests, and religious cults—most notoriously Falungong, on which the Communist government cracked down in 1999—are flourishing. Clearly, despite Weber's prediction, 'superstition' lives on in the modern world.

It was with 'superstition' in the modern world—and more particularly, 'superstition' in the non-western world—in mind that a conference was organized at the University of Essex in May 2005, sponsored by the journal *Past and Present* and the university's Department of History. *Superstition in Historical and Comparative Perspective* set itself the task of examining the meanings and practices associated with the term 'superstition' over a period of more than two millennia, beginning in classical Greece and ending in contemporary Cameroon, traversing classical Rome, early medieval China, medieval Islam, medieval and early-modern Europe, and modern Latin America and Africa en route.[4] Since the notion of *superstitio* was most influential in Europe, the conference was organized around a core of papers that dealt with superstition in medieval and early-modern Europe. This allowed for comparison of *superstitio* in Christendom with cognate notions and practices in societies where either the dominant faith tradition was non-Christian (Han China, medieval Syria) or where conversion to Christianity

---

[3] *The Times*, 15 May 2004.

[4] The title of the conference placed the word 'superstition' in inverted commas to signal that it was to be understood as a category of ascription. This is the sense in which the term is used in this introduction. It would be tedious, however, to put the term in inverted commas throughout.

was mediated through the experience of colonialism (Mexico, Cameroon, South Africa, Puerto Rico).[5]

In modern usage, superstition has a relatively clear sense. According to Collins Dictionary, it is 'irrational belief usually founded on ignorance or fear and characterised by obsessive reverence for omens, charms, etc.'[6] Most contemporary definitions point to irrationality as the central characteristic of superstition, the term generally denoting beliefs or practices founded upon a faulty, non-naturalistic understanding of cause and effect. This notion of superstition is very much a product of the Enlightenment. Prior to the eighteenth century, superstition signified 'bad religion' rather than 'bad science'.[7] If there were common elements in pre-Enlightenment conceptions of superstition, it is that the beliefs and practices so designated were either deemed to be impure or excessive from the standpoint of religious orthodoxy or were associated with the manipulation of occult—usually, demonic—powers. The modern understanding of superstition has generally lost this connection with religious orthodoxy, although it retains an association with magic. Much superstitious belief today is still rooted in a conception of the world as one animated by supernatural beings, forces or relations and, to that extent, may be seen as essentially magical in character. Much superstitious behaviour is premised on the assumption that certain powers are operative in human existence, often for ill, and that certain objects or formulae (a lucky bracelet, a St Christopher medal carried in one's car), certain actions (touching wood, crossing one's fingers), or the avoidance of certain actions (walking under a ladder, the number thirteen) can be used to deflect harm or promote good. Such practices are unlikely to derive any longer from a coherent magical world-view. They are more likely to spring from beliefs that are only partially articulated such as that luck can be manipulated or influenced by present behaviour; that coincidences have deeper meaning than random accident; or that elements of a situation—for example, at the start of a journey or at birth—can predict its outcome. Certain beliefs such as 'do not tempt fate', 'like cures like', 'begin well to continue well', 'anything unusual is likely to be threatening', seem to reflect a rather sombre view of existence, where death and injury are ever-present dangers,

---

[5] Dr Yahya Michot presented a paper to the conference on 'Superstition Between Entertainment and Religion: Ibn Taymiyya's Viewpoint' which will be published elsewhere.

[6] *Collins English Dictionary: Complete and Unabridged*, 6th edn (Glasgow, 2003), 1619.

[7] The phrase is taken from Mary O'Neil, 'Superstition' in Mircea Eliade (ed.), *The Encyclopedia of Religion* (16 vols.), vol. 14 (London, 1987), 165.

where pride, achievement, or good fortune risk being punished, and where neighbours are likely to be jealous of success.[8]

Once one moves beyond this cluster of beliefs, use of the term superstition becomes more contentious. Beliefs in witchcraft, vampires, or alien abduction would be seen by many as forms of superstition on the grounds that they are irrational beliefs rooted in fear or ignorance. Yet they are more articulate and coherent bodies of belief than, say, belief in lucky numbers or touching wood, and may often be held as a matter of intellectual conviction. This is even more true of systematic sets of beliefs such as those of astrology, which long passed out of the realm of legitimate science but which continues to provide the basis on which millions each day seek to descry their futures. Use of the term superstition would be still more contentious when applied to bodies of belief that do not directly invoke a notion of supernatural causation yet which conflict with mainstream science, such as many forms of alternative health therapy or belief in telepathy or extra-sensory perception. In view of the uncertain boundaries of the contemporary term, then, when organizing the conference we did not lay down any definition of superstition and were content to leave this to contributors to decide.

Historically, *superstitio*—along with its non-Christian cognates—has proved a remarkably flexible and capacious category that has performed a wide variety of ideological functions and communicated a wide variety of social concerns and anxieties. From a historical perspective, superstition appears primarily to be a pejorative label applied by adherents of a particular religious or ideological orthodoxy to beliefs and practices of which they disapprove, usually those of the less educated and less powerful members of society. As a category of ascription, it may tell us more about those doing the ascribing than it does about the people so described.[9] In his chapter Richard Gordon offers insight into the way in which in classical Rome use of the term served to bolster elite status by instantiating claims to belong to a 'community of sanctioned practice', legitimating its right to pass judgment on others, protecting its own intellectual claims from critical scrutiny and drawing attention away from areas of dispute, contradiction or anomaly. Looked at

---

[8] Steve Roud, *The Penguin Guide to Superstitions of Britain and Ireland* (London, 2003), x, xii.

[9] I use the term 'category of ascription', rather than, say, 'category of attribution' or 'category of evaluation', because in social theory ascription is a term generally encountered in discussions of social status, for example, in debate about 'achieved' versus 'ascribed' status. My use of the term is intended to signal that the attribution of the label 'superstitious' is not only about policing the boundaries of acceptable knowledge but also about the production and negotiation of status between differentially empowered groups.

historically, superstition was largely, in the words of Jean-Claude Schmitt, a 'discourse of authority, order and constraint', concerned with the ways in which defenders of orthodoxy used linguistic and institutional forms of power to police the bounds of acceptable knowledge.[10] Yet if the category of superstition is primarily one of ascription, this raises the interesting philosophical question of whether superstition is to be understood purely discursively, as a construct whose meaning is determined only within a specific historical and cultural field. If so, how does one account for the remarkable similarities between beliefs and practices classed as superstitious across different cultures and epochs? Does this justify treating superstition as a concept that denotes a class of really existing phenomena—ways of thinking about the way the world operates, particular practices designed to invoke forms of supernatural protection—that have features in common. Our contributors differ on this question. Most are content to treat superstition as a label, a historically changing category of ascription. In his contribution, however, Alan Knight offers a trenchant defence of superstition as a category that denotes real behaviour, specifically behaviour having a 'non-scientific, non-naturalistic, hence in some sense supernatural, rationale'. His view is broadly in line with that of contemporary psychologists and social scientists of an earlier vintage. Hugh Bowden, too, assumes that superstition has a referent in the real and makes the stimulating suggestion that the kinds of practices satirized as *deisidaimonia* in classical Greece would today be classed as obsessive-compulsive disorder. In the second part of this introduction, this issue is explored further through an examination of the overlap between superstitious beliefs and practices and those of magic and religion. First, however, let us try to trace the shifting discourse of superstition from the ancient world to the present day, seeking to demonstrate how superstition has been used to define and shore up issues of religious identity and authority, ideological orthodoxy and political power.

The development of the category of superstition

Like most ancient peoples, the Greeks worshipped a plethora of gods and inferior spiritual beings known as *daimones*, and sacrifices to these supernatural entities formed a key part of civic life. Hugh Bowden suggests that the term *deisidaimonia*, literally 'fear of the gods', was initially understood in a positive sense, to mean 'respectful piety'. Plato, Xenocrates, Aristotle and other philosophers assumed that beings who were superior in nature and

---

[10] Jean-Claude Schmitt, 'Les superstitions', in Jacques le Goff (ed.), *Histoire de la France religieuse*, vol. 1 (Paris, 1988), 423.

power would also be superior ethically, and they chose the word diamones to denote those lower spiritual beings, largely evil and certainly dangerous, who loomed large in popular belief.[11] From the late fourth century BCE, the term deisidaemonia thus took on a pejorative meaning, coming to signify an unhealthy attitude towards the gods. For Theophrastus (c.370–285 BCE), the *deisidaimon* was one who displayed an obsessive, fearful attitude towards supernatural beings; for Plutarch (c.46–c.120CE) he was someone whose fundamental orientation towards them was based on mistrust. *Deisidaimonia* thus acquired the sense of religion that had forgotten the necessity of balance and moderation. It is use of the term in this sense—which would be translated into Latin as *superstitio*—that inaugurated the tradition in which superstition served as a category buttressing a notion of 'true religion'. *Superstitiosus*, as an adjective, is found in Latin as early as the works of Plautus (254–184 BCE), where it is used in the context of divination, a practice at the heart of the *religio* of the Roman world. Subsequently, however, coloured by the Greek philosophers' critique of *deisidaimonia*, the term came to signify religion taken to excess.[12] As Richard Gordon explains, *superstitio* as a noun is of relatively late origin, appearing in extant Latin literature only in the work of Cicero in the first half of the first century BCE. For Cicero, Lucretius, and Seneca, it denoted excessive religious practices which, for Cicero, in particular, were associated with the lower orders: 'Those who spent whole days in prayer and offered sacrifices that their children might outlive them are called "superstitious"'.[13] These writers also used the term in a second sense to denote non-Roman religion, and by the first century BCE, *superstitio*, especially when applied to foreign religions, carried a sense of political threat, a connotation that *deisidaimonia* lacked entirely.[14] From the second century CE, *superstitio* was often used to denote the illicit cults, especially Christianity, that refused to honour the gods and the emperor, even by burning incense.[15] Tacitus (c.56–c.117CE) described the spreading Christianity of his day as a dangerous 'recurrent superstition' that had invaded Rome from Judea.[16] *Superstitio* thus came to focus political concern around the question of how the authorities should relate to religious beliefs and practices that were not part of state religion. At the same time, the term continued to carry earlier and broader

---

[11] Dale B. Martin, *Inventing Superstition: From the Hippocratics to the Christians* (Cambridge MA, 2004), 76–7.

[12] Denise Grodzynski, 'Superstitio', *Revue des études anciennes*, 76 (Jan–Jun 1974), 39.

[13] Cicero, 'On the Nature of the Gods', 2.28. Cited in Martin, *Inventing Superstition*, 130.

[14] Martin, *Inventing Superstition*, 131.

[15] Grodzynski, 'Superstitio', 47.

[16] Martin, *Inventing Superstition*, 2.

associations, referring to matters as diverse as divination outside the framework of Roman religion, magic and excessive religious fear.[17]

Though riven by division from the first, Christianity established itself rather early as a more centralized and institutionalized religion than other contemporary faiths. Spreading through the Roman empire in the third century, it succeeded in converting between 5 per cent and 10 per cent of the population by 300, mainly in the eastern provinces.[18] Fusing Jewish myths of the origin of evil with the *daemones* of the Graeco-Roman tradition, the early church fathers deployed the category of *deisdaimonia/superstitio* to denounce the Roman gods as idols and their oracles as the mouthpieces of *daemones*.[19] This redefinition of *superstitio* as idolatry was at first restricted to polemicists, but by the end of the fourth century it had become accepted as the paramount meaning of the term in Roman law. Constantine's bestowal of unrestricted freedom of worship on Christians by the Edict of Milan (313) caused it to grow rapidly, as urban and administrative elites were drawn to it by the prospect of social advancement. Church and state cooperated intermittently to root out paganism, although it was not until 438 that the eastern Emperor Theodosius II (c.408–50), at a time of repeated pressure from Attila and the Huns, issued a code that banned all pagan rites as *superstitio*.[20]

St Augustine of Hippo (354–430) played a seminal role in defining the Christian conception of *superstitio*, a conception that would remain authoritative for the next millennium. He construed *superstitio* within his larger theory of signs. Signs, he argued, are things whose significance exceeds their sensory appearance and are used to communicate. They are of two types: natural signs, such as smoke, and conventional signs (*signa data*), such as writing or music. Certain conventional signs, including superstitions, are superfluous or positively harmful since they are a medium through which men and demons can communicate. This idea of *pacta significationum*— 'pacts about certain meanings agreed with daemons by contract'—was to shape subsequent thinking about superstition, although it was not until St Thomas Aquinas that the idea of a pact with the devil acquired precision.[21]

---

[17] M. Salzman, 'Superstitio in the Codex Theodosianus and the Persecution of Pagans', *Vigiliae Christianae*, 41 (1987), 172.

[18] Frank Trombley, 'Overview: the Geographical Spread of Christianity' in Margaret M. Mitchell and Frances M. Young (eds), *The Cambridge History of Christianity, vol. 1, Origins to Constantine* (Cambridge, 2006), 313.

[19] Schmitt, 'Les superstitions', 430.

[20] Salzman, 'Superstitio', 176.

[21] Dieter Harmening, *Superstitio: Uberlieferungs- und theoriegeschichtliche Untersuchungen zur kirchlich-theologischen Aberglaubensliteratur des Mittelalters* (Berlin, 1979), 305–8.

Augustine reinforced the association of *superstitio* with the demonic, yet continued to use the term in the ways it had been used in the ancient world: to signal rites improperly performed or performed to excess and what he called 'thousands of the most frivolous practices', such as returning to bed if one sneezed while putting on one's slippers.[22] Even such silly practices, however, were a potential danger in Augustine's eyes, since human folly could easily be exploited by *daemones*.

By Augustine's time, the western Roman empire was disintegrating as a unified political entity as Germanic peoples from northern and eastern Europe moved in by migration and invasion. By the fifth and sixth centuries, western Europe had become Christian, but the Church was losing the support of strong central institutions, spiritual as well as temporal, as it ceased to be an urban religion and expanded into agrarian society. The effect of harsh laws against paganism was still felt—the destruction of pagan temples was still continuing 250 years after Constantine—but the triumph of the Church was essentially 'not one of obliteration but of widening embrace and assimilation.'[23] Much as it might fulminate against paganism, the Church was pragmatic enough to recognize that certain practices could be assimilated, with pagan heroes converted into Christian saints and pagan festivals converted to Christian festivals. The attitude was epitomized in the advice given by Pope Gregory the Great to Bishop Augustine on the eve of his commencement of missionary work in England (597–604): 'the temples of the idols . . . should on no account be destroyed'.[24] In general, it seems that public traces of paganism were indeed eliminated, whereas it proved much harder to curtail private practices such as the use of auguries, amulets, or witchcraft.[25] Churchmen, such as Caesarius of Arles (d.542) urged dogged pastoral work to eliminate the residues of Germanic and Celtic paganism and usually referred to these as *superstitio*. Homilies against *superstitio* increased during the sixth and seventh centuries and local church councils and bishops produced lists of forbidden practices—*indiculi superstitionum*—although punishments seem to have been fairly light. Churchmen might champion the superior efficacy of sacraments, blessings, and exorcisms against magic

---

[22] *De Doctrina Christiana*, 2:20. St Augustine, *The Confessions, The City of God, On Christian Doctrine*, 2nd edn (Chicago, 1990), 728.

[23] Ramsay Macmullen *Christianity and Paganism in the Fourth to Eighth Centuries* (New Haven, 1997), 158.

[24] Valerie Flint, *The Rise of Magic in Early Medieval Europe* (Princeton, 1991), 308, 205, 267, 213.

[25] Ian N. Wood, 'Pagan Religions and Superstitions East of the Rhine from the Fifth to the Ninth Centuries', in G. Ausenda (ed.), *After Empire: Towards an Ethnology of Europe's Barbarians* (Woodbridge, 1995), 253–68.

charms and amulets, but it is doubtful whether many of the laity appreciated the distinction between rites that drew on divine and those that drew on demonic power.[26]

From the seventh century, aided in the eighth century by the rising power of the Frankish kingdom, the papacy extended its control across western Christendom. In 742 a reforming church synod, whose decisions were widely circulated, forbade the casting of lots and other forms of divination along with the use of amulets and incantations. By the ninth century, with Charlemagne ruling most of western Christendom, the Church no longer seems to have felt threatened by paganism, although scholars disagree as to the extent to which paganism persisted among the laity. A handful of theologians were positively sceptical about the efficacy of magic. The *Canon Episcopi*, collected and formulated by Abbot Regino of Prüm (*c.*840–915), condemned pagan practices as *superstitio*, yet played down the danger of sorcery on the grounds that it implied that demonic powers could rival those of God. Rather later, King Kálmán of Hungary (r.1095–1116) passed a law that denied the existence of witches, a view for which he might have been hauled before the Inquisition five hundred years later.[27] Historians today question the notion of 'Carolingian scepticism'; but it seems that in this period the Church felt more confident that it could deal with the threat posed by *superstitio* than it would feel after 1000.[28]

By the time the Slavic peoples were converted to Christianity in the ninth and tenth centuries, relations between the Byzantine Greeks and the Latin West were under great strain, and tension came to a head with the Great Schism of 1054. Russia, which was converted by official fiat in 988, remained under the authority of the Greek patriarch of Constantinople even after that city fell to the Ottomans in 1453. Initially, Christianity was confined mainly to cities and monasteries but it gradually reached into the fields and forests.[29] The political and territorial consolidation of Muscovy encouraged greater assertiveness on the part of the Russian Orthodox Church, and in 1589 it established its own patriarchate. By the sixteenth century, the lives of the

[26] Karen Jolly, 'Medieval Magic: Definitions, Beliefs, Practices', in Marijke Gijswijt-Hofstra, Brian P. Levack, and Roy Porter (eds), *Witchcraft and Magic in Europe: the Middle Ages* (London, 2002), 17.

[27] Peter Dinzelbacher, 'Superstition', in Richard Golden (ed), *The Encyclopedia of Witchcraft: the Western Tradition* (Santa Barbara, 2006), 4, 1091–2.

[28] Michael D. Bailey, *Magic and Superstition in Europe: A Concise History from Antiquity to the Present* (Lanham, MA, 2007), 69, 91.

[29] Simon Franklin and Jonathan Shepard, *The Emergence of Rus 750–1200* (London, 1996), 230.

population were regulated according to the church calendar, rites of passage were marked by Orthodox sacraments, and the cult of saints and of miraculous icons was entrenched.[30] In the process of conversion, however, the usual compromises with paganism had been made, and in 1551 the Church Council (Stoglav) made a preliminary attempt to standardize ecclesiastical practice and reform public morals, condemning raucous popular amusements, demanding the execution of fortune-tellers, astrologers, and magicians, and inveighing against practices such as omen reading, dream interpretation, or bathing in a river or lake during a thunderstorm.[31] The Stoglav may tell us more about clerical concerns than about the resilience of supposed 'pagan' practices, but whatever its significance, its practical effect on popular religion was limited.

Of the world's faith traditions, Islam alone saw itself as a named entity from the first (the word 'Islam' occurs eight times in the Qur'ān). Within less than a century of the death of Muhammad (632), it had spread as far west as the Atlantic and as far east as Central Asia, but in the process of expansion the unity that had characterized its first decades was fractured by political conflict and socio-cultural division. Over the ensuing centuries, contrasting traditions emerged that ranged from the charismatic Shi'ite cult of saints and imams in Iran to the austere legalism of the followers of Muhammad ibn 'Abd al-Wahhab at-Tamimi (1703–92) in what would become Saudi Arabia. Different cultures became islamized, as the Qur'ān, the hadīth (traditions relating the words and deeds of Muhammad), and the five pillars of faith (the confession of faith, the five daily prayers, alms, fasting during Ramadān, pilgrimage to Mecca) took root, but at the same time, elements of pre-Islamic cultures became grafted on to the new religion.[32] Islam, for example, absorbed a rich culture of divination from Persia (although Shi'ites generally took a dim view of divination, as an irrational if not impious act). In due course, a sophisticated Arabic literature on divination developed that would become a source of fascination to intellectuals in twelfth-century Europe.[33] From Morocco to Indonesia, the use of charms and amulets (including texts

---

[30] Daniel H. Kaiser, 'Quotidian Orthodoxy', in Valerie A. Kivelson and Robert H. Greene (eds), *Orthodox Russia: Belief and Practice Under the Tsars* (University Park PA, 2003), 179–92.

[31] Robert O. Crummey, *The Formation of Muscovy, 1304–1613* (London, 1987), 119; Russell Zguta, *Russian Minstrels: A History of the Skomorokhi* (University Park PA, 1978), 61.

[32] Mark R. Woodward, 'Popular Religion', in John L. Esposito (ed.), *The Oxford Encyclopedia of the Modern Islamic World*, (New York, 2001), 336–8.

[33] Toufic Fahd, *La divination arabe: études religieuses, sociologiques et folkloriques sur le milieu natif d'Islam* (Leiden, 1966).

from the Qur'ān), the invocation of jinns, belief in the evil eye, sorcery, omens, and numerology became hallmarks of different Islamic cultures.[34] In South Asia, a sequence of Arab traders, central Asian and Afghan conquerors and migrants and, finally, Turkic Mughals introduced Islam where it interacted with the tribal customs and 'Hindu' faith to produce local forms characterized by the worship of charismatic saints (sufis), possessed of semimagical and healing powers, celebration of the birthday of Muhammad, music and dancing.[35] These or similar local practices were frowned upon by many of the ʿulamā', the religious scholars, and certainly by those of a more puritanical disposition such as the great medieval theologian Shaykh al-Islâm Ibn Taymiyya (1263–1328). He affirmed the primacy of scripture and the sharī'a and inveighed against deviations that he associated with *bid'ah* (innovation, reformation) and *shirk* (idolatry). He took particular exception to the veneration of saints, since it flew in the face of the Qur'ān's insistence on the absolute power and majesty of God. Centuries later, he would become a major influence on the theology of ibn 'Abd al-Wahhab, the inspiration of present-day Wahhabis.[36] 'His writings', a present-day scholar has written, 'were like a time bomb planted in the fourteenth and detonated in the eighteenth century whose shocks are still reverberating across the Islamic world'.[37] By no means all religious scholars were so intransigent in their attitudes to folk Islam. In South Asia and Indonesia, rural mullahs generally did their best to purge popular practice of un-Islamic innovations, yet their often imperfect knowledge of the sharī'a meant that they viewed, for example, the use of amulets as entirely orthodox.

China's pluralist religious field makes it distinct from that of medieval Christendom and Islam, although the absence of a central authority regulating religious affairs has parallels with the latter. Some scholars are reluctant to see the three traditions of Confucianism, Taoism and Buddhism—especially

---

[34] T. Fahd, 'Rukya (Charms)' *Encyclopaedia of Islam* VIII: 600a; Ph. Marçais, 'Ayn (Evil Eye)', ibid., VIII: 600a; T. Fahd, 'Fa'l' (Omens)', ibid.: II: 758b.

[35] Rafiuddin Ahmed, 'Popular Religion in South Asia', in *Oxford Encyclopedia of the Modern Islamic World*, 346–50.

[36] It is not without irony that Ibn Taymiyya should himself become the target 350 years later of another scourge of the superstitious, Pierre Bayle, who accused him of reinforcing 'sotte credulité' because of his hostility to the translation into Arabic of the Greek philosophers. Jonathan Israel, *Enlightenment Contested: Philosophy, Modernity and the Emancipation of Man, 1670-1752* (Oxford, 2006), 621.

[37] Frederick M. Denny, '"God's Friends": the Sanctity of Persons in Islam', in Richard Kieckhefer and George D. Bond (eds), *Sainthood: its Manifestations in World Religions* (Berkeley, 1988), 77.

Confucianism—as religions at all; yet they share certain family resemblances with the modern conception of religion insofar as they have canonical scriptures, a liturgy, clerical specialists and training centres. To complicate matters, the religion practised by most of the population corresponds to none of these traditions, although it is influenced by all three; and it fits much less well the modern conception of religion, since it is diffuse in nature and its local rituals are variable. Conventionally, the Han dynasty (206 BCE–220 CE), the subject of T. H. Barrett's chapter, is seen as the period when Confucianism was constructed as a set of cosmological and ethical doctrines serving the interests of state, although Barrett suggests that this is an oversimplification.[38] He deals mainly with the period of civil strife and rapid social change that accompanied the disintegration of the Han dynasty, a period when Buddhism and Taoism had not yet established themselves as separate, institutionalized religions. He suggests that official concern with *yin* practice—a term that connotes licentious, illicit, or excessive practices—particularly with the suppression of 'licentious cults' (*yinsi*), may mark a trend towards a more exclusive conception of religion. For more than 400 years following the collapse of the Han dynasty, China lacked a unified central government. This was a period of cultural efflorescence in which Buddhism and Taoism established themselves. Buddhism reached the peak of its influence in the early Tang dynasty (618–906), when unified government was once again re-established, and by the late Tang the impact of Taoism on popular religious culture was profound. Confucian polemics against the two religions erupted sporadically, and there were periodic efforts at suppression, but the state's policy in general was one of cooption. Indeed such was the potency of Confucianism as a socio-ethical orthodoxy that both religions accommodated to it.[39] Buddhist and Taoist elites from time to time sought to purge local practice of excesses and improprieties, but their efforts never went unchallenged; and by the time of the Song dynasty (960–1279), Buddhist elites were content to leave lay practice alone. Taoist elites proved rather more energetic in launching periodic drives to suppress 'licentious shrines' or 'licentious sacrifices' (*yinsi*), usually when these featured animal sacrifices, worship of unruly ghosts and nature spirits, or spirit mediums, but their capacity to reform local religion declined over time. More commonly, Taoism absorbed local deities into the orthodox pantheon, although it was probably less

---

[38] Kwang-ching Liu, 'Introduction' in Kwang-Ching Liu (ed.), *Orthodoxy in Late Imperial China*, (Berkeley, 1990), 4–5.

[39] Richard Shek, 'Taoism and Orthodoxy: the Loyal and Filial Sect' in Kwang-Ching Liu and Richard Shek (eds), *Heterodoxy in Late Imperial China* (Honolulu, 2004), 149.

successful in this than Christianity, not least because of the absence of a centralizing authority.[40]

During the Ming (1368–1644) and Qing (1644–1911) dynasties, the authorities sought to propagate Confucian values among the populace, chiefly through the promotion of ancestor worship. Scholar-officials and local gentry struggled for moral authority with Buddhist and Taoist monks, and all intervened at times to mould local rituals in ways they considered theologically, aesthetically and politically acceptable.[41] Elites ruthlessly suppressed the millenarian Buddhist sects that sprang up in this period, which they judged to be unequivocally 'heterodox' (*xie*), but proved more tolerant of cults they judged to be merely ignorant, deluded or wasteful. From time to time, magistrates shut down illicit temples or prosecuted illicit cults, such as that of the greedy and lascivious Wutong, god of wealth, and attacked spirit mediums, whose rituals of ecstatic possession offended Confucian norms of propriety. Yet the capacity of the authorities to purge popular cults of elements not in conformity with the canonical scriptures remained limited.[42] The gap between the rather austere Confucianism of elites and the more prodigal and expressive religion of the masses probably increased in the late-imperial period, just as the gulf between elite and popular culture widened in Europe at roughly the same time.[43]

From the tenth century, the population in western Europe grew and urban centres expanded for the first time since the break-up of the Roman empire. Ecclesiastical and secular elites imposed new forms of dependency on cultivators of the soil. During the twelfth century, intellectual life blossomed as cathedral schools and universities appeared, their growth spurred by the demand for clerics to staff the expanding bureaucracies of Church and state. Governments and legal systems became more structured and the Church, menaced by heretical challenges from the Waldensians and the Cathars from the late twelfth century, was pressed into clarifying the parameters of orthodox belief and practice.[44] As canon law developed and as ecclesiastical

---

[40] Paul R. Katz, 'Taoism and Local Cults: A Case Study of Marshal Wen', in Kwang-Ching Liu and Richard Shek, *Heterodoxy in Late Imperial China* (Honolulu, 2004), 175, 196.

[41] Romeyn Taylor, 'Official Religion in the Ming', in Denis Twitchett and Frederick W. Mote (eds), *Cambridge History of China*, vol. 8, part 2, *The Ming Dynasty, 1368–1644* (Cambridge, 1998), 886–9.

[42] Donald S. Sutton, 'Shamanism in the Eyes of Ming and Qing Elites', in Kwang-Ching Liu and Richard Shek (eds), *Heterodoxy in Late Imperial China* (Honolulu, 2004), 209–37.

[43] Katz, 'Taoism', 229. See Peter Burke on the loss of biculturalism of the elites: Peter Burke, *Popular Culture in Early Modern Europe* (London, 1978), 280–1.

[44] Bailey, *Magic and Superstition*, 77–9.

courts emerged, law increasingly became an instrument for regulating religious deviance, with specialised officials—inquisitors—appointed to root out heretics and violators of Church law. One facet of the twelfth-century renaissance was the development of an increasingly sophisticated and rarefied theology of the demonic by scholastic philosophers. William of Auvergne (c.1180–1249), bishop of Paris, and Albertus Magnus (1200–80), a German Dominican, combined Arabic learning with Aristotelian philosophy to defend a notion of 'natural' magic. Generally, however, magic came to arouse suspicion because of the fascination of a 'clerical underworld', to use Richard Kieckhefer's term, with black magic, alchemy and astrology.[45]

St Thomas Aquinas (1225–74), synthesising Aristotelian thought with Augustine's theology of signs, did much to firm up the association of *superstitio* with the demonic pact. *Superstitio*, he averred, is 'a vice opposed to the virtue of religion by excess . . . either because it offers divine worship to something not deserving of it; or it offers worship in some manner which is unfitting'.[46] The offering of worship to a being other than God was clearly idolatrous and represented an 'explicit' pact (*pactum expressum*) with the devil. The worshipping of God in an unfitting manner was less serious, but still represented an 'implicit' pact (*pactum tacitum*). Aquinas offered the following example in relation to the wearing of relics: 'If it is out of confidence in God and the saints, whose relics they are, this is not wrong. But if account were taken of some irrelevance, for example, that the locket is triangular and the like, which has no bearing on the reverence due to God and the saints, it would be superstitious and wrong.'[47] Such 'trivial nonsense' represented an implicit pact since by focusing on external signs, rather than on the worship of God, one left oneself open to the intrusion of demonic power. The problem was that since the Church itself dealt primarily in signs, Aquinas was forced back into arguing that only the Church could arbitrate between licit and illicit signs.

In this period, the prime concern of the Church appears to have been with heresy and magic, now understood as the deliberate manipulation of occult powers, rather than with *superstitio*. Nevertheless, the growth in the number of preachers, the appointment of inquisitors and the spread of annual confession after 1215 led to increased knowledge about the beliefs and practices of the populace, especially in the countryside. This fed the curiosity of the ecclesiastical authorities about the use of words, objects,

---

[45] Richard Kieckhefer, *Magic in the Middle Ages* (Cambridge, 1990), 12, 183.

[46] St Thomas Aquinas, *Summa theologiae, vol. 40, Superstition and Irreverence*, eds Thomas F. O'Meara and Michael J. Duffy (London, 1968), 5.

[47] Aquinas, *Summa*, 85.

gestures, and holy things for unauthorized purposes.[48] In his chapter, Michael Bailey shows that after 1400 the authorities revealed a new concern about the legitimacy of such practices as the use of charms, amulets, spells, or healing potions as they turned their gaze on *superstitio* among the laity. On the one hand, this reflected the increased capacity of church and secular courts to regulate popular practice and, on the other, a growing concern on the part of leading churchmen with the need for reform. The rise of learned demonology underpinned this intensified interest in the religious life of the people. By the early fifteenth century, the idea of witchcraft as a diabolic conspiracy, complete with sabbaths, sexual congress with the devil and marks of the devil, was fully elaborated.[49] By the middle of the century, it was being disseminated through sermons, ballads, and woodcuts, although historians disagree about the extent to which popular belief in *maleficium* (malevolent magic) was reconfigured by learned demonology. The convergence of belief in harmful magic with learned demonology, combined with the inquisitorial structures and procedures developed during the preceding two centuries, were factors that propelled the increase in the number of witch trials that began around 1430 in the western Alps. Stephen Bowd's chapter shows that witchcraft trials in the Val Camonica in northern Italy in the late-fifteenth and early-sixteenth centuries were fully articulated within the demonological paradigm. If learned demonology provided the intellectual rationale for witchcraft prosecutions, however, it is doubtful that it was the direct cause of the upsurge in witch trials, which peaked in the years between 1580 and 1620 and which was heavily concentrated in the fragmented territories of the Holy Roman Empire.[50] For most accusations of witchcraft were brought not by the authorities but by villagers and townsfolk who believed they were victims of *maleficium*. Increased popular anxiety about witchcraft appears to have stemmed primarily from social and economic factors, such as dislocation caused by crop failure, price inflation and epidemics—possibly connected to the Little Ice Age—and compounded after 1618 by the devastation of the Thirty Years War.[51]

With the Reformation, Protestants unleashed a ferocious onslaught on superstition of all kinds, massively expanding the category to embrace rituals that had hitherto been central elements of Christian orthodoxy, such as the seven sacraments, the invocation of saints, masses for the dead, vows and

---

[48] Harmening, *Superstitio*, 33–42.
[49] Bailey, *Magic and Superstition*, 127.
[50] Bailey, *Magic and Superstition*, 165.
[51] Behringer, *Witches and Witch-Hunts*, 88, 131; Alison Rowlands, *Witchcraft Narratives in Germany: Rothenburg, 1561–1652* (Manchester, 2003).

fasting. In accordance with the doctrine of justification by faith alone, reformers contended that humans could not access divine power through mere ritual acts, which must therefore be condemned as forms of idolatry. Calvin lambasted 'sacrileges' and 'abominations' from astrology—although he made an exception of what he called 'natural' astrology—to transubstantiation, condemning them as either 'pure human invention' or 'devilish phantasmagoria' that detracted from the glory of God.[52] Beneath the violent theological diatribes between Catholics and Reformers certain shared assumptions persisted. Both continued to believe that the devil operated within the natural world, although their remedies for dealing with the demonic differed: Catholics continued to rely on sacraments and rituals while Protestants relied on prayer and God's providence. As Alison Rowlands' chapter shows, however, Protestant clerics may have condemned recourse to spells or charms, yet Protestant layfolk were not prepared to give up practical ways of accessing magical power, which they creatively extended to include 'reformed' devices such as incombustible portraits of Luther.[53] Catholics and Protestants both continued to think of the material world as part of the cosmic order and thus susceptible to supernatural intervention; yet in attacking as idolatrous the notion that material objects and practices can transmit divine power, Protestant theologians helped to firm up the boundary between the spiritual and material realms.[54] A distinction emerged, for example, between supernatural 'miracles', where God intervened directly in creation, and 'marvels', or preternatural events, which depended on secondary causes, including the work of angels and demons. In the long term, this paved the way for a more materialist understanding of the operation of the natural world.[55]

After 1570, a process of confessionalization got under way in which competing Churches crafted clear-cut identities for themselves. The clergy of different denominations strove to instruct their members in the doctrines and forms of worship distinctive to their confession, often in tandem with

---

[52] Jean Delumeau, 'Les reformateurs et la superstition', in *Actes du colloque L'Amiral de Coligny et son temps*, (Paris, 1974), 451–87.

[53] Stuart Clark, *Thinking with Demons: the Idea of Witchcraft in Early Modern Europe* (Oxford, 1997).

[54] Carlos M. N. Eire, *War Against the Idols: The Reformation of Worship from Erasmus to Calvin* (Cambridge, 1986).

[55] Willem Frijhoff, 'Popular Religion', in Stewart J. Brown and Timothy Tackett (eds), *The Cambridge History of Christianity*, vol. 7, *Enlightenment, Reawakening and Revolution, 1660–1815* (Cambridge, 2006), 188–9.

secular elites who struggled to regulate behaviour in public places.[56] Johann Ludwig Hartmann, the ecclesiastical Superintendent of the Lutheran city of Rothenburg ob der Tauber, and the subject of Rowlands's paper, exemplifies the new brand of conscientious cleric seeking to enforce 'decency and good order' in worship and public morals. For both Protestant and Catholic reformers, a key aim was to deter ordinary folk from 'seeking success and security in their daily lives by their own efforts'.[57] With the Counter-Reformation, the regional offices of the Roman Inquisition subjected parish clergy to much closer scrutiny, concerned that many were unable to distinguish legitimate means of access to supernatural power, such as handwritten *brevi* containing biblical texts, from illegitimate ones, such as reciting verses from St John's gospel to cure fever. The number of prosecutions of Catholic layfolk for involvement in magical healing, divination and love magic increased in this period.[58] Superstitions—and the word was now invariably used in the plural—were defined and elaborated with increasing sophistication as reason came to organize the domain of Catholic theology.[59] With time, the field of rejected excesses became ever wider, as evidenced by the *Traité des superstitions* (1679) of Abbé Jean-Baptiste Thiers (1606–1703), which was designed to purge piety of credulity and belief in false miracles.[60] Yet if the laity on both sides of the Reformation divide acquired a much stronger sense of confessional identity, they proved at the same time ingenious in deflecting, adapting or reconfiguring top-down efforts to rid their faith of superstitious beliefs, customs, and festivals.

From around 1620, Russia's ecclesiastical and secular elites fell under the influence of ideas emanating from Kiev and other Orthodox centres of the Polish state, a process that gathered pace after 1650. The Polish word, *zabobony*, a translation of *superstitio*, was now occasionally used to denote beliefs and practices deemed to be at variance with Orthodoxy. Tsar Aleksei Mikhailovich (r.1645–76) took the lead in driving through reforms proposed by Patriarch Nikon to standardize worship and improve the morals of clergy and laity. In 1648, he drafted a decree, *On the Righting of Morals and the*

---

[56] Diarmaid MacCulloch, *Reformation: Europe's House Divided, 1490–1700* (London, 2003), xxiv.

[57] Clark, *Thinking with Demons*, 474.

[58] Mary R. O'Neill, 'Sacerdote ovvero strione: Ecclesiastical and Superstitious Remedies in 16th Century Italy', in Steven L. Kaplan (ed.), *Understanding Popular Culture: Europe from the Middle Ages to the Nineteenth Century* (Berlin, 1984), 60.

[59] Bernard Dompnier, 'Les hommes d'Église et la superstition entre XVIIe et XVIIIe siècles' in B. Dompnier (ed.), *La Superstition à l'âge des Lumières* (Paris, 1998), 13.

[60] Dompnier, 'Les hommes d'Église', 23–4.

Abolition of Superstition, which aimed to ensure that divine service at parish level was performed in full and to eliminate 'pagan' revels, especially those connected to folk entertainers (*skomorokhi*). Four years later, sorcery was made a capital offence.[61] By the 1680s, Church leaders had forced through the new liturgical order but at the expense of a schism that saw Old Believers set up communities to uphold the old liturgy. The hierarchy made an effort to assert its authority to recognize saints and miracle-working icons, but its capacity to impose its norms on lay piety remained limited, certainly by the standards of the confessionalizing Protestant and Catholic Churches.[62] Only at this time did church services begin routinely to include sermons; only in the early eighteenth century was annual confession made mandatory; and it was well into the eighteenth century before parish registers and confessional books became widespread.[63]

From the second half of the seventeenth century in western Europe, and from the eighteenth century in central and eastern Europe, the number of witch trials fell. This seems to have come about as a result of the secular authorities' increasing unease about the conduct of trials and the reliability of verdicts.[64] This development preceded the rise of intellectual scepticism towards witchcraft, which only began to be significant towards the end of the seventeenth century. In 1691–3, the Dutch Reformed pastor, Balthasar Bekker (1634–98) published *De Betooverde Weereld* (The World Bewitched). In the spirit of Descartes, this argued that the material and spiritual worlds cannot interact except through humans, a claim that many theologians and philosophers rejected vigorously since it seemed to contravene scripture.[65] Nevertheless, in the course of the eighteenth century, a growing mood of scepticism began to influence lawmakers. In 1766, Maria Theresa, Holy Roman Empress, outlawed witch-hunting in Austria-Hungary in order to 'uproot superstition and promote the rational judgement of crimes involving magic and sorcery'. The law referred sarcastically to the gullibility of the common people: 'Any event which seems to them hard to explain (although

[61] Robert O. Crummey, 'Ecclesiastical Elites and Popular Belief in Seventeenth-Century Russia', in James D. Tracey and Marguerite Ragnow (eds), *Religion and the Early Modern State* (Cambridge, 2004), 55–9.

[62] Paul Bushkovitch, *Religion and Society in Russia: the Sixteenth and Seventeenth Centuries* (Oxford, 1992).

[63] Valerie A. Kivelson and Robert H. Greene, 'Introduction', in Kivelson and Greene (eds), *Orthodox Russia*, 8.

[64] Bailey, *Magic and Superstition*, 173–4.

[65] Andrew Fox, 'Balthasar Bekker' in Richard Golden (ed.), *The Encyclopedia of Witchcraft: the Western Tradition* (Santa Barbara, 2006), vol. 1, 106–7.

caused merely by accident, science or speed) is ascribed to the activity of sorcerers and witches.'[66] Generally, the appeal to reason seems to have been connected more to changing standards of proof than to scientific developments, such as the advance of mechanistic philosophy that postulated objects as consisting of particles that interact in accordance with fixed natural laws.

Whether one may speak of a 'scientific revolution' in the seventeenth century remains moot. Some question whether anything akin to modern science existed in this period, arguing instead for a 'diverse array of cultural practices aimed at understanding, explaining and controlling the natural world.'[67] Nevertheless in all areas of natural philosophy, the older systems of logic, observation, and categorization associated with Aristotelianism were undermined by new modes of thinking such as the mathematical rationalism of Descartes or the empiricism of Francis Bacon.[68] John Locke aspired to do away with 'some of the rubbish that lies in the way of knowledge', insisting that only the evidence of the senses could lead to knowledge and that only a community of free men could evaluate this knowledge.[69] Such developments further served to call into question the idea that divine, demonic, or occult forces operate routinely in the sphere of nature.

The intensity of literature criticizing superstition increased between 1680 and 1725, which may be seen as the first phase of the Enlightenment. In advocating religious toleration on grounds of reason and natural morality, Pierre Bayle (1647–1706) polemicized against the 'idolatry' of the Catholic Church and against superstition in general.[70] Diderot and Voltaire initiated the more radical Enlightenment critique that consigned all organized religion, but especially the Catholic Church with its claim that ritual could activate divine power within the world, to the lumber-room of superstition. In the *Philosophical Dictionary* [1764] Voltaire linked superstition to tyranny

---

[66] Gábor Klaniczay, *The Uses of Supernatural Power: The Transformation of Popular Religion in Medieval and Early-Modern Europe* (Cambridge, 1990), 171.

[67] Steven Shapin, *The Scientific Revolution* (Chicago, 1997), 3. For a defence of the scientific revolution thesis, see Richard S. Westfall, 'The Scientific Revolution Reasserted', in Margaret J. Osler (ed.), *Rethinking the Scientific Revolution* (Cambridge, 2000), 41–58.

[68] Bailey, *Magic and Superstition*, 204; Barbara J. Shapiro, *Probability and Certainty in Seventeenth-Century England* (Princeton NJ, 1983), 271, 268.

[69] Roy Porter, *Enlightenment: Britain and the Creation of the Modern World* (London, 2001), 4.

[70] Anthony McKenna, 'Bayle et la superstition', in Dompnier (ed.), *La Superstition à l'âge des Lumières*, 49–65.

and reason to virtue and order in the body politic.[71] These radicals saw superstition as a syndrome rooted in dread and anxiety and argued that it produced intolerance and censorship.[72] In his fine defence of the radical Enlightenment, Jonathan Israel argues that it 'eradicated magic and belief in the supernatural from Europe's intellectual culture'.[73] Yet by no means all Enlightened thinkers subscribed to the assault on religion. In recent years, many historians have emphasized the role played by religion—Pietism in Germany, rational Dissent in Britain and Jansenism in France—in fostering the enlightened commitment to reform and progress. Such moderate thinkers, however, were no less hostile to superstition than the radicals, since superstition offended against their ideal of 'reasonableness' in religion.[74]

The French Revolution expanded on the political implications of the Enlightenment critique of religion and superstition, particularly following the subordination of Church to state in the Civil Constitution of the Clergy (12 July 1790) and the refusal of many Catholic clergy to swear an oath of loyalty to the Constitution. Superstition became more strongly attached to political 'fanaticism', to conspiracy by priests and tyrants against the people and to the slavish loyalty displayed by sections of the populace to throne and altar. In 1791, Saint-Just proclaimed: 'Fanaticism is the work of European priestcraft. A people which has suppressed superstition has made a great step towards liberty'.[75] As this suggests, the target of the revolutionaries was the Church, that is, organized, revealed religion, not least because of its hold over the nation's schools. But superstitious belief was also attacked, albeit never systematically, on the grounds that it conflicted with the canons of reason.[76] During the dechristianization campaign of 1793–4, the Jacobins accused priests of impeding the realization of equality by setting themselves up as an intermediate caste between God and man.[77] Robespierre's Cult of the

---

[71] Roy Porter, 'Witchcraft and Magic in Enlightenment, Romantic and Liberal Thought', in Marijke Gijswijt-Hofstra, Brian Levack, and Roy Porter (eds), *History of Witchcraft and Magic in Europe*, vol. 5, *The Eighteenth and Nineteenth Centuries*, (London, 1999), 222.

[72] Israel, *Enlightenment Contested*, 97.

[73] Jonathan Israel, *Radical Enlightenment: Philosophy and the Making of Modernity, 1650–1750* (New York, 2001), 11.

[74] Helena Rosenblatt, 'The Christian Enlightenment' in Stewart J. Brown and Timothy Tackett (eds), *The Cambridge History of Christianity*, vol. 7, *Enlightenment, Reawakening and Revolution, 1660-1815* (Cambridge, 2006), 283–301.

[75] Ruth Scurr, *Fatal Purity: Robespierre and the French Revolution* (London, 2006), 224.

[76] Emmet Kennedy, *A Cultural History of the French Revolution* (New Haven, 1989), 344, 360–1.

[77] Philippe Bourdin, 'Révolution et superstition: L'exemple du Puy-de-Dôme', in Dompnier (ed.), *La Superstition à l'âge des Lumières*, 213, 234.

Supreme Being was, according to Mona Ozouf, unconsciously influenced by the pre-revolutionary critique of superstition, insofar as it aimed to purge away all superfluity. 'For the Revolutionary cult to live, all that was needed, it seems, was a mass of renunciations'.[78]

Attacks on superstition became a staple of nineteenth-century radical politics. In the *Rights of Man* (1791) Thomas Paine classified governments as being founded on superstition, power, or the rights of man. While languishing in a French jail in December 1793, he commenced writing the *Age of Reason*, which begins: 'The total abolition . . . of everything appertaining to compulsive systems of religion . . . has rendered a work of this kind exceedingly necessary, lest, in the general wreck of superstition, of false systems of government, and false theology, we lose sight of morality, of humanity, and of the theology that is true.'[79] Paine's book gained notoriety for its attack on 'revealed religions' and became a founding charter for freethinkers and rationalists through the nineteenth century. Superstition became synonymous with resistance to progress, and reason and popular education were celebrated as its antidotes. The international socialist movement took up the cause of science and reason. The Internationale, penned by Eugène Pottier to celebrate the Paris Commune of 1871, proclaimed 'la raison tonne en son cratère', an emphasis still more pronounced in the English translation. 'For reason in revolt now thunders/And at last ends the age of cant/Away with all your superstitions/Servile masses arise, arise'. However, there were always currents on the left—from William Blake to Georges Sorel—that were sceptical if not hostile to what they perceived to be the sterile cult of reason. Marx's hostility to religion, moreover, sprang not from Enlightenment rationalism but from left Hegelianism. Nevertheless, in the second half of the nineteenth century, the dominant trend—exemplified by the Second International—was to marry Enlightenment faith in the liberating power of reason and science to a materialist epistemology. Engels typified this in his polemical counterposition of 'materialism' to 'idealism'.[80] Within this discourse, superstition possessed its modern sense of misplaced assumptions about causality derived from an erroneous understanding of nature. In the *Dialectics of Nature*, for example, Engels had great fun exposing the fraudulence of phrenology.[81]

[78] Mona Ozouf, *Festivals and the French Revolution*, trans. Alan Sheridan (Cambridge MA, 1988), 270.

[79] Tom Paine, *The Age of Reason* (London, 1938), ch. 1.

[80] Teodor Shanin, 'The Question of Socialism: A Development Failure or an Ethical Defeat?, *History Workshop*, 30 (1990), 68–74.

[81] Friedrich Engels, 'Natural Science and the Spirit World' (1878) in *The Dialectics of Nature* (London, 1940).

But the attack on superstition was by no means confined to the left. In the course of the nineteenth century, governments in Europe came to see themselves as having a mission to civilize their citizens, principally by providing schooling for the masses. A side-effect to elementary education, in addition to instilling rudiments of literacy, arithmetic and religious knowledge, was to convince children that magical forces had no power over their lives. In Prussia, for example, the government sought to combat the more egregious manifestations of folk religion and medicine through schooling, improved religious instruction, the popularization of medical knowledge and, in the longer term, through strengthening economic security and overcoming rural isolation. On occasion, it invoked the law to prosecute cunning folk, wise women, or fortune-tellers for 'fraud'. Following the unification of Germany, the offence of criminal mischief was extended to include the 'encouragement of superstition'.[82] The campaign by 'enlightened' European governments to persuade citizens that magical forces had no dominion over their lives complicated relations with the Catholic Church. In the Rhine province, annexed to Prussia in 1822, the Church supported the government's efforts to promote medical over magical treatment of illness by discouraging clergy from exorcising the mentally disturbed or by reading religious texts over the sick person (*Überlesen*). Yet demand from the laity for such services continued apace and clergy continued to provide them.[83] By the late nineteenth century, moreover, the Catholic Church, faced by the Kulturkampf in Germany and everywhere by the rising forces of secularism, deliberately embraced a less rationalistic, more emotional version of the faith that, inter alia, entailed a reaffirmation of miraculous apparitions.[84]

As Simon Dixon's chapter shows, in Russia paganism was only supplanted by superstition (*sueverie*) as the principal focus of ecclesiastical and secular concern under Peter the Great (r.1682–1725). The Spiritual Regulation of 1721, which embodied Peter's aspiration for a root-and-branch reform of the

---

[82] Nils Freytag, 'Witchcraft, Witch Doctors and the Fight against "Superstition" in Nineteenth-Century Germany' in Willem de Blécourt and Owen Davies (eds), *Witchcraft Continued: Popular Magic in Modern Europe* (Manchester, 2004), 29–45.

[83] Freytag, 'Witchcraft', 33–5.

[84] David Blackburn, *Marpingen: Apparitions of the Virgin Mary in Bismarckian Germany* (Oxford, 1993), 45–9. In France, too, the Church selectively supported miracles, prophecies, and local cults in its war against rationalism and free-thinking. Thomas A. Kselman, *Miracles and Prophesies in Nineteenth-Century France* (New Brunswick NJ, 1983), ch. 7; Ruth Harris, *Lourdes: Body and Spirit in the Secular Age* (London, 1999), 212–14. These authors all stress the 'feminization' of Catholicism as an element in this shift away from rationalism.

Church, expressed concern over 'superstitious practices' ranging from holy fools, 'shriekers' (*klikushi*), improbable versions of saints' lives, false miracles and icons, and bogus relics.[85] Its author, the Jesuit-educated but Protestant-influenced Ukrainian bishop, Feofan Prokopovich, aimed to reform popular piety by raising the educational standard of the parish clergy and by placing the Church under government supervision. He defined superstition as 'that which is superfluous, not essential to salvation, devised by hypocrites only for their own interest, beguiling the simple people, and like snowdrifts, hindering the passage along the right path of truth'.[86] The term *sueverie*, while focusing on the magical 'excesses' of popular piety, had broad connotations, and was used to condemn Old Believers or heretics such as Dukhobors, Muslims and Buddhists.[87]

Subordinated by Peter and expropriated by Catherine, the Orthodox Church entered the nineteenth century in a divided and disoriented state. From the 1820s, however, it became more assertive, as evidenced by its campaigns to convert Muslims and to assert central authority over local parishes and to catechise the laity.[88] The consequence was that by the 1880s the Orthodox Church had acquired a sharper sense of confessional identity. However, distaste for the rationalist reforms of Peter on the part of Church leaders, combined with still inadequate numbers of educated clergy, meant that the centralized regulation of popular piety had made only limited headway. In the last decades of the nineteenth century, moreover, faced by resistance from local communities and by a rising tide of Protestant and other religious dissent, the Church relaxed its reforming drive.[89] As in France and Germany, the hierarchy responded to the challenges posed by secularism, socialism and heresy by endorsing more emotional and expressive forms of piety.[90] By the time of the 1905 Revolution, as Dixon shows, churchmen

---

[85] Eve Levin, 'False Miracles and Unattested Dead Bodies: Investigations into Popular Cults in Early Modern Russia' in James D. Tracy and Marguerite Ragnow (eds), *Religion and the Early Modern State: Views from China, Russia and the West* (Cambridge, 2004), 257.

[86] Christine Worobec, *Possessed: Women, Witches and Demons in Imperial Russia* (DeKalb, 2001), 29.

[87] E. B. Smilianskaia, *Volshebniki, bogokhul'niki, eretiki: narodnaia religioznost' i 'dukhovnye prestupleniia' v Rossii XVIIIv.* (Moscow, 2003), 15.

[88] Simon Dixon, 'The Russian Orthodox Church in Imperial Russia, 1721–1917', in Angold (ed.), *Cambridge History of Christianity*, vol. 5, 328.

[89] Gregory Freeze, 'Institutionalizing Piety: The Church and Popular Religion, 1750–1850', in Jane Burbank and David L. Ransel (eds), *Imperial Russia: New Histories for the Empire* (Bloomington IN, 1998), 236.

[90] Nadieszda Kizenko, *A Prodigal Saint: St John of Kronstadt and the Russian People* (University Park PA, 2000), 285.

were caught between defending the miraculous against a sceptical and highly secular intelligentsia and invoking rationalist criteria when faced with what they saw as popular 'excesses'. Exactly similar tensions were evident in the Mexican Church, as Alan Knight shows.

It is likely that, as in Russia, most of the population in nineteenth-century Europe remained relatively untouched by Enlightenment rationalism, continuing to live in a world suffused with magical belief and practice. By the last quarter of the eighteenth century, the gulf between elite and popular cultures had become so wide that members of the educated classes became fascinated by the foreignness of popular culture. The term *Volkskunde* appeared in 1782 and around the same time the first chair in the subject was founded at Göttingen.[91] The fascination with popular culture reflected, on the one hand, a romantic reaction against the Enlightenment and, on the other, the growth of national sentiment. When the Brothers Grimm began to collect folktales (*Märchen*) in 1806 it was in the conviction that they constituted a repository of the wisdom of the Volk superior to the lucubrations of philosophers.[92] In her chapter Alexandra Walsham shows that in England the roots of the new scholarly discipline of 'folklore'—a term that came into existence in 1846—can be traced back to Tudor polemics against Catholic superstition and to interest in 'curiosities' of a slightly later vintage. The exponents of folklore were impelled by interest in the 'quaint remnants of a way of life that they were convinced was fading rapidly into oblivion', 'superstitions' representing a particular source of fascination. As a scholarly discipline folklore came to develop later in the nineteenth century within a fashionable evolutionary paradigm, magic, religion, and science being seen, respectively, as successive stages of human cognitive development. E. B. Tylor (1832–1917), Professor of Anthropology at Oxford from 1896, construed superstitions as 'survivals' or 'vestiges' of previous stages of development of the human species in its evolution 'from savage through barbaric to civilised life'.[93] Sir Laurence Gomme (1853–1916), a founder of the Folklore Society (1878), argued that superstitions represented 'the survival of traditional ideas or practices among a people whose principal members have passed beyond the stage of civilization which these ideas and practices once represented.'[94] Most notably, Sir James Frazer's, *The Golden Bough: A Study in Comparative Religion*, the third edition of which appeared in twelve volumes (1907–22), which construed magic and religion as primitive but precocious attempts at

---

[91] Frijhoff, 'Popular Religion', 204.

[92] Burke, *Popular Culture*, 11.

[93] Porter, 'Witchcraft and Magic', 265.

[94] George Laurence Gomme, *Folklore as an Historical Science* (London, 1908), 157.

scientific reasoning.[95] For these pioneers, it was precisely the irrationality of superstitions that proved they were survivals of an earlier stage of human development. The work of Tylor and Frazer focused scholarly interest in superstition as a key to understanding the 'primitive mind', an interest that would be maintained from Lucien Levy-Bruhl to Claude Levi-Strauss. Frazer distinguished between 'civilised' and 'savage' modes of thought, seeing the latter as groping, 'pre-scientific' attempts to comprehend nature. Levy-Bruhl recast the distinction as one between 'logical' and 'pre-logical' modes of thought, arguing that civilized thinking was rational, logical, and scientific, whereas primitive thinking was affective, poetic and magical.[96] This interest in the 'primitive mind' had a profound impact not only on the discipline of anthropology but also on the nascent disciplines of psychology and psychoanalysis. More generally, and in contrast to the *philosophes*, who had believed in the innate virtue of natural man and in the power of education, these trends signalled the rise of a darker view of man as naturally prey to passions and prejudice.

In the course of the nineteenth century, interest in superstitions—understood now as the lore of the Volk—came to be utilized in various ways by nationalists, especially those of a cultural or 'ethnic' type. In Greece, belief in demons, fairies and spirits known as *exotika* (literally, 'things outside or beyond'), though long frowned upon by the Orthodox Church, was still strong. This posed a problem for Greek nationalists since popular belief in these creatures, on the one hand, seemed to cast doubt on the self-identification of Greece as a Christian nation and, on the other, seemed to embody a link with ancient Greece. Nationalism appears to have become a vector through which belief in exotica continued into the twentieth century.[97] More typically, cultural nationalists engaged with superstition as a way of criticizing statist versions of the nationalist project. In Japan, anxiety that the traditional culture of the people was vanishing generated a critique of the Meiji definition of national identity in civic terms and of its programme of civilization and enlightenment.[98] In 1910, Yanagita Kunio published *Tales of Tono*, which purported to be a transcription of tales told to the author by inhabitants of this remote region in north-east Japan. Presenting these tales of the uncanny as an expression of what was enduringly Japanese, he used them

[95] Porter, 'Witchcraft and Magic', 266.

[96] Gustav Jahoda, *The Psychology of Superstition* (London, 1969), 99–100.

[97] Charles Stewart, *Demons and the Devil: Moral Imagination in Modern Greek Culture* (Princeton, 1991), 9.

[98] Gerald Figal, *Civilization and Monsters: Spirits of Modernity in Meiji Japan* (Durham NC, 1999).

to counter the Meiji emphasis on 'reason' along with its supposed containment of 'imagination'. As Marilyn Ivy notes, 'anxieties about cultural transmission, valorizations of the unwritten, discoveries of the marginal, and textual constructions of the 'folk' are replicable constituents of modern cultural nationalisms throughout the world.'[99]

Ideas of civilization and progress, as well as guns and trade, propelled European imperial expansion in the nineteenth century. Crucial to the civilizing mission was the work of Christian missionaries who came in the course of the nineteenth century to interest themselves in native 'superstitions'. Initially, in West Africa missionaries and travellers showed little interest in native 'paganism'—beyond noting its supposed obsession with the 'fetish'—dismissing it as 'a positive evil depressing society below the moral level attainable by unaided natural reason.'[100] Later, as the paternalistic project of moral improvement became overlaid by more racialized understandings of social development, missionaries became important cataloguers of indigenous religions, even as they dismissed it as idolatry and superstition.[101] Paradoxically, whilst missionaries presented themselves as opponents of magic and idolatry, they frequently appeared to indigenous peoples as remarkably effective manipulators of occult power. In the 1930s, the Dutch Montfort missionaries confounded the Muedans of Mozambique by telling them, on the one hand, that the spirit objects in their houses were worthless and that sorcery (*uwavi*) was superstition and, on the other, that uwavi was the work of Satan and a dangerous force.[102] Generally, however, African converts turned the 'civilization' and moral uplift offered by the missionaries to their own advantage, in a process described by the Comaroffs as one 'in which signifiers were set afloat, fought over, and recaptured by both sides of the colonial encounter'.[103] Much like the pagans of seventh-century Germany or the Mixtecs of Oaxaca after the Spanish conquest of Mexico, they 'converted Catholicism to themselves', recognizing Christ, Mary and the saints as versions of African

---

[99] Marilyn Ivy, *Discourses of the Vanishing: Modernity, Phantasm, Japan* (Chicago, 1995), 86, 73.

[100] Philip D. Curtin, *The Image of Africa: British Ideas and Actions, 1780-1850* (Madison, 1964), 496.

[101] See, for example, the valuable work by the French Jesuit, Henri Doré, *Recherches sur les superstitions en Chine*, 18 vols. (Shanghai, 1911–38).

[102] Harry G. West, *Kupilikula: Governance and the Invisible Realm in Mozambique* (Chicago, 2005), 126.

[103] John and Jean Comaroff, *Of Revelation and Revolution: Christianity, Colonialism and Consciousness in South Africa* (Chicago, 1991), 18.

gods and spirits, not so much in an act of conversion as one of cosmological augmentation.[104]

   Twentieth-century revolutions embraced Enlightenment confidence in the essential rationality and virtue of man and rejected all forms of irrationalism, not least the superstition incarnated in the Catholic Church. Like their French predecessors, the leaders of the Mexican Revolution were concerned to effect a moral regeneration of the people, to create modern citizens who were educated, secular and loyal to the state. As Knight explains, in 1926 Plutarco Elías Calles called for a radical anti-clerical revolution, a 'psychological revolution', which would break the hold of the Church over the masses. Initially, this plunged the nation into a religious civil war, the Cristero rebellion, which devastated much of central-western Mexico. Between 1930 and 1936, revolutionary leaders made a second, more sophisticated attempt to eliminate 'fanaticism' and superstition, using iconoclasm, civic rituals, education, theatre, language, art, and poetry.[105] Knight doubts that it had much impact, certainly never gaining the same level of support as the agrarian revolution. Perhaps because it was more short-lived, perhaps because it met with a greater level of popular resistance, cultural revolution in Mexico was even less effective than similar campaigns in Russia and China.

   The Bolsheviks, standing in the same Enlightenment tradition that championed reason as the source of progress in society, viewed the application of scientific knowledge to nature and society as the key to human advance. To this they added the 'scientific' materialism of the Second International. As in Mexico, their immediate concern was to break the institutional power of the Church. Between 1922 and 1925, and again during the 'cultural revolution' of 1928 to 1931, they launched a frontal assault on the Orthodox Church that significantly weakened its institutional base. At the same time, they began seriously to consider how best to spread 'science'—*nauka*, a word that connoted enlightenment and progress in general—among the 'dark' and 'backward' masses. In this endeavour, they were following in the footsteps of the liberal and radical intelligentsia of the nineteenth century who believed that social progress was dependent on raising the cultural level of the common people. In December 1921, the Central Committee set up an Anti-Religious

---

[104] West, *Kupilikula*, 126.

[105] Matthew Butler, 'Revolution and the Ritual Year: Religious Innovation and Conflict in *Cristero* Mexico', *Journal of Latin American Studies*, 38:3 (August 2006), 465–90; Adrian Bantjes, 'Burning Saints, Molding Minds: Iconoclasm, Civic Ritual and the Failed Cultural Revolution', in William H. Beezley, Cheryl English Martin, and William E. French (eds), *Rituals of Rule, Rituals of Resistance: Public Celebrations and Popular Culture in Mexico*, (Wilmington DE, 1994), 261–84.

Commission whose remit was to integrate anti-religious education and propaganda into 'general cultural and political-enlightenment work'. The objectives of anti-religious work were: 'first, the destruction of animistic understandings of natural and social phenomena; second, the dissemination of a materialist philosophical and natural-scientific and social-scientific outlook; third, a historical-materialist analysis and critique of religion.'[106] Yet the Bolsheviks never came close to fashioning a coherent strategy to realize these aims. There was no agreement on strategic questions such as the political importance to be assigned to the struggle against religion; whether that struggle was necessarily a matter of long-term education and propaganda or whether it could be speeded up through carnivalesque agitation of the kind favoured by the Young Communist League; or, finally, whether religion would simply wither away as the social conditions of the masses improved in the course of socialist construction. The various organizations charged with anti-religious education were at sixes and sevens on these matters. Schools and kindergartens were regularly condemned for ignoring the anti-religious education of children. The Young Communist League and the Pioneers initially favoured stunts designed to mock the religious, such as letting pigs loose in church, while the Union of Godless, formed in 1925, condemned such activities in favour of more systematic agitation.[107]

Following the brutal collectivization of agriculture (1929–33), which was accompanied by the arrest of priests and the closure of churches, commentators began to pay attention to the persistence of superstition among the rural populace. The traumatic changes unleashed on the countryside caused many to revitalize religious and folkloric idioms, such as those of the Antichrist and the Last Days, of miracle-working icons and 'heavenly letters', in an effort to put meaning on the upheavals that were tearing their lives apart.[108] Writing of children's anti-religious education, one prominent psychologist noted:

> We have conducted a broad and organised struggle (in the press, in schools, clubs etc.) against god and the emotions associated with

---

[106] Rossiiskii gosudarstvennyi arkhiv sotsial'no-politicheskoi istorii, f.17, op.69, d.438, ll.9–14.

[107] S. A. Smith, 'The First Soviet Generation: Children and Religious Belief in Soviet Russia, 1917–41', in Stephen Lovell (ed.), *Generations in Twentieth-Century Europe* (Palgrave, 2007), 79–100.

[108] Lynne Viola, *Peasant Rebels under Stalin* (Oxford, 1996), ch. 2; Steve Smith, 'Heavenly Letters and Tales of the Forest: "Superstition" against Bolsherism', *Forum for Anthropology and Culture*, 2 (2005), 316–39.

him, religious morality and rituals . . . and systematically or piece-meal this has influenced our children. But we have conducted almost no struggle against beliefs in house sprites, wood sprites etc., and the remnants of the ancient religion of clan society . . . . These are not mere trifles. They continue to live on through grand-mothers, grandfathers and mothers, servants and the like. They are transmitted to children, infecting their weak consciousness and burdening their emotions with heavy, oppressive fear.[109]

A 'broad and organized' struggle against superstition failed to materialize, not least because at a time of Terror and impending war, the state had more important things on its mind. A process of secularization got under way in the 1930s, as a consequence of the break-up of rural communities, urbaniza-tion, schooling, military service and—later—the general application of tech-nology to social life. Yet a recent historian has argued, 'there is no indication that scientific-atheistic propaganda made the slightest impact on the men-tality of the wider population'.[110]

Where a single powerful Church existed—as in Mexico or Russia—revo-lutionary states were compelled to confront it in order to establish a mono-poly of power. Nationalizing states in countries with pluralist religious traditions, however, sometimes sought to create national Churches or to promote religious institutions that adopted a modernist discourse on civil-ization and culture.[111] In Japan Meiji reformers attacked Buddhism and its local network of temple parishes at the same time as they created a national 'church', state Shinto, in an attempt to shift the religious loyalties of the populace from the local community to the nationalizing state.[112] Chinese nationalism, by contrast, was less mystical, less concerned with religion, more sympathetic to an Enlightenment discourse of 'science and democracy', the slogan taken up by New Culture radicals during the May Fourth Movement of 1919.[113] In 1898, the Qing dynasty, as part of its belated effort at reform, began to turn temples and traditional academies into modern schools.

---

[109] E. Perovskii, 'Antireligioznoe vospitanie v shkole: ob ateisticheskikh i religioznykh pre-dstavlenii detei', *Religioznik*, 1935, no.1, 26–31.

[110] Michael Froggatt, 'Science in Propaganda and Popular Culture in the USSR under Khrushchev (1953–64)', PhD, Oxford University, 2005, 60.

[111] Prasenjit Duara, *Sovereignty and Authenticity: Manchukuo and the East Asian Modern* (Lanham MA, 2003), 103–22.

[112] Helen Hardacre, *Shinto and the State, 1868-1988* (Princeton, 1991).

[113] Rana Mitter, *A Bitter Revolution: China's Struggle with the Modern World* (Oxford, 2004), 121.

The leading Shanghai newspaper, *Shenbao*, welcomed this on the grounds that the gods to whom Buddhists and Taoists sacrifice 'are all uncanonical absurd deities which no gentlemen would want to mention'.[114] The modern term for superstition, *mixin*—literally 'confused belief'—entered Chinese as a loan-word from Japanese at this time. In the very last years of the Qing dynasty, a rather surprising amount of energy went into 'reforming customs' (*fengsu gaige*) expressed in lectures, periodicals in the vernacular, pamphlets and novels.[115] Henceforward, a key component of reformist discourse in China—one that remains vital to the present day—would be that modernization entails the overcoming of 'feudal superstition'.

The republican government established in 1912 took aim at the field of popular religion, deeming it to fall far short of the implicitly western criteria of politically acceptable modern religion. The New Culture Movement (1915–20s) repudiated the Confucian tradition *tout court*, and stepped up the attack on superstition, which was now deemed to include ancestor worship and the other Confucian rituals.[116] Only with the formation of Chiang Kai-shek's Guomindang government in 1928, however, did the anti-superstition campaign take off in earnest. In the course of two years, a spate of directives was issued banning occupations linked to divination, astrology, fortune telling, geomancy and spirit mediumship (August 1928); methods of cure involving the gods (April 1929); and the making and selling of 'superstitious objects', such as paper money and talismans (March 1930).[117] The new Shanghai Municipal Government introduced regulations to eliminate 'feudal' elements in funerary rituals—such as the wearing of the uniforms of Qing officials or the carrying of banners announcing the arrival of an official—and to limit expenditure on such proceedings. In Zhejiang the provincial government declared: 'Superstition is a hindrance to progress. Appealing to the authority of the gods is a policy that keeps the people ignorant.'[118] The ability of the Guomindang government to enforce these ordinances, however, was patchy, and most remained a dead letter. Nevertheless by 1937, when Japan invaded mainland China it is estimated that one

---

[114] Vincent Goossaert, '1898: The Beginning of the End for Chinese Religion?' *Journal of Asian Studies*, 65:2 (May 2006), 311.

[115] Goossaert, '1898', 322.

[116] Daniel W. Y. Kwok, *Scientism in Chinese Thought, 1900–1950* (New Haven, 1965).

[117] Rebecca Nedostup, 'Religion, Superstition and Governing Society in Nationalist China', Columbia University PhD, 2001, ch. 6.

[118] *Shanghai shi zhinan* (Shanghai, 1933), 141–2.

half of the million or more temples that had existed in 1900 were no longer functioning.[119] The ideal of Enlightenment modernity entailed that the workings of society be made transparent through the application of reason to human action. However, as Peter Geschiere, Basile Ndjio and Lauren Derby show in their respective chapters, modernity in the late twentieth century was seen—especially by the poor in the indebted and dependent societies of the South—to generate 'the very opacities of power it claims to obviate'. In many parts of Africa, Latin America, and Asia, the effect of global capitalism has been to revitalize what Todd Sanders and Harry West call 'occult cosmologies', cosmologies that present the world as one animated by secret, unseen or mysterious powers.[120] In the words of these writers, 'belief in indecipherable power constitutes modernity's dark Other—an Other condemned as "superstition" '.[121] Peter Geschiere, in his pioneering work on Cameroon, demonstrated how witchcraft operates as an allegory that serves to conceptualize, cope with, and criticize modernity.[122] Different African societies deploy different occult idioms—allegories of cannibalism, vampirism, shape-shifting and money magic—and in different contexts, but they tend to identify exploitation with depraved and gluttonous consumption and to criticize the fact that people are commodified while money and possessions acquire the attributes of living things.[123] In his chapter, Basile Ndjio shows why it makes eminent sense for Cameroonians to conclude that the suddenly acquired wealth of a minority of formerly marginalized young men arises from the mystical theft of the vital powers of other people. Like peasants in Soviet Russia in the 1930s, Cameroonians and Puerto Ricans, the subject of Lauren Derby's intriguing chapter, are reconfiguring longstanding cultural idioms in order to make sense of new social and economic instabilities, psychological pressures and cultural uncertainties that accompany this latest phase of globalized capitalism. This suggests that while modernity

---

[119] Vincent Goossaert, 'Le destin de la religion chinoise au 20ème siècle', *Social Compass*, 50: 4 (2003), 436.

[120] Todd Sanders and Harry G. West, 'Power Revealed and Concealed in the New World Order', in Harry G. West and Todd Sanders (eds), *Transparency and Conspiracy: Ethnographies of Suspicion in the New World Order* (Durham NC, 2003), 16.

[121] Sanders and West, 'Power Revealed', 7.

[122] Peter Geschiere, *The Modernity of Witchcraft: Politics and the Occult in Postcolonial Africa* (Charlottesville VA, 1997).

[123] Elizabeth Isichei, *Voices of the Poor in Africa* (Rochester NY, 2002); James Kiernan, 'Introduction', in James Kiernan (ed.), *The Power of the Occult in Modern Africa* (Berlin, 2006), 1–18.

may have brought rationalization in many spheres, it has also bred its own forms of enchantment, a point to which I shall return in conclusion.

Some analytical issues

It is evident that the meanings of *superstitio* and its cognates in other cultures are broad, ranging from immoderation and excess, to vain or empty belief, to folly and irrationality, to the downright illicit or heterodox. In spite of this, certain features common to the discursive use of the term can be discerned. First, there is the sense of a norm being transgressed, often because the restraint deemed appropriate to encounters with the sacred is absent. Second, there is frequently an idea of beliefs and practices carried over from the past. This was already well established by the Middle Ages in Europe, where superstitio was associated with hangovers of pagan practice, an idea buttressed later by nineteenth-century evolutionism. Third, although the sense of superstition as 'bad science' is consolidated in the modern era, the idea of superstition as failure to think clearly is there from the first: evident in Theophrastus's satirization of those who respond to seeing a weasel by throwing three stones across its path. As Bowden points out, for Theophrastus, as for the moderns, such behaviour was essentially trivial, whereas from classical Rome through to the Enlightenment, *superstitio* often signalled belief and practice that was harmful and possibly dangerous. Tacitus called it 'deadly' (*exitiabilis*), Suetonius referred to 'new and evil superstition' (*superstitio nova ac malefica*), and the medieval Church increasingly saw *superstitio* as verging on the heretical.[124] Fourthly, notwithstanding huge variety across space and time, there is a surprising degree of consistency in the *kinds* of beliefs and practices that are classed as superstitious. Many appear to be rooted in an animistic or polytheistic view of the world that sees the human and natural worlds as an organic whole, energized by supernatural beings, forces, or relations. Within this world-view, the success or misfortune of the individual or of society is seen to depend on maintaining harmony with the supernatural entities that animate existence.[125] Much superstitious behaviour seems rooted in the assumption that the supernatural forces at work in maintaining cosmic order can be manipulated to deflect harm or to produce a desired outcome. In this respect, it overlaps significantly with magic. The semantic field in which the category of superstition has operated historically may be imagined

---

[124] L. F. Janssen, ' "Superstitio" and the Persecution of Christians', *Vigiliae Christianae*, 33 (1979), 134.

[125] Stephen Wilson, *The Magical Universe: Everyday Ritual and Magic in Pre-Modern Europe* (London, 2000), xvii.

as a triangular one, bounded at one corner by magic, at another by 'true religion', at another by rationality and science.

1) Superstition as magic

The first serious attempt to conceptualize magic was made by Frazer. Magic, he argued, is a technical act that depends on two laws: the law of similarity, where the practitioner imitates the desired effect so as to make it happen; and the law of contagion, where the practitioner acts upon an object that has been in contact with the thing he wishes to affect. Frazer saw both as forms of sympathetic magic in that they assume that things act on one another through secret sympathy, through some 'invisible ether'.[126] Scholars were not slow to point out that sympathetic magic by no means exhausts the range of magical practices. Divination, for example, is concerned with predicting an outcome or reaching a correct decision; and across many cultures, thoughts or words are believed to have the capacity to influence people or the material world, an insight seized on by Freud who argued that the magician and the obsessional neurotic share a belief in the omnipotence of thought. Roger Bastide charged Frazer with equating magic with the rules that govern its technique, that is, with mistaking its means for its end, and insisted that ritual is constitutive of magic, since it is ritual that mediates supernatural agency, and without which its efficacy cannot be guaranteed.[127] Marcel Mauss contested Frazer's assumption that magic is a hangover from the past, arguing that a practice can only be understood in terms of the social conditions that reproduce it in the present and fix its place within the contemporary ensemble of social practices.[128] Notwithstanding these differences, all these pioneers tended to agree that the fundamental characteristic of magic was that it entailed the manipulation of occult powers for the achievement—or avoidance—of practical effects.

Some historians may bridle at this essentially utilitarian conception, countering that the meanings of magic in historical context are far richer and more complex than this allows. Stuart Clark, for example, rejects the attempt to construct a general concept of magic for this reason: magic, he argues, is simply 'what in particular cultural settings it is construed to be.'[129] For much of European history, magic was defined very precisely by educated elites as an activity that involved the human invocation of demonic powers. This may seem to be a very culturally specific notion, yet the idea of magic as principally

---

[126] James G. Frazer, *The Magic Art* (2 vols), vol. 1, (London, 1902), ch. 3.

[127] Roger Bastide, *Éléments de sociologie religieuse* (Paris, 1935).

[128] Marcel Mauss, Henri Hubert, 'Introduction a l'analyse de quelques phénomènes religieux', Marcel Mauss, *Oeuvres*, vol. 1, (Paris, 1968), 22–6.

[129] Clark, *Thinking with Demons*, 216.

about the manipulation of demonic power is also there in Islamic and Chinese cultures. The central, though not exclusive, sense of the Arabic notion of magic (*sihr*) is action effected through solicitation of demonic forces. It comprises a very wide range of forms of knowledge about the causal mechanisms of nature and the affinities that bind mankind and the cosmos, but all, in the words of Toufic Fahd, represent 'the debris of celestial knowledge transmitted to mankind by fallen angels'.[130] In Chinese the words for magic—*moshu, wushu*—also imply the manipulation of occult, possibly demonic power; and the word for sorcery, *yaoshu*, has definitely evil connotations. There were, of course, many salient differences between magic in imperial China and magic in medieval Europe. For example, it is much harder to make a distinction between religion and magic in the Chinese case: over the centuries, the concern of classical Taoism with magic, alchemy and exorcism seeped into popular religion and, more crucially, popular religion is fundamentally concerned with improving the lot of the worshipper in this world. When a Taoist priest (*daoshi*) stages public ceremonies to call down gods to make rain or fine weather, or when a non-ordained Taoist 'rites master' (*fashi*) fashions charms and spells, or when a spirit medium (*wupo*) casts out evil spirits from the sick, it is doubtful that the average bystander sees these as activities intrinsically different from burning incense to the gods.[131] Magical activity of a private, individual kind existed in China, and often it worked according to the mimetic principles outlined by Frazer: for example, stabbing an image would bring harm to someone or placing the image of a tiger's head above a door would dispel spectres.[132] Generally, however, magic was a more public activity than in medieval Europe, and it was also one that was more specialized and professionalized.[133] In 1963, in Pi county in Sichuan province the authorities counted no fewer than twenty different types of practitioner of 'feudal superstition', including Taoist priests and rites masters, spirit mediums, sorcerers, many varieties of fortune-teller (those using the eight-character method, palm-reading, physiognomy etc.), yin-yang specialists, and feng shui specialists.[134] Finally, we may note that the

---

[130] T. Fahd, 'Sihr (Magic)' *Encyclopaedia of Islam*, (CD Rom) (Leiden, 2002), IX: 567b.

[131] J. J. M. de Groot, *The Religion of the Chinese* (Westport CT, 1980; orig. 1912), 56–7.

[132] Henry Doré S.J., *Researches into Chinese Superstitions*, trans. M. Kennelly, S.J., vol. 5 (Taipei, 1966; orig.1918), xiii; Ibid., vol. 4 (Taipei, 1966; orig. 1917), 478.

[133] Hsiao-Tung Fei, *Peasant Life in China: A Field Study of Country Life in the Yangtze Valley*, (London, 1939), 166–7.

[134] 'Pixian Xipu gongshe fengjian mixin huodong de qingkuang' ['Report on feudal superstitious activities in Xipu Commune in Pi County] 10 Jan. 1963, Sichuan Provincial Archive, 29–99.

make-up of the field of 'magic' in China was rather different from that in medieval Europe. There was less concern with *maleficium*—although malevolent witchcraft (*gu*) did exist – and more concern with discovering hidden and future things through forms of divination. In this respect, magic in imperial China was not dissimilar to magic in ancient Rome. Cultural differences in understandings of magic existed, therefore, and it is the task of the historian to attend to these, but it is not clear that historical and cultural variation, *ipso facto*, rule out a more abstract conception of magic: at the very least, some working definition appears to be a precondition for comparison across space and time.

In what is perhaps the most sophisticated treatment of magic to date, Stanley Tambiah argues that it should be understood as having a dual structure: on the one hand, it appears to imitate the logic of technical action by seeking to transform nature; on the other, it is performative in that it 'consists of acts to create effects on human actors according to accepted social conventions'.[135] He agrees with Bronislaw Malinowski (1884–1942) that although magic may be a false technical act, it is a true social act, insofar as it acts upon people rather than nature; and while not denying that magic aspires to be causally efficacious, he is concerned to point up its capacity to facilitate social communication, exchange and participation, as well as its capacity to organize experience into a coherent vision that can motivate social action. Several contributors to the volume emphasize these latter aspects, seeing magic and superstition primarily as activities that create meaning through ritual and through participation in a world of symbols. This perspective draws analytical attention away from the irrational character of superstition towards engagement with its potential for creating meaning. In her fine study of superstition in nineteenth-century France, Judith Devlin adopts just such a semiological approach. When people fling mud at a statue of Saint Laurent to obtain a cure for eczema, for instance, this action is only 'tenuously connected with the desired results' and should rather be understood as a form of catharsis that provides spiritual consolation and relief from psychological pressure.[136] Whether the fragmented activities we bundle together as superstition in the modern world, however, have the same capacity as traditional magic to engender social communication may be doubted.

---

[135] Stanley J. Tambiah, *Magic, Science, Religion and the Scope of Rationality* (Cambridge, 1990), 82.

[136] Judith Devlin, *The Superstitious Mind. French Peasants and the Supernatural in the Nineteenth Century* (New Haven, 1987), 54.

The consequence of too artificial a separation of the social from the cultural aspects of magic and superstition was evident in the debate between Keith Thomas and Hildred Geertz, sparked by publication of his magnum opus, *Religion and the Decline of Magic*.[137] Thomas connected medieval religion and magic to the powerlessness of people in the face of poverty, sickness, and disaster,[138] but Geertz criticized him for construing magic in essentially utilitarian terms. The implication of his argument, she averred, is that magical beliefs are discarded once they cease to be of practical value. In addition, she reproached him for not locating the meaning of magic in a coherent cosmology, insisting that magical beliefs possess an autonomous existence and systematic coherence. Thomas countered by agreeing that magical rituals may indeed be thoroughly permeated with meaning, but insisted that their function was essentially practical: 'they were meant to work'. The exchange echoed the debate as to whether magic is essentially a technical or a symbolic act. As we have seen, there is no reason to think it cannot be both. In respect of Geertz's claim that magical notions were embedded in 'covert, closed systems of ideas about reality', Thomas was surely correct to insist that this is an empirical question. Pointing out that magic in early-modern England consisted of layers sedimented over time—Christian, pagan, Germanic, and classical—he doubted the wisdom of over-emphasizing the coherence of its ideas and assumptions. It needed to be demonstrated, he argued, that those who believed in fairies or consulted astrologers saw these activities as systematically related.[139]

2) *Functions of superstition*

For those who believe that superstition is a category that refers to real beliefs and practices of a broadly magical type, the question arises as to what social or individual functions such beliefs and practices perform. Starting from the premise that magic 'fulfils some vital function, has some task to accomplish, represents an indispensable part of a working whole', Malinowski argued that it was essentially a means of coping with uncertainty and a lack of control over the environment: 'Man resorts to magic only where chance

---

[137] Hildred Geertz and Keith Thomas, 'An Anthropology of Religion and Magic: Two Views', *Journal of Interdisciplinary History*, 6 (1975), 71–110.

[138] Keith Thomas, *Religion and the Decline of Magic* (London, 1971), 761–2.

[139] Willem de Blécourt, 'On the Continuation of Witchcraft', in Willem de Blécourt and Owen Davies (eds), *Witchcraft Continued: Popular Magic in Modern Europe* (Manchester, 2004), 337–8.

and circumstances are not fully controlled by knowledge'.[140] Today, such functionalism is no longer fashionable, since it foregrounds the way that beliefs and practices secure order in society to the detriment of their intellectual content, treating ideas as instruments to the achievement of certain ends or as rationalizations of social necessity. Yet if there are problems with functionalism as a mode of explanation, it does not follow that a particular practice—however overdetermined with meaning—may not also fulfil a social function, including a latent one. Indeed most of our contributors assume that at the most general level superstitions serve, variously, to create a sense of predictability in an uncertain environment, to help people deal with feelings of powerlessness, to cope with personal or collective loss, or to create a sense of assurance as they pass through critical rites of passage. Such rudimentary functions registered, however, the historian's task remains that of interpreting the specific ways in which superstitious beliefs and practices serve to make such uncertainty or unpredictability meaningful.

Virtually all who write about superstition at some point allude to the affective states that inspire it: to the ways in which, for example, situations of uncertainty or social strain give rise to feelings of anxiety, vulnerability, or envy. This suggests that we may usefully look to psychology for insights into the functions and meanings of superstition. Malinowski, despite his functionalism (which in principle entails a rejection of psychological explanations of social phenomena), nevertheless had recourse to psychology when accounting for the magical practices of the Trobriand islanders. These practices, he argued, derived from an inability to master the environment, and this inability produced a state of tension—feelings of fear and anxiety—that magic served to resolve. It is because superstition so often has such an affective dimension that psychologists have been drawn to it. Like an earlier generation of social scientists, they treat superstition as a referential rather than an ascriptive category, that is, they assume that it describes real habits of mind and types of behaviour.[141] Unlike social scientists, however, they perceive it as fundamentally rooted in the satisfaction of emotional rather than social needs, and tend to be more concerned with the irrational behaviour of individuals than with the social significance of such behaviour. That said, there is little unanimity among them as to the psychological mechanisms that motivate irrational behaviour. Gustav Jahoda construes superstition largely as behaviour designed to reduce anxiety and promote a sense of order, regularity

---

[140] Bronislaw Malinowski, 'Anthropology', *Encyclopaedia Britannica*, First supplementary volume (London and New York, 1926), 132.

[141] Stuart A. Vyse, *Believing in Magic: the Psychology of Superstition* (Oxford, 1997).

and meaning, i.e. as a response to a sense of loss of control over one's environment. Rather tentatively, he also suggests that it may represent a regression to infantile emotional attitudes or a reversion to ideas and beliefs acquired during early emotional learning.[142] Jean Piaget, drawing a parallel between the thinking of children and the 'pre-logical thinking' of 'primitive' peoples as described by Levy-Bruhl, saw superstition as an extension of the animistic or anthropocentric thinking typical of small children. Children, he argued, cannot grasp the idea of physical necessity and assume that the physical world can be manipulated through thought or ritual. Superstitious behaviour emanates from the failure fully to transcend this stage of childhood development.[143] Behaviourist psychologists took a very different tack, seeing superstition as an expression of the human need to find patterns and regularities in the surrounding world, a need, they suggest, that has evolved as a survival mechanism. B. F. Skinner (1904–90), for example, conceived superstition as a conditioned response acquired as the result of an accidental connection between behaviour and reinforcement.[144] Human beings, he and others argued, have an innate tendency to assume causal relationships between experiences: thus the gambler who wears a certain tie when he wins the jackpot cannot resist wearing the same tie again, convinced that it is the tie, not luck, that has led to success.

Psychoanalytical interpretations of superstition focus much more on unconscious motivations. Freud's views, which evolved over time, were heavily influenced by the contemporary interest of anthropologists in the 'primitive mind'. In the *Psychopathology of Everyday Life* (1901) he construed superstition as the projection on to the external world of thoughts, fears, and desires that were the object of repression. By 1913, when he published *Totem and Taboo*, he drew an interesting analogy between the practitioner of magic and the obsessional neurotic: both, he argued, believe in their capacity to affect the external world through thoughts, feelings and wishes. For the neurotic individual, the projection of psychic motivations on to events in the external world derives from a failure to transcend the phase of narcissism. He wryly noted a similarity between his own thinking and that of the superstitious person: 'the compulsion not to let chance count as chance, but to

[142] Gustav Jahoda, *The Psychology of Superstition* (London, 1969), 146.

[143] Jean Piaget, *The Child's Conception of the World* (London, 1929), 169–70; Piaget, 'Causality and the Child' in Howard E. Gruber and J.Jacques Vonèche (eds), *The Essential Piaget* (London, 1977), 138–46.

[144] B. F. Skinner, ' "Superstition" in the Pigeon', *Journal of Experimental Psychology*, 38 (1947), 168–172.

interpret it, is common to us both.'[145] In 1939, Roger Money-Kyrle, a former analysand of Freud and a practising anthropologist, made an attempt to harness psychoanalysis and anthropology to the study of superstition. Drawing upon Melanie Klein's theory of child development, with its dark emphasis on infantile dependency, splitting, aggression, and illusions of omnipotence, he contended that the source of all irrationality lies in the inability to transcend a childish stage of development that sees things and persons as inhabited by spirits and things and persons as capable of emitting supernatural power. 'The infant's failure to distinguish between fantasy and reality leads to neurotic anxiety, perhaps the strongest and most persistent drive in his life'.[146] Superstition, like an obsessional symptom, was, he concluded, an irrational method for dealing with irrational anxiety. Finally, in an ingenious if ultimately unconvincing application of a Freudian perspective to the history of superstition, Nicole Belmont argues that superstition lies midway between the compulsive rituals of the neurotic, which are private and fragmented, and the systematic rituals of religion, which are stereotyped and communal, insofar as it shares the diversity of the former and the stereotypicality of the latter. Superstition caters to the collective need for exteriorization, a need to project on to the external world that which emanates from the unconscious and is censored by the conscious mind. However, in the wake of the Enlightenment, she contends, religion ceased to fulfil a function of exteriorization, coming to focus exclusively on 'interiorisation'—'un mouvement de retour sur soi-même'—thereby leaving superstition to provide the ritualized mechanisms through which unconscious needs and instincts could be externalized.[147]

3) Superstition and religion
The study of superstition can enable us better to understand the historical evolution of the category of 'religion', in that it focuses analytical attention on the authorizing processes by which religion is given form and meaning across time and space. A major problem in thinking about how religion and

---

[145] Sigmund Freud, *Standard Edition of the Complete Psychological Works of Sigmund Freud*, vol. 6, *Psychopathology of Everyday Life* (London, 1960), 257.

[146] Roger Money-Kyrle, *Superstition and Society* (London, 1939), 91.

[147] Nicole Belmont, 'Superstition et religion populaire dans les sociétés occidentales' in M. Izard and Pierre Smith (eds), *La Fonction symbolique: essais d'anthropologie* (Paris, 1979), 53–70. For pioneering works that apply psychoanalytic perspectives to the history of witchcraft, see Lyndal Roper, *Oedipus and the Devil* (London, 1994); John Demos, *Entertaining Satan: Witchcraft and the Culture of Early New England* (New York, 1982).

superstition mutually constitute one another is that our modern conception of religion cannot be mechanically applied to past societies. In the classical world neither *deisidaimonia* nor *superstitio* functioned as straightforward antonyms to civic religion although, as Hugh Bowden and Richard Gordon show, both were inseparable from an idea of appropriate ritual. *Religio* turns out to have been as polyvalent a term as *superstitio*, its meanings ranging from activities associated with worship of the gods, 'scrupulous attention to detail that links humankind to divinity by virtue of a code of conduct reciprocally binding on both sides' (Gordon), to something close to *superstitio* itself. A large part of the problem derives from the fact that in pre-modern societies religion did not occupy a clearly demarcated social space in the way that it does in modern societies, since the whole of social life was permeated by beliefs and practices we would class as religious. In a celebrated work, Wilfred Cantwell Smith argued that the modern conception of religion as a system of belief embodied in a bounded community did not appear until the seventeenth and eighteenth centuries, as fall-out from the polemics and apologetics unleashed by the Reformation and Wars of Religion. Prior to this, he contended, practitioners of different faith traditions spoke of 'faith', 'obedience', 'piety', 'truth' or 'the way'. In none of the classical languages except Arabic, he observed, is there a term that corresponds to the modern notion of religion. In particular, he suggested that practitioners could only think of their faith as a religion once they could see it from the perspective of outsiders.[148]

In the modern period, superstition plays a vital function in helping intellectuals and political leaders create a category of religion, as is evident in Asia. The Arya Samaj, a Hindu revivalist group founded in 1875, sought to constitute Hinduism as a 'purified' and 'rational' religion, based on ancient texts rather than 'superstition', that could both claim universality with Christianity and to be the national religion of 'Indians'.[149] 'Science was not locked in battle with religion but concerned with specifying its domain, disengaging it from what appeared as superstition.'[150] In Japan and China the creation of a modern category of religion was implicated in state-building and here, too, superstition served a vital function, coming to signify the unscientific excrescences of which traditional religion must be purged if it were to become

[148] Wilfred Cantwell Smith, *The Meaning and End of Religion* (London, 1962).

[149] Maria Misra, *Vishnu's Crowded Temple: India since the Great Rebellion* (London, 2007), 70–2.

[150] Gyan Prakash, 'Between Science and Superstition: Religion and the Modern Subject of the Nation in Colonial India' in Birgit Meyer and Peter Pels (eds), *Magic and Modernity: Interfaces of Revelation and Concealment* (Stanford, 2003), 41, 45.

a religion worthy of the modern nation. In Japan Buddhism struggled to reinvent itself as a modern, socially conscious, cosmopolitan, yet quintessentially Japanese religion in the face of persecution during the Meiji Restoration.[151] In China the modern idea of religion (*zongjiao*) arrived along with the notion of superstition at the end of the nineteenth century. As in Japan, it became a catalyst for the reconfiguration of Buddhism and Taoism as modern religions. Under the Guomindang, the two faiths strove to reconstitute themselves as institutionalized religions separate from the field of local popular practice, founding national associations to represent their interests, so that they might qualify for the freedom guaranteed to recognized religions under the constitution.

In drawing attention to the authorizing processes by which 'religion' is made and remade across time and space, superstition reminds us of the relationships between religion and power. Talal Asad is critical of the tendency of contemporary anthropologists to define religion in terms of belief and cultural meaning and to separate these issues from problems of power. Religion, he argues, must be construed as 'a concrete set of practical rules attached to specific processes of power and knowledge'.[152] This almost certainly gives too little weight to religion's symbolic dimension—Asad has Clifford Geertz in his sights—but it points up the inapplicability of the contemporary western ideas about religion to many cultures of the past. Ideas of the transcendent—of the divine as standing apart from the cosmos—for example are absent from many of the world's leading religions, including those of the Greeks, Romans and Chinese. The many-centred cults of Chinese religion are not usefully thought of as coherent systems of beliefs or symbols: indeed for China's rulers, belief, far from being the ground of social action, was construed as the expression of the correct performance of ritual.[153] The modern conception of religion fits Islam much better: here there was a word for religion—*dīn*—yet it related to how one lives more than to what one believes. 'The virtuous Muslim is not an autonomous individual who assents to a series of universalizable maxims but an individual inhabiting the moral space shared by all who are bound to God (the *umma*).'[154] Asad thus argues

[151] James Edward Ketelaar, *Of Heretics and Martyrs in Meiji Japan: Buddhism and Its Persecution* (Princeton, 1993).

[152] Talal Asad, *Genealogies of Religion: Discipline and Reasons of Power in Christianity and Islam* (Baltimore, 1993), 42.

[153] Evelyn Rawski, 'A Historian's Approach to Chinese Death Ritual' in James L. Watson and Evelyn S. Rawski (eds), *Death Ritual in Late Imperial and Modern China* (Berkeley, 1988), 28.

[154] Asad, *Genealogies*, 219.

that coherence in religious systems derives not from symbols but from acts of power by which authoritative institutions enforce standardized interpretations. What matters, he argues, is 'how authorizing processes represent practices, utterances or dispositions so that they can be discursively related to general (cosmic) ideas of order.[155] The relevance of this perspective to the study of superstition is obvious. As we saw in relation to the medieval Church, its authorizing processes ranged over a wide domain, including the repudiation or appropriation of pagan beliefs and practices, the legitimation of saints, shrines, and relics, as well as the designation of certain beliefs and practices as *superstitio*. In determining the boundaries of legitimate belief, *superstitio* was a critical means used by the Church to buttress its authority to determine truth from error. That the subtlety of its distinctions between, say, *superstitio* and heresy or, in the post-Tridentine Church, between sacraments and sacramentals, may have been lost on the faithful, does not invalidate the general point. Whether Asad is correct to reject religion entirely as a category of analysis is more moot. In an argument analogous to Clark's on magic, he argues that religion is not an analytical category, since it abstracts a set of practices from their historical context and subsumes them into a speciously universalist concept. Yet the fact that one falls back into using the term 'religion', even if in scare quotes, suggests that, as with magic, there are certain family resemblances between activities centred on supernatural beings and forces across different cultures.

4) Superstition and rationality

The modern conception of superstition seizes on irrationality as its defining characteristic, whether that is understood to mean a faulty understanding of the operation of cause and effect, a failure to distinguish appearance from reality, a failure to apply inductive reasoning, or simple ignorance. Just as study of superstition illuminates the processes whereby the category of religion was constituted in past societies, so it can shed light on past societies' understanding of what is reasonable and their criteria of rationality. In the modern West rationality is a very broad term whose connotations range from formal notions of efficiency and consistency to substantive notions of autonomy or self-determination.[156] Analytical philosophers tend to define the concept narrowly to denote the rules of logic and the constraints of consistency, coherence and non-contradiction in argument. Social scientists and philosophers disagree as to whether this conception of rationality has universal applicability. The late Richard Rorty was an eloquent exponent of the view

---

[155] Asad, *Genealogies*, 37.

[156] Jon Elster, *Sour Grapes: Studies in the Subversion of Rationality* (Cambridge, 1983), 1.

that what counts as rational is entirely determined by the language and culture of a particular community, and that the modern scientific conception of rationality is one conception among many, neither better nor worse than its competitors.[157] Peter Winch argued similarly that there is no 'norm for intelligibility in general': 'criteria of logic . . . are only intelligible in the context of ways of living or modes of social life.'[158] What counts as a good reason, in other words, is particular to context: Galileo relied on observation and experiment, Bellarmine relied on scripture. By contrast, scholars such as Alasdair MacIntyre, Ernest Gellner and Steven Lukes argue in different ways that rationality is a substantive concept, relating to rules of logic and inference and to values of consistency and non-contradiction, that has analytical applicability to other cultures.[159] Historians may feel sympathetic to contextualists such as Rorty or Winch, insofar as they know that standards of rationality in the past societies are grounded in values, norms, and expectations very different from our own. This is not, however, necessarily to concede the argument to contextualists. Charles Taylor, for example, recognizes that the opponents of Galileo had good reason for their beliefs, grounded as they were in fundamental assumptions about the ordering of the cosmos, yet he insists that a substantive distinction can be made between 'atheoretical cultures', where understanding the universe and attunement to it are inseparable, and modern scientific culture, where understanding and attunement are entirely dissociated. Moreover, he insists that modern scientific culture is self-evidently more effective in understanding and manipulating nature, although its claims for understanding the meaning of existence are by no means self-evidently superior.[160] From a different angle, MacIntyre argues that however much an investigator may seek to privilege native categories of thought and criteria of rationality, at best he or she can do so only in dialectical engagement with the categories of understanding he or she has inherited.[161] Alan Knight addresses this issue in his chapter.

The relevance of the rationality debate to the study of superstition lies in the fact that the latter, in illuminating the grounds on which champions of orthodoxy demean or debar forms of knowledge, reveals deeper criteria according to which a particular society deems something to be reasonable. In medieval Europe, Richard Kieckhefer argues that people saw magic as

---

[157] Richard Rorty, *Objectivity, Relativism and Truth* (Cambridge, 1991).

[158] Peter Winch, *Idea of a Social Science* (London, 1963), 100–1.

[159] See the essays in Bryan R. Wilson (ed.), *Rationality* (Oxford, 1974).

[160] Charles Taylor, 'Rationality', in Martin Hollis and Steven Lukes (eds), *Rationality and Relativism* (Oxford, 1982), 87–105.

[161] Alasdair MacIntyre, 'The Idea of a Social Science' in Wilson, *Rationality*, 128–30.

entirely rational: first, because it actually worked, that is, its efficacy was demonstrated by evidence recognized within the culture as authentic; and secondly, because its workings were governed by principles—of theology or of physics—that could be coherently articulated.[162] In China, as in classical Greece, there were thinkers who are often classed as 'rationalists'—although whether that is legitimate is touched on in T. H. Barrett's paper. The philosopher Wang Chong (27–c.100 CE), for example, scoffed at the idea that one could determine the will of Heaven by divination with stalks and ridiculed shamans for practising deceit on simple people.[163] Yet the principal criterion of reasonableness in imperial Chinese culture had little to do with understandings of causality in nature: rather it was concerned with how a particular belief or practice stood in relation to the 'right and correct teaching' (zheng) of the state, more specifically, to the Confucian 'doctrine of propriety and ritual' (lijiao). Categories of yin—understood as illicit or excessive—and xie-understood as outright heterodoxy—were defined in respect of the extent to which they deviated from correct teaching.[164] Rationality thus had little to do with rules of logic or non-contradiction in argument (which is not to say that these went unrecognized), and very much to do with Winch's 'ways of living or modes of social life'. Such 'context-dependent' rationalities,[165] while not meeting contemporary criteria of scientificity, could nevertheless accommodate naturalistic understandings of cause and effect or of inductive reasoning quite comfortably. E. E. Evans-Pritchard famously argued that witch beliefs among the Azande are explanations that supplement rather than deny natural causation. When a granary collapses on the men taking shelter beneath it, no one questions that this is due to termites eating through the poles on which it stands. But they point out that this does not explain why it fell on those particular men at that particular time.[166] Magic and superstition can work perfectly well in tandem with scientific modes of thought, since they

---

[162] Richard Kieckhefer, 'The Specific Rationality of Medieval Magic', *American Historical Review*, 99:3 (1994), 813–36.

[163] Michael Loewe, 'The Religious and Intellectual Background' in Denis Twitchett and Michael Loewe (eds), *Cambridge History of China*, vol. 1, *The Ch'in and Han Empires, 221BC – AD220* (Cambridge, 1986), 673, 681–2.

[164] Richard Shek, 'The Alternative Moral Universe of Religious Dissenters in Ming-Qing China', in James D. Tracy and Marguerite Ragnow (eds), *Religion and the Early Modern State* (Cambridge, 2004), 15.

[165] Steven Lukes, 'Some Problems about Rationality', in Wilson, *Rationality*, 194–213.

[166] E. E. Evans-Pritchard, *Witchcraft, Oracles and Magic among the Azande*, abridged with introduction by Eva Gillies (Oxford, 1976), 22.

serve better to explain the specificity of cause, and this remains as true in the contemporary West as among the Azande in the 1930s.

5) Elite versus popular

We have seen that the category of superstition was central to the articulation of relations between, on the one hand, the official, the orthodox, and the clerical and, on the other, the popular, folk, or lay. There was often a significant disjunction between these two levels, as many of our essays reveal: men (be they Dominican friars or Communist cadres) trained to uphold a textual tradition and oriented towards abstraction, came face to face with an unlettered populace, oriented to the world in more immediate, concrete ways. In classical Rome *superstitio* was already strongly associated with the *vulgus*; and following the fusion of the ecclesiastical hierarchy and the landed Gallo-Roman aristocracy in the fourth and fifth centuries, the distinction between privileged elites and the common people was sharpened, so that *paganus*, which meant 'pagan' by the fifth century, eventually produced the French words for 'peasant' (*paysan*) and 'pagan' (*païen*). In medieval Europe, *superstitio* continued to be strongly associated with *rustici, pauperes, populares* and *vetulae* (wretched old women), suggesting that elite discourse was permeated as much by male chauvinism as by class condescension.[167] This comes across clearly in Stephen Bowd's paper. In the discourse of superstition, rural folk generally, and women in particular, were overwhelmingly the target of elite scorn. Later, in a different way, the trope of survivalism within the discipline of folklore would reinforce this bias towards the rural.[168]

Historical study of superstition, however, provides as many challenges to the elite-popular distinction as it does endorsements of it. According to Peter Brown, the distinction between elite and popular religion was a product of the Enlightenment; David Hume, in particular, arguing that the popular classes were intellectually incapable of appreciating God's design in the rational universe, since their inability to think abstractly caused them to personalize as gods the unknown forces that governed their condition.[169] Several of our contributors are rightly cautious about counterposing elite to popular religion, not least because local elites themselves often subscribed to beliefs and

---

[167] Pierre Boglioni, 'Le sopravvivenze pagane nel medioevo' in Peter Slater (ed.), *Traditions in Contact and Change. Selected Proceedings of the XIV Congress of the International Association of the History of Religions* (Waterloo, 1983), 350.

[168] On charms, spells, mascots, and amulets in the London borough of Southwark, see Sarah Williams, 'Urban Popular Religion and the Rites of Passage', in Hugh McLeod (ed.), *European Religion in the Age of Great Cities, 1830–1930* (London, 1995), 216–38.

[169] Peter Brown, *The Cult of the Saints* (Chicago, 1981), 13–15.

practices castigated as superstitious by the defenders of orthodoxy. In medieval England, for example, the educated were as likely as the uneducated to use bits of paper on which prayers were written as charms.[170] Often we appear to be looking not at 'popular' variations or deviations from orthodox practice, but at 'local' or 'vernacular' practice. William Christian has advocated abandoning the term 'popular religion' in favour of 'local religion', which he defines as a style of religion shared by members of all social classes within a particular locale. In this view, local religion was not a 'little tradition' but a localization of the 'great tradition'.[171] As this formulation suggests, the relationship between the official and the local was by no means always one of opposition: local believers adjusted official doctrine and ritual to fit their needs and might find it in their interests to cooperate with the representatives of the 'great tradition'.[172] Secondly, even an official/local distinction may simplify reality in too dichotomous a fashion. As Tim Barrett shows in his paper, the terminology referring to 'licentious cults' in late Han China was not presented in terms of a two-tier distinction, but in terms of a gradation of religious observances appropriate to one's place in the social order. A similar linkage of religious practice to gradations of social status was apparent in the classical world. Thirdly, agency in the relationship between the official and the local/popular was by no means always top-down, that is, a straightforward matter of elites seeking to suppress or reform local belief and practice. Even in the long term, elites were not guaranteed to prevail in contests with popular practice. In Poland, for example, house sprites (*domowe*) were condemned as a species of inferior devil during the Counter-Reformation, yet by the nineteenth century the Church had been forced to embrace them, reclassifying them as guardian angels.[173] In thinking about superstition, then, we are not always dealing with a two-tiered, top-down relationship but with what Jean-Claude Schmitt calls a model of 'multiple poles and complex relations', with 'local theatres of ambition and conflict that bring into play a particular segment of society.'[174]

---

[170] Eamon Duffy, The *Stripping of the Altars: Traditional Religion in England, 1400–1580* (New Haven, 1994), 266–9.

[171] William Christian, *Local Religion in Sixteenth-Century Spain* (Princeton NJ, 1981).

[172] E. Badone, 'Introduction', in Ellen Badone (ed.), *Religious Orthodoxy and Popular Faith in European Society* (Princeton NJ, 1990), 5.

[173] A. C. Schiffmann, 'The Witch and Crime: the Persecution of Witches in Twentieth-Century Poland', *ARV: Scandinavian Yearbook of Folklore*, 43 (1987), 147–65.

[174] Jean-Claude Schmitt, *Le corps, les rites, les rêves, le temps: essais d'anthropologie médiévale*, (Paris, 2001), 19.

6) *Superstition and modernity*

Finally, we turn to the question of whether the onset of modernity leads to a decline in superstition; and if so, what the intellectual, technological, and social factors are that underpin any such decline. If we consider superstition in the narrow sense defined at the outset, and from the vantage point of the developed world, then Steve Roud is undoubtedly correct to conclude that: 'As a society we are immeasurably less superstitious than we used to be. We do not know so many superstitions, we do not believe so deeply, we do not act upon them so much, and the ones we still possess have been generally sanitised.'[175] The advance of modern science has discredited once widespread ideas that occult forces are operative in nature and that the supernatural regularly intervenes in the world. More generally, it has led to a scaling down of religion's claims to explain the realm of nature with respect to a whole range of issues such as the origins of the universe, the Earth and of mankind. The advance of science, however, has not led to the complete discrediting of religion: rather it has forced a redefinition of its sphere of competence from all-encompassing cosmology to a discourse concerned with questions of ultimate meaning and moral value. Moreover, it is not the scientific account of the world per se that has weakened supernatural understandings of the cosmos so much as the application of science to the natural and social worlds. The rise of modern farming methods, for example, means that in the developed world, at least, there is less need to worry about the potentially catastrophic effects of drought, floods, or invasions of pests, so magical practices concerned with protecting and ensuring the fertility of crops and livestock have been marginalized or else have vanished. Technology, however, cannot be separated from the wider socio-economic changes that have accompanied the rise of industrial capitalism. Keith Thomas, whilst arguing that magic first came under pressure from more coherent intellectual currents such as empiricism and rationalism, nevertheless attributed its decline primarily to socio-economic factors such as the growth of urban living, the spread of an ideology of self-help and increased control of the environment.[176] Thus the decline of superstitions associated with farming, for example, has been due not simply to the application of modern farming methods, it also reflects the steep decline in the numbers in the developed world who gain their livelihood from the land. The break-up of self-contained rural communities and the shift of population from the countryside to the towns have destroyed the contexts in which superstitious beliefs and practices connected with the agricultural and calendrical cycles once thrived.

[175] Roud, *Penguin Guide*, xviii.
[176] Keith Thomas, *Religion and the Decline of Magic*, 769–74.

That said, it is a moot point whether the modern world—menaced as it is by the threats of environmental or nuclear annihilation—is self-evidently a less risky place than the pre-modern world. As Anthony Giddens puts it: 'For hundreds of years, people worried about what nature could do to us—earthquakes, floods, plagues, bad harvests and so on. At some point, somewhere over the past fifty years, we stopped worrying so much about what nature could do to us and started worrying about what we have done to nature.'[177] Certainly, those in the developed capitalist world live longer and healthier lives than their forebears, but any enhanced sense of security may be offset by an enhanced sense of risk, brought about by the hectic pace of change to which our lives and environment are subject. To take one example: although the advance of modern medicine and the decline of epidemic disease have greatly improved our chances of living relatively healthy lives, the threat of disease or of a life-threatening accident are not ones against which we can calculate or control. Moreover the inherent complexities of modern medicine, combined with the fact that medical experts frequently disagree, mean that feelings of uncertainty about the efficacy of treatment or perceptions of risk attached to treatment and its side effects remain entrenched. It is thus not accidental that healthcare is an area where alternative therapies based on notions that conflict with western biomedicine flourish. Nor, more fundamentally, does science provide an answer to ethical questions or the ultimate questions of existence. And if we think of superstition in the broader sense—as beliefs and practices that conflict with the canons of scientific rationality—then the Enlightenment prognosis of a steady advance of reason and social progress looks much less persuasive. Writing of the urban legends—alligators in the New York sewers, the vanishing hitchhiker, spiked Coca Cola—that proliferate in the USA today, Linda Dégh writes of an 'irrationality explosion'.[178] Yet it is one that exists within a social world that is fundamentally organized by science and instrumental rationality. So whilst superstition in the narrow sense—those myriad beliefs and practices that have been traditionally mobilized to deflect harm or promote good—may have declined in the developed world, it is not self-evident that superstition in the wider sense of beliefs that conflict with science and rationality has been decisively eroded by the intellectual, technological, and socio-economic changes we associate with modernity.[179] Modernity has dramatically increased our understanding of the conditions under which we live and, in

---

[177] Anthony Giddens, 'Risk and Responsibility', *Modern Law Review*, 62:1 (1999), 3.

[178] Linda Dégh, *Legend and Belief: Dialectics of a Folklore Genre* (Bloomington IN, 2001), 21.

[179] For some statistics on the extent of superstitious belief in the USA today, see Vyse, *Believing in Magic*, 16–18.

many respects, at least in the developed world, has immeasurably increased socio-economic security, but in key areas of personal and social life we continue to live with risk and uncertainty and we continue to search for meaning beyond the sphere of quotidian existence. Indeed superstition, once associated with a world peopled by too many gods, may persist in part as a stubborn response to a world robbed of gods.

In the last analysis, however, we must be critical not only of seeing superstition as a kind of hangover from the traditional world but also of a binary way of thinking that sees modernity and superstition as fundamentally antithetical. Certainly, superstition has served as a powerful counterpoint to modernity, a foil against which modernity can be conceptualized. Yet as we saw in relation to the dependent societies of the 'south' and their encounter with globalized capitalism, in reality magic and the supernatural may be constitutive elements of modernity. Superstition, rather than being modernity's 'Other', is frequently inextricably entangled and complicit with it. Moreover, it is not only in the dependent societies of the south that modernity generates the opacities of power it is supposed to render transparent. As already noted, few of us understand the 'magic' of modern medicine or the communication technologies that govern our lives. More crucially, modernity produces its own forms of enchantment. We are all aware, for example, of the ways in which advertising promotes consumption through a kind of associative magic that invests products with powers and qualities they do not have. Similarly, modernity produces enchantment in the concealments of state power so ably discussed by Robin Derby, or in the ways that markets and commodities fetishize social relations, or in the wonders of modern technology, not least in computer-simulated virtual worlds. At best, then, Weber's 'disenchantment of the world' has been a highly uneven process. It may yet prove to characterize the general direction of global historical developments, but it could turn out that modernity is but the latest stage in an ongoing cycle of disenchantment or re-enchantment.[180]

---

[180] See the various essays in Meyer and Pels, *Magic and Modernity* (Stanford, 2003).

Before Superstition and After: Theophrastus and Plutarch on *Deisidaimonia*

Hugh Bowden

The earliest works on the subject of superstition were written by Greek philosophers in the Hellenistic and Roman period. While the presentation of superstitious behaviour and attitudes in these works was influential on later writers, they need to be understood in the context in which they were written. It is clear that what these writers condemned was much closer to the normal ritual activities of their contemporaries than they imply. The philosophical attack on superstition therefore can be seen as a polemical attempt to mark out a particular notion of 'proper religion', rather than a genuine attempt to isolate unacceptable activity. As this volume demonstrates, that attack has been taken up subsequently by other groups concerned with establishing their own idea of proper behaviour against what is popular practice. This paper goes on to show how deeply rooted popular practice is in human beings, and suggests that the campaign begun by the Greek philosophers is unlikely ever to end.[1]

I

It is a commonplace, but nonetheless significant, that there is no exact equivalent of the word 'superstition' in Greek. There is the word *deisidaimonia*, which was usually translated by Latin authors as *superstitio*, from which the English 'superstition' is derived.[2] That word literally means 'fear of the gods',[3]

---

[1] This paper has benefited from the contributions of all those who were involved in the conference on *Superstition in Historical and Comparative Perspective*, but in particular from those of my fellow scholars of the ancient world, Richard Gordon and Robin Osborne, and of the conference organizer, Steve Smith. I thank them all.

[2] On the general development of the notion in the ancient world see D. Grodzynski, 'Superstitio', *REA*, 76 (1974), 36–60.

[3] Strictly speaking 'fear of *daimones*'. I do not propose to discuss the possible range of meanings of *daimon* here. Plutarch writes in his essay about *to theion* (the divine) and *hoi theoi* (the gods), indicating that these are included in *deisidaimonia* as he understands the word.

Past and Present (2008), Supplement 3

and it is not always used in a pejorative sense: the adjective *deisidaimon* is regularly used in the same, respectful sense as the English phrase 'god-fearing'. However, from the end of the fourth century BCE onwards, and especially in the writings of philosophers, the word is used pejoratively, and in the two philosophical works that we will examine, Theophrastus' sixteenth *Character, Deisidaimon*,[4] written at the end of the fourth century BCE, and Plutarch's essay *Peri Deisidaimonias*, written near the end of the first century CE, we see it used in a way which corresponds reasonably closely to our term, 'superstition'.

Theophrastus was a pupil of Aristotle, and his successor as head of the Lyceum, a position he held for about thirty-five years until his death in *c*.287 BCE. He was the author of a number of philosophical and scientific works, but also of the *Characters*, a collection of about thirty sketches of different types of (exclusively) male behaviour. There is no scholarly agreement on what the purpose of these sketches was—although the idea that they were to spice up otherwise dull lectures has been accepted by a number of modern scholars (themselves usually lecturers)—or of exactly when they were composed, although it is generally agreed that they were written about Athenians, presumably in Athens, in the last quarter of the fourth century.[5] All the *Characters* are very short, and although number 16 is one of the longest, it short enough to give in full here:

Theophrastus, The Superstitious Man

2. The Superstitious man is the kind who washes his hands in three springs, sprinkles himself with water from a temple font, puts a laurel leaf in his mouth, and then is ready for the day's perambulations.

3. If a weasel runs across his path he will not proceed on his journey until someone else has covered the ground or he has thrown three stones over the road.

4. When he sees a snake in his home he invokes Sabazios if it is the red-brown one, and if it is the holy one he sets up a hero-shrine there and then.

5. Whenever he passes the shiny stones at the crossroads he pours oil from his flask over them and falls to his knees and kisses them before leaving.

---

[4] So J. Diggle, *Theophrastus Characters*, (Cambridge, 2004). J. Rustem, *Theophrastus Characters, Herodas Mimes, Sophron and other Mime Fragments* (Cambridge Mass. and London, 2003), 96, has *Deisidaimonias*.

[5] For recent work on Theophrastus see Diggle, *Theophrastus Characters*, 349–75; Rustem, *Theophrastus Characters*, 5–23; D. B. Martin, *Inventing Superstition: From the Hippocratics to the Christians* (Cambridge Mass. and London, 2004) 21–35; R. Lane Fox, 'Theophrastus' *Characters* and the Historian', *PCPS*, 42 (1996), 127–70.

6. If a mouse nibbles through a bag of barley he goes to the expounder of sacred law and asks what he should do; and if the answer is that he should give it to the tanner to sew up he disregards the advice and performs an apotropaic sacrifice.

7. He is apt to purify his house frequently, claiming that he is haunted by Hekate.

8. If owls *hoot* while he is walking he becomes agitated and says 'Athena is quite a power' before going on.

9. He refuses to step on a tombstone or go near a dead body or a woman in childbirth, saying that he cannot afford to risk contamination.

10. On the fourth and the seventh of the month he orders his household to boil down some wine, then goes out and buys myrtle-wreaths, frankincense and cakes, and on his return spends the whole day garlanding the Hermaphrodites.

11. When he has a dream he visits not only dream-analysts but also seers and bird-watchers to ask which god or goddess he should pray to.

12. He makes a monthly visit to the Orphic ritualists to take the sacrament, accompanied by his wife (or if she is busy, the nurse) and his children.

14. If ever he observes a man wreathed with garlic *eating* the offerings at the crossroads, he goes away and washes from head to toe, then calls for priestesses and tells them to purify him with a squill (sea onion) or a puppy.

15. If he sees a madman or an epileptic he shudders and spits into his chest.[6]

It is important to be aware of the tone and purpose of this sketch. It is part of a work that is essentially satirical. The reader is expected to laugh at the *Deisidaimon* rather than to condemn him, and in this respect it is obviously a different kind of work from the treatises on superstition produced by Christian authors in later centuries. For the same reason the behaviour described is to be seen not necessarily as deviant, but as extreme, and this is worth pursuing further.

To a modern reader the actions of the *Deisidaimon* are precisely what we would think superstitious behaviour would look like. There are lots of small, obsessive acts, extreme avoidance of certain animals and occasions, excessive fear of supernatural powers. However, when we set these actions against what

---

[6] Theophr. *Ch.* 16, trans. Diggle with minor adaptations. Words in italics are missing from the Greek text. There are a number of places where the text is open to a variety of readings and translations. The first sentence in the text, 'Superstition would simply seem to be cowardice with regard to the divine,' is generally considered a later interpolation, as is section 13, 'He would seem to be one of the people who scrupulously sprinkle themselves at the seashore'.

we know about classical Greek religious practices, the question of what marks this man out as 'superstitious' becomes less easy to pin down. There is no doubt, for example, that in the Greek world dead bodies and women in childbirth were perceived to be sources of pollution. It was necessary for certain people at certain times to avoid pollution, and any pollution that anyone incurred would need to be removed by an act of purification.[7] Dream-interpreters, seers (*manteis*) and bird-observers were all features of Athenian public life, although in practice *manteis* would combine the skills of reading entrails and observing the flight and sound of birds. *Manteis* were consulted regularly on official business in Athens, and dream-interpreters had a special role in some religious sanctuaries.[8]

Serious parallels can be found for even the more absurd examples in the sketch. So Theophrastus offers us a version of a well-worn joke:

> Q. What does it mean when a mouse has nibbled your sack?
> A. It means it is time to get a new sack.

But if a Roman were to ask, what does it mean when mice have nibbled the Lanuvian shields, the answer that a Roman diviner might give is that it portends civil war.[9] So it is not the actions themselves that are indicative of superstition, but their context. In general the dreams and household events of unimportant individuals would have been considered insignificant, but the *Deisidaimon* reacts as if they are of vital importance; he treats every day as if it were extremely inauspicious; and so on.

Theophrastus' description has nothing to say about public ritual activity, despite the fact that it was an important part of Greek life. This silence is made clearer by the frequent references to behaviour around sacrifices found in others of Theophrastus' *Characters*. Turn up at a sacrifice and when you are tucking into the meat you are apparently likely to find the *Tactless Man* choosing to use the moment to mention the interest you owe him on a loan, while the *Shabby Profiteer* takes a double portion. The *Man of Petty Ambition* will nail the skull of the ox he has sacrificed above his door, and garland it, so that you know he has sacrificed an ox, as opposed to a smaller animal like a sheep. The *Shameless Man* will already have carried out his own sacrifice

---

[7] On pollution in Greece see R. C. T. Parker, *Miasma: Pollution and Purification in Early Greek Religion* (Oxford, 1983).

[8] On divination in ancient Greece see S. I. Johnston and P. T. Struck (eds), *Mantikê: Studies in Ancient Divination*, (Leiden, 2005); H. Bowden, 'Oracles for Sale' in P. Derow and R. C. T. Parker (eds), *Herodotus and his World*, (Oxford, 2003), 256–74.

[9] Cic. *Div.* 1.99, 2.59; Diggle, *Theophrastus Characters*, 359.

at home and salted and stored all the meat for himself, and then turned up to benefit from someone else's sacrifice. If the occasion is a wedding then the *Illiberal Man* will sell off the meat rather than give it to the guests. When you send some of the meat to the *Self-centred Man* he will make it clear that you will get nothing in return, and when you send some to the *Ungrateful Grumbler* he will just complain that he wasn't invited to the party. A number of other Characters behave in unsatisfactory ways during public festivals.[10] Clearly it is poor social behaviour at public festivals and sacrifices that is being satirized in these examples: the actual ritual activities are seen as part of normal life. And it is not suggested in any of these cases that significant offences against the gods are being committed.

Because of this it has been suggested that the contrast between public and private ritual is central to the question of what distinguishes 'superstitious' behaviour. To quote another recent commentator, Theophrastus 'is satirizing personal over-reaction and "unofficial" types of religiosity, but he never makes fun of a recognized civic cult. He draws a line, which others recognize, and does not make fun of what lies inside it.'[11] But this I think is a misunderstanding, because it again suggests that there is a distinction between 'acceptable' and 'unacceptable' religious *practices*. But even while he is describing practices, what Theophrastus is concerned with is clearly attitudes. It is his fearfulness that most obviously characterizes the Superstitious Man, and that fearfulness leads him to take to extremes a set of practices that, in other contexts, might be seen as reasonable. This of course takes us back to the meaning of the word *deisidaimon*, 'fearing the gods': it is precisely this fear that Theophrastus is illustrating.

II

The mental state of the *Deisidaimon* is the concern also of Plutarch's essay *Peri deisidaimonias*, written probably latish in the first century CE.[12] Plutarch puts

---

[10] Theophrast. *Ch.* 12.11, 30.4, 21.7, 9.2, 22.3, 15.5, 17.2; cf. 10.3, 19.4, 19.9, 21.11.

[11] Lane Fox, 'Theophrastus' *Characters*', 152.

[12] Plut. *Mor.* 164e–171f. See Martin, *Inventing Superstition*, 93–108; H. Görgemanns, *Plutarch, drei religionsphilosophische Schriften: Über den Aberglauben, Über die spate Strafe der Gottheit, Über Isis und Osiris* (Düsseldorf, 2003); M. Smith, 'De Superstitione, Moralia 164e–171f', in H. Betz (ed.), *Plutarch's Theological Writings and Early Christian Literature* (Leiden, 1975), 1–8; H. A. Moellering, *Plutarch on Superstition, its Place in the Changing Meaning of Deisidaimonia and in the Context of his Theological Writings* (Boston, 1963); H. Erbse, 'Plutarchs Schrift Περὶδεισιδαιμονίας', *Hermes*, 80 (1952), 296–314.

forward the case that both atheism and *deisidaimonia* are the result of the same lack of understanding about the gods—atheism being the response of the hard-minded, *deisidaimonia* that of the soft-headed:

> Ignorance and lack of understanding of the gods divides itself from the start into two streams, one of which produces in resistant characters, as with hard soils, atheism, and the other of which in tender characters, as with moist soils, produces *deisidaimonia*. All false judgements, especially in these matters, are distressing, but where emotion is involved they are most distressing. For any emotion is likely to be a festering delusion. And just as dislocations of the joints accompanied by laceration are most difficult to deal with, so are distortions of the soul accompanied by emotion. (164e-f)

He goes on to paint a picture of the mental anguish unnecessarily endured by the victim of *deisidaimonia*, and suggests that *deisidaimonia* is even worse than atheism. The essay is somewhat repetitive and not very subtle, and it is universally reckoned to be an early work of Plutarch—and indeed some scholars have suggested that it is inauthentic, or perhaps half missing. It is an essay that seems particularly to have bothered scholars who are concerned in discovering the nature of Plutarch's 'religious faith'. The fact that this essay so clearly states that *deisidaimonia* is worse than atheism is the most worrying aspect of it. It doesn't help that in a later essay, '*That it is not possible to live happily while following the precepts of Epicurus*', he states just as clearly that atheism is worse than *deisidaimonia*,[13] while in *On Isis and Osiris* he says that *deisidaimonia* and atheism are equally bad.[14] However, this is an issue that need not delay us here. As Paul Veyne has pointed out, it all depends on who you are (philosopher or common man), what you mean by *deisidaimonia*, and what you mean by 'worse'.[15] Plutarch's different essays argue the point in different ways, and in the essay under discussion his main concern appears to be the harm the *deisidaimon* will inflict on himself, rather than, for example, the threat he poses to others.

For Plutarch, *deisidaimonia* is absolutely a matter of fear—indeed terror—of the gods. And this fear is a result of ignorance about what the gods are like. This ignorance is shared by the atheist, but the outcome is different.

---

[13] *Mor.* 1101c–1102c. Cf. A. G. Nikolaidis, 'Plutarch's Contradictions', *CM*, 42 (1991), 164–7.

[14] *Mor.* 378a.

[15] P. Veyne, 'Prodiges, divination et peur des dieux chez Plutarque' *Revue de l'Histoire des Religions*, 216 (1999), 437–42.

The atheist simply does not accept that there are any gods, and gets on with living his life on that basis. The *deisidaimon* on the other hand, not only accepts that the gods exist, but assumes that they are out to get him. He is incapable of accepting the possibility that the gods might be benevolent. This is spelled out at the start of the essay, and then repeated frequently thereafter:

> And so to our subject: atheism, the feeble judgement that nothing is blessed and incorruptible, seems to lead to some kind of lack of feeling, through lack of faith in the divine, and the end it achieves through not recognising the gods is not fearing them; *deisidaimonia* as the name itself indicates, is a notion full of feeling and an assumption that produces fear which humbles and crushes a man as he considers that there are gods, and that they are the cause of pain and distress. The atheist then appears unmoved regarding the divine, while the *deisidaimon* is moved in ways in which he ought not to be twisted about. For ignorance produces in the one lack of faith in something that can help him, and in the other it generates the added opinion that it can harm him. From which it follows that atheism is falsified logic, while *deisidaimonia* is emotion generated from false logic. (165b–c)

One reason why, in this essay, superstition is presented as worse than atheism is that it is not simply a case of ignoring the gods, but actively attributing to them bad qualities. As the author puts it later on in the essay—the unique case of Plutarch's name appearing in his own works:

> Why for my part I should prefer that men should say about me that I have never been born at all, and there is no Plutarch, rather than that they should say 'Plutarch is an inconstant fickle person, quick-tempered, vindictive over little accidents, pained at trifles. If you invite others to dinner and leave him out, or if you haven't the time and don't call on him, or fail to speak to him when you see him, he will set his teeth into your body and bite it through, or he will get hold of your little child and beat him to death, or he will turn the beast that he owns onto your crops and spoil your harvest.' (169f–170a).

As was the case with Theophrastus, at first glance Plutarch's argument may seem reasonable. If we start from the notion that God or the gods are all-knowing and ultimately love mankind, then behaving as if they were the opposite would seem irrational. But evidence and experience, and above all Greek tradition, might be said to point in another direction. Greek poets from Homer to Euripides and beyond have painted a rather different picture.

The gods are presented by these authors precisely as fickle and vindictive,[16] and quite often threaten to destroy the harvest;[17] and it must be said that throughout Greek history there is no shortage of examples of cities acting collectively to make sure that the gods are never excluded from public dinners, and are called on and spoken to on a regular basis.[18]

An earlier passage is similarly problematic. Plutarch appears to disapprove of too much attention being paid to cult images. He complains of the *deisidaimones* that:

> They put their trust in bronze-casters, and stone-carvers and wax-workers who make anthropomorphic figures of the gods, and they have such things made, and they decorate them and make obeisance to them; but they scorn philosophers and politicians who are engaged in revealing the solemnity of the gods with their goodness and magnanimity and gentleness and solicitude. (167d–e)

Festivals that involved decorating and parading cult statues were a central part of the religious life of Greek cities, and were the responsibility precisely of those politicians Plutarch appears to be referring to here.[19] It may be that Plutarch has private practices in mind, but it is not obvious that this is the case. It does appear that Plutarch's idea of proper religious behaviour, what he refers to as *eusebeia*, did not correspond to the normal religious practices of Greek communities.

It is important to distinguish here between 'superstition' and 'impiety'. Greek cities did have procedures to punish impiety, for which we have the Greek word *asebeia*: the kinds of action considered as *asebeia* were fairly easily identifiable. They included damaging sacred objects, polluting sacred places, or killing suppliants at altars, and other similar activities. As a rule they were not specific to any particular cult or community—there was a shared understanding of what was or wasn't considered appropriate behaviour, even if there could sometimes be disputes about whether impious acts had been committed.[20] It has been suggested that there was an increased concern about impiety in Athens in the later fifth century BCE, although the evidence

---

[16] E.g. *Iliad* 11.72–83, 14.153–362; Eur. *Hipp.* 1–57, 1416–30.

[17] E.g. *Homeric Hymn to Demeter* 305–11; Hesiod, *Works and Days*, 238–47.

[18] On public dinners see P. Schmitt Pantel, *La cité au banquet: histoire des repas publics dans les cités grecques*, (Rome, 1992), 121–43. On speaking to the gods see S. Pulleyn, *Prayer in Greek Religion* (Oxford, 1997).

[19] An example would be the Athenian Panathenaia, on which see J. Neils, *Goddess and Polis: the Panathenaic Festival in Ancient Athens* (Princeton N.J., 1992), esp. 17, 103–117.

[20] On shared attitudes see Hdt. 8.144.2. Dispute: Thuc. 4.97–8.

is not straightforward.[21] If this were the case, it is more likely to have been a response to the city's misfortunes, which included plague and war, than the result of a change in general understanding. Any such change would be further evidence that fear of angering the gods was indeed a factor in the public administration of Greek religion.

III

It appears from the examination of these two texts that Theophrastus and Plutarch, far from offering an understandable critique of the behaviour and attitudes of the misguided, are actually offering a challenge to the religious norms of their time. In fact this challenge can be traced back at least to the fifth century BCE, and it has its clearest exposition in Plato's *Laws*, written in the mid-fourth century. In a discussion of the laws about religion that are to operate in the ideal city of Magnesia, Plato's central character, referred to as 'the Athenian', says this:

> No-one who believes that the gods are as the law directs (*theous hēgoumenos einai kata nomous*) ever voluntarily commits an unholy act or lets any lawless word pass his lips. If he does, it is because of one of three possible misapprehensions:
>
> (1) as I said, he does not believe [that the gods are],
> (2) that the gods are (*ontas*) but do not concern themselves with mankind,
> (3) that they are easily influenced by sacrifices and persuaded by prayers.

(*Laws* 885b4–9)

As we have already seen, the third of these so-called misapprehensions represents the normal view of Greek communities and of the poetic tradition back to Homer. The first misconception I will return to later. It is the second that is of most interest at the moment. The speakers in the *Laws* agree without difficulty that the gods are essentially unchanging, all wise and benevolent. In Plato's *Timaeus* the divine form is further described as spherical and fiery, these being the purest shape and form of matter:

> The divine form he made mostly of fire so that it should be as bright and beautiful to look at as possible; and he made it spherical like the universe . . . It is beyond our powers to know or tell about the birth of the other gods; we must rely on those who have told the story

[21] R. Garland, *Introducing New Gods: The Politics of Athenian Religion*, (London, 1992); R. C. T. Parker, *Athenian Religion: A History* (Oxford, 1996).

> before, who claimed to be the children of the gods, even if they give
> no probable or necessary proof of what they say: we must conform
> to custom and believe their own family history . . .
> (*Timaeus* 40a2–4, 40d6–41a3)

The idea of a single non-anthropomorphic god presented here is being explicitly contrasted to the polytheism implied by Greek cult and described in the authoritative poetry of Homer and others, a fact which Plato acknowledges, but does not really concern himself with.

It is not clear that this philosophical image of the gods had any more merit to it than the traditional position to which it offered a challenge. If it were the case that Greek philosophical and 'scientific' writings were necessarily characterized by 'rationality', it might follow that even in the sphere of religion their theories are to be preferred.[22] However, it is increasingly recognized that this is not the case.[23] The widely-held idea that Greece in the sixth and fifth centuries BCE experienced an intellectual 'Enlightenment', revealed most obviously in the writings of the Presocratic philosophers and the Hippocratic medical corpus, has been challenged by the argument that what was erected as an alternative to traditional views was in fact an illusion.[24] The idea that the gods (or God) were necessarily well-disposed to humans, as Plato and others argued, was not an obvious truth, or a conclusion drawn from the study of any evidence, but was an untested hypothesis; furthermore, as we have seen, it was a hypothesis that flew in the face of plentiful evidence that the gods were not well-disposed towards mankind—it was a form of religious Panglossianism.

This picture of the gods appears to be based on analogy. It developed in tandem with a political change in Greece, in particular with the appearance of the term *isonomia*, 'equality under the law'—a term that was associated with the new Athenian democracy. *Isonomia* required obedience to the law from all citizens regardless of wealth or birth. If that were required of all citizens, it should surely be expected of the gods too—and indeed, since more was expected of those who had more to offer, the gods should be expected to be most well-disposed to the community. This was a view that never really won widespread acceptance outside the philosophical classes, and was abandoned even by them not long after Plutarch's time, partly perhaps because

---

[22] E.g. G. E. R. Lloyd, *The Revolutions of Wisdom: Studies in the Claims and Practice of Ancient Greek Science* (Berkeley, 1987), esp. 176–81.

[23] E.g. P. Kingsley, *Ancient Philosophy, Mystery and Magic: Empedocles and Pythagorean Tradition* (Oxford, 1995).

[24] The 'Grand Optimal Illusion' in the words of Martin, *Inventing Superstition*.

Christianity began to offer a significantly different view, but also because the notion of *isonomia* and the social issues that went with it were so clearly being abandoned under the growing autocracy of the Roman empire.[25]

One may note here that just as Plutarch's idea of *deisidaimonia* is essentially a philosophical construct, so too is the other extreme he discusses, atheism. In the essay atheism is presented as an intellectual position, and one that is held by a particular philosophical tendency, Epicureanism. In the essay mentioned earlier, *That it is not possible to live happily while following the precepts of Epicurus*, as in the essay on *Deisidaimonia*, Plutarch suggests that denying that there are gods makes life less comfortable, but he does not really see it as more threatening than that.[26] Plato in the *Laws* does consider atheism a more serious problem, but primarily because it can lead in some people to other crimes.[27]

In contrast, in the real world atheism was not a rational position to hold. To be *a-theos* was originally not so much to be an unbeliever as to be godless or ungodly. The most notorious atheist in the ancient world was the fifth-century Diagoras of Melos. Although he was later supposed to have been a writer, the earliest references to Diagoras are accusations that he revealed the secrets of the Eleusinian Mysteries to non-initiates.[28] Such an action would not only have been impious, but also reckless, given the punishment he could expect both from the Athenians and from the goddesses of Eleusis. If Diagoras' reputation as *atheos* rested on this action, as it would seem to, rather than on writings later attributed to him, then the label 'atheist' would appear to be a condemnation of his behaviour rather than a description of his intellectual position. On the other hand, Plato presents a man supposed not to believe in the existence of gods, Anaxagoras of Clazomenae, as a figure of ridicule rather than a threat to anyone.[29]

We can perhaps still recognize as valid Plutarch's attempt to locate *eusebeia*, his true religion, between the poles of *deisidaimonia* on the one side and atheism on the other, but we would have to conclude that in real life it lay a great deal closer to the former than the latter.

IV

Although their critique of *deisidaimonia* may not tell us anything about the views of their contemporaries, one aspect of Plutarch's and Theophrastus'

---

[25] Martin, *Inventing Superstition*, 226–43.

[26] *Mor.* 1102b-c.

[27] *Laws* 908b-909d.

[28] L. Woodbury, 'The Date and Atheism of Diagoras of Melos', *Phoenix* 19 (1965), 178–211.

[29] Plato, *Apol.* 26d.

depiction of the *Deisidaimon* may help us towards an understanding about superstition in general. As we have seen, the *Deisidaimon*'s actions differ from those of his 'normal' contemporaries in their extremity rather than anything else. As the most recent commentator on the *Characters* puts it, 'his actions and his attitudes, taken one by one, would probably not have seemed abnormal to the average Athenian. What sets him apart is the obsessiveness and compulsiveness of his behaviour.'[30] Behaviour so described can be the result of a pathological condition, known as obsessive-compulsive disorder (OCD), and this condition has become a subject of interest to anthropologists of religion in recent years. Now I am not in any way suggesting that Theophrastus is describing a case of OCD. Indeed, there is no reason to suppose that Theophrastus' description of the *Deisidaimon* is based on observation at all— it is far more likely to be an imaginative exaggeration of some types of religious behaviour. But this is where the interest lies—because that is more or less what OCD is too. Recent studies by psychologists have identified a significant correlation between features in the behaviour of OCD patients and ritual activities described by anthropologists in a wide range of cultures.[31] The list of such features includes a high proportion that would describe the behaviour of Theophrastus' *Deisidaimon*. It is worth quoting the list in full, to make the parallels clear. Those items in italics are features found in OCD behaviour and ritual that were significantly more rarely identified in activities other than ritual or work. After each item I have indicated section numbers of Theophrastus' text that correspond to it—in some cases the identifications are more obvious than others:[32]

- *Lucky or unlucky numbers or numbers with special significance* (2, 3, 10);
- *colours with special significance* (4);
- *repeating activities* (2, 7, 12 and *passim*);
- measures to prevent harm (6, 7, 9);[33]
- *ordering or arranging (things or people) in a definite configuration*;
- *saying special prayers or incantations in a set manner* (4, 8);
- *attention to a threshold or entrance* (cf. 5);
- washing or grooming (2, 13);

---

[30] Diggle, *Theophrastus Characters*, 350.

[31] S. Dulaney, and A. P. Fiske, 'Cultural Rituals and Obsessive-Compulsive Disorder: Is there a Common Psychological Mechanism?', *Ethos*, 22 (1994), 243–83; A. P. Fiske and N. Haslam, 'Is Obsessive-Compulsive Disorder a Pathology of the Human Disposition to Perform Socially Meaningful Rituals? Evidence of Similar Content', *Journal of Nervous and Mental Disease*, 185 (1997), 211–22.

[32] The list is from Fiske and Haslam 'Is Obsessive-Compulsive Disorder a Pathology?'

[33] These are the cases where prevention of harm is explicitly mentioned.

- concern with illness or disease (14);
- concerns about rules, right and wrong, morality;
- touching, tapping or rubbing;
- *telling, asking or confessing* (6, 11, 12);
- concern or disgust with bodily wastes or secretions;
- repetition of special words, sounds or numbers (8);
- cutting hair (head, face, body);
- *concern with pollutants, unclean things* (7, 9, 13);
- cleaning things (7);
- *other measures to prevent or remove contact with contaminants* (2, 7, 9, 13, 14);
- *making nonsense sounds, words or music;*
- fear of harming others if insufficiently careful.

Almost all the actions of the *Deisidaimon* can be identified in this list, and most of the items on the list are found in the behaviour of the *Deisidaimon*. This is of course not surprising, since this is a list of actions found in ritual, and, as we have seen, it is not the types of action, but the excessive perform-ance of them, that characterizes the behaviour of the *Deisidaimon*. Nonetheless, the implications of this parallel are worth pursuing. It is sug-gested that:

> The psychological proclivities that may underlie cultural rituals may be closely related to the mechanism that is malfunctioning in OCD patients. In rituals, these actions are socially legitimated and meaningful, while OCD patients are driven to perform actions that have no cultural meaning—except that they mark the person as 'crazy.'[34]

Anthropologists working in the cognitive science of religion have considered the 'psychological proclivities that may underlie cultural rituals', and ex-plained them convincingly by reference to human evolution. Certain kinds of action, often, but not always, related to avoiding contamination or illness, helped the survival of the human species, and natural selection has produced a tendency in human beings to be drawn to certain types of behaviour. This has two distinct but related consequences: human beings are generally attracted to certain kinds of behaviour, and thus will more readily adopt them as rituals; and for some individuals, a pathological condition (OCD) leads them to perform the actions to excess. Thus OCD effectively reveals what kind of actions human beings are instinctively drawn to, and the fact that these

---

[34] Dulaney and Fiske, 'Cultural Rituals' 247.

often resemble religious ritual behaviour explain why certain rituals are readily adopted, whether or not they are officially sanctioned.[35]

V

This work on ritual is part of a larger project in the anthropology of religion. The same approach can explain why other features of religion appeal to human beings. Essentially the reactions that developed to help the survival of early humans make us receptive to certain types of ideas. These include the notion of the existence of powerful invisible supernatural beings—referred to as spirits or ancestors in most modern anthropology of traditional societies, but essentially similar to gods in the polytheistic systems of the ancient world.[36]

The case being made by the cognitive science of religion is substantial, but it should not be oversimplified. The claim is not that religious rituals or beliefs are the direct result of natural selection. Nor is it that the emergence of religion or superstition assisted the survival of the human species. Nor is it that all religious activities or beliefs can be explained as simply the result of human evolution: it is important to note that evolutionary approaches do not explain the concept of a single all-powerful creator God, nor do they address the asking of fundamental questions about existence, or life after death. Rather, the claim is that feelings that human beings have evolved through natural selection, such as the urge to wash when dirty, or a heightened sense of anxiety when seeing a dead body (which may indicate the presence of a predator in the immediate area), make certain forms of action, and certain beliefs, or ways of interpreting the world, particularly appealing. Human beings are therefore instinctively drawn to religious practices, or superstitions, which make use of these feelings.

This anthropological approach has important implications for our study. First of all it is clear that ancient Greek religion, characterized by a great deal of ritual activity, and acknowledging the existence of a large number of supernatural beings who need to be placated, is very much the kind of religious

---

[35] P. Boyer, *Religion Explained: The Human Instincts that Fashion Gods, Spirits and Ancestors* (London, 2001), 262–302.

[36] Boyer, *Religion Explained*, 155–231. For applications of these ideas to ancient religion see D. L. Gragg, 'Old and New in Roman Religion: A Cognitive Account', in H. Whitehouse and L. H. Martin, (eds), *Theorizing Religions Past: Archaeology, History and Cognition* (Walnut Creek, Cal., 2004), 69–86; R. Beck, 'Four Men, Two Sticks, and a Whip: Image and Doctrine in a Mithraic Ritual', in Whitehouse and Martin, *Theorizing Religions Past*, 87–103; R. Beck, *The Religion of the Mithras Cult in the Roman Empire: Mysteries of the Unconquered Sun*, (Oxford, 2006), esp. 88–101.

system that one would expect to develop in human society as a result of these evolutionary tendencies. And indeed it is a system very similar to that of the rest of the ancient world, including ancient India and China.[37] That is not to deny the major cultural influences on the development of polytheistic religious systems in these societies, but to argue that as they are practised—and this is probably even more the case in the area of private religious activity—they appeal to the emotions and instincts of their participants. This stands in contrast to later monotheistic 'religions of the book', which lay stress on 'teachings', which are addressed more to the intellect. It follows that the philosophical critique of this kind of behaviour as *deisidaimonia* can be seen as an intellectual reaction against behaviour that is fundamentally rooted in human nature.[38]

Over time however, the philosophers triumphed. This can be seen not only in the rise of 'rationalism' and science, but also in religion. The Greek philosophical tradition was one of the roots of Christian doctrine, and the philosophical condemnation of *deisidaimonia* lies behind the Church's condemnation of superstitious beliefs and practices, explored in several of the papers in this volume.[39] But although physical scientists and religious authorities have attacked superstition—not incorrectly—as irrational, they have not managed to extinguish it. The ease with which human beings are able to accept the existence of powerful spirits—whether embodied in magical statues, saints' relics, or anything else—and the human propensity to adopt apparently meaningless rituals as a way of coping with the uncertainties of life, are—according to cognitive scientists—the result of natural selection, and are therefore part of what it is to be human. For that reason, superstition is unlikely to disappear.

There is one more point to note. The mechanism by which these 'superstitious' beliefs and activities are made attractive is not intellectual,

---

[37] For the Mediterranean and the Near East see S. I. Johnston (ed.), *Religions of the Ancient World: A Guide* (Cambridge Mass, 2004); for China see Poo Mu-chou 蒲慕州, *In Search of Personal Welfare: A View of Ancient Chinese Religion* (Albany, 1998); M. J. Puett, *To Become a God: Cosmology, Sacrifice, and Self-divinization in Early China* (Cambridge Mass., 2002).

[38] For a similar intellectual reaction to the same phenomenon in China, see T. H. Barrett, this volume.

[39] For what might be considered an authoritative, albeit controversial, assertion of the role of Greek philosophy in Catholic Christianity, see Benedict XVI, 'Faith, Reason and the University: Memories and Reflections', delivered at the University of Regensburg in September 2006, http://www.vatican.va/holy_father/benedict_xvi/speeches/2006/september/documents/hf_ben-xvi_spe_20060912_university-regensburg_en.html (consulted 27 September 2006).

but emotional. Rituals are adopted to some extent because they bring comfort, but also because not to carry them out can produce feelings of anxiety—in OCD patients 'non-performance creates a strong feeling of fear and anguish'.[40] In other words it can be argued that it is indeed fear that drives superstitious behaviour: to that extent Theophrastus and Plutarch were right.

---

[40] Boyer, *Religion Explained*, 274.

Superstitio, Superstition and Religious Repression in the Late Roman Republic and Principate (100 BCE–300 CE)

Richard Gordon

Rather more than a century ago, Georg Wissowa, editor of the multi-volume encyclopaedia of Classical Antiquity, *Paulys Realencyclopädie*, commissioned for the first volume of the new enterprise an article on Superstition, 'Aberglaube', from the respectable and industrious Ernest Rieß. Rieß duly turned in an article of 64 closely-printed columns in which he listed hundreds of bizarre ancient beliefs and practices, from meteorological phenomena to birth and death, from magical stones to plant-remedies, many of them culled from the Elder Pliny's *Natural History* (written around 70–75 CE).[1] For example, if you wash your mouth twice a month in the forenoon with pounded lettuce-leaves mixed with vinegar, you will not be troubled by tooth-ache; if you take a living bat, carry it three times around the house and nail it head-down over the window, it will protect you and your household, especially the sheep-pens, from witchcraft.[2]

Rieß noted that the Greek word *deisidaimonia* and the Latin *superstitio* do not coincide fully with the semantic range of German 'Aberglaube'. He defined the last as 'ideas about the supernatural, that have sunk down out of the realm of living religious consciousness and become to some extent petrified, and the associated ritual practices'. Properly conceived, superstition is one form of religious or mythological thinking, and can usually be explained by means of historical research. For example, belief in the werewolf can be accounted for by tracing it back to a cult involving human sacrifice, and beyond that, to the semantic link in Indo-European pre-history between the (Greek) word for wolf, *lykos*, the god of Light (Latin *lux, lucere*), and the god's birth, as Zeus Lykaios, on Mount Lykaion in Arcadia in the central Peloponnese. A routinized philological historicism thus underlay Rieß' confidence that superstitions could in principle be explained without residue. It was simply a matter of seeing the historical connections.

---

[1] E. Rieß, s.v. 'Aberglaube', *RE*, 1.1 (1894), 29–93.

[2] Pliny, *HN*, 20.58; 29.83.

Typical of scholars of his day, and still of most ordinary people nowadays, Rieß took it for granted that superstition is an unproblematic, well-nigh universal descriptive category for a wide variety of sunken beliefs. The contents of the category can only be enumerated; it consists in particular instances of petrified usages. It has no theory. By contrast, however, if one looks up 'Aberglaube' in the modern replacement of Wissowa's encyclopaedia, *Der Neue Pauly*, compiled in the 1990s, one finds no entry at all. Instead there is a reference to the two ancient words, *deisidaimonia* and *superstitio*, which it is reckoned to translate. Superstition has ceased to appear to be a natural category. It is not simply that the mass of material collected by Rieß has been re-classified under other heads: the very notion that superstition might be a scientific term now, after the 'anthropological turn' inaugurated by the Annales school, appears laughable. Whereas the key interpretative metaphor used to be petrification, which legitimated the claim that history was the privileged mode of understanding such beliefs while characterizing *das Volk*, the Folk, as the Romantically-authentic carriers of such unchanging lore, 'superstition' now almost always wears inverted commas, and has become an actor's or positional word, demoted from the ineffable throne of Science down to the muddy fray of *parti pris*.

As Steve Smith's Introduction makes clear, the Wivenhoe conference invited participants to reflect on this relatively new, operational aspect of superstition, its situational, argumentative or vituperative use, and the problems arising: the nature of the anxieties expressed, the boundaries policed, the relation between superstition and other negative words, whether 'reason' or 'rationality' figure in the debate. At the same time it was suggested that it might be worth looking at the value of superstitious beliefs to those who hold them; whether they are always popular, of the Folk; how far they may be implicated in struggles over the legitimacy of religious innovation; what superstition may have to do with the ability of a religious system to maintain the very category of the sacred. This programme involves going beyond semantic enquiry in order to examine overt conflicts concerning the use of, or admission to, sacred symbols, conflicts which may in turn conceal differing attitudes towards a range of other issues.

In this contribution on Rome between *c.*100 BCE and 300 CE, I have chosen to concentrate on the self-understanding, and anxieties, of the socio-political group (essentially the members of the great families that dominated the Senate) that came to define an imagined, or ideal, community of right belief-and-practice in terms of *superstitio*. It was the struggle to maintain the imagined community in the wider context of the striking changes—political, military, ideological, and religious—brought about by Rome's acquisition of a Mediterranean empire that accounts for the word's semantic vagaries. The underlying issue, however, as I see it, is relatively simple: the socio-political elite had a sharply different interest in the religious system from that of the mass of the population, day-labourers and peasant-farmers. Thanks to its domination of public rhetoric, it enjoyed the social power of representing 'Roman religion' as the engine of Roman imperial success. Although that religion was acknowledged to be a construction over time, created in its main lines by certain grand figures of the remote past—the legendary Romulus, Numa, and Servius Tullius—but constantly refined by famous experts in pontifical law such as P. Mucius Scaevola (elected *pontifex maximus* in 130 BCE), its drift was consistent. From the point of view of this elite, itself of course the real driving-force behind territorial expansion, the gods smiled on Rome because she was equipped with the best religious institutions.[3] As the poet Propertius put it, the Romans owed their empire not so much to their military prowess as to their religious observance.[4]

Since the Roman concept of *superstitio* is in my view so closely linked with the ideological interests of a competitive but non-hereditary elite, I here completely ignore an alternative view, developed by Hellenistic philosophers, and picked up by their Roman imitators (such as Cicero towards the end of his life, wearing his philosopher's hat), that understood superstition as the clean inverse of religion. Such an opposition depended upon a premise quite foreign to mainstream Greek and Roman religious discourse, namely that just because the gods are blessed and immortal they cannot also be angry or partial.[5] This account saw superstition as based upon a false view of the nature of the gods; but the only way of substantiating the claim was to redefine them as constituents of nature (Ceres = grain) or forms of a single Deity, who is inherently and solely beneficent.[6] In a polytheistic context, this was strong stuff: it was not for nothing that the Stoics chose to deal with theology at the very end of years of philosophical study. And in my view this theological account of superstition was both irrelevant and, indeed, incomprehensible both to elites and to masses in the period under discussion, at any rate until

---

[3] The clearest expression is Cotta's speech in Cicero, *Nat. deor.* 3.5f; cf. P. A. Brunt, 'Laus imperii', in P. D. A. Garnsey and C. R. Whittaker (eds), *Imperialism in the Ancient World* (Cambridge, 1978), 159–91 at 164–8.

[4] Propertius 3.22.21: *quantum ferro tantum pietate potentes stamus.*

[5] E.g. Cicero, *Nat. deor.* 1.45; 55f; 2.63; 71f.; *Div.* 2.149. This is the discourse that D. B. Martin, *Inventing Superstition: From the Hippocratics to the Christians* (Cambridge, MA and London, 2004) sees as central; to my mind it is peripheral to the main problems (cf. my review in *Gnomon*, 78 (2006), 521–6).

[6] E.g. Cicero, *Nat. deor.* 2.63–70.

the rise of Christianity in the second half of the third century CE made the idea of a single truly beneficent god appear less outlandish.[7] In the Roman case, then, it makes most sense to view the notion of superstition as a strategy for delimiting an imagined community by claiming the existence of consensual frontiers between traditional/sanctioned/proper and non-traditional/unsanctioned/improper/religious action.[8] The sociopolitical locus of the claim that a given religious expression or act is superstitious is thus of central importance. On that basis, we can discern at least four types of cognitive interest in asserting the existence of such boundaries.[9]

1. Self-definition: Tacitly or explicitly, the speaker claims to be a member of, indeed spokesman for, a community of sanctioned religious practice. To invoke superstition is to align oneself with an implied authority, whether 'traditional', legal or moral.

2. Drawing the boundaries: Use of the negative discrimination implies that the speaker has the right to determine where the boundary between sanctioned and unsanctioned practice is to be set. Each intervention is therefore at the same time an assertion of the speaker's authority or right to impose the discrimination at this point. Whatever the local criteria for superstition may be, the speaker affirms their validity as *the* appropriate criteria.

3. The right to judge: The use of the negative discrimination implies the superiority of the speaker's claimed point of reference, without his being

---

[7] Cf. the critique of the Stoic account of divinity put into the mouth of C. Aurelius Cotta at *Nat. deor.* 3.38ff. On the different forms of Hellenistic philosophical theology, see J. Mansfeld, 'Theology', in K. Algra et al. (eds), *The Cambridge History of Hellenistic Philosophy* (Cambridge, 1999), 452–78.

[8] B. Anderson, *Imagined Communities: Reflections on the Origin and Spread of Nationalism* (London, 1983).

[9] 'Cognitive interest' is the conventional translation of the German *Erkenntnisinteresse*, a concept that has a central role in Max Weber's reflections on the methodology of the social sciences, e.g. 'All knowledge of cultural reality . . . is always knowledge from particular points of view': ' "Objectivity" in Social Science', in M. Weber, *The Methodology of the Social Sciences*, trans. and ed. E. A. Shils and H. A. Finch (New York, 1949), 49–112 at 81 (= 'Die ‹Objektivität› sozialwissenschaftlicher und sozialpolitischer Erkenntnis', in *Max Weber, Soziologie, Universalgeschichtliche Analysen, Politik*, ed. J. Winckelmann (Stuttgart, 1992), 186–262 at 224; = *Gesammelte Aufsätze zur Wissenschaftslehre*, ed. J. Winckelmann (Stuttgart, 1988), 148–214 (original published 1904)). The issue was generalized by Jürgen Habermas, *Erkenntnis und Interesse* (Frankfurt am Main, 1968), translated by J. J. Shapiro as *Knowledge and Human Interests* (Boston, 1971, repr. Cambridge, 1987).

required to show or specify the grounds or even the nature of that claim. Since the charge of superstition operates by arousing an essentially emotional response, the logical basis of the claim is protected from examination.

4. Safeguarding the imagined community: Accusations of superstition at the margin serve to distract attention away from areas of dispute, contradictions or anomalies within the claimed community of belief-and-practice. The implied or explicit centre can thus be defended as a whole, without reference to embarrassing detail. Just as vernacular nationalisms shore up archaic conceptions of power and privilege, so superstition maintains useful fictions, say the total adequacy of a world-view, or stability of belief within the imagined community, and legitimates the transfer of the impure reality of shifting needs and interpretations onto the outside.

It is difficult to judge whether, or how far, the Roman elite was aware of these functions of its concept of *superstitio*. We hardly need to be reminded of the world-constructing power of religious systems, and sub-systems. As I point out later, it is easy enough to find examples of individuals claiming the sufficiency of traditional Roman religion while at the same time acting to innovate within it, for example by introducing new deities or even entire cults, such as that of the Mater Magna; indeed there existed institutions, such as the reading of the Sibylline Books, intended to facilitate precisely that.[10] Double-thinking here merges with reality-principle. It would perhaps be best to appeal to the notion of social script: forms of religious behaviour that could loosely be described as 'unmanly' or 'un-Roman' were subsumed under a single script that both expressed and reinforced the exclusionary thinking of a society based on orders.[11] The implication that such unmanliness is inborn is simply an instance of the naturalization of its own arbitrariness practised by every established order.[12] Scripts, being stereotypes, resist reflection. *Superstitio* was thus understood not so much as a judgement of others' behaviour as a label for a supposed weakness of the mind

---

[10] On the role of the Oracles in mediating the introduction of new cults, and their negotiating value, see M. Monaca, *La Sibilla a Roma: I libri sibillini fra religione e politica* (Cosenza, 2005), 197–278, with a useful collection of texts.

[11] I have adapted the notion of scripts from narratology, though it originally derives from cognitive psychology; cf. M. Kaiser, 'Die Schematheorie des Verstehens fiktionaler Literatur', *Vierteljahrsschrift für Literaturwissenschaft und Geistesgeschichte* 56 (1982), Sonderheft, 226–48. The advantage of the narratologists' version is that it starts from the reader's perception of small units of described and implicitly evaluated behaviour, which can be grouped to form more complex units that carry 'inherent' meaning.

[12] Cf. P. Bourdieu, *Outline of a Theory of Practice*, trans. R. Nice (Cambridge, 1977), 164.

(*levitas animi*) that produced such behaviour; then as the behaviour itself and, by extension, entire religious traditions based upon such 'weakness'.

Although the English words superstition and superstitious derive from the Latin *superstitio* and *superstitiosus*, their ranges only partly overlap. Nowadays, for example, it is not uncommon to find 'superstitious' used as a humorous self-deprecation. At Rome, however, no member of the politico-social elite would have dreamed of describing himself as *superstitiosus* in connection with religion. The adjective would only be used in connection with a personal enemy (even a 'bad' emperor); about those of inferior social or gender status, *de haut en bas*, within Roman society; or to depreciate the cult practices of foreigners or provincials, usually en masse. Again, *superstitio* never has the modern sense of a belief one can take or leave; nor did it imply a shallow, insincere, or opportunistic belief. Moreover, outside the philosophical discussion I have mentioned, at Rome *superstitio* did not imply an irrational belief or practice, one that science, 'organized religion', or some other authority has shown to be false, untrue or meaningless. The word had no, or virtually no, reference to intellectual claims.[13] It was rather a dismissive way of referring to what in the speaker's opinion appeared excessive, dishonourable, unmanly, sometimes simply new and unfamiliar, sometimes actually wicked, forms of religious action or expression. In other words, the condemnation or distance it asserted was nicely calibrated with the self-image of the Roman politico-social elite in matters relating to religious practice. Roman *superstitio* can thus be defined as religious action producing the inverse of Bourdieu's notion of distinction.[14]

[13] It is therefore rather dismaying to find that the standard modern dictionary, the *Oxford Latin Dictionary*, ed. P. W. Glare (Oxford, 1968–82), defines its first sense (1a) as 'an attitude of irrational religious awe or credulity, superstition'. As I understand the matter, the Roman concept of *superstitio*, outside narrowly philosophical argument, involved neither rationality nor belief. It was focused on *ends* and the *style* appropriate to attaining those ends.

[14] 'Because the appropriation of cultural products presupposes dispositions and competences which are not universally distributed (although they have the appearance of innateness), these products are subject to exclusive appropriation, material or symbolic, and, functioning as cultural capital (objectified or internalized), they yield a profit in distinction, proportionate to the rarity of the means required to appropriate them, and a profit in legitimacy, the profit par excellence, which consists in the fact of feeling justified in being (what one is), being what it is right to be': P. Bourdieu, *Distinction: A Social Critique of the Judgement of Taste*, trans. R. Nice (London, 1984), 228 (= *La distinction: critique sociale du jugement* (Paris, 1979), 252).The French is much easier to understand.

In the two sections of this paper, I first explore a little further the range of uses of Latin *superstitio*, and examine the nature of the categories and boundaries it sought to safeguard within the context of the expansion of the Roman Republican empire.[15] It is especially important here to observe its relation to the slippery word *religio*, whose meaning can range between the scrupulous attention to detail that links humankind to divinity by virtue of a code of conduct reciprocally binding on both sides, through the totality of actions conventionally regarded as appropriate in the worship of the gods, to being more or less synonymous with *superstitio*.[16] The second section explores how the imagined community that the Republican term was intended to protect, itself inherently imprecise and unstable, began to crumble under the disorderly pressures unleashed by the sheer success of territorial empire. The establishment of an autocratic regime in which the emperors and their interests came to dominate the forms and the ends of the traditional religious system meant that *superstitio* came to register new types of inappropriate behaviour, and indeed sometimes to become virtually synonymous with the terms that mark the negative pole of the continuum of religious belief-and-practice, impiety, atheism, and magic. These senses were not wholly new in the semantics of *superstitio*, but they now become far more prominent.

I

Before embarking on a sketch of Latin usage, I should stress the extreme bias of the surviving literature in favour of the 'classical' literature of the Roman elite that seemed in the fifth to the eighth centuries CE worth preserving. In particular very little survives from the entire history of the Republic apart from Plautus (active *c.*218–186 BCE) and Terence (active *c.*170–60 BCE), and Cicero, Lucretius, Catullus, and Caesar in the first century BCE. The conclusions we draw about the range of reference that *superstitio* and its cognates might have had are to an unknowable extent influenced by the type of texts preserved and the social status of their authors.

The earliest surviving example of the noun *superstitio* occurs in a lengthy legal document composed by Cicero as a youngish man (*c.*70 BCE), but never

---

[15] I cite just a small selection from the exhaustive trawl now made possible by the Latin database of the Packard Humanities Institute, CDRom #5.3.

[16] 'The term *religiosus* was applied to people who allowed themselves to be taken over by an excessive, superstitious *religio*, and such behaviour was considered disgraceful': Aulus Gellius, *Attic Nights* 4.9.11f. (*c.*180 CE). On the senses of *religio*, see M. Sachot, 'Religio/ superstitio: Historique d'une subversion et d'un retournement', *Revue de l'Histoire des Religions* 208.4 (1991), 355–94.

actually delivered as a speech in a law-court. It is used to describe the mixture of horror, outrage, and religious apprehension felt by the Greek-speaking inhabitants of the Roman province of Sicily at the removal by the rapacious governor C. Verres of a famous cult-statue of Demeter from the temple at Enna.[17] Cicero is here doubtless translating the Greek word *deisidaimonia*, fear of god, awe, from the testimony of one of his Greek clients, but in doing so he gives it a slight twist: he chooses to emphasize the Sicilians' anxiety lest the goddess return the Roman governor's insult by sending them a succession of poor harvests—Demeter was the goddess of harvested grain, and Enna had been her main cult-centre on the island for more than three centuries. Implicit in the word here is the Roman aristocrat's—in the young Cicero's case, would-be Roman aristocrat's—'involuntary' disdain for the subject peoples. And it requires no great penetration to see that, had he been defending Verres rather than prosecuting him, Cicero could have used the same word in a more openly negative sense to mean 'unmanly panic prompted by fear of divine retribution'. Indeed, one of the most vituperative examples of *superstitio* in the extant literature occurs in another early speech, delivered only four years later, in defence of an evidently extremely unpleasant character accused of poisoning his own stepfather. Employing a smear-tactic common in Roman courts, Cicero depicts his client's wealthy mother, who had instigated the prosecution, as a ghastly witch who would stop at nothing to fix his client, even including *nocturna sacrificia*, by implication necromantic human sacrifice or offerings to Hekate, the goddess of nefarious magic. These sacrifices to further her unspeakable crimes are described as *contaminata superstitio*, foul, polluted practice, the inverse of proper cult.[18]

The very earliest extant occurrences of the word *superstitio* thus reveal three features that remained central to its illocutionary force. Firstly, it refers to religious acts or practices, and the anxieties or fears that inspired them, but never to particular fixed, widespread, conventional beliefs that can be shown to be false. 'Superstitious' rituals are not necessarily ineffectual acts vis-à-vis the gods. Secondly, its antonyms are the key pro-words of religio-political discourse: *pietas* (due observance), *religio* (cult according to the traditional

---

[17] Cicero, 2 *Verr.* 4.113; cf. A. Vasaly, *Representations: Images of the World in Ciceronian Oratory* (Berkeley, 1993), 157–72.

[18] *Pro Cluentio* 194. For the associations of nocturnal sacrifices, see H.-G. Kippenberg, 'Magic in Roman Civil Discourse: Why Rituals could be Illegal', in idem and P. Schäfer (eds), *Envisioning Magic. A Princeton Seminar and Symposium* (Leiden, 1997), 137–163; on the moral, community-building, functions of invective, cf. Cicero, *Rep.* 5.6, *Philipp.* 9.13 etc. with A.Corbeil, 'Invective,' in J. M. May (ed.), *Brill's Companion to Cicero: Oratory and Rhetoric* (Leiden, 2002), ch. 7.

rules, written and unwritten), *iustae preces* (appointed or customary supplications).[19] All of these pro-words imply adherence both to a set of moral expectations and to tacit prescriptions relating to normative physical self-presentation, in French *tenue*. A key mark of *superstitio* is weeping, wailing, loss of dignity, the open expression of fear and distress in a religious, but non-funerary, context. Thirdly, it marginalizes a set of practices, definable only in concrete situations, and yet characteristic of certain kinds of person: *superstitio* is the behavioural correlate in the context of religion of the refusal or inability to live up to proper standards. The masses, Greek-speaking provincials, and women of all kinds are just the sort of people from whom such behaviour is to be expected. They may know how to behave, but one cannot bank on it.

These early Ciceronian usages imply an already-established semantic field covering both psychological attitudes and misuse of religious ritual. When the word *superstitio* emerged in this sense is unknown. Nothing can be achieved by appealing to etymology.[20] About a century earlier than these two speeches, the adjective *superstitiosus* seems to have meant 'inspired' or 'frenzied'.[21] It is generally believed that noun and adjective alike derive from *superstes*, relict, that is, 'remaining after the rest has been removed'. However the logic remains quite opaque.[22] In my view it is far more likely that the abstract noun *superstitio* is a back-formation from *superstitiosus* when that word began to be used to reflect the usual ambivalence towards low-level, unpretentious forms of divination with a high failure-rate.[23] Once the noun came into being, the adjective must quickly have lost its older sense

---

[19] As will become clear later, the relation between *superstitio* and *religio* is far from simple.

[20] Cicero, *Nat. deor.* 2.72 suggests that the word was developed from *superstes*, 'surviving': the adjective *superstitiosus* would then have been applied originally to parents who spent all day long praying and sacrificing in the hope of their children surviving them. The most elaborate discussion of the semantic development is L. F. Janssen, 'Die Bedeutungsentwicklung von *superstitio/superstes*', *Mnemosyne* NS 28 (1975), 135–88.

[21] Used of the prophetess Cassandra, doomed never to be believed (Pacuvius, frg. 216 Ribbeck), and of the Pythia at Delphi (*Trag. incert.* 19 Ribbeck).

[22] E. Benveniste suggested that the connection might be that the seer speaks of an event in the past 'as if it were before his eyes'; *superstitio* would then be the gift of second sight which allows one to know the past as if one had actually been present: *Le vocabulaire des institutions indo-européennes* (Paris, 1969), 2: 273–9, repeating an idea he had already published in 1938. However the passage of Plautus he cites in evidence only shows that *superstitiosus* might already have a negative connotation in the late third century BCE.

[23] As already in Plautus, *Amphitryo* 321–3, *Curculio* 397, *Rudens* 1139, all from the 190s, the decade after the end of the Second Punic War, a period of intense stress and uncertainty which had seen a number of outbreaks of *superstitio*.

of 'inspired'. This would imply that the noun *superstitio* came into existence already in the first half of the second century (which would explain Cicero's confidence in using it about a century later).

It can, I think, be assumed that the word already then reflected the anxiety of the politico-social elite regarding the ability of the Senate, as the constituted authority in matters of legitimate religious practice, to control popular religious movements, prophetic outbreaks, moral scares. We shall see that this is the pattern implied by Livy's stereotyped account of the regal and early Republican periods, in which motifs from the second century BCE model alleged events in earliest Roman 'history'.[24]

The two primary areas in which the Latin term *superstitio* was applied are popular fears of divine anger, manifested in epidemic illness, strange untoward events and so on, and by extension 'unmanly' apprehensions by individuals, including even emperors, of magical attack, misfortune or murder; and the religions of foreign peoples.

Like the negative sense of Greek *deisidaimonia* in Theophrastus' *Characteres* 16 (late fourth century BCE) and Plutarch's *De superstitione* (*c*.70 CE), *superstitio* could mean 'excessive religious apprehensions or fears'. Thus Livy records that the third *lectisternium* (a Greek ritual of feasting the gods) in the history of Rome was performed in 364 BCE in order to put an end to a plague believed to be due to divine anger; and when that had no effect, and the people became even more frightened (*victis superstitione animis*), stage-plays were ordered to be performed as an additional placation of divinity.[25] Roughly contemporary with Livy, the funeral address in honour of an unnamed upper-class woman lists her domestic virtues of modesty, obedience, obligingness, her skills at weaving, and her ability to dress without ostentation; and adds her *religio sine superstitione*, her religious observance free of that excess—or emotionality—associated with female religiosity.[26] Pliny the Younger mentions an enemy of his, a well-known litigant and legacy-hunter named M. Aquilius Regulus (d. *c*.105 CE), who was so in the grip of anxieties when he spoke in court that he used to ward off magical spells

---

[24] E. T. Lansford, *Augustan Ideology in Livy's First Pentad* (Ann Arbor, 1994); G. B. Miles, *Livy: Reconstructing Early Rome* (Ithaca, 1995); G. Forsythe, *Livy and Early Rome: A Study in Historical Method and Judgement* (Stuttgart, 1999).

[25] Livy 7.2.3. On Livy's account of early Roman religion, cf. B. Liou-Gille, *Une lecture 'religieuse' de Tite-Live, 1: Cultes, rites, croyances de Rome archaïque* (Paris, 1998).

[26] *Laudatio 'Turiae'* (= Dessau, *ILS* no. 8393) 30f. By the mid-first century CE we find the rhetorician Quintilian using *superstitio* and the adverb *superstitiose* in a totally secular context to describe the behaviour of students who stick blindly to the rules instead of creatively learning from them, e.g. *Inst. or.* 4.2.85; 10.6.5; 12.10.14.

(designed to make him fall suddenly dumb, what we would call stagefright) by painting a line round one eye and placing a white patch alternately over one or other eyebrow; and ask *haruspices*, people who could divine the future, about how his cases would go.[27] 'Extravagant superstition' (*a nimia superstitione*), says Pliny gleefully, but I suppose one can say that he took his role in court seriously![28] Suetonius, at about the same date, describes Nero, a 'bad' emperor, as 'in the grip of superstition' (*superstitione captus*), in the context of gossip that he actually used to sacrifice to a female statuette that had been sent him as a talisman against conspiracy.[29] A rescript of the emperor Marcus Aurelius, in the third quarter of the second century CE, decreed that anyone who acted in such a way as to excite people's apprehensions in relation to a divinity (*quo leves hominum animi superstitionis numinis terrentur*), that is, as a religious prophet, was to be relegated to an island.[30]

In this context, the word is usually (though, as it happens, not in these cases) in the plural, and often linked to *religiones*, also in the plural, which means much the same, a tendency to have recourse to supposedly extravagant ritual through fear of divine anger. Thus Livy tells how the legendary early King Tullus, in a time of plague, himself became ill, and, from being a regular fire-eater, suddenly changed tack, 'fell prey to all manner of religious fears great and small', and filled his subjects with similar anxieties.[31]

---

[27] Similar fears are known among other Roman orators, proving that 'superstition' was not merely a matter of class and education. The forehead and eyebrows are specifically mentioned as targets in the two longest Latin curse-tablets listing body parts (*IDefixAudollent* 135; *CIL* I² 2530).

[28] Pliny, *Epist.* 6.2.2; cf. 2.20.3–5. By contrast, when Cicero (whose account of the derivation of *superstitiosus*, cited in n.16, was written at about the same time) lost his only daughter, aged 33, in 45 BCE and spent much of the rest of the year making and unmaking plans for building a temple to her as a kind of divinity at his country villa (*ad Atticum* 12.12.1; 36.1), his friend Atticus called his behaviour stupid, mistaken folly (*ineptiae; stultitia; error...*) but not *superstitio*.

[29] Suetonius, *Nero* 56; likewise Domitian, another 'bad' emperor, is said to have worshipped Minerva superstitiously (*superstitiose colebat*): *Domit.* 15.3; cf. J. Scheid, 'Religion et superstition à l'époque de Tacite: quelques réflexions', in AA.VV., *Religion, superstición y magia en el mundo romano* (Cádiz, 1985), 19–34.

[30] Modestinus, *de poenis*, ap. *Digest.* 48.19.30.

[31] *Omnibus magnis parvis superstitionibus obnoxius degeret ... religionibus ... populum impleret* (Livy 1.31.6); also 6.5.6 (after the sack of Rome by the Gauls in 390): *in civitate plena religionum, tunc etiam ab recenti clade superstitiosis principibus ...*, at Rome all kinds of religious anxieties were making the rounds, and the faith of the leading men in the efficacy of religion was shaken by the recent defeat.

The second area where we regularly find the word *superstitio* is as a term to describe non-Roman religions. No particular distinctions in time or distance can be discerned in this context, for we find the word used with reference to Italic tribes as well as about exotic peoples such as the Egyptians, the Chaldaeans (for astrology), the Gauls, and the Germans. But there is a tendency for *superstitio* to denote what we would call the religion of exotic peoples, whereas in the case of those more integrated into the Roman world-picture, it denotes particular practices or rituals.

Thus, while the Samnites were off 'busy with their mumbo-jumbo' (*operati superstitionibus*) in 293 BCE, the consul Sp. Carvilius Maximus seized the opportunity to capture the town of Amiternum and massacre about 2,800 men.[32] *Superstitio*, claims Cicero, is worshipping cats and dogs, as the Egyptians do.[33] In his concern to keep up indigenous Italic religious tradition, the emperor Claudius proposed in 47 CE to create an official college of Etruscan *haruspices* (diviners) at Rome; this knowledge, he explained, has suffered recently under public neglect 'and the spread of foreign religions'.[34] Pliny the Elder would have liked to describe the Greek magico-medical incantations associated with Thracian Orpheus as *superstitio*, but he knew there was no magic in Thrace.[35] According to Tacitus, the Baltic tribe of the 'Aestii' [= Eistr/Esten] worshipped the Mother of the Gods, and therefore used the emblem of a boar 'as a sign of their faith'.[36] The emperor Antoninus Pius (138–61 CE) permitted provincials to take oaths according to their local religious usage, described as *superstitio*.[37]

---

[32] Livy 10.39.1–2.

[33] Cicero, *De leg.* 1.32. The geographer Pomponius Mela specifies human sacrifice as a typical mark of superstition: *gentes superbae superstitiosae aliquando etiam immanes adeo, ut hominem optimam et gratissimam diis victimam crederent*, proud and superstitious peoples tend to be really brutal, inasmuch as they believe that a human being is the best sacrificial offering of all, and the most acceptable to the gods (*De chorogr.* 3.14, *c*.40 CE).

[34] *Et quia externae superstitiones valescant*: Tacitus, *Ann.* 11. 15. 1. Given the divinatory context, I assume he had astrology mainly in mind, though the cult of Egyptian Serapis encouraged dream-divination.

[35] Pliny, *HN* 30.7.

[36] *Insigne superstitionis*: Tacitus, *Germ.* 45.3. Presumably the deity was a form of the Germanic goddess Nerthus-Freyja, whose favourite, Óttarr, sometimes took the form of a boar with golden bristles. However, no such emblems are known in the archaeology of East Prussia/the Baltic lands.

[37] *Quod propria superstitione iuratum est, standum rescripsit*: Ulpian, *ad edictum praetoris*, ap. *Digest*. 12.2.5.1.

It is worth noting here that even among these few citations there is a range of implied attitudes, between Antoninus Pius' neutral distance (he is interested only in ensuring the maximum authority for oaths, given their crucial role in contracts and law-courts; it is thus improbable that *superstitio* here has a belittling sense); through Livy's implied judgement, that it served the Samnites right for being so preoccupied with religion when there was a war on;[38] to the outright hostility of Cicero's contempt for the Egyptians. So far as I know, and for what it is worth given the nature of our sources, the earliest extant example of this markedly negative usage occurs in a legal speech, also by Cicero, delivered in 59 BCE in relation to the requirement upon Jews to send money annually to Jerusalem.[39] It becomes more common, however, from the middle of the first century CE.[40]

These two usages are both expressions of the idea that there existed a traditional set of public and private practices, instituted by Romulus and Numa, that had unique authority as the *religio Romanorum*. In reality, of course, the institutions, rituals and inflections of Roman religion were subject to historical change over both the long and the short term. Some of the most typically 'Roman' gods, Mercury, Saturn, Hercules, Minerva, Diana, Ceres, Venus, for example, as well as many ritual practices and festivals, were, or were believed to be, Etruscan or Greek, absorbed into Roman cult during the early history of the city. Some changes, such as the building of new temples, the introduction of new deities, for example Venus Eryx from Sicily or Aesculapius from Epidaurus, or increases in the number of specialist roles ('priesthoods'), were indeed marked and recorded by the collective memory, inasmuch as they were related to competition between the members of the elite and the furtherance of their ends, personal and collective. For example, among the information recorded by the official Roman calendars, beginning in the late Republic, are the foundation dates of temples, many of them to abstract deities of great significance for the self-representation of the aristocracy, such as Salus, Victoria, Honos, Virtus, Fides, Fortuna huiusce diei

---

[38] Beyond that, of course, his choice of the word is intended to deflect the accusation that Maximus had broken the rules of war, quite apart from making a mockery of the Roman claim to particular *pietas*. The scheme is derived from a *topos* in Greek history familiar from the genre of *Strategems*, e.g. Peisistratus at Athens, Syloson at Samos (Polyaenus, *Strat*. 1.20; 6.45).

[39] *Huic barbarae superstitioni . . . severitatis*: Cicero, *pro Flacco* 67. Note that this attack has nothing to do with belief (in a single god, for example) but with a customary financial obligation.

[40] The classic account of the process of intensification, which I summarize at the end of this article, is D. Grodzynski, 'Superstitio', *Revue des Études Anciennes*, 76 (1974), 36–60.

(Security from Attack, Victory, Honour, Manliness, Keeping one's Word, Today's Good Fortune), that were erected and paid for 'privately' by individual consuls and generals with the proceeds of booty. But many, perhaps most, changes in the religious field occurred below this level, and so went unrecorded.[41] This focus on political action is fully in keeping with the more general character of 'Roman religion'.

In the traditional perception, inspired by Theodor Mommsen's reconstruction, or perhaps rather invention, of the system of Roman public law (*Staatsrecht*), there was a Roman 'state religion', contrasted with the 'private religion' of the family.[42] It is now considered mistaken to conceptualize the Roman Republican order as though it were even remotely comparable to the nineteenth-century national state; and, as a corollary, that Roman religion, likewise, cannot be thought of as a state religion, but should more properly be seen as the religion of the Roman elite, and especially that of the noble families represented in the Senate.[43]

At the same time, the territorial expansion of Rome, the direct consequence of the internal competition of the aristocracy for prestige, status, and wealth, brought with it suzerainty, exploitation and dominion over other peoples with non-Roman cults and beliefs. The temple of Jupiter on the Capitoline acted as a perpetual reminder of Rome's conquering mission, and was recognized as such by the subject peoples: when it burned down in 69 CE, during a skirmish between the soldiers of the reigning emperor Vitellius and those of the successful pretender Vespasian, the event was hailed by native prophets in Gaul as boding the end of the Roman empire and the beginning of a Celtic one.[44] This intimate association between Roman religion and

---

[41] J. Rüpke, *Religion of the Romans* (Cambridge, 2007), 39–61.

[42] The first volume was published in 1871; the standard, much enlarged, edition is T. Mommsen, *Römisches Staatsrecht* (3 vols. in 5, Leipzig, 1887–8); cf. the shorter version prepared by Mommsen himself: *Abriß des römischen Staatsrechts* (Leipzig 1907; first published 1893). On Mommsen's view of the Roman 'state' and its public law, see A. Giovannini, 'De Niebuhr à Mommsen: remarques sur le genèse du "Droit public"', *Cahiers du Centre Glotz*, 3 (1992), 167–76; W. Nippel and B. Seidensticker (eds), *Theodor Mommsens langer Schatten* (Göttingen 2005). Mommsen's counterpart in the field of Roman religion was Georg Wissowa, *Religion und Kultus der Römer* (Munich, 1912).

[43] Cf. K.-J. Hölkeskamp, *Senatus Populusque Romanus. Die politische Kultur der Republik. Dimensionen und Deutungen* (Stuttgart, 2004), 11–83; idem, 'Rekonstruction einer Republik: Die politische Kultur des antiken Rom und die Forschung der letzten Jahrzehnte'. *Historische Zeitschrift*, Beihefte NS 38 (Munich, 2004), 19–56; Rüpke, ibid. (see n. 41) 24–29.

[44] Tacitus, *Hist.* 3.71–2; 4.54.

Roman imperial success made it inevitable that the former be used as one of the boundary-markers in mapping the differences between Rome and her subjects. The extension of territorial control, out into Italy, then into Sicily and the Gaulish Po valley, then into Gallia Narbonensis, Hispania, Macedonia, and the organized Hellenistic monarchies of Asia Minor, the Near East and North Africa, to say nothing of trade with the eastern Mediterranean through the island of Delos, created a variety of contacts with other religious systems, deities, and rituals; and of course with differing conceptions of the proper nature and ends of religious practice.

In principle polytheistic systems, such as the Roman, are extremely open to new modes of religious action, whether in the form of individual cults or new modes of ritual expression; and, as I have mentioned, the Roman elite did indeed develop several institutions for admitting new cults and knowledge-practices into the system. Nevertheless the sheer scale of these territorial acquisitions, which occurred largely between 300 and 50 BCE, and increasingly rapidly in the century between 150 and 50, together with the displacements of populations (slaves; long-serving legions; colonists) that they involved, made it increasingly difficult to maintain a balance between an ideal-typical 'Roman religion', largely in the service of an imperialist ideology, and the concerns of the rest of the Roman population, to say nothing of the subject provincial populations. In this situation, the notion of *superstitio* neatly accommodated polytheistic openness to the exorbitant variety of actually worshipped divinities with sound, non-theological, reasons for retaining a commitment to an ill-defined, essentially pragmatic, concept of 'our ancestral religion', the religion of the Roman elite persuasively identified with that of the people of Rome.

II

In ancient societies, the ideal form of religious knowledge-practice was encoded in the performance of civic sacrifice, which in turn was imbricated in the sets of norms governing perceptions and judgements of civilized versus savage life. Civic sacrifice itself was embedded in the calendar of civic festivals (themselves the meeting-point of formal laws or rules of organization and of aetiological myth) and in the sacred topography of the city and its surrounding territory. All claims to religious knowledge outside or beyond this normative core were more or less problematic, but could be tolerated, even incorporated into 'tradition', so long as their challenge to the norms inscribed in civic sacrifice remained indistinct. The inverse of legitimate religious knowledge-practice took three quite different forms: rejection of some part of established religious knowledge, or the rules that express it, which is impiety; denial of the very possibility of religious knowledge, which is atheism;[45] and malign sorcery, the reversal of the norms contained in legitimate knowledge. All ancient states had institutionalized means, consisting usually in the death penalty, or at the least exile, of sanctioning such extreme forms of illegitimacy. Both in Greece and in Republican Rome, however, superstition represented a form of religious practice some way away from that pole. It marked a boundary, not a total exclusion from the civilized order.

The problem lay rather in the type of exclusions the concept of superstition attempted to impose. At Rome, one way of marking the illegitimacy of the religious knowledge connoted by the term was to note its 'vacancy', its absence of force or authority. 'This annual ritual of ours that you are witnessing is no *vana superstitio*, no empty show', explains the exiled Arcadian King Evander to Aeneas on the future site of Rome, 'it commemorates Hercules' defeat of the monster Cacus'.[46] Sanctioned practice was thus conceptually 'full'. The stereotypical carriers of 'empty' religious knowledge were the classificatory marginals, first women, then strangers. Trying to explain why people indulge in mourning, Cicero suggests that one reason is that men adopt 'a sort of female excess (*muliebris superstitio quaedam*), imagining that, having been dealt a blow by the gods, they are more likely to pacify them by ostentatiously showing themselves humbled and crushed'.[47] Still more specifically, the ideal-typical superstitious person is an old woman (Lat. *anus*, adj. *anilis*), the folly of her beliefs and practices rehearsing her prescriptive social marginality. Indeed, *anilis superstitio* was a cant expression. Listing the Academic arguments against divination, for example, Cicero claims: 'The very notion of fate is just an old wives' tale, utterly superstitious'.[48] Old women are the type of the superstitious because they lack courage, moderation and steadiness, they have 'light' or 'weak' minds, tremble, weep, worry. Some people, says Cicero to his brother Quintus in the same dialogue, believe that dreams foretell the future, but how many more are there who 'despise them and think that such a belief is the superstition of a feeble, old woman's spirit?'[49] According to Livy, it was the Senate's refusal to reveal when Africa was to be invaded towards the end of the Second Punic War, that made people anxiously ready to claim to have seen portents: two suns in the sky at the same time, a comet, city gates struck by lightning. 'All this filled people's minds with fears (*impleverat ea res superstitionum animos*), and they

---

[45] Plutarch defines atheism as 'imperviousness to the divine' (*de superst.* 6, 167e7f.).

[46] Vergil, *Aen.* 8.187f.

[47] Cicero, *Disp. Tusc.* 3.72.

[48] *Anile sane et plenum superstitionis fati nomen ipsum*: Cicero, *De divin.* 2.19.

[49] *Superstitionem imbecilli animi et anilis* (ibid. 2.125).

were all the more ready to spread gossip about prodigies and to believe in them'.[50] As we saw earlier, Marcus Aurelius' rescript relegating religious agitators likewise linked their success to the *animi leves* of their adherents, the 'lightness' of their minds, their inability to resist fear or anxiety about the gods.

In this context, the overt objection to *superstitio* was that, even when demonstrated by men, it was a form of religious knowledge typical of that half-other, woman, and most especially old women. By definition, such persons did not belong to the imagined community of courageous, moderate and steadfast adult males, the community of sanctioned practice. Old womanliness was thus an apt metaphor for the inadequacy or 'vacancy' of the religious knowledge summarized in the notion of *superstitio*. But a completely different criterion of exclusion might also be applied. It was not merely 'light minds' that bothered the ideological centre, it was the rituals they appealed to. The Senate, or rather, the politico-social elite of Rome, desired a folk whose religion they could dominate inasmuch as it mirrored or imitated their own; what they got, especially at times of war, epidemic, natural disaster, was superstition. This desire for an obedient, manageable community that looks to the elite for its sanctioned practice is mostly occluded. It becomes explicit only in the invented history of the early Republic that I mentioned earlier. The best example is a report by Livy of the supposed events of 429 BCE. A prolonged drought caused cattle and sheep to expire in the dried-up watercourses. The country people were forced into the towns. At the same time, an outbreak of 'mange' (*scabies*) spread from the animals to human beings. 'Not only were their bodies seized by the affliction, but their minds; all manner of superstitious fears (*multiplex religio*), mostly foreign, overcame them; people's imaginations were overwhelmed by religious dread (*sunt capti superstitione animi*) spread by individuals who, in order to make themselves rich, introduced novel forms of sacrifice and of divination into private houses, until the collapse of public morale (*publicus pudor*) reached the ears of the government.' In this mythical version of early Roman history, when Roman men were still manly, courageous, moderate and steadfast, all the government needs to do is send in the Aediles, who issue a proclamation that only Roman gods may be worshipped, and only in a Roman manner (*ne qui nisi Romani di neu quo alio more quam patrio colerentur*).[51] In this limning of the Bacchanalian affair of 186 BCE, when the Senate savagely repressed the adherents of Bacchic cult, which had for years been peacefully practised in Italy and

---

Rome, authentic salvation is to be found only in the *cultus patrius*, traditional Roman religion. That cult alone is the locus of 'full' religious knowledge. The unstable contours of the Senate's imagined community will by now be sufficiently clear. However, the deeper difficulty had nothing to do with manly minds or old-womanly fears, but with fundamentally different interests in the religious system. Whatever the origins and complex earlier history of Roman religion, by the second century BCE, as I have sketched, it had become a system whose main function was to legitimate the imperial expansion driven by the competition of the aristocracy. It thus offered a classic Weberian theodicy of good fortune (*Theodizee des Glücks*), confirming the legitimacy of 'the internal and external interests of all rulers, property owners, victors, and physically healthy people'.[52] The successful and healthy owed their success and their health to their piety; thanks to the religious institutions created by the early kings, and maintained by the Senate, Rome itself was the most pious polity imaginable. The mass of the population however had a mainly instrumental attitude towards religion: for them, its function was the 'magical' (again in Weber's sense) guarantee of agrarian productivity and protection from evils, above all serious illness. On this view, collective suffering is the result of divine anger, individual illness evidence of attack by a spirit (or by a witch). Such instrumentalism positively requires new ritual forms of protection, which makes specialization in this area exceptionally attractive to the charismatic as a means of upward mobility; and tends to be brutal towards failed divinities.[53] The expansion of the Roman state into Italy, especially the Greek areas of Southern Italy and Sicily, and later into the eastern Mediterranean, provided ample means of culture-contact and so access to new modes of religious action, grist to the mill of instrumental needs.

The basic issue therefore was the extent to which a public religious system primarily orientated towards justifying the good fortune of the socio-political elite could control and channel the demand for 'magical' protection. As I

---

[52] The citation is from M. Weber, 'Einleitung in die Wirtschaftsethik der Weltreligionen', in *Max Weber, Soziologie* (see n.9 above), 398–440 at 403 = *Gesammelte Aufsätze zur Religionssoziologie*, ed. Marianne Weber (Tübingen, 1920–1), 1: 237–75 (= 'The Social Psychology of the World Religions', in *From Max Weber: Essays in Sociology*, trans. and eds H. H. Gerth and C. Wright Mills (London, 1948), 267–301 at 271. First published in 1916). (The essay is oddly omitted from the standard collection in English: Max Weber, *The Sociology of Religion*, tr. E. Fischoff, intro. T. Parsons (London, 1966)). Weber here uses 'theodicy' in a sociological, not theological, sense to mean 'legitimation (of good fortune) by representing it as a result of divine approval', and contrasts it with the more familiar 'Theodizee des Leidens', theodicy of misfortune.

[53] Weber, 'Einleitung', 403–8 (= 'Social Psychology', 271–6).

have mentioned, some efforts were made; numerous healing cults are known from the Republican period. But the sum of human misery is always greater than such efforts can channel. Sociologically speaking, the concept of *superstitio* negotiated the gap between a theodicy of good fortune and religious instrumentalism. It admitted that there were other religious ends than the legitimation of good fortune, but sought to minimize the threat of such claims to effective religious knowledge by identifying them with the stereotype of the foolish old woman, the slave, and the foreigner, people who don't count, thus underlining their marginality to what really mattered, 'our religion', 'our values'.

The safeguard function of Roman *superstitio* is thus clear. Moreover, the case of Cicero's daughter Tullia, who died in 45 BCE aged 33, reminds us that the limits of a theodicy of good fortune are everywhere visible; Cicero's constant public projection of himself as a member of the imagined community of the justified rubs uneasily against his project of erecting a temple to Tullia, a project that his own closest friend is too polite to call *superstitio*. Moreover, by the late Republic at any rate the educated elite (perhaps not a large number of men) was familiar with the thought that public religion is merely an instrument of domination, a means of fooling the people. But they were forced to the same conclusion as Cicero at the end of *On divination*, where, after spending the second book reworking the Academic demolition of the possibility of divination, he lamely concludes that the Roman elite cannot cut off the branch it sits on: the public religious system depends absolutely on the assumption that its means of discovering the will of the gods is effective. Whatever we may believe privately, we have no alternative but to maintain the traditional system of worship, of which divination is part.[54] Here again, *superstitio* provided welcome paper for the cracks down the centre of the imagined community.

With the crisis of the Late Republic and the protracted civil war which gave birth to the Principate in 29 BCE, the theodicy of good fortune naturally received a fair number of knocks; the literature of the period is full of lamentations about how Rome has been abandoned by the gods, how the altars are empty of offerings, and only *superstitio* abounds.[55] In religious terms, the Principate effected a restoration of both the imagined community and the theodicy of good fortune by forging a direct link between Jupiter Optimus

---

[54] M. Schofield, 'Cicero for and against divination', *Journal of Roman Studies*, 76 (1986) 47–65.

[55] P. Jal, *La guerre civile à Rome: Étude littéraire et morale* (Paris, 1963), 231–54; 360–488; A.W. Lintott, 'Imperial Expansion and Moral Decline in the Roman Republic', *Historia*, 21 (1972), 626–32.

Maximus, the high god of the state, and the Princeps, whose personal status fluctuated perpetually between Here and There, depending on context, and whose dead predecessors, with some exceptions, were lumped together to form a new type of collective godhead, the *divi*.[56] Images, votives, and prayers to Jupiter Optimus Maximus and the Princeps/*divi* outnumbered those to all other divinities put together.

In this context, the instrumentalism of popular religion ceased to threaten the validity of traditional cult, guaranteed as it was by the person of the Emperor. The old-woman model of *superstitio*, without disappearing, thus lost much of its value.

In this situation, it was the second aspect of the Republican notion, the notion of foreigners as *superstitiosi*, that came to the fore. In the early first century BCE, the peoples of Italy had forced Rome to grant them admission to the 35 tribes and other rights of Roman citizens. With the continuing vast territorial expansion of the empire, the demand to redefine the imagined community beyond Rome, even beyond Italy, grew further, culminating in the extension of Roman citizenship to all free inhabitants by the emperor Caracalla in 212 CE. We have already noted some examples of depreciatory attitudes towards provincials and foreigners; but there are many others. Aulus Gellius, for example, describing how the renegade Roman pro-praetor Q. Stertorius (d.72 BCE) had used a tame hind to impress the Lusitanians with his magical powers, remarks, 'Thus was the barbarians' well-known credulity of great value to Sertorius in high matters'.[57] This assumption of credulousness encouraged the belief that foreign peoples were superstitious. Prominent among these foreigners were the Jews, whose innumerable 'food restrictions... circumcisions and excisions'[58] forced a second connection to Roman *superstitio*, the sense of over-scrupulous observance of religious rules as an end in themselves. Moreover, alone of all the populations within the Roman Empire, the Jews were able, and determined, to use their religion as a bargaining counter with the Romans; with the result that when, in 66–70 CE (and again in 133–5) the internal conflicts within Judaism could only be resolved

---

[56] P. Herz, 'Der römische Kaiser und der Kaiserkult: Gott oder primus inter pares?', in D. Zeller (ed.), *Menschenwerdung Gottes—Vergöttlichung von Menschen*. Novum Testamentum et Orbis Antiquus 7 (Fribourg/Suisse and Göttingen, 1988), 115–40; M. Clauss, *Kaiser und Gott: Herrscherkult im römischen Reich* (Stuttgart and Leipzig, 1999); I. Gradel, *Emperor Worship and Roman Religion* (Oxford, 2002).

[57] Aulus Gellius, *Noct. att.* 15.22.9. *Credulitas* however has nothing to do with religious belief; it is rather a virtual synonym of *levitas animi*.

[58] Strabo, *Geogr.* 16.2.37, 761C; cf. Apuleius, *Florida* 6: *Iudaeos superstitiosos*; the word refers here not to their monotheism but to their dietary rules and observance of the Sabbath.

by rebellion, the Romans responded by abolishing the official Temple cult and selling thousands of Jews into slavery. A fictional speech of dramatic date 69 CE, but written in *c*.220, declares: 'The Jews rebelled long ago not only against Rome but against all mankind; people who have devised an unsociable way of life, with no food, libations, prayers or sacrifices in common with other men are further away from us than Susa, Bactria, and the Indians beyond that...'.[59] Already at the time of the first revolt, the handful of early Christians in Rome, closely connected with Judaism, were likewise branded *superstitiosi*. Nevertheless the criteria remained essentially the same, focused upon the practice of civic sacrifice, and its constituent parts, prayer, libation, the communal eating of sacrificial meat: that is the point of Apollonius' complaint against the Jews. In just the same way, the guilt of the Christians lay in their refusal to sacrifice, their refusal to act as members of the imagined community should—they might sing and pray and be as morally good as they liked, but the fact that they would not sacrifice meant that they wilfully refused membership in that community. The reasons for this refusal, including their belief in a different sort of god to whom sacrifice was unacceptable, were not at issue.

It was therefore the need for a new version of the imagined community in the altered conditions of the Principate, and especially from the early second century CE, that made it plausible to emphasize the second meaning of *superstitio*, that of 'foreign credulity/religion'. This new community, at least from 212 CE, encompassed all the free population of the Empire throughout the provinces, from Armenia to Britannia, from Lower Germany to Upper Egypt. By this time it was clear that traditional Roman religion as Varro had understood it in the mid-first century BCE existed only as a citation, its partial reproduction in each Roman colony a mere mark of privileged status. Roman religion outside the city of Rome now meant in practice the cult of the emperor, of Jupiter Optimus Maximus, and any Roman or 'Roman' divinity whose cult local elites and groups of private worshippers cared to institutionalize. *Superstitio* came to connote religious practice outside this flexible, not to say muddy, notion of 'our religion', and thus tended to shift its dominant meaning towards the extreme pole of impiety, atheism, and malign magic.[60]

---

[59] Philostratus, *Vit. Apollon. Tyan.* 5.33.

[60] Atheism here is not the claim that there are no gods (a claim limited in antiquity to a handful of philosophers, mainly Cynics) but not accepting the ordinary civic gods. Euhemerus, for example, was widely considered an atheist, although he simply argued that the gods had once been important human benefactors of humankind, thus preparing acceptance of Hellenistic kings as gods. Christians too were denounced as atheists, because they refused to sacrifice.

The later notion of *superstitio* was thus a response to the pragmatic impossibility of defining the religion of the Roman empire in anything but the vaguest terms focused upon the one common denominator, the practice of animal sacrifice.

Two developments gave a particular pregnancy to this use. First, the Roman habit of identifying their own Empire with the scope of *humanitas*, ambiguous between humane and human; it was for example Roman *humanitas* that suppressed the Druids, who practised human sacrifice.[61] The slide towards equating those who rejected this *humanitas* with 'non-humans' was easy. Second, as Marie-Theres Fögen has argued, the vulnerability of the individual *Princeps* to conspiracy rendered the institution intensely suspicious of divination directed towards the outcome of an imperial illness or the date of the emperor's death. Illicit religious knowledge (we are not talking about belief, but knowledge) therefore tended to be identified with divination, especially astrology and magic, relating to the *Princeps* and so the security of the realm.[62] Under these conditions, the connotations of *superstitio* shifted, above all from the period of the Severans (first quarter, third century), from 'foreign credulity' towards 'hostility to human-kind', and justified the persecution of the Christians by Decius (249–51 CE) and by Diocletian (Great Persecution, 303–5 CE), and the violent rhetoric of the latter's law against the Manichaeans (297, 298 or 302 CE). The place of *superstitio* on the notional continuum of religious knowledge-practices thus shifted in the later Principate decisively towards the negative pole of total illegitimacy. The Christians, in their turn, simply inverted the same language to describe non-Christian worship. Constantius II's law of late 341 against pagan sacrifice begins: 'Let superstition cease, let the madness of sacrifice be abolished'.[63]

The final transformation of *superstitio* worth noting here, however, was not this justification for mutual persecution but a formulation by Lactantius, written soon after the end of the Great Persecution. After dismissing

---

[61] Pliny, *HN* 30.13; cf. É. Aubrion, 'Humanitas et superstitio dans la littérature latine du début de l'époque antonine', in J. Dion (ed.), *Culture antique et fanatisme. Études anciennes* 13 (Nancy and Paris, 1996), 77–94.

[62] M.-Th. Fögen, *Die Enteignung der Wahrsager: Studien zum kaiserlichen Wissensmonopol in der Spätantike* (Frankfurt, 1993), 254–321.

[63] *Cesset superstitio, sacrificiorum aboleatur insania*: Cod. Theod. 16.10.2.; cf. *absque ullo sacrificio atque ulla superstitione damnabili exhiberi populo voluptates . . . decernimus*, (we command that public entertainments be mounted without performing sacrifice or any (other) execrable pagan ritual): *Cod. Just.* 1.11.4 (399 CE).

Cicero's etymology, the Christian professor of rhetoric makes short work of the distinction between *religio* and *superstitio*:

> Religion is of course the worship of what is true, and superstition is the worship of what is false . . . . 'Superstitious' is the word for those who worship quantities of false gods, and 'religious' is for us who pray to the one true God.[64]

Even the Hellenistic philosophers could never have hit upon such an opposition, based on the ontological status of the object of worship: for them, after all, the pagan gods were real enough, albeit mere aspects of a higher deity who sustained the cosmos. Lactantius' solution shifted the criterion of difference decisively away from the issue of performance of specific rituals, above all animal sacrifice, to that of the truth-content of claims about divinity. From that perspective, Augustine was wholly justified in claiming that the Roman state never was a *res populi*, a true commonwealth, as Cicero makes Scipio claim in the *Republic*. For a *res populi* must be based on justice, and there can be no justice if those who live in it do not serve God but sacrifice to evil and impure demons, *malis et inpuris daemonibus*.[65] What is *De civitate Dei* but the laborious effort to create a new imagined community amid the desolation wrought by Alaric's Goths in 410 CE?

---

[64] *Inst. div.* 4.29.11; 16.
[65] Cicero, *De repub.* 3.43; Augustine, *De civitate Dei* 19.21.

Superstition and its Others in Han China

T. H. Barrett

Any discussion of the history of superstition in a broadly comparative context must inevitably begin with a few words of linguistic explanation, in order to assure the reader as to the extent to which like is being compared with like when materials in completely unrelated languages are being used. This is of course a topic on which it might be possible to philologize indefinitely, but in order to move as rapidly as possible to the contemplation of an actual slice of human history, a few words of introductory explanation must suffice. The contemporary East Asian term for 'superstition', *mixin* (meaning literally 'deluded faith') in Chinese, would appear to be a comparatively recent coinage, and may well reflect a Christian analysis of the religious situation. Dictionaries—admittedly a rather fallible source for such information—list no examples that antedate the Christian missions of the seventeenth century, whilst a Jesuit essay in Chinese entitled 'A discussion of people's deluded faith (*mixin*) in *fengshui* and *dili* (i.e. "earth patterns", an element in what we now include under the broader term fengshui)' is still preserved in Paris, suggesting strongly the likely provenance of this coinage.[1]

But there was a terminology widely used throughout most of the two millennia and more of Chinese imperial history that did function in much the same way as 'superstition' and its equivalents in European languages have always done, as a system of labelling that immediately denigrated certain forms of religious activity as inferior and thereby, though perhaps less immediately, made them the legitimate target for reform, control or ultimately outright persecution. We even find the terminology exported beyond China to Korea, where in the eighteenth century, for example, condemnation of popular religious behaviour, using expressions equivalent to the Chinese terms and written with the same Chinese characters, was *de rigueur* for those

---

[1] Not seen; the work is listed in Xu Zongze, *Ming-Qing jian Yesu huishi yizhu tiyao* (Beijing, 1989 reprint of 1949), 444.

wishing to assert their high social status.[2] Most prominent of the terms used in Chinese, and the one upon which the following remarks will chiefly focus, was the compound *yinsi*, often translated 'licentious cult', or more concretely, 'licentious sacrifices'.

These English equivalents—though I shall use them here myself—are by no means unproblematic. A number of other translations into English that have been preferred by other scholars will be introduced below and briefly discussed, to give some further sense of the problem to the reader unfamiliar with the pitfalls of translating from classical Chinese. The range of variation in translations is in this case far from accidental, since exactly what constituted a 'licentious cult' in Chinese history is usually quite impossible to tell, especially for the formative period of the concept that forms the topic of this study. For the writers of Chinese history, condemnation was always more important than description. So rather than revealing the nature of superstition itself in the China of two thousand years ago, our sources allow a far better perspective on who was using the label and why. This turns out to be a question of some delicacy especially for the second century CE, when China's first age of empire was stumbling towards its ruin. At this point, just as in Europe, new religious forces were on the rise, though in China the resulting conflict was much more rapid and even more bloody. A religious group known from their identifying headgear as the 'Yellow Turbans' rose in massive revolt in 184 CE, obliging the imperial government to allow extraordinary powers to the generals charged with their suppression. The powers granted were never surrendered: after the rebel movement was broken, a generation of internecine warlord conflicts resulted in the collapse of the unified empire and the division of China into three competing kingdoms.

These political developments and their antecedents have not in the past been seen as of any great relevance to a history of superstition. When one hundred years ago the founding fathers of twentieth century sinology looked at the statutes still in force against cults that were labelled by the technical vocabulary of superstition in Chinese as 'licentious'—apparently implying during this period both the sense that they were unlicensed by the state and that they were (in terms of the sensibilities of educated persons) morally excessive—it was only natural for them, given the prevailing view of China as an unchanging society mired in centuries of tradition, to write as though the state attitude to popular superstition went back all the way in an unbroken

---

[2] See Boudewijn Walravens, 'Popular Religion in a Confucianized Society', in JaHyun Kim Haboush and Martina Deuchler, (eds), *Culture and State in Late Choson Korea* (Cambridge, MA, 1999), 160–198 at 169.

line to the formative stage of Chinese civilization in the first millennium BCE.[3] And in truth more recent research has in some ways vindicated this assumption, for example by stressing that the early expansion through conquest of the core of Chinese civilization brought under the control of Chinese rulers populations of a quite distinct cultural type whose religious practices were viewed from the start with considerable suspicion.[4] That one such area is today particularly associated with the career of Confucius only goes to show how successful Chinese high culture has been in effacing all consciousness of its originally quite geographically restricted scope. But even much later in that formative millennium we find hostile descriptions of those local cults— in modern scholarship loosely termed 'shamanic'—that are evidently intended to mark cultural difference in areas plainly within the Chinese orbit but equally plainly still considered outside the Chinese heartland.[5] With the unification of China by the First Emperor in 221 BCE one might have expected this discourse about local religious culture and its shortcomings to fade, but the rapid collapse of the First Emperor's dynasty in fact ushered in a lengthy period during which the tensions between the high tradition of Chinese culture and religious influences seen as alien and inferior became the topic of yet more intense—if decidedly guarded—debate.

This was because the beneficiaries of the collapse of the First Emperor's dynasty were a family of far humbler origins than his who ruled with much greater success for about four centuries, under the dynastic name of Han (206 BCE–220 CE). The Han founder's roots, moreover, were precisely in the local society of one of those pre-imperial problem areas, with the result that he and his immediate descendants had very little exposure to the high culture of the pre-imperial period, and a far more natural interest in religious practices that many of their better educated officials would have frowned upon, though of course, it was not an easy matter to condemn utterly the religious observances of the emperor's friends and relations. The demise of the First

---

[3] The classic statement of this view may be found in J. J. M. De Groot, *Sectarianism and Religious Persecution in China* (Taipei, 1963 reprint of 1901), 17–19, 25–6.

[4] E. G. Pulleyblank, 'Zou and Lu and the Sinification of Shandong', in P. J. Ivanhoe, (ed.), *Chinese Language, Thought and Culture: Nivison and His Critics* (Chicago/La Salle, IL, 1996), 39–57.

[5] See Gopal Sukhu, 'Monkeys, Shamans, Emperors, and Poets', in Constance A. Cook and John S. Major (eds), *Defining Chu: Image and Reality in Ancient China* (Honolulu, 1999), 145–65 at 149, where the author notes however that the practices condemned in the region concerned were rife elsewhere in early China. Note also—in the light of the argument outlined below—that some (but not all) of the terminology adduced by Sukhu derives from a source that actually dates to almost three centuries after the unification.

Emperor's ruthlessly anti-traditional regime has been regarded as heralding the triumph of Confucianism, at least in the conventional historiography taken over from Chinese sources into modern non-Chinese conceptions of the main narrative of Chinese history. But recent research has increasingly come to see this as a gross oversimplification, especially for the first part of the Han dynasty. During that time it might be more accurate to think of a ruling group relatively untouched by the preoccupations of the educated coexisting very uneasily with a scholar-official group whose intellectual loyalties were to a cultural heritage that had already suffered considerable losses as the result of the First Emperor's ruthless policies.

Only now, thanks to fresh sources uncovered by archaeology, are we beginning to see the extent to which the scholars of Han times, in retrieving what they could of the old China as a model for their overlords of the Han dynasty, engaged in a reinvention of tradition so thoroughgoing as to shape—and perhaps warp—our whole understanding of what had gone before. Terms like Confucianism and Taoism that seemed to have a clear meaning a generation ago now appear to specialists in the Han period to be highly problematic—even the very notion of 'China', so insouciantly deployed several times already in this essay, begins to look like a construct of rather doubtful utility to contemporary historians of the Han.[6] Once, however, we abandon our past assumptions about unities and continuities, a close reading of the discussions of religious activity that took place at the Han court during the first two centuries of its existence reveals some unexpected features, which may help in tracing developing attitudes to 'superstition'. Most notably our sources appear to exhibit a complete failure to use the word *yinsi* to describe phenomena that would most definitely have merited the label in later times. The arguments of certain scholars writing during the Han dynasty who wished to curb the religious enthusiasm of the imperial court for a vast variety of cults they themselves despised, and the counter-arguments of other scholars of a less prescriptive disposition, have been closely examined in modern scholarship. Nowhere in the original documents as cited by later historians—whatever their own vocabulary in describing these past arguments—do we find the term *yinsi* deployed.[7] If it already existed, its absence from our texts may be because it was a term far too pejorative to apply to cults supported by the imperial family. The closest one finds to the condemnatory language of

---

[6] Some idea of the pace of change in the study of Han times may be gathered from a collection of essays edited by Michael Loewe and Michael Nylan, *China's Early Empires*, (Cambridge, 2008).

[7] For the debates in question, see Michael Loewe, *Crisis and Conflict in Han China* (London, 1974), 134–92.

later times is in a passage in the *Shi ji*, the great history of China up to his own times written circa 100 BCE by Sima Qian, a man whose criticism of his own emperor had resulted in his castration, and in the composition of his master work as 'a text that not surprisingly exhibits a fascination with the problem of how to criticize rulers and yet survive unscathed'.[8] Just as he implicitly criticizes the religious activities of the First Emperor rather than say a word concerning the identical activities of the Han emperor of his own day, when it comes to popular cults he studiously avoids any obvious comment on the Han situation.[9] But writing of conditions under a tyrant of ten centuries before his own times, he reports as the observation of a witness to those distant times that the population 'belittle and are excessive in sacrifices to the gods of Heaven and Earth'. This language looks very much like the deliberate rewriting of earlier material, in the light of his personal preoccupations. For his source still survives, and it contains no word for 'excessive', as the translator renders the adjective *yin* in this context.[10] Evidently the uncontrolled flourishing of popular religion was something that worried him, yet he had to depend on the reader to understand the extent to which his history was contemporary history,

This may seem a merely fanciful interpretation. Certainly the significance assigned to the absence of more explicit terminology concerning superstition in our surviving materials may depend ultimately on an argument from silence. If, however, the term *yinsi* did exist during the first half of the Han, it is still somewhat strange to find no one hostile to popular cults quoting the source that in later ages was seen as the *locus classicus* embodying the verdict of Confucius on their spiritual value: 'A sacrifice which it is not proper to offer, and which yet is offered, is called a licentious sacrifice. A licentious sacrifice brings no blessing'.[11] This dictum may be found in the *Record of Rites*, one of several collections of materials on matters of ritual made in Han times on the basis of what survived of pre-imperial practices. But nothing similar occurs in the rest of the surviving corpus of ritual materials, and it may not be accidental that current scholarly opinion sees the *Record of Rites* as having achieved its final form remarkably late in the process of canon formation,

---

[8] Grant Hardy, *Worlds of Bronze and Bamboo: Sima Qian's Conquest of History* (New York, 1999), 19.

[9] Hardy, *Worlds of Bronze and Bamboo*, 186.

[10] Compare William H. Nienhauser (ed.), *The Grand Scribe's Records, Volume V.1: The Hereditary Houses of Pre-Han China* (Bloomington, IN, 2006), 269, and James Legge, *The Chinese Classics*, vol. 3 (Hong Kong, 1961), 277.

[11] James Legge, *The Li Ki*, vol. I (Oxford, 1899), 116.

perhaps in the first century CE.[12] Of course the dictum may not have been a last moment addition, and it is at any rate quoted in the *Discussions in the White Tiger Hall*, purportedly the record of court debates in 79 CE concerning the 'Confucian' Canon as it was then constituted.[13] But unfortunately not all are agreed that this text does in fact date back to 79 CE.[14] Later sources also put the dictum in the mouth of an official named Diwu Lun, who undertook a suppression of 'licentious sacrifices' in the area under his jurisdiction in 53 CE.[15] One does not know if these sources report his *ipsissima verba*, but they do at any rate clearly date back to the Han dynasty.[16]

By the mid-first century CE, the ruling house had distanced itself completely from its humble origins, for after an episode during which it had been replaced by a usurper, a rather distant relative had revived the dynasty as the 'Eastern' or 'Later' Han. There is however one reason for supposing that the concept of *yinsi* dated back earlier than this, to a period when arguments still needed to be mounted quite carefully against what were still the religious predilections of the ruling house. For in its original context the term is not so much about 'bad' religion as 'inappropriate' religion. As formulated in the *Record of Rites* the distinction between types of sacrifice is not even presented in a two-tier fashion at all, but rather related to a gradation of different religious observances deemed appropriate at different levels of society. Thus in terms of the 'Confucian' Canon as it came into being in Han times it was just as 'licentious' for an aristocrat to conduct a sacrifice reserved for a king as for a commoner to perform a sacrifice proper to an aristocrat—or vice versa. It should of course be admitted that though the canonical texts were repeatedly cited until the end of the imperial system in the twentieth century, these specific distinctions of rank, rooted as they were in the society of pre-imperial times, had lost their precise relevance as soon as the society they reflected was swept away in the consolidation of the imperial system. But the Han classicists responsible for recreating an image of pre-imperial times for their own age

---

[12] See Michael Loewe (ed.), *Early Chinese Texts: A Bibliographical Guide* (Berkeley, 1993), 294.

[13] Tjan, Tjoe Som, *Po hu t'ung, The Comprehensive Discussions in the White Tiger Hall*, vol. 2 (Leiden, 1952), 376–7.

[14] Loewe, *Early Chinese Texts*, 348–50.

[15] Diwu Lun was also concerned about the popular enthusiasm for various types of divination: see Michael Loewe, *Divination, Mythology and Monarchy in Han China* (Cambridge, 1994), 188.

[16] See the editorial collation notes of Wang Liqi to Ying Shao, *Fengsu tongyi jiaozhu* (Beijing, 1981) 9, 401.

seem to have been quite careful to build in—or resurrect—notions of gradated hierarchy.

The resultant regime, by now also wedded to the conception of the Emperor as ruling in accord with the Mandate of Heaven, cannot be characterized as in any way sympathetic towards popular cults, as Diwu Lun's actions attest.[17] Indeed, material elsewhere in the ritual corpus shows that as an agent of the emperor an imperial official such as Diwu would have possessed full spiritual authority delegated to him to suppress lesser cults, because the Emperor is treated in ritual terms as both human and divine.[18] There was, in short, in imperial China no conception of religious authority separate from political authority: in the invisible spirit world in which the dead found their home, no differently from the visible world they had once inhabited, the writ of their emperor still ran with equal validity. Lesser spirit powers around which cults tended to form were of course seen as inferior to higher spirit powers, including ultimately the power of Heaven, by whose authority the emperors of the Later Han now reigned. But that authority put these petty gods—just as much as their worshippers—firmly under the rule of the emperors also. There was an element of flexibility in the canonical notion of 'appropriate' religion, at least in Han times, in that no definitive list of approved objects of worship seems to have been maintained by the state, so that leniency could quite readily be shown to errant imperial relatives, for example. But the authority for the imperialistic use of force was always there, if need be.

Whatever the precise timing of the incorporation of the word *yinsi* as a key term into this analysis of power and belief, it is certainly well in place there before the end of the first century CE in China. Ban Gu (32–92), who is the chief author of the *Han shu*, the history of the first half of the Han dynasty that follows up Sima Qian's work in the *Shi ji*, uses it several times, though unfortunately not in any context where it forms part of a passage that has seen extended translation into English.[19] But for example where Sima had talked of the 'excessive' religious behaviour of people ruled by an early despot, Ban notes that after his overthrow '*yinsi* had prohibitions against them', and likewise the usurper who briefly supplanted the Han before its re-foundation is described as having esteemed *yinsi*, whilst in a further allusion to early

---

[17] For the late development of the Mandate of Heaven as the justification of Han rule, see Loewe, *Divination, Mythology and Monarchy*, 90.

[18] John Steele, *The I-Li, or Book of Etiquette and Ceremonial*, vol. 1 (London, 1917), p. xxi.

[19] For Ban Gu and his history, see Loewe (ed.), *Early Chinese Texts*, 129–36, which includes a finding list of the main translations. All the Han authors cited below are also in Loewe's bibliographical guide.

history illustrating the importance of rulers setting a moral example, the influence of a queen fond of shamans is blamed for a rise at the time in *yinsi* among the people.[20] His only apparent reference to contemporary conditions concerns the people of one of the regions formerly less than perfectly 'Chinese', who are still described as 'much addicted to lewd religious rites'—a translation that again represents *yinsi*.[21] Here the translation certainly captures the moral indignation implicit in the term, but since it is impossible to tell exactly what outrages against morality worshippers committed, their activities might not merit the description of lewdness in contemporary English.

But if this is over-translation, then it is equally arguable that the English translation of *yinsi* in the writings of one of Ban's contemporaries, Wang Chong (27–c.97 CE) as 'unauthorized sacrifices' somewhat underplays the freight of opprobrium that the word carried.[22] The translator, however, was working while the imperial system still held sway in China, and perhaps his choice of words reflects the more dispassionately bureaucratic attitudes of the traditional Chinese state in its very last phase. At any rate Wang's frequent and passionate aspersions on the credulity of his contemporaries have more recently won him a privileged place in Chinese Marxist accounts of the national record of opposition to obscurantism.[23] Even less sanguine assessments of his commitment to rationalism would at least see him as the father of the Chinese polemical essay.[24] Or is something else beginning to become apparent in Wang's writings? Yet a third view would see him, whatever his own view of his role, as in retrospect occupying an important position at the start of a trend towards a new religious dichotomy between 'good' and 'bad' religion.

Even so, do we see the establishment thereafter of a clearly binary use of the terminology, in which it is used in a more straightforward fashion to mark off the 'superstitious' from the acceptable? Was there a point at which the

[20] Ban, *Han shu* 25A (Beijing, 1962), 1194; 25B, 1270, and 81, 3335.

[21] The translation is that of Sukhu, as above, n. 5.

[22] Alfred Forke, *Lun-Heng* (New York, 1962, reprint of first edition of 1907), 524.

[23] A full bibliography of the publications in this vein would be quite lengthy. For a typical example from a prominent scholar published at an important turning point in the evolution of scholarship on religion in China, see Ren Jiyu, 'Cong Wang Chong dao Xiong Bolong', in Zhongguo wushenlun xuehui (ed.), *Zhongguo wushenlun wenji* ((Wuhan), 1982), 52–61. The compilers of this volume were the Society for Atheism, and Ren Jiyu was at this point their president, and simultaneously president of the Society for the Study of Religion: see Radiopress, Inc., *China Directory, 1983* (Tokyo, 1982), 240.

[24] In this role he is accorded a brief but pointed sketch in David Pollard, *The Chinese Essay* (London, 2000), 4.

gradated approach to what was appropriate in religion gave way to a clearer dichotomy of the type implied by our use of the word 'superstition' in discussing the history of Europe?

Ultimately, yes. Wang's writings have been cited as the starting point of a demonstration of the tensions between popular religion and the religion that later came to be called Taoism - or more recently Daoism, in deference to the standard *pinyin* system of romanizing Chinese, though here the older, more familiar form is retained.[25] This religion, like its rival, the imported creed of Buddhism, eschewed animal sacrifice—a practice otherwise at the very heart of Chinese religious life—whether such sacrifice was 'licentious' or even in Confucian terms canonically licit.[26] Taoist texts moreover provide religious, 'theological' grounds for taking a superior stance with regards to other, lesser forms of religion, quite independent of the sanction of the high tradition of pre-imperial (or supposedly pre-imperial) ritual that we have discussed so far.[27] In Taoist writings *yinsi* are seen as symptomatic of an age of decline, as in Sima Qian and Ban Gu, but this decline is now seen as part of a distinctive religious history: the religion's primordial divine ruler is represented as saying 'After I left, people's minds became decadent, and there were orgiastic cults and deviant deities, with offerings that included blood sacrifices'— where 'orgiastic cults' represents a particularly negative translation of *yinsi*, influenced (though perhaps to an unacceptable degree) by the polemical context.[28]

Now all scholars would probably agree that the Taoist religion has its roots in the religious turmoil of the end of the Han, in the same environment that gave rise to the Yellow Turbans (184 CE), though continuities are easier to trace with another contemporary movement in West China known as the Way of the Celestial Masters. Taking matters a full century back, as far as the writings of Wang Chong, does however look a little tendentious, especially as Wang prefaces his remarks on sacrifice quite conventionally with references to the *Book of Rites*.[29] Even as unrest grew as the age of the Yellow Turbans

---

[25] This study was published as R. A. Stein, 'Religious Taoism and Popular Religion from the Second to Seventh Centuries', in Holmes Welch and Anna Seidel (eds), *Facets of Taoism* (New Haven, 1979), 53–82.

[26] On this question, see Terry Kleeman, 'Licentious Cults and Bloody Sacrifices: Sacrifice: Reciprocity and Violence in Traditional China', *Asia Major*, 3rd ser., 7.1 (1994), 185–211.

[27] This has been argued by Chi-tim Lai, 'The Opposition of Celestial Master Taoism to Popular Cults during the Six Dynasties', *Asia Major*, 3rd ser., XI.1 (1998), 1–20.

[28] Livia Kohn, *Laughing at the Tao: Debates among Buddhists and Taoists in Medieval China* (Princeton,1995), 111.

[29] Forke, *Lun-Heng*, 516.

approached, and new religious cults began to multiply alarmingly, one still finds plenty of scholars fully committed to the notions of appropriate religious observance enshrined in that text. A close reading of a later Han writer such as Wang Fu (c.78–163 CE) shows that the standpoint adopted is still very much that of canonical orthodoxy: it is hierarchically inappropriate religious behaviour that is condemned.[30] His complaints therefore are couched in such terms as 'Nowadays, ordinary men toy with divination and sacrifice to spirits that are not their own' and 'Just as ranks of nobility exist among men, there are honourable and base spirits'.[31] Likewise but even later, Xun Yue (148–209) delivers a prescription for the perfect society built on the image of the Golden Age already found in the Confucian canonical literature: 'Cut out trivial taboos, discontinue unorthodox cults, and do away with strange superstitions, then apparitions and falsehood will cease to exist', where 'unorthodox cults' represents yet another translation of *yinsi*.[32] Elsewhere too the same pattern prevails.[33]

This is not to deny that momentous changes were afoot in the second century CE, possibly precipitated by a worsening natural climate that gave rise to more natural disasters and epidemics, and hence to healing cults in particular, since both the Yellow Turbans and the Celestial Masters seem to have been much preoccupied with the problem of disease.[34] For the first time, moreover, it is possible to see that outside influences were entering the Chinese religious sphere in the form of Buddhism, a world religion already well used to making converts outside its South Asian homeland. Indeed, one might suspect that the very notion of a 'religion' as a separate doctrine and set of associated practices standing outside traditional social arrangements came into China only with the arrival of Buddhist believers. For in the hierarchically ordered visible and invisible worlds we have described the Chinese as inhabiting in early Han times, it is hard to detect any form of specifically

---

[30] For Wang Fu and his position in literary history, see Anne Behnke Kinney, *The Art of the Han Essay: Wang Fu's Ch'ien-fu lun*, (Tempe, Arizona, 1990).

[31] Thus Wang as rendered by Kinney, *Han Essay*, 107 and 113.

[32] The translation is that of Ch'i-yün Ch'en, *Hsün Yüeh and the Mind of late Han China; A Translation of the Shen-chien with Introduction and Annotations* (Princeton, 1980), 104–129.

[33] For example in Ying Shao (c.140—before 204), *Fengsu tongyi*, 9, pp. 386, 394. As noted above, n. 16, Ying also commends the activities of Diwu Lun.

[34] The following two paragraphs are based on an interpretation of the late Han that I have tried to outline in a broader fashion in a chapter on religious change in Loewe and Nylan (eds), *China's Early Empires*. For climate change as a possible driving factor in change at this time, see Mark Elvin, *The Retreat of the Elephants: An Environmental History of China* (New Haven and London, 2004), 5.

religious authority existing beyond the authority of the emperor, especially after his recognition as Son of Heaven. The very spirit world by Han times seems to have been conceptualized as simply another bureaucratic empire, staffed by imperial officials of the Lord of the Dead, unseen colleagues to the officials of the Han emperor. Yet the Buddha, in the eyes of his devotees, is regularly proclaimed a 'teacher of both gods and men', a 'god of gods', as high above the great deities of the Hindu pantheon as they are above mankind, while a 'son of heaven' a *devaputra*, is in Buddhist texts no more than a mere junior god. The fact that the Buddha seems to have been identified on his arrival in Later Han China as somehow the same figure as the ancient sage Laozi, the reputed author of the *Daode jing*, who was certainly co-opted as founder of the Taoist religion by its later adherents and may well have been cast in a similar role by the Way of the Celestial Masters and the like, would further seem to suggest that the notion of a high god independent of their ruler had become available to the native Chinese imagination too.

No wonder then that one Chinese scholar, Liu Yi, in a brilliant synthesis of the evidence from the closing years of the Han dynasty and beyond, has characterized the overall shift in religious thought of the period as constituting a movement from 'Revering Heaven' to 'Worshipping the Dao', where the last term is the Way, the *dao* of Taoism, the unseen immanent power behind all things manifested in such powerful figures as Laozi.[35] It is clear that whatever happened, a separate non-political religious sphere did not come into being at this point in China, for the Taoist tradition was in its early days—and even thereafter—organized still along lines highly reminiscent of an imperial bureaucracy. Indeed, the whole conception of the spirit world that later Taoism inherited is shot through with notions of bureaucracy apparently of Han date, and that world is consistently deemed to run on bureaucratic lines that only an educated priest with the requisite clerical skills is qualified to approach as an intercessor.[36] Rather than transferring their allegiance in a wholesale way to some other conception of religious authority, it would seem that the denizens of late Han China, once they realized that the empire to which they were subjects was beginning to fall apart, turned in the first instance to the unseen empire of the spirits: yellow, the colour that identified the Yellow Turbans, is in early Chinese thought associated with the world of the dead.

[35] Liu Yi, *Jing Tian yu chong Dao*, (Beijing, 2004).

[36] The best short study to bring this out is undoubtedly Angelika Cedzich, 'Ghosts and Demons, Law and Order: Grave Quelling Texts and Early Taoist Liturgy', *Taoist Resources*, 4.2 (1993), 23–33, an essay that gives full credit to the pioneering research of the late Anna Seidel in this area.

All this is not to deny the importance of Buddhism as a force for religious change in late Han times, but it certainly cannot be claimed that the status of the *yinsi* was directly affected by Buddhism, if only because overt opposition to local cults and popular religion does not seem to have been a matter of any concern to the first wave of Buddhist translators. Of course Buddhists in South Asia saw their religion, the dharma of the Buddha, as in quite another class from local cultic activity, and in time at least one Chinese Buddhist visiting South Asia found it appropriate to use the term *yinsi* in his own description of phenomena there. 'The kingdom of Simhala formerly was addicted to immoral religious worship', runs a Victorian translation of the seventh-century travels of Xuanzang, where the last three words provide yet another English-language gloss on the term.[37] But the digitization of the Chinese Buddhist canon shows that no translator from Han times onwards ever used the term to represent any Indian word in any scripture, commentary, or doctrinal treatise of Indian composition. Buddhists saw a clear division between their path and other forms of belief, and possessed a terminology to characterize heterodoxy, but as newcomers to the late Han religious scene they avoided aggressive polemics.

And if we turn from the Buddhists to what we know of Chinese beliefs at this point, there are plenty of indications that religion was frequently not a dichotomized activity, but one in which both high and low within society could join together, perhaps even to a greater degree than hitherto.[38] This seems to have been particularly the case with the cults of the *xian*, variously translated as 'transcendents' or 'immortals', individuals whose religious practices had freed them from the bonds of a normal human lifespan. Tales about *xian* form an important element in the later Taoist religion, even though their individualistic and often reclusive lifestyles made them difficult to fit into any bureaucratic paradigm of organization in the spirit world. One way of reconciling the two was provided by the later notion of the 'banished immortal', the mysterious holy man or even poetic genius who was allegedly once an official with responsibilities in the spirit world before some infringement

---

[37] Samuel Beale, *Si-yu Ki: Buddhist Records of the Western World*, vol. 2 (London, 1884), 246.

[38] Lydia Thompson puts forward this view on the basis of a study of a corpus of surviving visual materials, on page 27 of her 'Confucian Paragon or Popular Deity? Legendary Heroes in a Late-Eastern Han Tomb', *Asia Major*, 3rd ser., 12.2 (1999), 1–38. Others have suggested that this phenomenon, while documented elsewhere for the late Han, may also be found just as well earlier in the dynasty: see Donald Harper, 'Contracts with the Spirit World in Han Common Religion: The Xuning Prayer and Sacrifice Documents of A. D. 79', *Cahiers d'Extrême-Asie*, 14 (2004), 227–267, at 231.

of other-worldly regulations entailed a period of exile amongst mankind.[39] The possibility that one might as a result encounter someone of supernatural abilities leading an ostensibly ordinary life was obviously one to fire the imagination, and in late imperial China the imagery of the 'Eight Immortals', the best known of their kind, became part of popular culture.

But during the Han dynasty such developments lay well in the future. Han immortals have about them not the least air of whimsy: many people during this period apparently saw the *xian* as having won a prize that was quite straightforwardly open to all through diligent pursuit of a variety of macrobiotic techniques. Since one of the common qualifications for success in their endeavours involved meritorious service on behalf of the community, one can see that even those who felt obliged to take cognizance of the Confucian Canon would have felt able to celebrate their lives.[40] This illustrates the degree of flexibility built into the prescriptions of the *Book of Rites*, as noted above. Even in the terms of that body of literature, meritorious individuals who had benefited the places in which they lived were considered legitimate candidates for posthumous sacrifices by those who were not descended from them, thus enlarging the scope of what was 'appropriate' within a system of religious observances largely structured around 'ancestor worship'.[41] This may explain why in the case of the best-known cult of an immortal from the second century there are clear indications that its adherents were drawn from a range of social positions.[42] Furthermore, the ability of a cult of this type to play a socially integrative role may in turn explain why a compilation of biographies of *xian* that would appear to go back to the late Han period lists a very large number as having become the focus of posthumous religious observances.[43]

---

[39] Unfortunately this engaging idea has so far not been explored much in English; in Chinese Li Fengmao, *Wuru yu zhejiang* (Taibei, 1996), 247–85, gives a good account of its manifestation in the fiction of the Tang dynasty.

[40] Robert Ford Campany, *To Live as Long as Heaven and Earth: A Translation and Study of Ge Hong's Traditions of Divine Transcendents* (Berkeley and Los Angeles, 2002), 92–4, gives a very useful summary of this aspect of the pursuit of immortality, albeit one based on somewhat later materials.

[41] Legge, *Li Ki*, I, 274.

[42] This is made clear by Donald Holzman, 'The Wang Ziqiao Stele', *Rocznik Orientalistyczny*, 47.2 (1991), 77–83; cf. also Campany's discussion of the late Han cult of Tang Gongfang, *To Live as Long as Heaven and Earth*, 107.

[43] Thus M. Kaltenmark, *Le Lie-sien tchouan* (Pékin, 1953), 74, 76, 81, 90, 95, 104, 107, 109, 115, 125, 132, 139, 148, 152, 157, 161, 168, 175, 179, and 187—a significant proportion of the total number of seventy-two biographies included in this source.

The cult of the *xian*, however, may be an unusual case, in that it is a variety of the cult of the holy person, who not just in second-century China, but frequently elsewhere as well tended to bring into local society wider religious perspectives whilst in his or her person making them intelligible to preexisting local understandings of religion. Thus while the *xian* figure became an important element in later, plainly self-consciously Taoist hagiographical traditions of writing, these accounts retain—even more than in the case of Chinese Buddhist hagiography—an element of ambiguity.[44] For the centuries immediately following the late Han, the dual or even multiple roles potentially available in biographical writing to one and the same *xian* as a result of the different standpoints from which their lives might be described has been effectively demonstrated by recent research.[45] But to the educated observer of the religious scene of the late Han it was not so much the popular capacity for worshipping holy persons that raised questions for them about the effects of misguided religiosity as the distinctly more baffling popular propensity for finding holiness in the most improbable inanimate objects—not simply trees or wells, but even fish heads.[46] The former type of object of worship could be incorporated into the Taoist tradition, as it was later constituted; the latter definitely could not. And for all that has been said so far, there still survive from this period a number of passages concerning the suppression of popular cults—not necessarily containing the term *yinsi*—that have been identified by the Canberra-based Chinese scholar Liu Cunren as possibly signifying, for whatever reasons, a shift of attitudes, compared to the conventions of earlier times, towards a more exclusive religion.[47]

---

[44] Stephen Peter Bumbacher, *The Fragments of the Daoxue zhuan*, (Frankfurt am Main, 2000). For a study of early Chinese Buddhist hagiographical materials, see John Kieschnik, *The Eminent Monk: Buddhist Ideals in Medieval Chinese Hagiography*, (Honolulu, 1997).

[45] This task has been well executed by Benjamin Penny, 'Jiao Xian's Three Lives', in Benjamin Penny (ed.), *Religion and Biography in China and Tibet* (Richmond, Surrey, 2002), 13–29.

[46] For some rather dated translations of a couple of these stories, see James R. Ware, *Alchemy, Medicine and Religion in the China of A.D. 320: The Nei P'ien of Ko Hung* (Cambridge, MA, 1966), 160–2. The annotation provided to these tales in Wang Ming (ed.), *Baopuzi neipian jiaoshi* (Beijing, 1985, revised edition), 181 (text on 175) shows that they derive from the late Han author Ying Shao, mentioned above, n. 33.

[47] See below, n. 51, for Liu's remarks, which form a part of his researches into early Celestial Master Taoism. For some reason the main source for the period in question, the *Hou Han shu*, while it does use the term *yinsi* on occasion, seems frequently to prefer another term *fangsi* literally 'sacrifices indoors', which appears to differentiate substantial built shrines from outdoor altars, to judge from the seventh-century commentary on the passage cited

The first such passage is in the biography of the late Han official Luan Ba, as contained in the *Hou Han shu*, the Standard Dynastic History of the period that follows on from Ban Gu's work. This history reached its final form more than two centuries after the end of the dynasty but it is normally taken as a reliable record based on contemporary documentation. The biography has Luan Ba at some point between 150 and 160 CE 'destroying all the superstitious shrines' under his jurisdiction with complete spiritual impunity, thanks to his knowledge of the 'art of the Tao' which gave him power over demons.[48] Later tradition, however, apparently refused to countenance the statement that Luan was eventually forced to commit suicide after complaining about government execution of two of his fellow officials, promoting him instead to the ranks of the *xian*. Indeed in a second biography, contained in another early hagiographical source devoted to such figures, one finds even more dramatic accounts of Luan's dealings with the supernatural.[49] This leads one to wonder whether perhaps by the time of the compilation of the dynastic history legends about Luan Ba had already started to colour accounts of his bureaucratic career. There is however one intriguing detail that occurs not only in his dynastic biography but also twice in other parts of the *Hou Han shu* not directly concerned with him at all, which in all likelihood must be authentic. In 142 he was selected as part of a group of eight officials tasked with traversing the empire and checking on local conditions.[50] Liu Cunren has pointed out that this event seems to have made a deep impression in religious circles, in that there are clear allusions to it in a Taoist source of the early fifth century, even though Luan Ba is not mentioned.[51] Liu further notes that quite possibly Luan Ba's suppression of popular religion simply stemmed

---

in n. 48, below. This may signal some new religious development of the age—dictionaries list no earlier source—but as with all matters concerned with these cults, it is impossible to be sure.

[48] The translations here are drawn from that on page 92 of the article by Hisayuki Miyakawa, 'Local Cults around Mount Lu at the Time of Sun En's Rebellion', in Welch and Seidel (eds), *Facets of Taoism*, 83–101; the original text may be found in Fan Ye, *Hou Han shu* (Beijing, 1965), 57, 1841. Stein, 'Religious Taoism and Popular Religion', 79, cites the same source. The word 'superstitious' here derives not from the underlying Chinese text, but from an interpretative gloss of the translator, while 'arts of the Tao' reproduces one of the rather vague terms in Han usage that do not allow us to suppose that they indicate anything as definite as a connection with something called 'Taoism'.

[49] Campany, *To Live as Long as Heaven and Earth*, 252–5, and text notes, 451–3.

[50] Fan, *Hou Han shu*, 6, 272, and 61, 2029.

[51] Liu Cunren, 'Was Celestial Master Zhang a historical figure?', in Benjamin Penny (ed.), *Daoism in History* (London, 2006), 189–253, esp. section 4, 219–26.

from 'traditional' motives like those that had earlier motivated Diwu Lun, and one may indeed suspect that his biography was simply co-opted by later Taoists and re-read in the light of their distinctive religious attitudes. But he also points to another, slightly later instance of the destruction of popular shrines that is less easy to interpret in that way.

This slightly later suppression was carried out at the behest of the Emperor Huan (r.146–167). The entry describing it in the emperor's annals under the year 165 is sparse enough, but fortunately a remark in the biography of an earlier meritorious official whose shrines were spared shows that the move was connected with other innovations in the ruler's religious observances.[52] Concerning these innovations we are fairly well informed, and so they do provide a somewhat more detailed picture of a religious context other than adherence to the dictates of the Confucian classics that could have stimulated attacks on sites of popular worship.[53] It has already been pointed out both that the identification of the emperor with the Son of Heaven came much later than generally imagined, and that a shift from respect for Heaven to worship of the Way appears to have taken place. The object of worship favoured by Emperor Huan consisted of a god or gods named Huang-Lao, literally 'Yellow' and 'Old', though most have assumed that the latter term, 'Lao', refers to the divine Laozi. It cannot be readily identified with any figure from earlier tradition, although it is true that the term is not unprecedented. At the start of the dynasty, a political philosophy was in vogue that drew on writings ascribed not only to Laozi but also to Huangdi, the Yellow Emperor of remote antiquity. This strain of thought, however, which has been much discussed in recent years because of newly discovered texts, seems to have faded from the scene long before, and there is no evidence at all of its per-petuation through a cult of any sort.[54]

There are some good reasons to believe that at this point the emperor was worshipping a single divinity, Huang-Lao, not least because there is ample documentation to show that this Huang-Lao was paired in joint worship with the Buddha, whom we have already noted as a figure associated with Laozi well before this point. This is particularly clear in a memorial to the emperor in 166 CE from an individual named Xiang Kai, though other sources also confirm the identification.[55] There are, besides, ways of explaining the

---

[52] Fan, *Hou Han shu* 7, 314; 76, 2470.

[53] See Loewe, *Divination, Mythology and Monarchy*, 136.

[54] On Huang-Lao thought, see e.g. the summary in Loewe, *Divination, Mythology and Monarchy*, 127–9, which advances some possible causes for its eclipse.

[55] See, for a full English translation of Xiang Kai, Rafe de Crespigny, *Portents of Protest in the Later Han Dynasty* (Canberra, 1976), esp. 29–30, and notes on 82–3.

element 'Huang' or 'Yellow' without invoking the Yellow Emperor. It may for example—as already pointed out—be taken as a reference to the world of the dead, but 'Yellow' simultaneously has directional associations with the centre. A high god known as 'Huang-Lao of the Central Pole' occurs in at least one later religious text apparently drawing on Han tradition.[56] Mention elsewhere in the same text of a 'Yellow Spirit' has moreover been seen as perhaps providing some reflection of the supreme deity of Han popular belief, though the relationship between these two gods—assuming they were not in some sense identical—remains to be clarified.[57] At this point, it is only possible to speculate about the role of the Buddha in all this, but since he seems at times to have been regarded not simply as a high god but as a lord of the dead—a role in which we occasionally find Laozi also soon after the Han—the likelihood is that in 166 CE the emperor considered that he was propitiating two beings of unusual spiritual power.

There is just one other mention from 173 CE of two individuals worshipping a god or gods named Huang-Lao jun ('Lord Huang-Lao') who is said to have been capable of bestowing good fortune and longer life, but there is no mention of the Buddha here and the reference is not detailed enough to clarify the nature of the deity any further.[58] Whether or not this was a jealous god who might order the suppression of lesser rivals we cannot tell, but Liu Cunren certainly seems to suspect as much. In any case the deity did not do much for the emperor himself, who died very shortly thereafter, or for the Han, which was thrown into irremediable turmoil in 184 by the Yellow Turbans, whose slogan, whatever its significance, is widely agreed to have been 'The Blue Heaven is already dead, the Yellow Heaven is about to arise!'[59]

The third passage on the suppression of *yinsi* concerns these Yellow Turbans and their relations with Cao Cao, the military leader of relatively undistinguished origins who proved best able to capitalize upon the chaos

---

[56] This god is listed in Kristofer Schipper, 'The Inner World of the *Lao-tzu chung-ching*', in Chun–chieh Huang and Erik Zürcher, (eds), *Time and Space in Chinese Culture* (Leiden, 1995), 114–131, at 122. For a more recent look at this work, see also John Lagerwey, 'Deux écrits taoïstes anciens', *Cahiers d'Extrême-Asie*, 14 (2004), 139–71. I am grateful to Mr. Frederick Chen of St. Cross College, Oxford, for drawing my attention to the importance of this text.

[57] Lagerwey points this out in his study 'Deux écrits', 162, and n. 63, citing Donald Harper's work on Han manuscripts.

[58] Fan Ye, *Hou Han shu*, 50, 1669.

[59] On this slogan, see Loewe (ed.), *Cambridge History of China*, vol. 1 (Cambridge, 1986), 876.

and civil war that ensued, so as to lay the foundations of a successor regime.[60] Cao Cao may have been the first figure since Diwu Lun to have used the authority of the Confucian canon to destroy 'licentious shrines', rather than simply rail against them, as scholars like Wang Chong, Wang Fu and others did. As we have seen, the Emperor Huan's suppression did not cite the *Book of Rites*, though an earlier entry in the imperial annals for *circa* 105 CE does so, but only as an argument for removing shrine officials who strayed from the canonical norms.[61] One early source, however, suggests that Cao Cao's actions stemmed neither from ritual tradition nor from newer, more exclusive religious beliefs, but rather from his practical hostility to excessive expenditure on religion.[62] Even so, a later encounter with the remnants of the Yellow Turbans in 192, which our sources depict as a unilateral surrender on their part but which modern historians suspect was a carefully negotiated compromise, has allowed the preservation of a very interesting gloss by their leaders on these earlier exploits of his.[63] 'Formerly when you were in Jinan and you destroyed the spirit altars, this way of behaving was the same as that of Zhonghuang Taiyi, the Central Yellow Supreme Unity: it seemed that you understood the Way, but now you have become confused. The course of the Han is over; the Yellow House (*jia*) will be established. The great cycles of Heaven are not the sort of thing that your individual talents and strength are able to sustain'.[64]

Here we have the name of a jealous god—apparently a high god—who had inspired an entire attempt at creating an alternative empire, and once again the title is one that bears careful analysis. The notion of a central divinity connected with the power of the colour yellow we have already encountered, and noted too its background in earlier Han belief and subsequent influence within the Taoist tradition. Taiyi, the 'Supreme Unity', was a high god much more conspicuous in our conventional historical sources in the early years of the Han, before the rise of the imperial worship of Heaven.[65] His survival in later Taoist tradition is also well attested, though a scholarly description of

---

[60] For a succinct introduction to Cao Cao in English, see Rafe de Crespigny, 'Man from the Margins: Cao Cao and the Three Kingdoms', The Fifty-first George Ernest Morrison Lecture in Ethnology, (Canberra, 1990).

[61] Fan, *Hou Han shu*, 10A, 422.

[62] See the commentary to Chen Shou, *San guo zhi* (Beijing, 1959) 1, 4.

[63] For a recent view of this incident, see the translation and notes in Rafe de Crespigny, *To Establish Peace: Being the chronicle of Later Han for the years 189 to 220 AD as recorded in Chapters 59 to 69 of the Zizhi tongjian of Sima Guang*, vol. 1 (Canberra, 1996), 108.

[64] Chen, *San guo zhi*, 1, 10.

[65] Loewe, *Divination, Mythology and Monarchy*, 114.

the way in which his presence is manifested there suggests a far from simple picture: 'The Great One can thus be found on all levels of this universe. He is the same, he is always identified as "One", yet he assumes a great variety of different names and guises'.[66] This Protean capacity for changing his outward form, as it were, would also seem to characterize his appearance in texts associated earlier in the Han with popular religion. In this environment, as revealed by recent research, the guises may vary, but this high god's overall position, as the controller of supernatural punishments, does not.[67] Under such circumstances, in which a number of different names may be taken to indicate the same divine reality, it is naturally conceivable that the Huang-Lao worshipped by Emperor Huan and the god of the Yellow Turbans could have been either one and the same, or in some broader sense versions of the same figure, even if so far no evidence to clinch this identification has been brought forward.

Whatever the nature of the supernatural authority invoked in these cases of the persecution of superstition, Liu Cunren brings together all three passages, and suggests hypothetically that they may be linked. He points out that Luan Ba, after all, was originally employed as a eunuch according to the *Hou Han shu* before regaining his virility, and there are some indications that the Yellow Turbans had links with the eunuchs in the imperial palace, which might explain how Emperor Huan came to be a convert to their beliefs. We might thus see these three sources as between them tracing the rise in the late Han of a type of religion that was in Liu's word (he uses the English term) 'exclusive', and more sweeping in its condemnation of lesser gods than anything seen hitherto.[68] The hypothesis is certainly attractive, but it awaits confirmation by more substantial evidence.

With our present sources we cannot know anything about the content of 'superstition' under the Han, and we still do not know enough to make more than an educated guess about the alternative to superstition that was emerging in the late Han to vie with the 'traditional' (though itself perhaps relatively recent) view presented in the *Book of Rites*. It might, therefore, seem that the account of the late Han yields nothing of any interest to the comparative study of superstition elsewhere. There is, however, one aspect of the Chinese situation that is quite distinctive, and deserves comment. Thanks to the beliefs about authority in the seen and unseen worlds introduced earlier, even if the details of both superstition and its others remain unclear in

[66] Schipper, 'The Inner World', 128.
[67] Harper, 'Contracts with the Spirit World', 261–2.
[68] Liu, 'Celestial Master Zhang', 222–3.

religious terms, the function of both emerges quite unambiguously in relation to the contestation of political power.

Though we must reluctantly lay aside the biography of Luan Ba, at least until we can be sure what forces have shaped its transmission in its currently known earliest form, the persecution of superstition by both the emperor Huan and the Yellow Turbans as claimed in their remarks to Cao Cao can only be interpreted as displays of authority over the spirits that were a prerequisite for establishing legitimacy. The emperor needed such a demonstration because he was attempting to shift the ideology of the Han regime away from the Mandate of Heaven toward some new spiritual basis, possibly because he accepted that Heaven was no longer a power strong enough to maintain the Han. The Yellow Turbans likewise needed to show that they ruled in the name of an unseen power—whether the same as that of the emperor or different—that gave them authority in the spirit realm. Where Cao Cao stood in this contest cannot be known: the suggestion that his actions were purely pragmatic might after all reflect a later attempt to distance him from the religious struggle of the time, or it might represent a partial truth: as an emerging warlord, confiscating any wealth built up by cultic shrines would have both increased his resources and usefully demonstrated his authority at the same time. All three cases of persecution (if we assume that the Yellow Turbans did what they commended Cao Cao for having done) can thus be construed as a show of force: in modern China such an exemplary persecution of a scapegoat is known as 'killing a chicken to show (or to scare) the monkeys'.[69] Perhaps similar motives in the persecution of superstition could be found elsewhere. We should bear in mind, moreover, that in Han China would-be successful rulers had monkeys temporal and spiritual, this-worldly and other-worldly, in view. Whether exactly the same holds true anywhere else I do not know, but the identification of 'superstition' as the target of demonstrations of authority in worlds visible and invisible is surely one worth considering in a comparative context.

---

[69] See Wen Duanzheng (ed.), *Zhongguo suyu dacidian* (Shanghai, 1989), 766, and cf. John S. Rosenow, *A B C Dictionary of Chinese Proverbs* (Honolulu, 2002), 25, entry D14, 27, entries D41, 42.

Concern over Superstition in Late Medieval Europe

Michael D. Bailey

Late medieval Europeans inhabited a world replete with spells, charms, blessings, and other rites intended to invoke and manipulate supernatural power. Whether these people regarded such practices as 'magical' or not, they typically believed them to be capable of producing real effects.[1] Innumerable rites existed, mostly to achieve basic goals, such as to heal or ward off disease, or to avoid misfortune.[2] Despite such simple, quotidian, and beneficial supposed effects, these practices could raise grave concerns and spark significant debate. At the beginning of the fifteenth century, for example, a woman in the upper Rhineland, in the diocese of Speyer, was worried about her son. He had injured his finger, and while she knew of various rites that might heal him, she feared they were impermissible. Certain clergy in her hometown of Neustadt an der Haardt, less than fifteen miles west of Speyer, had strongly condemned such practices. Not content with this prohibition, however, she found occasion to bring her son to an Augustinian friar and lector in theology at nearby Landau (some ten miles south of Neustadt). This man, Werner of Friedburg, encouraged her to do all she could to heal her boy.[3]

Werner, it seems, believed that many common spells could be used 'licitly and without sin', and this belief, among other questionable positions that he held, eventually caused him to be summoned to the court of the bishop of Speyer and subsequently brought before the theological faculty of the nearby university at Heidelberg in January and February 1405. Under questioning,

---

[1] Richard Kieckhefer, *Magic in the Middle Ages* (Cambridge, 1989), 3–6, 8–17.

[2] Kieckhefer, *Magic*, 69–74; Karen Louise Jolly, 'Medieval Magic: Definitions, Beliefs, Practices', in Bengt Ankarloo and Stuart Clark (eds), *Witchcraft and Magic in Europe: The Middle Ages* (Philadelphia, 2002), 30–53.

[3] Werner described the encounter in a *revocatio* of his errors in Munich, Bayerische Staatsbibliothek, Clm 4721, fo. 198r–v; see also the slightly earlier *responsio* edited in Robert E. Lerner, 'Werner di Friedberg intrappolato dalla legge', in Jean-Claude Maire Vigeur and Agostino Paravicini Bagliani (eds), *La parola all'accusato* (Palermo, 1991), 279–81.

he admitted to approving of all charms and blessings, so long as they did not appear to invoke 'malign spirits'. He even supported such practices in public sermons. Asked by the Heidelberg theologians whether he knew any 'superstitious blessings', he replied that he knew one, recited in vernacular German: 'Christ was born, Christ was lost, Christ was found again; may he bless these wounds in the name of the father and of the son and of the holy spirit'. No doubt sensing the risk such admissions entailed, Werner stated that he did not 'firmly believe' that this blessing was effective. Nevertheless, he immediately continued, he had been made healthy when he had used it on himself. He also defended his positions that a charm bearing the names of the three magi would protect people from epilepsy, and that the phrase *verbum caro factum est* would drive away demons.[4]

Werner's case most likely originated as part of a purely local, ad hoc inquiry into possible error.[5] When brought before the Heidelberg faculty, however, the case became part of a major current of late medieval religious anxiety, namely rising clerical concerns, particularly in German lands, over the danger posed to the faith by superstitious practices.[6] The chief Heidelberg theologian, Nicholas Magni of Jauer, who authored the official refutation of Werner's positions, also wrote one of the earliest, most widely circulated, and most influential treatises on superstition in the fifteenth century, perhaps at least partly inspired by Werner's errors.[7] Nor was Nicholas alone in focusing his attention on supposed superstition. In the early years of the fifteenth century, the influential chancellor of the University of Paris, Jean Gerson, wrote several tracts on these subjects, beginning with his *De erroribus circa artem magicam* in 1402. Between 1405 and 1425, the Heidelberg theologian Johannes of Frankfurt, an anonymous author who was probably a theologian from Cologne, and Heinrich of Gorcum, another Cologne theologian, all wrote on superstition and superstitious invocations of demons. Subsequently the German theologians Nicholas of Dinkelsbühl and Johannes Nider dealt with such subjects in their treatises on the Ten Commandments, since invoking demons could entail a form of idolatry. By the mid-1400s, Martin of Arles,

---

[4] Werner, *Revocatio*, fo. 198r; Lerner, 'Werner di Friedberg', 280.

[5] Lerner, 'Werner di Friedberg', 271.

[6] Cf. Kathleen Kamerick, 'Shaping Superstition in Late Medieval England', *Magic, Ritual, and Witchcraft*, iii (2008), 29–53.

[7] On Nicholas, see Adolph Franz, *Der Magister Nikolaus Magni de Jawor: Ein Beitrag zur Literatur- und Gelehrtengeschichte des 14. und 15. Jahrhunderts* (Freiburg im Breisgau, 1898), 151–95. More recent is Krzysztof Bracha, *Teolog, diabel i zabobony: Świadectwo traktatu Mikolaja Magni z Jawora 'De superstitionibus' (1405)* (Warsaw, 1999); a German translation is under way.

a canon in Pamplona, and Johannes of Wünschelberg, a professor at Leipzig, both added treatises *De superstitionibus*, and Denis the Carthusian, a native of the Low Countries, wrote *Contra vitia superstitionum.*[8] The practices defined by these men as superstitious—mainly common spells, blessings, and charms—were widespread in this period, as throughout the Middle Ages. Yet their wide diffusion would have been of no concern had authorities not begun to deem them dangerously illicit. In fact, many of these practices were based on ecclesiastical rites, often drawing on standard prayers and elements of the liturgy, and many modern scholars regard them as evidence of sound and vibrant lay religiosity.[9] Although the medieval church was never so benign in its view of lay appropriations of ecclesiastical ritual, high medieval religious authorities had generally not focused so intently on issues of superstition.[10] By the early 1400s, however, the topic had become an explicit concern for a number of authors. This article examines this fifteenth-century resurgence, some roots of which lie in previous centuries. After briefly outlining the meaning of superstition and the various ways in which this category was employed during earlier periods, I will attempt to discern more general issues underlying authoritative discussions of superstition in the late Middle Ages. I will then explore developments in late medieval religious and intellectual culture that caused authorities to focus their concern on lay appropriations of ecclesiastical prayers, rites, and blessings, and on the common use of spells and charms. I will argue that deeply rooted concerns about the nature of spiritual being and power combined with certain

---

[8] Edward Peters, 'The Medieval Church and State on Superstition, Magic and Witchcraft: From Augustine to the Sixteenth Century', in Ankarloo and Clark (eds), *Witchcraft and Magic in Europe*, 228–9; Lynn Thorndike, *A History of Magic and Experimental Science*, 8 vols. (New York, 1923–58), iv, 274–307; Françoise Bonney, 'Autour de Jean Gerson: Opinions de théologiens sur les superstitions et la sorcellerie au début du XVe siècle', *Le Moyen Age*, lxxvii (1971), 85–98; Jan R. Veenstra, *Magic and Divination at the Courts of Burgundy and France: Text and Context of Laurens Pignon's 'Contre les devineurs' (1411)* (Leiden, 1998), 143–53; Werner Tschacher, *Der Formicarius des Johannes Nider von 1437/38: Studien zu den Anfängen der europäischen Hexenverfolgungen im Spätmittelalter* (Aachen, 2000), 269–91.

[9] Eamon Duffy, *The Stripping of the Altars: Traditional Religion in England 1400–1580* (New Haven, Conn., 1992), 266–98; R. N. Swanson, *Religion and Devotion in Europe, c.1215–c.1515* (Cambridge, 1995), 182–90.

[10] On superstition through the thirteenth century, see Dieter Harmening, *Superstitio: Überlieferungs- und theoriegeschichtliche Untersuchungen zur kirchlich-theologischen Aberglaubensliteratur des Mittelatlers* (Berlin, 1979); also Jean-Claude Schmitt, 'Les "superstitions"', in Jacques Le Goff and René Rémond (eds), *Histoire de la France religieuse*, vol. 1, *Des dieux de la Gaule à la papauté d'Avignon* (Paris, 1988), 417–551.

intellectual developments and the growth of specific intellectual structures in the early fifteenth century caused religious authorities to examine common beliefs and practices more closely than had previously been the case. These concerns then impelled them to see dangerous superstition in the many spells, blessings, and other rites that had long been diffused throughout medieval society.

I

Whereas in the modern West, at least since the Enlightenment, superstition usually implies an irrational belief or action not grounded in a proper scientific understanding of the world—a 'perversion of reason'—in medieval Europe *superstitio* meant a 'perversion of religion'.[11] Roman authorities had coined the term in antiquity, and had used it most often to describe improper or excessive forms of divination or other cultic rites, as well as the actions of suspicious foreign cults. Early Christians, for example, were often criticized as superstitious. Christian authorities later returned the favour by categorizing all pagan rites as *superstitio*.[12] The basis for this manoeuvre was the Christian conviction that pagan deities were actually demons in disguise, and so all pagan rites were diabolical perversions of the proper devotions that should only be shown to the Christian God. The categorization of all forms of paganism as inherently demonic and superstitious culminated in the early fifth century with the greatest of the Latin fathers of the church, Augustine of Hippo.[13] The writings of Augustine and other fathers were extremely influential on Christian authors who then perpetuated the discourse on superstition in the sixth century, such as Caesarius of Arles and Martin of Braga, and these men in turn became authoritative for later writers.[14] Thus as Christianity spread away from the Mediterranean and across northern Europe, the category of superstition remained linked not just to paganism, but in many ways to the particular forms of paganism that Christianity had initially encountered in the Roman Empire.

[11] Harmening, *Superstitio*, 5. On the Enlightenment reclassification of superstition, see Martin Pott, *Aufklärung und Aberglaube: Die deutsche Frühaufklärung im Spiegel ihrer Aberglaubenskritik* (Tübingen, 1992).

[12] Dale B. Martin, *Inventing Superstition: From the Hippocratics to the Christians* (Cambridge, Mass., 2004).

[13] Schmitt, 'Les "superstitions" ', 428–30.

[14] See Caesarius of Arles, *Sermons*, trans. Mary Magdeleine Mueller, 3 vols. (The Fathers of the Church xxxi, xlvii, and lxvi, New York, 1956, and Washington, D.C., 1964, 1973); Martin of Braga, 'Reforming the Rustics', in *The Iberian Fathers*, trans. Claude W. Barlow (The Fathers of the Church lxii, Washington, D.C., 1969), 71–85.

There is considerable debate about how real a problem superstition was for Christian authorities in the early medieval period. Throughout the Merovingian and Carolingian eras, down to the tenth century, sermons, penitentials, and lists of superstitions (*indiculi superstitionum*) condemned superstitious practices. Yet these writings strongly echoed earlier authorities.[15] Some scholars maintain that such resonance with earlier sources need not impugn the accuracy of later accounts. Rather, they contend that ancient pagan beliefs and practices in fact remained vibrant among large segments of the European population, enduring under a thin veneer of Christianity, in some places perhaps even into the twelfth century.[16] Other scholars vigorously oppose this interpretation, however, maintaining that there is no reliable evidence of significant pagan survivals even in the Merovingian period, let alone into the Carolingian period and beyond.[17] In fact, while ever-expanding Christendom continued to encounter pagan peoples at its borders, the Christianization of more in-lying regions seems to have been a fairly thorough process. Christianization did not necessarily mean the eradication of all previously pagan folk practices, but these practices—many of which took the form of spells, charms, or other magical acts—were now understood and employed, by clergy and laity alike, within an essentially Christian framework.[18]

Thus while superstition remained a rhetorical concern for early medieval religious authorities, activities they typically described as *superstitio*—undiluted remnants of pagan rites and cultic practices—may well have been fairly rare in most of Western Christendom, and those acts that were widespread—spells and charms, methods of divination, and so forth, that integrated traditional folk-practices into a system of Christian belief—were not decried as superstitious.[19] In the high Middle Ages, superstition became even less of a direct concern. Beginning in the eleventh century, when Christian authorities looked for deviance and error within their own communities,

---

[15] Ian N. Wood, 'Pagan Religions and Superstitions East of the Rhine from the Fifth to the Ninth Century', in G. Ausenda (ed.), *After Empire: Towards an Ethnology of Europe's Barbarians* (Woodbridge, 1995), 254.

[16] Schmitt, 'Les "superstitions"', 441–51.

[17] Yitzhak Hen, *Culture and Religion in Merovingian Gaul A.D. 481–751* (Leiden, 1995), 154–206.

[18] Karen Louise Jolly, *Popular Religion in Late Saxon England: Elf Charms in Context* (Chapel Hill, N.C., 1996). Cf. Valerie I. J. Flint, *The Rise of Magic in Early Medieval Europe* (Princeton, N.J., 1991).

[19] Bernadette Filotas, *Pagan Survivals, Superstitions and Popular Cultures* (Toronto, 2005), 46, argues that scholars may be 'too pessimistic' about the possibility of linking literate descriptions of superstition to contemporary practices, but acknowledges this essential problem.

they found it not in pagan-derived superstition but mainly in heresy.[20] While heretics were sometimes labelled superstitious, heretical deviance was qualitatively different from the supposed superstitions of earlier centuries. Even serious superstition might rest as much on mistaken practice as erroneous belief. Heresy, on the other hand, implied the deliberate denial of fundamental church doctrines. While ecclesiastical officials had often regarded superstition as mere foolishness arising from lack of proper instruction, they came to regard heresy as a far more deliberate and pertinacious form of deviance necessitating focused efforts to investigate, uncover, and eradicate.

Particularly in the wake of the Fourth Lateran Council in 1215, religious authorities began to undertake more systematic inquiries into common beliefs and practices, and in 1231 Gregory IX first authorized papally designated inquisitors.[21] These men undertook sweeping investigations that might well uncover superstition, now more typically described as deviant Christian practice than the remnants of paganism.[22] Yet concern, while rising, was still far from its peak. In the thirteenth century, for example, the Dominican inquisitor Stephen of Bourbon uncovered a popular cult devoted to a dog, the 'holy greyhound' Guinefort. Yet even in this extreme instance of deviant belief, the inquisitor seems to have been more fascinated than horrified, and although he worked to eradicate the cult, he did not treat those he found guilty of this superstition with anything like the severity he reserved for heretics.[23] In the early fourteenth century, the inquisition launched by Jacques Fournier, bishop of Pamiers, uncovered numerous unorthodox beliefs among the people of the village of Montaillou, but the motivating concern behind this inquisition was the perceived threat of heretical Catharism, not superstition.[24] Only a few years later, in his great inquisitor's manual,

---

[20] R. I. Moore, *The Origins of European Dissent* (1977; reprint Toronto, 1994); Malcolm Lambert, *Medieval Heresy: Popular Movements from the Gregorian Reform to the Reformation*, 3rd edn, (Oxford, 2002), 14–51.

[21] Lambert, *Medieval Heresy*, 99–114. On the establishment of an 'inquisitional culture' following Lateran IV, see Dyan Elliott, *Proving Woman: Female Spirituality and Inquisitional Culture in the Later Middle Ages* (Princeton, N.J., 2004), esp. 11–21. Krzysztof Bracha, 'Der Einfluß der neuen Frömmigkeit auf die spätmittelalterliche Kritik am Aberglauben im Reformschrifttum Mitteleuropas', in Marek Derwich and Martial Staub (eds), *Die 'Neue Frömmigkeit' in Europa in Spätmittelalter* (Göttingen, 2004), 226–7 and 229, links late medieval pastoral activity to currents emerging from Lateran IV.

[22] Schmitt, 'Les "superstitions"', 502, 510.

[23] Jean-Claude Schmitt, *The Holy Greyhound: Guinefort, Healer of Children since the Thirteenth Century*, trans. Martin Thom (Cambridge, 1983), 33–4.

[24] Emmanuel Le Roy Ladurie, *Montaillou: The Promised Land of Error*, trans. Barbara Bray (New York, 1979).

the Dominican Bernard Gui touched on the sort of spells and charms that later authorities would frequently characterize as superstitious, but he devoted only a few pages of his enormous work to this subject.[25] Intellectual authorities also dealt with superstition during the thirteenth and fourteenth centuries. Indeed, the rapid growth of schools and universities in these years led to a reinvigoration of theological discussions of the category of *superstitio*.[26] In his *Summa theologiae*, the thirteenth-century theologian Thomas Aquinas produced the foundational definition of superstition for the remainder of the medieval period—superstition entailed either rites or devotion directed toward God, but improperly, or devotions properly owed to God that were instead directed toward some creature.[27] Aquinas's older contemporary William of Auvergne also wrote important works on superstitious divination and demonic magic.[28] Yet, particularly as William's work demonstrates, these men mainly focused on erroneous astrology and demonic magic among the clerical elite. Only in the early fifteenth century would concerns about common practices fully merge with more refined intellectual anxieties about superstition.

II

Authoritative writing on superstition in the first decades of the fifteenth century was not only far more focused on this topic than the works of preceding centuries, it was also more practical in approach. That is, rather than treating superstition purely as a theological abstraction, authorities now engaged with particular manifestations of superstitious practice. Nicholas of Jauer, for example, was involved in the case against Werner of Friedberg, while Jean Gerson apparently wrote *De erroribus circa artem magicam* to chastise the university medical faculty at Paris, because physicians, he felt, were setting a dangerous example for common people by casually accepting and employing common healing charms.[29] Beyond such changes in focus and approach, a change of tone can be detected in the authors of the early fifteenth century. They no longer judged superstition a matter of simple error; rather they saw in potentially superstitious practices a profound and dangerous deviance. Certainly some superstitions remained mere foolishness. Just as

[25] Bernard Gui, *Practica inquisitionis heretice pravitatis* 5.6.1–2, ed. C. Douais (Paris, 1886), 292–3.

[26] Schmitt, 'Les "superstitions" ', 503.

[27] Aquinas, *Summa theologiae* 2.2.92.2.

[28] Especially his *De fide et legibus* and *De universo*, available in *Guilielmi Alverni Opera Omnia*, 2 vols. (1674; reprint Frankfurt, 1963).

[29] Thorndike, *History of Magic*, iv, 125–6.

Augustine in the patristic era, late medieval authorities ridiculed people who believed that if a boy ran between two friends walking together in the street their friendship would dissolve unless they caught and beat the boy.[30] Other practices, however, involved dangerous misuse of aspects of the divine cult. Above all, authorities feared that many common spells and charms involved engaging, either knowingly or not, with demonic power, and offering to demons some form of devotion properly owed to God—the very definition of intolerable superstition.[31]

That concern over express or tacit invocations of demons should run through Christian writings about superstition is hardly surprising. The church fathers had strongly demonized paganism and deemed all pagan rites superstitious. In late antiquity, however, Christian condemnations of superstition were clearly motivated first by the need to combat deeply entrenched pagan cults, and then by fear of supposedly persistent pagan practices. In the late Middle Ages, authorities again focused intensely on superstitious practices, but these now entailed mainly lay appropriations of Christian ritual or liturgy that needed to be forcefully recast as demonic. In so doing, these authors reveal a highly intellectualized obsession with the nature, extent, and possibility of demonic power in the world.[32] Given the emphases apparent in their writings, this concern seems more likely to have preceded and motivated authorities' new (or renewed) focus on superstition, rather than concern about potentially superstitious practices leading them of necessity into discussions of the demonic.

The desire to use cases of superstition, spells, and charms primarily as mechanisms through which to address issues of demonic power is evident in Jean Gerson's highly influential *De erroribus circa artem magicam*. He began this work not with any consideration of magical arts per se, but with a discussion of demons and, initially, of the basic fact of demonic existence. Having established the reality of demons, he then treated the nature and extent of their powers.[33] All of this was done fairly cursorily, but considering

---

[30] Martin of Arles, *Tractatus de superstitionibus* (Rome, 1559), fo. 19r, citing Augustine's *De doctrina christiana*.

[31] Detailed especially in Nicholas Magni of Jauer, *Tractatus de superstitionibus*, University of Pennsylvania, Codex 78, fos. 56v-57r. I have compared this copy to Vatican Library, Pal. Lat. 679, fos. 164r–205r, and Pal. Lat. 719, fos. 64r–77v.

[32] Alain Boureau, *Satan hérétique: Histoire de la démonologie (1280–1330)* (Paris, 2004), 17–18, 125–33, argues that, while earlier authorities wrote extensively about demons, systematic demonology only developed in the fourteenth century.

[33] Gerson, *De erroribus*, in P. Glorieux (ed.),*Gerson, Oeuvres completes*, 10 vols. (Paris, 1960–73), x, 78–81.

the brevity of the work overall, the focus is significant. If a separate declaration condemning various articles of magic and superstition made by the Paris theological faculty in 1398 that Gerson appended to his work is excluded, close to half the original material in *De erroribus circa artem magicam* deals solely with demonic existence and power.[34]

Nicholas of Jauer's *De superstitionibus* is far more extensive than Gerson's work, but follows the same pattern. Although Nicholas eschewed the need to argue for the basic existence of demons, he began his treatise with a discussion of the nature and extent of demonic power, in particular the degree to which demons might be able to affect the human mind, or even more insidiously the human soul. He concluded, drawing on many standard theological sources, that their direct abilities in this area were extremely limited, basically restricted to the power of illusion and deception.[35] In particular, Nicholas noted, demons could not know human thoughts or intentions, although they might detect sinful desires via physical signs, much as physicians diagnosed illnesses by their symptoms.[36] Long an issue within Christian thought, even from the time of Augustine, was the manner in which demons might know the future, and thus the extent to which they might lurk behind divinatory rites. Nicholas followed Augustine in maintaining that demons could never know the future directly, but through their vast knowledge and experience they could often predict future events based on present evidence.[37] He then turned to another essential point regarding the nature of demonic power, namely, whether humans could compel demons to perform certain tasks by special words, spells, or ritual actions. If specific rites exerted power over demons, then those rites might not be superstitious, since they need not entail worshiping or supplicating demons. Again drawing on longstanding Christian doctrine, he concluded that demons were never compelled by such means, but only acted because of devotions shown to them, and above all because such rites consecrated a pact, either explicitly or tacitly, between them and anyone who engaged in such superstition.[38] Only at this point did Nicholas begin to discuss specific superstitious acts he wanted to condemn.

[34] On this declaration, see Jean-Patrice Boudet, 'Les condemnations de la magie à Paris en 1398', *Revue Mabillon*, xii (2001), 121–57.

[35] Nicholas of Jauer, *De superstitionibus*, fos. 35r–36r.

[36] Nicholas of Jauer, *De superstitionibus*, fo. 37r.

[37] Nicholas of Jauer, *De superstitionibus*, fos. 39r–40r, referring to Augustine, *De divinatione daemonum*.

[38] Nicholas of Jauer, *De superstitionibus*, fos. 42v–43r.

The point where Nicholas of Jauer concluded his discussion of demonic abilities was the very point at which another Heidelberg theologian, Johannes of Frankfurt, began. He authored a *quaestio*, a point of theological disputation, concerning the power of characters, figures, or spoken words to compel and control demons.[39] From this initial question, however, he backtracked so as to cover many of the same issues as Nicholas of Jauer and Jean Gerson. The first topic with which he actually engaged was the nature of demonic existence, focusing particularly on how essentially spiritual beings could nevertheless act in physical ways. Some of his language echoed Gerson, although direct influence is difficult to determine, given that these issues were fairly standard in late medieval demonology. He then moved to the nature of demonic knowledge, akin to Nicholas of Jauer, and he ultimately concluded, as Nicholas had, that words and written characters or figures, such as those employed in superstitious spells, could not compel demons to act. Rather, demons responded to these as signs of supplication.

Only after they had discussed the basic nature of demonic power did these authors turn to particular spells, charms, or other potentially superstitious practices. Here they sought to determine whether such practices drew on demonic power, that is, whether they entailed either deliberate or inadvertent invocation or supplication of demons. Such determinations were difficult to make with absolute certainty. If healing spells or protective charms involved using herbs, plants, or stones, any supposed effects might be attributed to these substances' natural properties, and no superstition need be entailed. Some authorities were grudgingly willing to concede that such practices could be legitimate, while others were less so.[40] Astral forces were also problematic, for they too were essentially natural and could be legitimately exploited. Yet authorities feared that most actions claiming to draw on astral power actually involved demons, and they spent considerable effort trying to determine the limits of natural astral effects.[41] Spoken words and

---

[39] 'Quaestio utrum potestas cohercendi demones fieri posit per caracteres, figures atque verborum prolationes', in Joseph Hansen (ed.), *Quellen und Untersuchungen zur Geschichte des Hexenwahns und der Hexenverfolgung im Mittalalter* (1901; reprint Hildesheim, 1963), 71–82.

[40] Nicholas of Jauer, *De superstitionibus*, fo. 56r–v, allows the possibility of such natural effects; similarly Johannes Nider, *Preceptorium divine legis* 1.9.e and 1.11.ii (Milan, 1489) (no pagination); Johannes Hartlieb, *Das Buch aller verbotenen Künste, des Aberglaubens und der Zauberei*, ed. and trans. Falk Eisermann and Eckhard Graf (Ahlerstedt, 1989), 78–80. Martin of Arles, *De superstitionibus*, fos. 25v–26r, is more suspicious.

[41] Nicholas of Jauer, *De superstitionibus*, fos. 52v–53v; Martin of Arles, *De superstitionibus*, fos. 15v–16v. Hartlieb, *Buch*, 38, is more suspicious. Gerson wrote an entire work on

written characters were also troubling. Since the formulas used in questionable rites often derived from official prayers, blessings, or elements of the liturgy, one could argue that divine rather than demonic power was being invoked, and for certain rites no clear authoritative consensus existed. For example, the Heidelberg theological faculty, led by Nicholas of Jauer, had forced Werner of Friedberg to recant his tolerance for such healing spells as 'Christ was born, Christ was lost, Christ was found again', as well as the use of talismans bearing the names of the three magi to ward off epilepsy. Only a few years later, however, the Cologne theologian Heinrich of Gorcum wrote that protective talismans bearing the names of the three kings were entirely legitimate, and near the middle of the fifteenth century the Zurich canon Felix Hemmerlin, trained in law, argued at length that the 'Christ was born' spell was perfectly licit.[42]

While most late medieval authors writing on superstition dealt first with the nature of demons and demonic power before moving to specific cases, some began with individual incidents and then moved to general considerations. Around the middle of the century, for example, the canon of Pamplona, Martin of Arles, began his treatise *De superstitionibus* by addressing a single questionable practice. In times of drought the clergy of a nearby town would stage a procession in honour of Saint Peter and perform masses over an image of the apostle. This image would then be submerged in water, and this action was supposed to cause rain.[43] Asked by another cleric whether this practice was legitimate or superstitious, Martin moved into a consideration of superstition more generally, and throughout his treatise he more often proceeded from specific events to their more theoretical, theological implications, rather than the reverse.[44] Nevertheless, as with other authorities, he always returned to a consideration of demonic power.

What even this cursory survey of late medieval treatises on superstition suggests is that those authorities who turned their attention to this subject did so because it allowed them to discuss their real concern: the prevalence of

---

astral superstition, *Trilogium astrologiae theologizatae* (*Oeuvres completes*, x, 90–109), cited by Martin of Arles, *De superstitionibus*, fo. 57r–v.

[42] Heinrich of Gorcum, *De superstitiosis quibusdam casibus* (Blaubeuren, 1477 or before), fo. 4r (this passage also edited in Hansen, *Quellen*, 87); Felix Hemmerlin, *Alius tractatus exorcismorum seu adiurationum*, in Hemmerlin, *Varie oblectationis opuscula et tractatus* (Strassburg, *c*.1497), fos. 106v–107v.

[43] Martin of Arles, *De superstitionibus*, fos. 1r–2r.

[44] Martin discussed other popular rites (fos. 6v–7v), belief in auspicious or inauspicious days (fo. 11r–v), the use of magical images and talismans (fos. 15r–16r), and even the effectiveness of the 'evil eye' (fos. 23r–24v).

demonic power in the world. Fear of the devil was clearly rising in the late medieval period, manifesting in fears of demonic magic and witchcraft, but also in intensifying concern over visions, which could be subject to demonic deception, and in authoritative conceptions of the experience of demonic possession, which grew darker in these years.[45] Certainly changing conceptions and representations of demons reflected broad and multifaceted developments within medieval culture.[46] Yet Walter Stephens has suggested one possible, and provocative, interpretation of late medieval authorities' growing obsession with ideas of demonic witchcraft. Rather than arising straightforwardly from increased conviction in demonic reality and power, he argues, such obsessions masked authorities' growing doubts about demonic existence itself. Officials turned especially to suspected witches' (often coerced) testimony of sex with demons to bolster their wavering conviction in the physical reality of demons.[47]

That late medieval authorities might doubt demonic existence and power is not so extraordinary as it perhaps initially sounds. In his history of the devil, Jeffrey Russell has noted that several major intellectual and religious currents in the late Middle Ages, including nominalism, neoplatonism, humanism, and mysticism, all downplayed the active power of the devil. Only traditional scholasticism stressed demonic power as an important component of its world-view.[48] Walter Stephens' argument removes even this bastion of certainty. He centres doubts about demonic reality in scholastic demonology developing since the twelfth century. As authorities strove to comprehend how spiritual creatures could affect the physical world within an increasingly strict Aristotelian framework, they encountered incongruities that shook their faith in their own positions. They overcame these discrepancies by various intellectual manoeuvres, but underlying anxieties remained.

To whatever degree authorities felt anxiety about the reality of spiritual presence and activity in the world (and we need not posit that they consciously doubted basic elements of their faith), they would have perceived the existence and frequent toleration of superstitious practices as disquieting evidence of the failure to acknowledge the prevalence of demonic power.

---

[45] Boureau, *Satan hérétique* (passim); Nancy Caciola, *Discerning Spirits: Divine and Demonic Possession in the Middle Ages* (Ithaca, N.Y., 2003), 274–319; Elliott, *Proving Woman*, 264–96.

[46] Jeffrey Burton Russell, *Lucifer: The Devil in the Middle Ages* (Ithaca, N.Y., 1984), 274–301; Robert Muchembled, *A History of the Devil From the Middle Ages to the Present*, trans. Jean Birrell (Cambridge, 2003), 21–7.

[47] Walter Stephens, *Demon Lovers: Witchcraft, Sex, and the Crisis of Belief* (Chicago, 2002).

[48] Russell, *Lucifer*, 274–95.

It was bad enough that common people were employing spells and charms without any understanding of the forces on which they drew, but some clerics and educated men were aiding and abetting them. In Paris, Jean Gerson scolded the medical faculty for its toleration of superstitious healing rites; in Heidelberg, Nicholas of Jauer was aghast that Werner of Friedberg, a man with good theological training, would support the use of superstitious spells; Martin of Arles argued against a superstitious rain ceremony performed by local clergy near Pamplona.[49] Addressing the issue of superstition allowed these men to assert the reality and extent of demonic power. In doing so they were not simply giving voice to an elevated fear of the devil that infused late medieval society, but responding, in a particular fashion, to what they saw as dangerous laxity in necessary and salubrious fear of the demonic.

III

The subject of superstition, linked to both error and the demonic since the earliest days of the church, provided a somewhat natural focus for authorities concerned about erroneous perceptions of demonic power. Yet it was hardly a necessary focus. If these men were motivated by a general concern about demons, could they not simply have written more general, abstract demonological treatises? The answer, quite simply, is that such an approach to theological problems was no longer in favour. Fifteenth-century schoolmen adopted what Daniel Hobbins has described as a new literary genre— rather than the sprawling *summa* or abstract *quaestio*, the short and issue-specific 'tract'. The great innovator of this genre was Jean Gerson, and his influence was felt throughout European learned circles.[50] Not all the works discussed here could accurately be labelled tracts. Nicholas of Jauer's *De superstitionibus*, for example, was a long treatise, while Johannes of Frankfurt wrote a traditional *quaestio*. Nevertheless, all certainly conform to Hobbins' insight that late medieval theological writings tend to address specific and practical problems, rather than confronting major issues abstractly.

This approach to theological writing was grounded in a new approach to theology itself that was influential in this period. First identified in German scholarship as *Frömmigkeitstheologie* (literally the theology of piety), this trend called for authorities to focus more on promoting common piety and ensuring sound pastoral care, rather than addressing abstract points

---

[49] Nicholas of Jauer, *De superstitionibus*, fo. 57r, particularly criticized clerics who allowed superstitious rites to go uncorrected; also Martin of Arles, *De superstitionibus*, fo. 59v; Hartlieb, *Buch*, 104.

[50] Hobbins, 'The Schoolman as Public Intellectual: Jean Gerson and the Late Medieval Tract', *American Historical Review*, cviii (2003), 1308–37.

of doctrine.[51] Once again, Jean Gerson was an important innovator, and he exerted a significant influence, especially over theological faculties in several recently founded universities in the German Empire—Prague (founded 1347/48), Vienna (1365), Heidelberg (1385), and Cologne (1388).[52] At Prague in particular, growth of interest in superstition in the late fourteenth century was also spurred by the currents of religious and spiritual reform developing in Bohemia that would eventually give rise to the Hussite movement. Nicholas of Jauer, who both studied and taught in Prague, can be seen as the culmination of this rising concern, although, of course, he wrote his major treatise on superstition in Heidelberg, where he had moved in 1402, thus exemplifying the lines of communication by which such concerns could spread.[53] In fact, from each of these schools emerged practitioners of pastoral theology who would write important works about superstition and sorcery, the power of demons, and the proper discernment of good from evil spirits.[54]

The new pastoral theology in the universities of Germany, and even more basically the relatively recent establishment of those universities, played a major role in allowing late medieval concerns over superstition to reach their peak. In 1300, there were around fifteen universities in Europe, and none in German lands. By 1378, this number had doubled to around thirty, including the first German universities at Prague and Vienna. Across Europe, seven more came into existence between 1378 and 1400 (an additional eighteen were established in the first half of the fifteenth century).[55] These newer universities were, in contrast to many older ones, founded by kings and princes, and they existed more directly to serve immediate political and religious

[51] Berndt Hamm, 'Frömmigkeit als Gegenstand theologiegeschichtlicher Forschung: Methodisch-historische Überlegungen am Beispiel von Spätmittelalter und Reformation', *Zeitschrift für Theologie und Kirche*, lxxiv (1977), 464–97. Karin Baumann, *Aberglaube für Laien: Zur Problematik und Überlieferung spätmittelalterlicher Superstitionenkritik*, 2 vols. (Würzburg, 1989), i, 201–2, connects this theological approach to concern over superstition.

[52] Krzysztof Bracha, 'Kritik an den Glaubens- und Verhaltensformen und an der Aberglaubenpraxis im kirchlichen reformatorischen Schrifttum des Spätmittelalters', in Paweł Kras and Wojciech Polak (eds), *Christianity in East Central Europe: Late Middle Ages* (Lublin, 1999), 272–3; also Bracha, 'Einfluß der neuen Frömmigkeit', 227–9.

[53] František Šmahel, 'Stärker als der Glaube: Magie, Aberglaube und Zauber in der Epoche des Hussitismus', *Bohemia*, xxxii (1991), 325–9; also Bracha, 'Kritik', 276–7.

[54] Tschacher, *Der Formicarius*, 216–20, 279–82.

[55] Jacques Verger, 'Patterns', in Helen de Ridder-Symoens (ed.), *Universities in the Middle Ages* (A History of the University in Europe i, Cambridge, 1992), 57; Heinrich Denifle, *Die Entstehung der Universitäten des Mittelalters bis 1400* (1885; repr. Graz, 1956), 219.

needs.[56] The profusion of universities also broke the previous theological monopoly exerted by Paris.[57] These newer institutions and their faculties were eager to assert their authority within their more limited territories, and to serve their political masters by working to maintain proper social and religious order in their regions. The issue of superstition served these goals. The case of Werner of Friedberg, heard ultimately by the Heidelberg theological faculty, is illustrative. Werner was clearly espousing some questionable or at least provocative beliefs. Moreover, he deliberately contradicted the teachings of other clergy in his region.[58] Perhaps because of such challenges, he was initially questioned by representatives of the bishop of Speyer, but was able to defend himself fairly well. Twenty years earlier, there might have been no recourse for the confounded episcopal officials, but now Werner's case could be transferred to the erudite faculty of Heidelberg.

IV

The increased involvement of religious authorities in the lives of ordinary Christians in the late Middle Ages and authorities' growing concern over common lay beliefs and practices have long been noted. Since the early 1970s, some historians of popular religion have argued that the vast majority of Europe's population was not really Christianized until the sixteenth century, and for most of the Middle Ages a sharp divide separated relatively small Christian elites from the common laity, who practised a predominantly pagan folk religion.[59] Other scholars have strongly contested this view, maintaining that Europe was fully Christianized early in the medieval period, and cautioning against drawing any sharp division between clerical elites and common masses in terms of essential beliefs or practices.[60] Late medieval concerns over superstition have sometimes been interpreted in terms of the former view of Christianization, as evidence that clerical authorities were for the first time taking a deep, almost anthropological interest in belief systems

---

[56] A. B. Cobban, *The Medieval Universities: Their Development and Organization* (London, 1975), 118–19; Jacques Verger, *Les universités au Moyen Age* (Vendôme, 1973), 140–3.

[57] Verger, *Les universités*, 112.

[58] Lerner, 'Werner di Friedberg', 270–1.

[59] Jean Delumeau, *Catholicism Between Luther and Voltaire: A New View of the Counter-Reformation*, trans. Jeremy Moiser (London, 1977); Robert Muchembled, *Popular Culture and Elite Culture in France, 1400–1750*, trans. Lydia Cochrane (Baton Rouge, La., 1985).

[60] See John Van Engen, 'The Christian Middle Ages as an Historiographical Problem', *American Historical Review*, xci (1986), 519–52, and literature cited there; also Van Engen, 'The Future of Medieval Church History', *Church History*, lxxi (2002), 497.

they regarded as unfamiliar and essentially unchristian.[61] Late medieval writings on superstition can feed into this view, insofar as their authors frequently drew on the language of the church fathers to describe superstition in terms of residual paganism.[62] Such references were purely formulaic, however, and in fact these men were chiefly interested in the abuse of clearly Christian practices. Moreover, they did not focus exclusively on uneducated and potentially unchristianized rustics. That Jean Gerson, Nicholas of Jauer, and Martin of Arles wrote (at least partly) against superstitious clerics has already been noted. Denis the Carthusian addressed his *Contra vitia superstitionum* expressly to parish clergy, lest they share the superstitious beliefs of their flocks.[63] The German court physician Johannes Hartlieb's *Buch aller verbotenen Künste* dealt with common spells and witchcraft to some degree but concerned primarily learned, courtly magical practices and superstitious beliefs.[64]

The approach these men took was in some sense anthropological, but they were not field anthropologists immersed in a foreign society. Rather, they were observers and critics of their own culture. Their descriptions of superstition convey not the shock of discovery but dismay over what they regarded as noticeable deterioration in familiar customs. They repeatedly expressed the fear that recourse to superstitious practices was growing increasingly common in their day. Gerson opened *De erroribus circa artem magicam* by asserting that such errors were becoming more and more pronounced, and Nicholas of Jauer compared contemporary Christians to biblical Jews in their predilection for idolatry.[65] This rhetoric of the degradation of present days and need to stem a growing tide of iniquity indicates that late medieval writings about superstition were, to a large degree, a manifestation of the broad impulse for religious reform evident throughout the late-fourteenth and fifteenth centuries.[66]

---

[61] Schmitt, 'Les "superstitions" ', 423; Schmitt, *Holy Greyhound*, 1–7.

[62] E.g. Nicholas of Jauer, *De superstitionibus*, fos. 43v–44r, 45v, 48v, 60v, 62v.

[63] Denis the Carthusian, *Contra Alchoranum et sectam Machometicam libri quinque, De instituendo bello adversus Turcas, et de generali celebrando Concilio, Contra vitia superstitionum* (Cologne, 1533), 599.

[64] Frank Fürbeth, *Johannes Hartlieb: Untersuchungen zu Leben und Werk* (Tübingen, 1992).

[65] Gerson, *De erroribus*, 77; Nicholas of Jauer, *De superstitionibus*, fo. 44r.

[66] On reform as an issue throughout the Christian era, see Christopher M. Bellitto, *Renewing Christianity: A History of Church Reform from Day One to Vatican II* (New York, 2001). A foundational study remains Gerhart B. Ladner, *The Idea of Reform: Its Impact on Christian Thought and Action in the Age of the Fathers* (Cambridge, Mass., 1959).

The issue of late medieval religious reform in all its varieties, from institutional reforms envisioned by Church councils at Constance and Basel, to reforms within many religious orders, to more generalized impulses for moral and spiritual regeneration throughout Christian society, is vast.[67] Yet one important connection to arguments already advanced here can be drawn. Late medieval religious reformers were deeply concerned with demonic power, which they regarded as motivating most forms of religious deviance and actively resisting any sort of reform.[68] Thus reformist impulses can be seen to coincide with concern over superstition particularly when superstition is recognized as a subject that attracted and focused concerns about demonic power.

Like authorities writing about superstition, religious reformers in general feared not only growing demonic power in the world but also what they regarded as a dangerously widespread failure to recognize the reality and scope of that power. The notion that most people were so inured to sin that they casually ignored signs of demonic activity was a frequent theme of sermons.[69] The famous reforming preacher Bernardino of Siena, for example, who railed against superstitious healing spells and charms, among many other forms of perceived immorality, was deeply concerned to call attention to the operations of demonic power.[70] Bernardino's fiery preaching gave rise to numerous trials for superstition, sorcery, and witchcraft, and indeed concern over superstition in the first few decades of the fifteenth century is usually seen as

[67] On councils, see Johannes Helmrath, 'Reform als Thema der Konzilien des Spätmittelalters', in Giuseppe Alberigo (ed.), *Christian Unity: The Council of Ferrara-Florence, 1438/39-1989* (Leuven, 1991), 75–152; Jürgen Miethke, 'Kirchenreform auf den Konzilien des 15. Jahrhunderts: Motive—Methoden—Wirkungen', in Johannes Helmrath and Heribert Müller (eds), *Studien zum 15. Jahrhundert: Festschrift für Erich Meuthen*, 2 vols. (Munich, 1994), i, 13–42. On religious orders, see Kaspar Elm (ed.), *Reformbemuhungen und Observanzbestrebungen im spätmittelalterlichen Ordenswesen* (Berliner historische Studien xiv, Ordensstudien vi, Berlin, 1989). On general concepts, see Gerald Strauss, 'Ideas of *Reformatio* and *Renovatio* from the Middle Ages to the Reformation', in Thomas A. Brady Jr., Heiko A. Oberman, and James D. Tracy (eds), *Handbook of European History, 1400–1600: Late Middle Ages, Renaissance, and Reformation*, 2 vols. (Leiden, 1994–5), ii, 1–30.

[68] Michael D. Bailey, *Battling Demons: Witchcraft, Heresy, and Reform in the Late Middle Ages* (University Park, Pa., 2003), 115–16; Tschacher, *Der Formicarius*, 379–87, 457–8.

[69] Larissa Taylor, *Soldiers of Christ: Preaching in Late Medieval and Reformation France* (Oxford, 1992), 118.

[70] Franco Mormando, *The Preacher's Demons: Bernardino of Siena and the Social Underworld of Early Renaissance Italy* (Chicago, 1999), 89–97.

an important precursor to ideas of conspiratorial, diabolical witchcraft and the earliest European witch hunts beginning in the 1430s.[71]

For the rest of the fifteenth century, and for several centuries thereafter, concern over witchcraft was also deeply enmeshed with ideologies of religious reform, and clerical writings on witchcraft frequently focused on explicating the powers of demons, detailing the intimate connections between witches and demons, and decrying those who failed to recognize the many forms demonic power could take. The infamous *Malleus maleficarum*, for example, the pre-eminent late medieval treatise on witchcraft, began its long catalogue of horrors by condemning first and foremost not witches themselves but those who failed to believe in the real existence of witches; that is, those who did not accept the intensely diabolized interpretation of the operations of common sorcery that the *Malleus* would present.[72]

V

By the end of the fifteenth century, concern over common spells and charms had largely been subsumed into concern over witchcraft, which only intensified during the sixteenth and early-seventeenth centuries. Also in these years, condemnation of superstition was recast into Reformation-era polemics, as Catholics and Protestants accused each other of practising foul superstitions, and policed belief within their own confessions.[73] These forces may well have generated concern over superstition even if none had existed before, but significant concern had, in fact, already developed in the late Middle Ages. A number of specifically late medieval factors contributed to the increased attention religious authorities paid to matters of common belief and practice. A new form of pastoral theology caused schoolmen to address practical matters of common religiosity, and new theological faculties, especially those in central Europe, focused more on particular instances of local practice and on maintaining local religious order, rather than on addressing abstract theories. Above all, the widespread impulse for reform that reverberated through all levels of late medieval religious culture, and which is too

---

[71] Peters, 'Medieval Church', 228–9.

[72] Heinrich Kramer (Institoris), *Malleus maleficarum: Nachdruck des Erstdruckes von 1487 mit Bulle und Approbatio*, ed. Günter Jerouschek (Hildesheim, 1992), fo. 4r.

[73] Stuart Clark, *Thinking with Demons: The Idea of Witchcraft in Early Modern Europe* (Oxford, 1997), 472–88; R. W. Scribner, 'Sorcery, Superstition and Society: The Witch of Urach, 1529', in Scribner, *Popular Culture and Popular Movements in Reformation Germany* (London, 1987), 257–75; R. W. Scribner, 'Magic and the Formation of Protestant Popular Culture in Germany,' in Scribner, *Religion and Culture in Germany (1400–1800)*, ed. Lyndal Roper (Leiden, 2001), 323–45.

often and too easily passed over as a mere prelude to the great themes of the sixteenth century, inspired authorities to engage with common belief and practice even as it filled them with dread about the supposed state to which those beliefs and practices had sunk.

For each of these developments and tendencies, superstition was a more or less obvious focal point. Yet while these factors certainly gave form and expression to late medieval concern over superstition, we will not fully understand the nature and importance of that concern if we explain it purely in terms of new intellectual or ecclesiastical structures. As with religious reform, ultimately a matter of deep conviction and belief that is not adequately explained only by intellectual and institutional developments, so too the issue of superstition resonated so powerfully in the fifteenth century because it spoke to some of the deepest concerns of this age, and allowed authorities to give voice to those concerns. At issue in late medieval debates over supposed superstition were the nature, extent, and indeed reality of demonic power, and concomitantly of divine power as well. In subsequent centuries, questions of spiritual reality and power continued to impel debates associated with the Reformation, Scientific Revolution, and Enlightenment. Concern over 'medieval' superstition would resonate through much of later European history.

'Honeyed Flies' and 'Sugared Rats': Witchcraft, Heresy, and Superstition in the Bresciano, 1454–1535

Stephen Bowd

I

In 1426 the republic of Venice seized the Bresciano region in northern Italy from the control of the Visconti duke of Milan, and in 1454 the area was conclusively recognized as a part of the Venetian empire by the Treaty of Lodi. As was the case in its other subject cities Venice entered into a 'constitutional pact' with Brescia that granted a large degree of local autonomy in return for directly appointed Venetian rectors, a *podestà* and *capitano*, with powers of arbitration and management.[1] In 1455 Brescia had a population of around 28,000 rising to 50,000 by the end of the century—making it one of the most populous cities in Italy. A contemporary Venetian visitor noted that the city was 'in a wonderful state of opulence and growth' and was '[well] furnished with fountains, bells and whores'.[2] Richly endowed with mineral resources and strategically important to the defence of the Venetian empire's vulnerable western flank Brescia was heavily taxed as well as heavily fortified.

The Venetian conquest of Brescia serves as a reminder that internal politics in all Renaissance cities, courts, and communes were a hostage to external fortune. However, it is also true that the fortunes of the political community could turn on the whim of local interest groups or factions keen to apply pressure over particular issues, including heresy and witchcraft. Neighbouring Alpine valleys such as the Valtellina, Val Chiavenna, and Val Leventina, were among the first areas in Europe to witness the prosecution of heretics and witches on a significant scale from the latter half of the fourteenth century. Not surprisingly, the Bresciano was one of the first regions south of the Alps to follow suit and what might be called the 'plurality of power' manifested itself in the witch-hunts of the fifteenth and sixteenth centuries as popes, bishops, inquisitors, Brescian councillors, and Venetian governors

---

[1] Ann Katherine Isaacs, 'States in Tuscany and Veneto', in Peter Blickle (ed.), *Resistance, Representation, and Community* (Cambridge, 1997), 302.

[2] Marin Sanudo, *Itinerario di Marin Sanuto per la terraferma veneziana nell'anno MCCCCLXXXIII* (Padua, 1847), 70, 73.

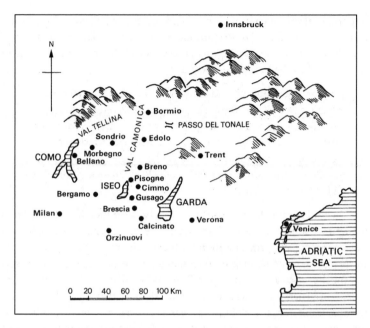

Fig. 1. Centres of inquisitorial action against witchcraft, 1454–1534 (map courtesy of Ray Harris)

all sought to impose their authority on the Val Camonica—a seemingly benighted, superstitious, and demonic area.[3]

The Val Camonica was (and still is) the longest valley in Italy, and runs for 90 km to the Alpine pass of Tonale north of Brescia.[4] It provided the most

---

[3] Richard Kieckhefer, *European Witch Trials: Their Foundations in Popular and Learned Culture, 1300–1500* (Berkeley and Los Angeles, 1976), 123, 132; Giovanni Giorgetta, 'Un Pestalozzi accusato di stregoneria', *Clavenna: bollettino del centro di studi storici valciavennaschi*, xx (1981), 58–72 (*estratto* at <http://www.paoloportone.it/giorgetta1/giorgetta1.htm> accessed 12 June 2007); and Giovanni Giorgetta, 'Documenti sull' Inquisizione a Morbegno nella prima metà del secolo XV', *Bollettino della società storica valtellinese*, xxxiii (1980), 59–83.

[4] Previous studies of witchcraft in the area include: 'Atti del convegno eretici e streghe, quando e come. Cemmo, 6 marzo 1999' in *Synopsis. Quaderno di approfondimenti storici*, i (2000); Roberto Andrea Lorenzi (ed.), *Sante, medichesse e streghe nell' arco alpino. Atti del convegno promossa dall'Università popolare di Val Camonica—Sebino, 24-25 aprile 1993* (Bolzano, 1994); Giorgio Tortelli, 'Inquisizione e stregoneria a Brescia e nelle valli. La difficile convivenza fra autorità laiche e religiose nei primi decenni del XVI secolo', in *Scritti in onore di Gaetano Panazza* (Brescia, 1994), 259–68; Maurizio Bernadelli Curuz, *Streghe Bresciane. Confessioni, persecuzioni e roghi fra XV e il XVI secolo*

important means of communication between the Bresciano and the Tyrol, and it was claimed in 1520 that around 50,000 souls could be found there.[5] An educated local observer, giving an account of the witch hunts there in 1518, described the Val Camonica as a

> place of mountains more than plains, more sterile than fertile, and inhabited by a people who are largely ignorant, goitrous, and almost entirely deformed and lacking all the finer points of civil society. Their customs are rustic and wild, and there are few who know, let alone obey, the commandments of God. So these valley dwellers are as different from other Brescians as the Portuguese are from those [inhabitants] of Calicut.[6]

The cliché of rustic oafishness, isolation, and backwardness has persisted into modern accounts of the witch-hunt. Hugh Trevor-Roper argued that Brescia was interesting as a prime location for the 'witch-craze' as an unassimilable social phenomenon because of its mountainous location. However, Brescia was much less isolated than Trevor-Roper believed and its isolation was less crucial in generating witch-hunting than the fact that the Val Camonica formed, in his suggestive phrase, a 'sensitive social frontier'.[7] Another historian has argued that the Alpine 'witch-craze' owed a great deal to economic and political change in the valleys and was 'an accompanying phenomenon of opening, not of isolation'.[8] Indeed, the Val Camonica formed a significant economic centre and its relative autonomy was recognized by the governments of the Visconti and Venice. They both initially granted the valley

---

(Desenzano, 1988); F. Odorici, *Le streghe di Valtellina e la santa inquisizione* (Milan, Venice, and Verona, 1862); and *Le cronache bresciane inedite dei secoli XV–XIX*, ed. Paolo Guerrini, 2 vols. (Brescia, 1922), i, 183–7. See also P. Burke, 'Witchcraft and Magic in Renaissance Italy: Gianfrancesco Pico and his *Strix*,' in S. Anglo (ed.), *The Damned Art: Essays in the Literature of Witchcraft* (London, Henley, and Boston, 1977), 32–52.

[5] Paola Lanaro, 'Economia cittadina, flussi migratori e spazio urbano in terraferma veneta tra basso medioevo ed età moderna', in Donatella Calabi and Paola Lanaro (eds), *La città italiana e i luoghi degli stranieri XIV–XVII secolo* (Rome, 1998), 74; *relazione* of Pietro Tron, former *podestà* in Brescia, noted in Marino Sanudo, *I Diarii*, 58 vols (Venice, 1879–1903), xxix, col. 334.

[6] Giuseppe da Orzinuovi to Ludovico Querini, 1 Aug. 1518, Sanudo, *Diarii*, xxv, col. 602.

[7] H. R. Trevor-Roper, *The European Witch-Craze of the Sixteenth and Seventeenth Centuries* (London, 1988. First publ. 1967), 29, 32, 38.

[8] Arno Borst, 'The Origins of the Witch-craze in the Alps', in Brian P. Levack (ed.), *New Perspectives on Witchcraft, Magic and Demonology*, vol. 2 *Witchcraft in Continental Europe* (New York and London, 2001), 310.

privileges distinct from those of Brescia while castellans in the Val Camonica responded to local as much as Brescian or Venetian concerns throughout this period.[9] The Val Camonica was also a centre for the spread of newly reformed clerical orders concerned with eradicating 'superstition' and reinvigorating popular faith. For example, Franciscan spirituals led by the Portuguese João Mendes de Silva founded a number of convents in the Val Camonica after 1460. Mendes was based in Milan and it is important to note that Milanese and Lombard Franciscans were in the forefront of promoting new measures for poor relief in the region from the 1480s onwards, notably the *monte di pietà* which provided a licit Christian alternative to Jewish moneylenders.[10] The Franciscan preachers who visited Brescia during the fifteenth century argued that the moral reform of the city required the expulsion of the Jews. The council sought this expulsion, which it compared to the liberation of the city from the tyranny of the Visconti dukes of Milan.[11] When news of the 'martyrdom' of the child Simon at the hands of the Jews in the town of Trent reached Brescia it was quickly printed and was complemented by a number of edifying frescoes depicting Simon on the walls of Franciscan churches in Brescia and throughout the Val Camonica.[12] It is no coincidence that such an area of intense anti-semitism fuelled by mendicant spirituality was also the site of fears about these 'synagogues of satan', the witches' sabbat.[13]

---

[9] A. Menniti Ippolito, 'La dedizione di Brescia a Milano (1421) e a Venezia (1427): Città suddite e distretto nello stato regionale', in Gaetano Cozzi, (ed.), *Stato, società e giustizia nella Repubblica Veneta (sec. XV–XVIII)* 2 vols. (Rome, 1980–5), ii, 29–54.

[10] Gabriella Ferri Piccaluga, 'Economia, devozione e politica: immagini di francescani, amadeiti ed ebrei nel secolo XV', in *Il Francescanesimo in Lombardia: storia e arte* (Milan, 1983), 107–22; Brian Pullan, *Rich and Poor in Renaissance Venice: The Social Institutions of a Catholic State, to 1620* (Oxford, 1971), 202.

[11] Agostino Zanelli, 'Predicatori a Brescia nel quattrocento,' *Archivio Storico Lombardo*, 3rd ser., xv (1901), 143.

[12] R. Po-Chia Hsia, *Trent 1475: Stories of a Ritual Murder Trial* (New Haven, 1992), esp. 33, 53–7; D. Rigaux, 'Antijudaïsme par l'image: l'iconographie de Simon de Trente (d. 1475) dans la région de Brescia,' in D. Tollet (ed.), *Politique et religion dans le judaïsme ancien et médiéval* (Paris, 1989), 309–18; and Elia Capriolo, *Chronica de rebus brixianorum* (Brescia, n. d., [c.1505]), fol. LXXIXv.

[13] Compare the inquisitor of Como's report from Bormio which describes how, at the instigation of a Franciscan preacher a Jew was burned in 1483 and 42 witches were shaved and burned in 1485: Giovanni Giorgetta, 'Processi di stregoneria a Bormio tra il 1483 ed il 1486', *Bollettino della società storica valtellinese*, xxxvi (1983), 153–67 (<http://www.paoloportone.it/giorgetta2/giorgetta2.htm> accessed 12 June 2007).

The immediate source of the idea of the sabbat and many of these more demonological concerns lay with the Dominican inquisitors charged by the papacy since the thirteenth century with rooting out heresy. Their activities were directed by the head of the Lombard order from Milan, which was an early centre of heresy and witchcraft trials and a base for the composition and dissemination of Dominican tracts on witchcraft and the demonic.[14] The classic stereotype of the witch, which emerged in Europe after c.1400 and fused inversions of Christian belief and practice with pagan or classical ideas, was disseminated by Dominican texts and preaching and is evident in almost all of the cases of witchcraft found by investigators in the Val Camonica. As these inquisitors, together with bishops and lay governors, combatted witchcraft in the Val Camonica from the middle of the fifteenth century they discovered hundreds of cases of deliberate and obstinate heresy which they frequently attempted to burn out of society. In common with the prosecutions in other Alpine areas 'manifest heresy', including the adoration of the devil and the abuse of sacraments and the sacramental, or 'superstition', was increasingly accompanied in the Bresciano by evidence of *maleficium* (harmful action usually prompted or aided by demons) and by new and alarming reports and confessions of the presence of thousands of valley dwellers at the witches' sabbats, participation in feasts and orgies, and demonic pacts.[15]

While the demonic aspect of the new heresy of witchcraft, especially the sabbat, has received ample scholarly treatment, the role of 'superstition' in the persecution of witches has received much less attention until recently. Superstition, or 'superfluous and vain religion' as the fifteenth-century canon of Pamplona Martín de Arles put it, was regarded in early modern Europe as a less calculated and serious sin than heresy. However, as a form of 'false' or exaggerated religion superstition could be dangerous to the untutored Christian and lead him or her into heresy or the suspicion of heresy.[16]

---

[14] For example, works by the Milanese Dominican Girolamo Visconti, *Opusculum de striis, videlicet an strie sint velud heretice iudicande* (c.1460) and *Lamiarum sive striarum opusculum* (c.1460), both published in Milan in 1490; Giordano (Jordanes) da Bergamo, *Quaestio de strigis* (c.1470); Bernardo Ratengo of Como, *De strigiis* (c.1510). In general see, Michael Tavuzzi. *Renaissance Inquisitors. Dominican Inquisitors and Inquisitorial Districts in Northern Italy, 1474–1527* (Leiden and Boston, 2007).

[15] On the formation of the European witch see Norman Cohn, *Europe's Inner Demons* (London, 1975); Kieckhefer, *European Witch Trials*; and Carlo Ginzburg, *Ecstasies: Deciphering the Witches' Sabbath*, trans. Raymond Rosenthal, ed. Gregory Elliot (London, 1991).

[16] Martín de Arles quoted by Ruth Martin, *Witchcraft and the Inquisition in Venice, 1550–1650* (Oxford, 1989), 124. On the link between superstition and heresy see ibid., 74 n. 149.

As the influential theologian Thomas Aquinas pointed out in the thirteenth century, superstitious practices were usually based on false and vain opinions which could be exploited by demons, whether a man entered into a demonic pact or not.[17] In this way there were normally good grounds for treating superstition as a minor fault but the way was open for subsequent theologians and inquisitors to suspect that it formed a link in the chain which led from ignorance to devil worship.

Inquisitors might be aided in their construction of this demonic link by the fact that in its more common and non-demonic usage 'superstition' was an elastic term that could include, or exclude, a large number of beliefs and practices which might be associated with common strategies for protection from harm, as well as learned or clerical magic, and witchcraft.[18] This normative process could vary according to the prejudices and aims of the observer or investigator, and was also moulded by local circumstances and it was in this conceptual elasticity that a confusion of *religio* and *superstitio* sometimes arose. However, it can also be argued that this was an ordering confusion: in other words, the definition of superstition was contingent upon the delineation of religion and vice versa.[19] As clerics attempted to clarify or impose doctrine in key matters of faith, superstition was given some weight in their sermons and actions.

Critical to both concepts was a similar systemic duality of the natural and the supernatural. The communication between natural and supernatural worlds was a given in the whole spectrum of beliefs and practices from church liturgy to folklorized or magical ritual but the precise boundary between the natural and the supernatural was contested throughout the medieval and early modern periods as fierce debates about the eucharist, miracles, the immaculate conception, and demonic power demonstrate.[20] For example, in 1462 Brescia was the setting for debates about the incarnation of Christ in which a local inquisitor—who instigated the prosecution of

[17] St Thomas Aquinas, *Summa theologiae*, pt. 2 (second pt.), qu. 92–6.

[18] On 'superstition' as a broadly defined 'catch-all label' in fifteenth-century Italy see Bernadette Paton, ' "To the fire, to the fire! Let us burn a little incense to God": Bernardino, Preaching Friars and *Maleficio* in Late Medieval Siena', in Charles Zika (ed.), *No Gods Except Me: Orthodoxy and Religious Practice in Europe, 1200–1600* (Melbourne, 1991), 15. See also eadem, 'Preaching Friars and the Civic Ethos: Siena, 1380–1480', doctoral thesis (University of Oxford, 1986), 272–81. Microfilm.

[19] See the contributions to this volume by Hugh Bowden and Richard Gordon.

[20] On the role of demonic theory in the defence of natural and supernatural aspects of Christian theology see Walter Stephens, *Demon Lovers: Witchcraft, Sex and the Crisis of Belief* (Chicago and London, 2002).

witches in the city a few years before—played a leading role.[21] Robert Scribner has shown how these varied and often colourful or tangible emanations of the sacred in the profane were persistent aspects of 'popular religion' before and after the Reformation.[22] A similar spectrum of ritual and belief in early modern Terra d'Otranto, in the heel of Italy, has been named a 'system of the sacred' by David Gentilcore who describes the role of catholic clergy in the strictly liturgical, the para-liturgical, and the frankly magical aspects of popular religion which has been revealed there.[23] Evidence of a similar sacred system in northern Italy has been suggested by Carlo Ginzburg and recently by many other historians, especially those who have worked on inquisition records of trials for witchcraft.[24]

Superstition was also the target of a number of works produced by educated clerics and laymen as a part of their efforts to reform and reinvigorate religious belief and practices. For example, speakers at the Fifth Lateran council summoned by Pope Julius II in 1512 outlined the duties of both clerics and laymen, and stressed the need for a reform of morals and the abolition of superstition.[25] The Venetian noblemen turned hermits, Vincenzo Querini and Tommaso Giustiniani, asserted, in a reform document drafted on the occasion of the council and addressed to the pope in c.1512–13, that there was scarcely a single household unaffected by some form of superstition. They alleged that the laity and clergy had been led into superstitions by the Jews, and by books on the interpretation of dreams and on the divining arts. The authors of these works ought to be condemned by the pope, and the

---

[21] See Giacomo della Marca, *De Sanguine Christi*, ed. D. Lasic (Falconara Maritima, 1976); Archivio di Stato, Brescia, Archivio Storico Civico (hereafter ASC), 496, fos. 222v, 224r–v, 227v (16 and 19 Aug. 1454, 6 Sept. 1454, pencil foliation); ASC 497, fos. 6v, 34r, 84r, 197r–v (6 Feb., 4 May, and 3 Dec. 1455, 19 Feb. 1457, first foliation); ASC 498, fo. 3v (11 Jan. 1458, first foliation).

[22] R. W. Scribner, 'Cosmic Order and Daily Life: Sacred and Secular in Pre-Industrial German Society', in idem, *Popular Culture and Popular Movements in Reformation Germany* (London and Ronceverte, 1987), 1–16; and idem, 'Ritual and Popular Belief in Catholic Germany at the Time of the Reformation', in ibid., 17–47.

[23] David Gentilcore, *From Bishop to Witch: The System of the Sacred in Early Modern Terra d'Otranto* (Manchester, 1992).

[24] Guido Ruggiero, *Binding Passions: Tales of Marriage, Magic, and Power at the End of the Renaissance* (Oxford, 1993), and Anne Jacobson Schutte, *Aspiring Saints: Pretense of Holiness, Inquisition, and Gender in the Republic of Venice, 1618–1750* (Baltimore and London, 2001).

[25] Antonio Pucci, *Oratio habita per Reverendum Patrem dominum Antonium Pucciu[bus] Camere Apostolice Clericum: in Nona Sacrosancti Lateranensium Concilii Sessione. Tertio Nones Maii. M. d. xiiii* (n. p., n. d., [Rome? 1514?]), sig. Cv.

books destroyed. People who practised the black arts ought to be burnt alive or sent into perpetual exile if they were not repentant. Querini and Giustiniani also condemned astrology and astrologers, and wrote that the sick ought to be forbidden to go to so-called 'doctors' who used bogus cures, charms, words, and poems. In short, the hermits scorned the idea that certain prayers, poems, or magical words could heal specific parts of the body and they ridiculed the idea that miraculous images and pictures carried in procession or on one's own person could heal the sick, induce rain, or promote fertility in cows—although such practices were widespread in Italy.[26]

In a similar fashion, the hermits' friend Gasparo Contarini asserted in his 1517 treatise on the ideal bishop, written for the new bishop of Bergamo, that the bishop's congregation should be prevented from straying from correct religious practices by legal sanctions and episcopal guidance. Contarini described how the people were affected by impiety and superstition, and he seems to have associated the former with the educated and the latter with uneducated peasants. The former vice arose from the arts of prediction such as magic and astrology, which were opposed to religion and went by the name of wisdom although they were, in effect, a form of idolatry. However, superstition was distinguished as another sin that could lead to impiety for it consisted of 'too much religion' and the worship by country folk of 'a god of fever and a god of pestilence, a goddess of glaucoma and of eye disease'. The peasants also 'set up gods for cows, sheep, and grains', and in times of need 'they all immediately exasperate the saints, even the statues of the saints, with most of their prayers, just as each one pleases'. This quasi-pagan impiety, he wrote, must be destroyed by the bishop using 'a certain gentleness' in order to 'recall the whole people to the true worship of the one God and of Jesus Christ'. Those who were in thrall to superstition accepted prayers for good fortune and health, and apocryphal writings just as if they were canonical texts. Women were particularly singled out for censure: 'I pass over women, for whom nothing is without superstition!'[27]

Such superstition could arise from ignorance which was not confined to lay women: Querini and Giustiniani alleged that there were scarcely two out of one hundred of the clergy who understood Latin, and Contarini thought the

---

[26] T. Giustiniani and V. Querini, 'Libellus ad Leonem Decem', in *Annales Camaldulenses ordinis Sancti Benedicti*, ed. J. B. Mittarelli and A. Costadoni, 9 vols. (Venice, 1755–73), ix, cols. 670, 674–88.

[27] Gasparo Contarini, *The Office of a Bishop* (De officio viri boni et probi episcopi), ed. and trans. John Patrick Donnelly, S.J. (Milwaukee, 2002), 105–9, 129–33. The bishop is warned against practising 'superstitious disciplines such as magic and skill at divination, whether from the stars or from anything of that sort' at ibid., 83.

Dominicans and Franciscans most superstitious in their excessive devotion to their founding saints.[28] Fifteenth-century clerical writers on superstition, following Thomas Aquinas, noted that it was also bound up with demonism whose force they defined more broadly and whose scope they extended in their efforts to reform religion and religiosity. Clerical necromancy, which had been seen as one of the principal conduits for demonic power in the human world during the Middle Ages, was increasingly accompanied by a more general demonic threat which was embodied in the new heretical sect of witches.[29] The inquisitors of the Bresciano elaborated on the nature of this demonic threat, identified the clergy partly responsible for its spread, and extracted confessions which led from admissions of superstitious practices such as medicinal healing, to admissions of diabolical practice.

In the 1450s, the decade of the earliest surviving evidence, the local inquisitor presented the problem of practices and beliefs in the Val Camonica to the pope and to Venice as one predominantly of heresy and clerical superstition. Given the traditional medieval concern with heresy and superstition in clerical necromancy, as expressed for example by the inquisitor Nicolau Eymeric in his well-known 1376 *Directorium Inquisitorum*, this is not entirely unexpected, and clergy appeared in many subsequent cases.[30] However, the documentation also reveals some evidence of *maleficium*. In 1455 at Edolo, a town near the head of the valley, the Dominican inquisitor Antonio found heretics 'who refuse the sacraments, sacrifice children, [and] worship the devil', and two years later clerics who practised superstitious conjurations and invocations or 'nefarious arts' likely to encourage the laity to fall into deviations were reprimanded.[31] The Brescian council appealed to the doge and apostolic nuncio in Venice in 1494 against the 'multa maleficia' committed daily by ordinary clerics, and in 1508 condemned clerics who led shameful lives and committed crimes, including unspecified 'diabolica fraude'.[32]

---

[28] Giustiniani and Querini, 'Libellus ad Leonem', cols 674–6; Contarini, *Office of a Bishop*, 131.

[29] On clerical necromancy see Richard Kieckhefer, *Magic in the Middle Ages* (Cambridge, 1989), 151–75.

[30] A woman interrogated in 1518 confessed that demons had appeared to her at the sabbat in the guise of monks: Sanudo, *Diarii*, xxv, cols 639–40.

[31] Joseph Hansen, *Quellen und Untersuchungen zur Geschichte des Hexenwahns und der Hexenverfolgung im Mittelalter. Mit einer Untersuchung der Geschichte des Wortes Hexe von Johannes Franck* (Bonn, 1901), 472, 19–20.

[32] ASC 514, fo. 112v (10 Dec. 1494, second foliation); ASC 521, fo. 6r-v (23 Oct. 1508, third foliation).

Similarly, around 1480 the Dominican inquisitor Fra Antonio de Petosellis revived the case of one Stefano from Bellano (a town on the east side of Lake Como) who had been investigated for heresy by the inquisition in 1467 and again in 1476. The inquisitor acted on 'new and extremely serious' depositions made by witnesses against Stefano who was found to have relapsed into his previously abjured heresies, and to have fallen into many which were much worse. On two occasions, as Stefano confessed, he had gone to a house in Brescia where he had invoked and worshipped the devil, denied the faith, and later refused the sacrament. For nine years Stefano was transported to a sabbat (*ludum*) 'realiter et corporaliter' while wide awake. There the devil appeared in the form of a 'queen', and every week at this place Stefano denied God and the faith, refused the sacraments and worshipped this queen who seems to have been attended or associated with a 'holy angel' who, Stefano believed, guarded the gates of paradise.[33] Stefano was sentenced in the presence of a large number of people to public decapitation (his head was to be burned), and then handed over to the secular arm in the form of the *podestà* Giovanni Moro for execution.[34]

A similar example of the new demonic witch was displayed by the inquisitor in Brescia around the same time: Maria 'called the doctor' of Vicenza, but living in Calcinato, east of Brescia. Maria fulfilled every requirement for the classic stereotype of the witch. Her many 'errors and enormities' included attendance at the sabbat, worshipping the devil, and denying the faith. However, the record of her crimes was much fuller and, presumably, more worrying for the authorities than those of Stefano. She denied God, refused Christ, received cures and 'maleficiatis' from the devil, celebrated masses for the devil using the blood of murdered babies, made animal sacrifices, abused the sacrament, and bewitched (*streavit*) thirty boys and girls, half of whom subsequently died.[35]

On this occasion the episcopal and secular authorities were in agreement with the inquisitor and the sentence of death was carried out. However, cases of witchcraft in the Val Camonica during this period were often marked by conflicts of jurisdiction and authority within and between the ecclesiastical and secular authorities. First, I would argue that in respect of these judicial disputes the dual nature of law in the Venetian republic was key.

---

[33] Guerrini, *Cronache inedite*, i, 185–7.

[34] The description of Stefano's sentencing is taken from a contemporary copy of a report on this case by the inquisitor to the archdeacon and episcopal vicar: Biblioteca Queriniana, Brescia (hereafter BQB), MS. H.V.7, fos. 133r–134v.

[35] Guerrini, *Cronache bresciane*, i, 183–5.

Venice largely preserved the body of positive law, whether communal or Roman, which it found practised in the conquered *terraferma*. Instead of wholesale centralization or regularization of law and procedures to suit the city's emphasis on traditional practice, experience, and divine justice the Venetians issued ad hoc edicts, entertained appeals in different courts, or left rectors to deal with local disputes. This opened the way to Venetian intervention in moral or spiritual matters, as well as meddling in local affairs. Consequently there was some jockeying for authority among several different organs of state in the Venetian mainland.[36]

Second, there was doubt about elements of *maleficium* and the classic witch stereotype, which some observers found 'scarcely credible'.[37] However, while 'manifest heresy' remained largely immune to overt criticism (and indeed after 1535 supplanted witchcraft in the inquisition's list of concerns) the opponents of witch persecution among Venetian lawmakers found that 'superstition' offered a much more attractive opening for attacks on the inquisition. Both the jurisdictional conflicts and the arguments about the demonic and superstitious in witchcraft will be the focus of the rest of this essay. An examination of individual Brescian cases and a comparative study of the work of the best known inquisitor of the new era of witch-hunting will demonstrate the origins, nature and significance of these disputes and the respective roles of the demonic and superstitious in the heresy of witchcraft.

II

In December 1485 the Dominican friar Antonio, active in the Val Camonica, told Doge Barbarigo in Venice that:

> By the goodness and mercy of God many persons leading a heretical life have been discovered in . . . Edolo. Among other things, they renounce the Catholic faith and spurn the sacraments. They choose the devil for their god, spit and trample on the cross of Christ, and continue ceaselessly to sacrifice babies and to cast spells. They grind up the body of Christ in a mortar and exhume the corpses of babies, and with this flesh they make sacrifices to the devil and other detestable things.[38]

---

[36] See James S. Grubb, *Firstborn of Venice: Vicenza in the Early Renaissance State* (Baltimore, 1988), 28-35, 105–6.

[37] See below, p. 149 and n. 51.

[38] Doge to Brescian rectors, Venice, 10 Dec. 1485, Odorici, *Streghe di Valtellina*, 125–6. See also Archivio di Stato, Venice (hereafter ASV), Senato Terra, registro 9, fo. 164; ASV, Capi del Consiglio di Dieci, Lettere, filza 5, no. 10; and Sanudo, *Diarii*, xxvi, cols. 32–3.

The inquisitor saw a danger to the faith in heresy and diabolism of this kind and insisted that the rectors strive to extirpate them. The doge therefore instructed his rectors, who had been reluctant to act, to arrest every person indicated by the inquisitor, and to conduct them under close escort to Brescia, where they should be thrown into prison. While the doge urged the rectors to use all diligence and zeal, and to punish the accused severely according to their crimes, nevertheless they were also to act 'with prudence and the circumspection which seems appropriate to you, with the understanding that justice will be followed'.

However, justice moved with feet of lead, and the matter dragged on through the following year. It seems as if the Brescian council or the bishop attempted to hinder the process. Certainly, higher ecclesiastical authorities in the shape of the apostolic legate and the patriarch were called in to investigate the inquisitorial procedure against several heretics. As Doge Agostino Barbarigo informed the new rectors in the autumn of 1486, the legate and patriarch had affirmed that the trial had been properly conducted in law and that the accused ought to be handed over quickly to the secular arm for sentencing. As a harbinger of future problems, the ducal decision was rapidly followed by a papal brief addressed to the bishop and the inquisitor rejecting the civil officials' wish to review the process before passing sentence. The brief affirmed that the crime of heresy was 'an entirely ecclesiastical matter', and instructed the officials to act in the matter within six days, on pain of excommunication.[39]

Paolo Zane, the bishop of Brescia, went to view matters for himself, and he told the doge that no sentence should be passed without his consent.[40] Blocked by some of the highest local authorities in this way, the inquisitor turned on the closest and most vulnerable lay representative: the rector's vicar Alberto de Albertis. The notary was denounced from the pulpit of the Dominican church and accused of providing hostile advice to the rectors in the matter of the 'heretical women'. Still worse, the inquisitor accused Alberto of heresy and called for *his* trial, possibly in Rome. While the doge advised the rectors to demand that Alberto be left in peace, in fact in the spring of 1487 the Dominicans lured another notary, whom they blamed for the filibustering tactics of bishop and council, into their monastery and held him there.[41]

Inquisitors could also work with Venice and Brescia against the pope. For example, it was on the recommendation of the inquisitor in 1499 that the

[39] Odorici, *Streghe di Valtellina*, 128–30.

[40] Ibid., 129; Curuz, *Streghe Bresciano*, 52.

[41] Odorici, *Streghe di Valtellina*, 130–3.

special council of Brescia agreed to imprison for life two more heretics of the Val Camonica; on this occasion, 'two wicked and impious priests'.[42] The sentences against Martino and Hermano, and a third man who escaped, Don Donato de Buzolo, exhibit the familiar mixture of outrageous crimes: including attendance at a 'ludum Sathanae' on Monte Tonale, worship of the devil, denigration of the cross, misuse of hosts and holy oil, and copulation on the cross with women; all over a period of ten to twenty-five years.[43] In this case it was the inquisitorial vicar who in September 1499 forwarded the confessions and complained to Venice that the judges appointed by the pope were locally infamous men and asked for the rectors to intervene and suspend matters for several months. Although the doge was highly incensed [*molto caldo*] in his opposition to this affair, causing the letters to be left unread in the meeting of the *collegio*, nevertheless he was eventually prevailed upon to ask the rectors in Brescia to insist that the papal judges act strictly according to the instructions issued to them by the pope.[44]

Venetian hostility towards Roman interference in ecclesiastical matters was well known and occasionally erupted into serious conflict, as in 1483–4 when the republic and the papacy were at war over Ferrara. In Brescia, these were opening shots in a period of marked hostility between the communal council and Venice on the one hand, and the local Dominicans on the other. The tensions between clerical and secular priorities resurfaced dramatically during the first decade of the sixteenth century in a dispute over funerals that prompted a pamphlet war between the conventual Dominicans and local humanists.[45] These pamphlets addressed local concerns about the alms or 'fees' paid to mendicant mourners, but they also considered the lay use of ecclesiastical property and debates about the role of religion and the religious in civil society more broadly. One of the pamphleteers made a point of condemning the Dominican inquisitors' treatment of witches in the Val Camonica and accused the Dominicans of using the Church's weapons

> to satisfy your uncontrollable lusts, frightening a people of pure and simple faith, who fear God and the Church, with all the dreadful bogies of excommunication. Your aim is that this terror may shock

---

[42] ASC 516, fo. 1r (26 Mar. 1499, second foliation).

[43] The clerics misused the holy oil to perpetrate 'ignominiosas superstitiones et scelera'. Sanudo, *Diarii*, ii, cols. 1204–8. Much of the same material was copied by Sanudo into his diary nineteen years later at the time of a new outbreak of witch hunting: ibid., xxvi, cols. 34–7.

[44] Ibid., ii, cols. 1207–8.

[45] Stephen Bowd (ed.), *Vainglorious Death: A Funerary Fracas in Renaissance Brescia*, trans. J. Donald Cullington (Tempe, AZ, 2006).

them into casting themselves and everything they own at the feet of you greedy and haughty people,[46] who give yourselves such airs by using a certain title of the Inquisition—a title weighty in itself, and rightly established by our forebears long ago, but now weak and hollow thanks to you—or rather, lucrative, for according to popular gossip you use it for profit.

You use the office (such is your vanity and pride) almost as a kingdom and, lest it lie idle, you seize from the Val Camonica certain old women who are stupid and frozen in a kind of mental daze, and you interrogate them about their faith, the Trinity, and other such topics. You bring in scribes and drag out the proceedings; you conduct examinations under torture so that, by inflicting pain and torment on women who are admittedly little different from brutish beasts, you may appear as guardians of the Christian faith.[47]

Bishop Zane and the inquisitor initiated a more intense phase of witchcraft persecution in the Val Camonica in June 1518 when news reached them of heretics who denied the faith, took the devil as their god, and thereby caused many deaths.[48] The bishop and inquisitor went up the valley to eliminate this heresy accompanied by preachers who exhorted the people to confess their errors against faith. Those who did so were given a light penance and absolved of their sins, but others remained obstinate and told similar alarming stories.[49] Seven women and one man were excommunicated and expelled as heretics from the Church on the eve of the feast of St John. They were handed over to the secular authorities for judgement and as a result of their 'excessi' they were sentenced to be burned alive.

The trial record of sixty-year-old Benvegnuda 'ditta Pincinella' of Terra di Navi, in the Val Camonica, who was burnt as a witch in August 1518 sheds light on this inquisitorial procedure: having heard of her quarrels in the area the inquisitor excommunicated the whole of Navi and commanded everyone

---

[46] An allusion to Acts 4: 34–7.

[47] Anonymous [Elia Capriolo?], *Defensio populi Brixiani rei violatae ecclesiasticae libertatis ob decretum ab eo factum de ambitione et sumptibus funerum minuendis, accusantibus Fratribus Sancti Dominici* (Venice?: Giorgio de' Rusconi?, 1506?), sig. Avr. The translation is in Bowd and Cullington, *Vainglorious Death*, 49, 51.

[48] ASV, Consiglio dei Dieci, Misto, registro 44, fos. 63r–64r, 69r, 85r–v (pencil foliation); Santo ufficio, processi, busta 160; ASC 1552, fos. 1v–2r; Sanudo, *Diarii*, xxv, cols. 537–8, 541, 545–8, 572–4, 574–5, 585, 586–8, 602–8, 609–11, 632–50; xxvi, cols. 23, 29–32, 32–3, 34–7, 55–6, 95; xxviii, cols. 144, 273, 287; xxix, cols. 65, 211, 465, 506–7; xxx, cols. 13, 15.

[49] Sier Carlo Miani, Castellan of Breno (in the Val Camonica), to Sier Marin Zorzi, 24 Jun. 1518: Sanudo, *Diarii*, xxv, col. 545.

who knew of Benvegnuda's activities should come before the inquisition in Brescia and give their testimonies. In all, twenty-four testimonies were taken down over four days at the Dominican convent of San Domenico in Brescia or by a public notary in the town of Gusago (west of Brescia). Benvegnuda had already been punished by the inquisition for earlier offences connected with 'medicine superstitiose' as well as 'incantamenti et diaboliche superstitiose', which she believed were the reason for her detention in this instance, but over four days of interrogation she gradually revealed details of the demonic orgies on Monte Tonale, storm raising, and harm caused to children. It is worth speculating how far she was prompted by her interrogators and by the application, or threat, of torture: her admissions grew more 'diabolical' over time, and on the last day of questioning she was asked if she dreamt of her trips to the Tonale. She is reported to have replied, in a suspiciously flat contradiction of the early medieval *Canon Episcopi* in which the nocturnal flights of the followers of the goddess Diana were attributed to dreaming: 'I truly know that I go bodily and not in my dreams'.[50]

Outright scepticism of such details emerges in the letter written by a certain Giuseppe da Orzinuovi in which he gave a friend in Venice a lengthy and learned account—full of classical pagan allusions—of what the bishop and inquisitor had found in the Val Camonica. A plague of witches had spread from Albania (an area commonly associated with the Bogomil heresy) and for many years had been encouraged by demonic priests who refused to baptise many thousands of valley dwellers and in fact led them into evil with the temptations of pleasure and wealth. These 'rebels against God' gave themselves body and soul to the devil who presided over an 'epicurean paradise' in the forest with palaces, parties, and all manner of good things not found in Portugal, Calicut or Alexandria such as 'honeyed flies' and 'sugared rats'. At these 'zuogi' or sports on Monte Tonale the many thousands of disciples of the devil were given magic powders and unguents, which they used to cause harm, transform themselves, and enchant objects of desire. They also subverted the sacramental rituals of the church when they attended by using secret signs and prayers.

Even as they burned alive, the witches, including a chancellor of the valley who had punctiliously kept their 'libri ordenari' for thirty years and a courier who had taken their messages into Spain and France, were tricked by the devil into believing they could survive the fires since he appeared to them in the guise of the Virgin Mary to reassure them. However, as the flames charred

---

[50] Ibid., xxv, cols. 632–50, 'e cognosso veramente che vado corporalemente et che non me insonio [*sic*]'. This material is reproduced in full as 'Processi di streghe', *Archivio storico lombardo*, anno xvi, vi (1889), 625–45.

their flesh the women cried: 'O Devil you have deceived us.' As Giuseppe da Orzinuovi exclaimed at the end of his letter, such things had not been heard of since the time of the sorceress Medea and were 'scarcely credible.' He dismissed outright as 'fables' [*fabula*] rather than 'history' [*istoria*] accounts of unseen armed battles in the Bergamasco.[51]

Similar scepticism was expressed by a number of others. Dr Alessandro Pompeio of Brescia concluded his account of the sabbat on Monte Tonale saying that he would write no more to his patrician correspondent 'because your magnificence would not believe it unless you had seen it'.[52] The castellan of Breno (another town in the Val Camonica) speculated whether these confessions of attendance at the sabbat derived from demonical delusions or from bodily experiences, and he wondered if the accused should be consigned to the flames alive. In the absence of any other civilized company with whom he could discuss the matter, as he said, he turned to canon law for guidance and discovered several passages which indicated that these were all the delusions of the ignorant.[53]

Piero Tron, the Venetian *podestà* of Brescia, even met some of the witches condemned at Pisogne by the inquisitor's vicar Bernardino de Grossis. Despite inquisitorial resistance he managed to interview them and to discover that the inquisitor had used undue force and trickery to extract the fatal confessions. Describing the sexual antics of the condemned women, who had been pleasured at once by the anus and the vagina on a cross by the devil with his bifurcated penis, the *podestà* ended a letter to the Council of Ten with baffled resignation: 'These all seem grave and strange matters, rather beyond me, which I believe and I don't believe.'[54]

---

[51] Giuseppe da Orzinuovi to Lodovico Querini, 1 Aug. 1518, Sanudo, *Diarii*, xxv, cols. 602–8. The courier is mentioned, along with the chancellor 'missier Pasino', in a letter written by an eyewitness to the interrogations and burnings: Dr Alessandro Pompeio to Zuan Zustignan, Brescia, 28 July 1518, ibid., cols. 574–5.

[52] Dr Alessandro Pompeio to Zuan Zustignan, Brescia, 28 Jul. 1518, Sanudo, *Diarii*, xxv, col. 575.

[53] Ibid., col. 548. This doctor of laws naturally turned to the *Decretum* (compiled by Gratian *c.*1140), *Causa* 26, *quaestio* 5 for the text of the *Canon Episcopi*, which condemned as illusory the belief that one could ride out at night with the goddess Diana; to the canon law collection of Dionysius Exiguus (*c.*500); to the commentary of St Thomas Aquinas to Book IV, distinction 34 of Peter Lombard's *Sentences* where he noted that many did not think demons existed outside the imagination of ignorant, uneducated people; and to an unspecified passage of St Augustine (probably *De civitate Dei*, bk. 7, ch. 21) where he asserted that God did not permit to demons any supernatural power.

[54] Sanudo, *Diarii*, xxv, col. 588.

In this instance, the pressure to apply the brakes to the inquisitorial process seems to have come from the Council of Ten in Venice who read the *podestà*'s letter and instructed him to act discreetly with the bishop ('cum ogni secreteza') and peruse the trial documentation before sending it to Venice. Several hundred case notes (now lost) were sent to Venice, and the Ten interviewed the offending inquisitor Bernardino de Grossis, and notified the pope that he ought to be removed. The council referred the matter to the apostolic nuncio (Altobello di Averoldi) who visited the Val Camonica in the company of the bishop of Famagosta (the Brescian Matteo de Ugonibus) in September 1518. The nuncio returned with a learned priest ('uno prete leterato') held in Brescia accused of witchcraft who described how his lust for a certain woman had driven him to the sabbat on the Monte Tonale. Questioned by the doge and other patricians he was reported to have replied that there 'were devils with horns on their heads and hands like goose hide'.[55]

The Ten responded by appointing justices against *maleficium* in Brescia.[56] The Brescian council voted almost unanimously to ask their orators in Venice to support the actions of the messengers from the Val Camonica, the patriarch and legate there and to give officials in Brescia every necessary freedom and authority to make opportune provision for the conservation of the Catholic faith and the punishment of witches ('strigas') and other 'perfidious and maleficent persons', whether in the Val Camonica or in the city.[57] Matters were then complicated by the inquisitor's zealous vicar who arrested a person already detained for heresy without consulting the bishop or the rectors. The Brescian *podestà* informed the Ten that when he sent his secretary to the inquisitorial vicar to protest, he had been insulted. The Ten therefore ordered action to be taken against those who made the arrests. When the detainee in question was moved to the public prison it was discovered that the vicar had extorted money from him. The vicar was questioned and then released, but the Ten advised the rectors to act carefully, especially in the matter of asking the inquisitor how the goods of those who had been burnt were shared out.

By February 1520 around sixty women and twenty men had been burnt but further inquisitorial activity was hindered by the Ten while it examined the paperwork at length in several stormy meetings in Venice at the beginning of 1521. At one of these meetings the bishop's trial records were read, confirming the 'truth' about the witches in the Brescian valley. In opposition to this one member of the council, Luca Tron, denied that they contained the truth. Dismissing the inquisitor from a post that he had held so briefly the Ten then

[55] Ibid., cols. 55–6. The priest's case is also mentioned in an anonymous letter at cols. 29–32.

[56] ASV, Consiglio di Dieci, Misto, registro 42, fos. 36v, 72v.

[57] ASC 527, fo. 117r–v (21 Oct. 1519, second foliation).

considered a papal complaint about Venetian interference in what was an ecclesiastical matter. Tron was once again vehement in his opposition, asserting that 'these pathetic creatures [*meschini*] died martyrs, and nothing happened on Monte Tonale'.[58] As the Ten condescendingly put it: 'These poor creatures of the Val Camonica are simple people with the coarsest understanding, and have no small need of preachers and prudent instruction in the Catholic faith.'[59] A new inquisitor was sent to Brescia but, as with some of the earlier cases, it is not entirely clear how the matter was resolved although it is interesting to note that the evidence of cases in Sondrio (in a neighbouring Alpine valley) in 1523 indicates that sentences were more lenient while the apostolic nuncio to Venice in 1534 found that senators were more concerned about Lutheran heresy than about witchcraft.[60]

III

This survey of the cases of witchcraft in the Val Camonica after 1454 reveals that worship of the devil and denial of the faith were associated with heresy in the way outlined by medieval authorities such as Eymeric. Heresy was defined as an 'error of belief persistently and perniciously held', with apostasy regarded as a 'subspecies' of heresy in which a false belief replaced faith, for example, the worship of the devil. In this respect, witchcraft was clearly a heresy and, moreover, involved apostasy and idolatry.[61] However, the range and nature of the witches' apostasy in the fifteenth-century Val Camonica surpassed or differed from medieval heresy in some striking ways. If both old and new shared many characteristics such as the sabbat or an emphasis on carnality, as well as the presence of superstition, there were other, newer, elements that complicated the picture, raising doubts in the minds of men such as Luca Tron and Giuseppe da Orzinuovi.

To take superstition first, its traditional association with women seems to have had an interesting role in fifteenth-century witch persecutions.[62]

---

[58] Sanudo, *Diarii*, xxx, col. 13.

[59] ASV, Consiglio di Dieci, Misto, registro 44, fo. 8r (pencil foliation).

[60] Odorici, *Streghe di Valtellina*, 91–116; Girolamo Aleandro cited by Martin, *Witchcraft and the Inquisition*, 15. For the nuncio's views on the problems in the Val Camonica at this time see also the *Nunziature di Venezia*, ed. Franco Gaeta (Rome, 1958), i, 77, 97, 155.

[61] Indeed, the title of Bernardino of Siena's fifteenth-century treatise on witchcraft and superstition is *De idolatriae cultu*. See Franco Mormando, *The Preacher's Demons: Bernardino of Siena and the Social Underworld of Early Renaissance Italy* (Chicago, 1999), 82.

[62] Hans Peter Broedel, *The* Malleus Maleficarum *and the Construction of Witchcraft. Theology and Popular Belief* (Manchester, 2003).

Thus, in an area with a tradition of prosecuting heresy, such as Lausanne, the episcopal inquisitors applied the heretical stereotype to the witch with the result that men formed the majority of cases of witchcraft persecutions there between 1300 and 1499. In neighbouring Lucerne secular judges rather than ecclesiastical personnel dealt with witches and consequently they seem to have relied more heavily on the accusations of rural witnesses about incidents of *maleficium* than on the articles of canon law or any direct experience of trials for heresy. Although some elements of the new demonic witch stereotype such as the sabbat were absent, just over ninety per cent of those accused in Lucerne in the same period were women.[63]

Superstition, and especially its association with women, was also crucial for Heinrich Institoris (Krämer) the Dominican inquisitor and author of the *Malleus Maleficarum* (1487). It is worth looking at this work since it was cited approvingly by Silvestro Mazzolini da Prierio who was inquisitor in Brescia between 1508 and 1512.[64] Two related grounds for Institoris's attack on witchcraft have been highlighted by recent studies of his text. In the first place, women are notably predominant in certain key aspects of the analysis of witchcraft. Although it is by no means the case that the *Malleus* was simply, or even primarily an attack on women Institoris revised the book in order to emphasize demonic copulation with women as proof of the existence of demons. In doing so he inserted a list of female moral failings drawn from a standard range of misogynist medieval sources.[65]

It is also important to note Institoris's decision to give selective credence to 'popular' counter-magical practices, which many church reformers classified as superstition and sought to control or eradicate.[66] Institoris seems to have regarded the use of such countersacramentals as handy proof of the existence of the supernatural. By arguing that the validity and effectiveness of sacramentals were dependent on the operator Institoris used a strategy very similar

---

[63] Susanna Burghartz, 'The Equation of Women and Witches: A case study of witchcraft trials in Lucerne and Lausanne in the fifteenth and sixteenth centuries', in Brian P. Levack, (ed.), *Articles on Witchcraft, Magic, and Demonology. A twelve volume anthology of scholarly articles*, vol. 10. *Witchcraft, Women and Society* (New York and London, 1992), 67–84. Burghartz admits (at 72) that 'it has not been possible to carry out a systematic investigation of the Lausanne records'.

[64] Silvestro Mazzolini [Prierias], *De strigimagarum demonumque mirandis libri tres* (Rome: Antonio Bladis de Asula, 24 Sept. 1521). He mentions witches in Como and Brescia in bk. 2, ch. 1.

[65] Stephens, *Demon Lovers*, ch. 2.

[66] Euan Cameron, 'For Reasoned Faith or Embattled Creed? Religion for the People in Early Modern Europe', *Transactions of the Royal Historical Society*, 6th ser., viii (1998), 165–6.

to that employed when he dealt with copulating witches as witnesses of the demonic: he highlighted the moral character of the participant.[67] Institoris pushed the 'character issue' in a witchcraft trial at Innsbruck in 1485, although this move was unsuccessful and encountered stiff episcopal resistance there.[68] The author of the *Malleus*, smarting from the rebuff at Innsbruck then sought to by-pass this episcopal 'interference' by promoting the superior claim of papal authority in matters of witchcraft by placing at the beginning of his work the papal bull *Summis desiderantes affectibus* (1484), which authorized and extended his activites and described the harm caused by heretics who have given themselves to devils. Institoris also claimed in the *Malleus* that he had secular support in the form of the local archduke, as well as the emperor, and he played up the terrible nature and pressing danger of the witch. Finally, Institoris argued that while both secular and episcopal authorities would normally be involved in inquisitorial activity they could also act independently of each other.

This latter argument, if put into practice, was likely to provoke some confusion and conflict, and certainly did so in Innsbruck; and what is more, in Brescia. In the former case the bishop sought to hinder the investigation by questioning the procedures employed by Institoris as inquisitor. The bishop also explicitly cited the *Canon Episcopi* which described the diabolical experiences of women such as night rides as delusions or dreams and not real experiences. We may recall that similar tactics were used at Brescia: as bishops or councillors questioned the methods and process of the inquisition the inquisitor emphasized that the sabbat had been experienced 'really and bodily' and not simply in a dreaming sleep. It is interesting to note in this regard the importance attached to the *Canon Episcopi* by the Brescian inquisitor Silvestro Mazzolini da Prierio. He was also at pains to distinguish the modern sect of witches from the sorcerers mentioned in the *Canon*.[69] Finally in the Brescian case, appeals were made to Rome and, just like Institoris,

---

[67] Broedel, Malleus Maleficarum, esp. 146–58.

[68] Richard Kieckhefer, *Repression of Heresy in Medieval Germany* (Liverpool, 1979), 105–6; Broedel, Malleus Maleficarum, 1–3, 12–20; and Eric Wilson, 'Institoris at Innsbruck: Heinrich Institoris, the *Summis Desiderantes* and the Brixen Witch-Trial of 1485', in Bob Scribner and Trevor Johnson (eds), *Popular Religion in Germany and Central Europe, 1400–1800* (Basingstoke, 1996), 87–100.

[69] Mazzolini, *De strigimagarum*, bks 1, 2. Note also the similar argument used by him in the entry 'Haeresis III' in his *Summa silvestrina* (1515, completed 1507), and in a 1507 sermon 'De strigibus': Michael Tavuzzi, *Prierias: The Life and Works of Silvestro Mazzolini da Prierio, 1456–1527* (Durham NC, 1997), 55–60, 122–7.

papal briefs emphasizing alarming and dangerous 'superstitions' were sent to bolster inquisitorial authority in the Val Camonica.[70]

The similarity in these cases may not be entirely coincidental. Although no Brescian cases of witchcraft are cited in the *Malleus* it is interesting to note that a larger cluster of recent cases at nearby Bormio is mentioned and that the route Institoris most likely took from Rome to Innsbruck in December 1484 would have taken him through Brescia or nearby Verona.[71] The Brescian council often asked Dominicans or Franciscans to preach in the city at this time, and it is possible that Institoris could have taken advantage of a similar invitation as he did in Innsbruck.[72]

It is likely that the inquisitors, just like the authors of the *Malleus*, prompted by new demonological speculations highlighted the demonic in order to support the urgency of their work. It may also be the case that inquisitors and their vicars were genuinely concerned about the spread of 'superstition' in the Val Camonica. Superstitious practices such as herbal remedies and incantations were much more easy to identify and could serve, as we have seen in the cse of Benvegnuda da Navi, as a starting point for the investigation of more serious crimes. Dominican inquisitors may also have been troubled by the growing presence of the rival Franciscan order in the Val Camonica during this period, and the assertion of their traditional role may have formed part of an attempt to establish a position of influence. Conversely, notions of female credulity and superstition were certainly used by Brescians, and probably by Venetians like Tron, to *diminish* the claims of the inquisitors in the Val Camonica. It is no coincidence that the anonymous Brescian who denounced Dominican persecution of ignorant women as witches was also at pains to lavish praise on Franciscan spirituality.[73]

The better known sin of *maleficium* was, like superstition, a double-edged weapon. It is not mentioned explicitly in all of the cases but was clearly implicit in almost all of them in the harm caused to children and adults. As a crime of concern to both secular and ecclesiastical authorities the presence of *maleficium* in these cases may in fact have encouraged conflict. It may be no

---

[70] A brief addressed to the bishop of Brescia and the inquisitor Antonio was sealed on 30 Sept. 1486; another brief addressed to the Venetian bishops was sealed on 15 February 1521. For their contents see Hansen, *Quellen und Untersuchungen*, 29–30, 32–4.

[71] Henricus Institoris, *Malleus maleficarum* (Speyer, 1487), sig. pir. See also Giovanni Giorgetta, 'Processi di stregoneria a Bormio tra il 1483 ed il 1486', *Bollettino della Società Storica Valtellinese*, xxxvi (1983), 153–67 (<http://www.paoloportone.it/giorgetta2/giorgetta2.htm> accessed 12 June 2007).

[72] Zanelli, 'Predicatori a Brescia', 83–144.

[73] Bowd and Cullington, *Vainglorious Death*, 29, 53, 71.

coincidence that the evidence of the inquisition in Venice in the century after 1550 reveals little or no concern with *maleficium* and hardly any references to the main elements of the classic stereotype such as the sabbat and demonic pact.[74] Ruth Martin, who has studied the cases of witchcraft brought before the Venetian inquisition during the latter period, has concluded that this lack of a concern with *maleficium* and indeed the absence of any Venetian 'witch craze' on the scale of northern and central Europe in the later sixteenth and seventeenth centuries can be attributed to the strength and independence of the Venetian inquisition and the secular courts in relation to the Catholic church.[75] The sabbat, demonic pact, and cannibalism, if mentioned at all, were regarded with scepticism or as elements of rural society.[76] Therefore, after 1550, in place of strife we find broad agreement between inquisitors and Venetian governors on the nature and predominance of superstition in the cases examined, and as a result very few executions and many lighter penalties. Moreover, after *c.*1580 the evidence of the sabbat became less important to the inquisition in Rome and witchcraft was treated as a spiritual or judicial battle in which exorcism and the correction of superstition played the key roles.[77]

The control of the relationship between spiritual and natural worlds in this way drew on Catholic tradition. In 1517 Gasparo Contarini advised his new bishop that he should exercise prudence in order to avoid 'new and superstitious arts', and that he should 'gently' lead the superstitious back to the worship of God. Indeed, he did not make much, if anything, of human sin, or the snares of the devil, although *human* trickery and snares were severely condemned.[78] In a similar fashion, Silvestro Mazzolini da Prierio was

---

[74] Martin, *Witchcraft and the Inquisition*, esp. ch. 5.

[75] On the law in Venice and the *terraferma* see Gaetano Cozzi, *Repubblica di Venezia e stati italiani: politica e giustizia dal secolo XVI al secolo XVIII* (Turin, 1982).

[76] Martin, *Witchcraft and the Inquisition*, 207–13.

[77] Giovanni Romeo, *Inquisitori, esorcisti e streghe nell'Italia della controriforma* (Florence, 1990); Cameron, 'For Reasoned Faith'.

[78] Contarini, *Office of a Bishop*, 57, 129, 133. Here Contarini may betray the fact that he was 'deeply influenced' by his Paduan tutor Pietro Pomponazzi whose Aristotelian natural philosophy left no room for demons according to Stephens, *Demon Lovers*, 77–9; quotation from Elizabeth G. Gleason, *Gasparo Contarini: Venice, Rome and Reform* (California, 1993),79. His respect for the philosopher was maintained even when Pomponazzi's assertions about the immortality of the soul occasioned a printed dispute between the two men in 1517. Thomism strongly influenced Contarini's theological position. See ibid., 76–81. It is also interesting to note that Contarini firmly emphasized divine worship to the exclusion of angelic, saintly, or demonic concerns, citing Augustine and the angel Raphael's rejection of Tobit's praise. Contarini, *Office of a Bishop*, 131, 133. As Michael D. Bailey argues in his contribution to this volume, 'fascinated horror' with the demonic

prepared to argue that those guilty of certain minor superstitions ought not to be associated with formal heresies and should be treated leniently.[79] This may also be why Reformation ideas revising the relationship between the natural and supernatural worlds and reordering the links between *religio* and *superstitio* failed to find a lasting place in the religiosity of Renaissance Italy. The local religion traced here sustained a reciprocal relationship between men and God which was expressed in a bricolage of miracles, prayers, and saintly veneration. This system of the sacred united and strengthened the religion of early modern Italy but it was inherently unstable given the conceptual elasticity of 'superstition'.[80]

---

seems to be more evident in the writings of clerics associated with the new universities of the German empire.

[79] Tavuzzi, *Prierias*, 127.

[80] On Reformation Germany see Scribner, 'Ritual and Popular Belief'.

'Superstition', Magic, and Clerical Polemic in Seventeenth-Century Germany

Alison Rowlands

As soon as a power or effect is attributed to an object, which the object has received neither from God, nor from nature, nor from other known natural causes, then this is sorcery and superstition.[1]

The Protestant Reformation spawned an unprecedented attempt on the part of the clerical elite first to define clearly what constituted superstition, and second to stop the 'common people' from holding superstitious beliefs and indulging in superstitious practices. The aim of this essay is to analyse the impact of this attempt for the Lutheran imperial free city of Rothenburg ob der Tauber and its rural hinterland by the late-seventeenth century, using the works of Johann Ludwig Hartmann, a cleric and the foremost ecclesiastical official (or Superintendent) of Rothenburg, as a starting point. The sweeping definition of superstition given above is Hartmann's, and comes from *Greuel des Segensprechens* (*The Horror of Speaking Blessings*), his 1680 fulmination against the contemporary habit of using blessings (spoken or written formulae, often religious in origin, and used on their own or with other rituals) to attempt to cure disease, protect against witchcraft and misfortune, and find lost and stolen goods and missing persons. In a second part to the book Hartmann also criticized belief in the efficacy of three specific types of profit-making magic: the use of the mandrake root to increase wealth, the use of the severed thumbs of executed thieves to improve trade, and the conjuring of spirits to assist in various tasks, such as the production of goods. Hartmann's 352-page *Greuel* was the sequel to a shorter but equally polemical pamphlet,

---

[1] '... so ist es eine Zauberei und Aberglauben so bald einem Ding eine Kraft und Würckung zugemessen wird, die es aber weder von Gott noch von der Natur oder andern bekanten natürlichen Ursachen empfangen hat', Johann Ludwig Hartmann, *Greuel des Segensprechens* (Nuremberg, 1680), 54 (hereafter *Greuel*). Many of Hartmann's published texts are held in the Rothenburg Stadtarchiv (hereafter RStA) in the Konsistorialbibliothek collection, Th. 450–460. For *Greuel*, see RStA Th. 456. It may have been published posthumously, as Hartmann died on 18 July 1680.

Neue Teuffels-Stücklein (*New Tricks of the Devil*), he had published in 1678.[2] The 'new tricks' Hartmann criticized here were the magical practices employed by soldiers to protect themselves against injury in battle which had, according to Hartmann, spread to the civilian population of Rothenburg and its rural hinterland in the course and aftermath of the Thirty Years War. Hartmann was, by Rothenburg standards, an exceptionally talented cleric, as his rapid rise to prominence demonstrated. He was born into a distinguished line of Lutheran clerics in Rothenburg on February 3 1640 and attended the city's grammar school and then Wittenberg University. He returned to Rothenburg to become pastor of the hinterland parish of Spielbach in November 1660, then rector of the city's grammar school in January 1662. He was appointed Superintendent of the city and its rural parishes by the city council in March 1666, aged just twenty-six.[3] Despite the pressures of pastoral and administrative work and his relatively early death at the age of 40 (in July 1680), Hartmann was a prolific author with at least eighty-one published texts to his credit, including collections of sermons, books of instruction for parish pastors, theological disputations, and anti-Catholic polemics. He also published a range of books aimed at the 'common people' that focused on what he regarded as the worst sins of his age, explaining why they were incompatible with Lutheranism and how they were to be eradicated: examples include his *Alamode-Teuffel* (*Fashion Devil*, 1675), *Tantz-Teuffel* (*Dance Devil*, 1677), *Spielteuffel* (*Gaming Devil*, 1678), and *Sauff-Teuffel* (*Drunkenness Devil*, 1679).[4] These works constituted a late flourishing of the Lutheran genre of 'devil books' which had emerged in Germany in the mid-sixteenth

[2] Johann Ludwig Hartmann, *Neue Teuffels-Stücklein* (Frankfurt, 1678), RStA Th. 458 (hereafter *Stücklein*).

[3] Two short biographical articles on Hartmann exist, see Paul Schattenmann, 'Dr. Ludwig Hartmann, Superintendent von Rothenburg (1640–1680)', *Jahres Bericht des Vereins Alt-Rothenburg* (1920/21), 13–79; and Heinrich Schmidt, 'Dr. Johann Ludwig Hartmann', *Fränkischer Feierabend* (October 1960), 79–80; (November 1960), 81–8. For a summary biography of Hartmann and other clerics from the Hartmann family, see also Wilhelm Dannheimer, *Verzeichnis der im Gebiete der freien Reichsstadt Rothenburg o. T. von 1544 bis 1803 wirkenden ev.-luth. Geistlichen* (Nuremberg, 1952), 64–6. Hartmann's predecessor as Superintendent had been Daniel Rücker, who died aged 60 in March 1665 after holding the post for just 10 months. See Ludwig Schnurrer, 'Daniel Rücker (1605–1665). Theologe', *Fränkische Lebensbilder*, 20 (2004), 101–19, esp.113–15.

[4] Hartmann's publications are listed thematically by Schattenmann, 'Dr. Ludwig Hartmann', 72–7. Two texts by Hartmann -*Greuel* and *Reine Lehrer und feine Zuhoerer* (Rothenburg ob der Tauber, 1679) are also discussed briefly in Hans-Christoph Rublack, 'Success and Failure of the Reformation: Popular "Apologies" from the Seventeenth and Eighteenth Centuries', in Andrew C. Fix and Susan C. Karant-Nunn (eds),

century and in which individual vices were presented as the result of tempta-
tion by specific devils.[5] Hartmann's two works discussing superstition and
the role of the devil in encouraging superstition were also aimed at a popular
audience and belong partly to this 'devil book' genre and partly to the genre
of Protestant demonology identified by Stuart Clark as emerging in the writings by clerics of reformed churches across Europe from 1520 onwards.[6]
Hartmann's third claim to fame was thus that he was the only Rothenburger
ever to publish a demonology: jurist Georg Christoph Walther wrote a short
tract on witchcraft in 1652 that never made the transition from manuscript
to print.[7]

Like the earlier Protestant demonologists identified by Clark, Hartmann's
main concern in *Greuel* and *Stücklein* was with the white magic still used by
many nominal Lutherans, rather than with the black magic of alleged witches,
and his aim was pastoral and didactic: to convince his flock once and for all
that the use of magical ritual was wrong and imperilled their souls. In order to
teach this lesson he adopted a standard line in Protestant providentialism,
articulated in most detail in *Greuel*: all things, including misfortune, came
from God and were part of God's plan for humankind, so the only proper
response of the good Lutheran in the face of loss, suffering or accident was
to wait patiently for divine assistance. To resort to blessings or other magical
rituals instead in order to try to solve problems was evidence of supreme
arrogance (as it implied that human beings could bend God's power to their
own will) and also contravened the Biblical injunction (Deuteronomy,
Chapter XVIII, verses 10–11) forbidding the use of divination and

---

Germania Illustrata. Essays on Early Modern Germany Presented to Gerald Strauss
(Sixteenth Century Essays & Studies, Volume XVIII, Kirksville, Missouri, 1992), 141–65.

[5] August Schnizlein, 'Allerlei aus alter Zeit', *Jahres Bericht des Vereins Alt-Rothenburg*
(1902/03), 25–37, esp. 27–8. For general discussion of this genre, see Charles Zika,
Exorcising Our Demons. Magic, Witchcraft and Visual Culture in Early Modern Europe
(Brill, 2003), 500–2.

[6] Stuart Clark, 'Protestant Demonology: Sin, Superstition, and Society (*c*.1520–*c*.1630)', in
Bengt Ankarloo and Gustav Henningsen (eds), *Early Modern European Witchcraft.
Centres and Peripheries* (Oxford, 1993), 45–81.

[7] For the Walther tract, see Staatsarchiv Nuremberg (hereafter StAN) Rothenburg Repertorium 200/III Konsistorialakten, vol. 2087 fos. 99r–113r: it is discussed in Alison Rowlands, *Narratives of Witchcraft in Germany: Rothenburg, 1561–1652* (Manchester, 2003),
esp. ch. 2. A sermon against sorcery preached by Hartmann's predecessor as Superintendent, Daniel Rücker (see above, n. 3), was published in *Die vermumbte verkehrte Welt*,
a collection of Rücker's sermons published posthumously in Bad Windsheim in 1688
(RStA Th.652).

consultation of enchanters, witches and necromancers. Moreover, given that many blessing rituals incorporated either the name of God or names and words from the Bible, their use broke not only the Second Commandment (not to take the Lord's name in vain), but also the Third (to keep the sabbath holy, which in Lutheranism involved honouring the preaching and teaching of God's word). To Hartmann, this misuse of scripture was worse than the fact that some blessings (the use of the Ave Maria and prayers to saints) were obvious hangovers from Catholicism, although he criticized their use as well, noting that those who declared themselves Lutheran but clung to such 'popish horrors and idolatry' in their hearts were hypocrites.[8]

The crux of Hartmann's criticism of blessings was, of course, that they were superstitious and diabolic: people who used them contravened the First Commandment by putting their trust in the devil instead of God. Mere words or ceremonies had no innate power to bring about certain effects, Hartmann explained, and they could not be given such power by the arts of humans. Should anything appear to have been effected by blessings or other magical rites that went against nature and God's word, then this could only have been achieved by the intervention of the devil. Even if people used blessings without realizing the extent of the sin they were committing—and Hartmann was charitable or judicious enough to allow that this might be the case—this was nonetheless evidence of a secret pact with the devil. Here Hartmann drew on the writings of St. Augustine to emphasize that all magic (white as well as black) involved a pact of some sort between people and the devil. Hartmann did, however, 'rank' white and black magic. One of his arguments against the speaking of blessings was that it constituted a first step on a slippery downward slope to malevolent witchcraft, a point implying that, while he feared the corrupting influence of white magic on an individual, he viewed harmful magic employed on the basis of an explicit pact with the devil as the greater sin.[9]

Hartmann's fulminations were underpinned by his belief that the speaking of blessings was still a general practice in late-seventeenth century Rothenburg, defended by many (erroneously, of course, in his opinion) as permissible.[10] This was despite the fact that, since the formal adoption of

---

[8] Hartmann, *Greuel*, 1–2, 5–7, 16–17, 21–2, 25–6, 76, 94, 114, 139–40, 162, 177, 193, 217–19. The reference to 'päpistisch. Greuel und Abgötterei' is on 218, but Hartmann was also anti-Semitic, claiming that blessings were commonly used by Jews as well (ibid., 212–16).

[9] Ibid., 29–31, 32–3, 36–7, 76, 151–78.

[10] Ibid., 3. While Hartmann identified certain people as particularly prone to using blessings (see n. 25), he also said that the problem affected all social groups, see ibid., 3, 43, 46.

Lutheranism by the Rothenburg City Council in 1544, various measures had been put in place to try to combat the problem of popular use of magic. For example, the instructions issued by the council in 1558 for formal visitations of its urban and rural parishes listed sorcery amongst the deviations from Lutheran orthodoxy that were subject to ecclesiastical and secular censure,[11] while consultation of cunning folk and use of magic had been defined as apostasy and prohibited on pain of punishment in a series of ordinances promulgated from 1612 onwards.[12] Moreover, the main thrust of Hartmann's *Stuecklein* was that things had become worse instead of better in the course of the seventeenth century as a result of the spread of soldier-magic to the civilian population in the Thirty Years War. Hartmann's portrayal of what he saw as the lamentable moral laxity of his contemporaries can, of course, be seen as a continuation of the 'chorus of disenchantment' voiced by earlier Lutheran reformers over their perceived failure to persuade their flocks to live up to their own rigorous standards of pious belief and behaviour.[13] However, by setting Hartmann's writings in the context provided by a range of other sources (ordinances issued by the city council; criminal court cases; minutes of the Consistorium, the city's ecclesiastical administrative body; and visitation records) we can see that the picture he painted of magical practices as still widespread in Rothenburg and its hinterland by about 1680 was fairly accurate. His method in writing, then—although influenced by the 'devil book' and demonological genres discussed earlier—was very much that of the clerical anthropologist, who drew on first-hand experience in the field in order to illustrate his arguments as vividly as possible.[14] This experience would have been gained by Hartmann during the fourteen months he spent as pastor of the hinterland village of Spielbach as well as in the course of the

---

[11] Emil Sehling, (ed.), *Die evangelischen Kirchenordnungen des XVI. Jahrhunderts*, vol. XI: Bavaria, Part I: Franconia (Tübingen, 1961), 561–616, esp. 612–13. See Paul Schattenmann, *Die Einführung der Reformation in der ehemaligen Reichsstadt Rothenburg ob der Tauber (1520-80)* (Gunzenhausen, 1928), for a narrative account of the early Reformation in Rothenburg.

[12] Rowlands, *Narratives of Witchcraft*, 68–75, esp. 70–1.

[13] Gerald Strauss, 'Success and Failure in the German Reformation', *Past and Present*, 67 (May 1975), 30–63, esp. 31–3.

[14] Here Hartmann had much in common with the other Lutheran pastors discussed by Rublack, who drew on their personal pastoral experience in their 17th- and 18th-century publications, many of which focused on the apparent 'failure' of the Reformation to live up to clerical expectations, see Rublack, 'Success and Failure of the Reformation'. Cf. also Alan Macfarlane, 'A Tudor Anthropologist: George Gifford's *Discourse and Dialogue*', in Sydney Anglo (ed.), *The Damned Art: Essays in the Literature of Witchcraft* (London, 1977), 14–155.

visitations to the urban and rural parishes of the Rothenburg territory he led as Superintendent between 1666 and 1680.[15]

Hartmann began *Greuel* with various anecdotes drawn from recent personal experience as a way of establishing the scale of the problem of popular use—and defence—of magic. For example, Hartmann recounted a visit to a sick soldier during which he had had great difficulty in persuading the soldier to admit that he had been wrong to try to cure his fever by means of a charm worked by a barber-surgeon, involving a blessing written onto a piece of paper and then thrown into flowing water. Next Hartmann recalled the case of a schoolmaster whom he had encountered during an inspection of Rothenburg's rural schools who had written the name of Saint Nicasius over the doors of his school-house to keep out mice. Again, Hartmann emphasized the difficulty he had had in convincing the schoolmaster, who claimed to have learned the charm from his own father fifty years earlier, to wash off the words, and to concede that it was probably his mousetraps rather than the saint's name that kept the school mouse-free.[16] Hartmann had observed bits of birch-wood (put up as part of a Shrove Tuesday ritual to protect cattle against vermin) and pieces of parchment bearing house blessings (presumably put into door-lintels or under thresholds) in the course of rural visitations,[17] and had also handled other items of magical paraphernalia. These included a mandrake root, surrendered to him by a baker from one of the hinterland villages (which Hartmann burned), and an Austrian *Kunstbüchlein*, or 'little book of arts' (a printed or handwritten collection of blessings and charms), confiscated from a cunning man.[18]

---

[15] Visitations were formal inspections of all aspects of religious, educational, and moral life in parishes, from the material structure of the church to the orthodoxy of pastors and parishioners. They were supposed to take place annually but were disrupted significantly in the 17th century, especially in the rural hinterland, by warfare. Hartmann presided over rural visitations in 1666, 1667, 1668, 1672, 1674, 1675 and 1679, Schmidt, 'Dr. Johann Ludwig Hartmann', 84. On the general practice of visitations, see Alison Rowlands, *Women, Gender and Power in Rothenburg ob der Tauber and its Rural Environs, 1500–c.1618* (Ph.D. dissertation, Cambridge University, 1994), 18, n. 59; 359, n. 51.

[16] Hartmann, *Greuel*, Introduction. Nicasius, 5th-century Bishop of Reims, had been beheaded by 'barbarians' as he stood at the door of his cathedral trying to save his flock, David Hugh Farmer, *The Oxford Dictionary of Saints* (5th edn, Oxford, 2003), 384. This was doubtless why Nicasius was believed to be a powerful protector of thresholds.

[17] Hartmann, *Greuel*, Introduction, 114–15.

[18] Ibid., 325, 114–15. Hartmann also recalled being given a book containing rituals of protective magic by a repentant soldier, see *Stücklein*, 13.

Use of magic was not merely a rural problem for Hartmann: indeed, in the discussion of profit-making magical rituals involving mandrake roots, thieves' thumbs and the conjuring of spirits that constituted the second part of *Greuel*, examples drawn from the urban milieu of craftsmen predominated.[19] In these, as in his earlier anecdotes, Hartmann was careful to avoid naming names (doubtless in order to avoid being thought overly censorious or even libellous), but it is occasionally possible to identify the people to whom he referred from other sources. For instance, in the chapter on thieves' thumbs he mentioned 'an innkeeper from a prominent city' who had tried to work magic using a thief's thumb, to the utmost peril of his soul.[20] This was almost certainly an allusion to Hans Wilhelm von Berg, master-brewer and landlord of the Black Bear pub in Rothenburg, who had been banished for four years from the city and its hinterland in 1672 after admitting that he had bought a thief's thumb from Hans Martin Cranz, an executioner's assistant from the town of Marktbergel in the neighbouring principality of Brandenburg. Von Berg had rubbed the severed thumb three times round the taps of the barrels in his cellar then put it into a hole above the cellar threshold as a magical method of improving the takings from his sale of beer and wine. Cranz had cut the thumb off the body of malefactor Georg Hillebrandt, who had been executed and left to rot on the wheel at the Marktbergel gallows.[21] In 1672 the Rothenburg Consistorium, chaired by Hartmann, had also investigated an allegation that the healthy profits enjoyed by another master-brewer of Rothenburg, Michael Henninger of the Crown Inn, were the result of magic that he had worked with a mandrake root. The investigation against Henninger petered out due to lack of evidence but Hartmann's first-hand knowledge of these two cases, which must have been the talk of Rothenburg in 1672, helps explain why he devoted specific chapters to these types of magic in his book about blessings.[22]

In addition to craftsmen, who had an obvious interest in improving their profits and who (according to Hartmann) gained knowledge of such magical practices while travelling as journeymen, Hartmann identified two other 'professions' as particularly likely to turn to 'profit-making' magic. These were robbers (who used the severed hands or fingers of executed thieves or dead children as magical lights to help them commit their nocturnal crimes)

---

[19] Hartmann, *Greuel*, 312–52.

[20] Ibid., 335, 'Ein Gastgeber in einer vornehmen Stadt'.

[21] For the von Berg case, see RStA Urgichtenbuch A908 (unpaginated), bundle of 16 documents dated 27 June 1672–3 March 1673.

[22] For the Henninger case, see StAN Rothenburg Repertorium Konsistorialakten 200/III, vol. 2087 fos. 513r–524v.

and men who studied and who might use their knowledge to conjure spirits to their advantage.[23] This then was a markedly masculine world of 'superstition' that depended partly on literacy and access to ritual magic in books, partly on the possession of books of ritual magic and other material objects necessary for working profit-making magic (which were often, as in the case of mandrake roots and severed thumbs, associated with the gallows), and partly on the networks created by male professions that gave access to such knowledge and objects and that were formed either licitly (in the case of craftsmen or students) or illicitly (in the case of criminals). Elsewhere in *Greuel* Hartmann tried to redress this portrayal by suggesting that women were more likely than men to fall into the sin of speaking blessings.[24] However, this seems to have been an expression of the standard Protestant view that women were weaker than men and more prone to the devil's temptations on Hartmann's part rather than a reflection of actual practice, as the list of those he identified as especially prone to use blessings in the course of their work was also dominated by men: barber-surgeons, huntsmen, smiths, herdsmen, doctors of livestock (male), as opposed to midwives and childbed attendants (female).[25]

In addition to first-hand experience, Hartmann also encountered the problem of magic in his capacity as chair of the Consistorium, the main ecclesiastical administrative committee in Rothenburg whose other five members consisted of two other urban clerics and three city councillors, including one of the ruling mayors. The first item discussed at Hartmann's first Consistorium meeting on April 25 1666 was a list of complaints brought by five rural pastors about the ungodly behaviour of their parishioners, which included the frequent use of sorcery, superstitious practices and blessings.[26] The Consistorium members agreed that superstition was spreading and that harsher preaching and edicts were needed to combat it. They singled out one particularly popular cunning man called Saü Classen (who was probably a herdsman in the hinterland), and his wife for criticism: they used magic to find buried treasure and had a crystal by means of which they could affect

[23] Hartmann, *Greuel*, 335–7, 344.

[24] Ibid., 172–3.

[25] Ibid., 3, 43, 100. On this standard Protestant view as it was articulated in Protestant writings on witchcraft, see Rolf Schulte, *Hexenmeister. Die Verfolgung von Männern im Rahmen der Hexenverfolgung von 1530–1730 im Alten Reich* (Frankfurt am Main, 2nd edn, 2001), 166.

[26] StAN Rothenburg Repertorium Konsistorialakten 200/III, vol. 2093, fo. 1r. The rural parishes in question were Adelshofen, Neusitz, Steinsfeld, Schweinsdorf and Gattenhofen.

men's virility.[27] The 'sinfulness' uncovered during the summer visitation of the rural parishes in 1666 prompted the city council, on the recommendation of the Consistorium, to issue an edict in October to exhort its rural subjects to desist from swearing, drinking to excess, profaning the sabbath, and seeking help from infamous sorcerers and speakers of blessings, on pain of an unspecified but severe punishment.[28] Much the same catalogue of sins was in evidence during the rural visitation two years later, however, including the case of Barthel Best, the schoolmaster of Leuzenbronn. Best admitted that he had employed a cunning man to work a ritual that involved boring a hole into a tree in Best's garden, in order to try to cure Best's grandson of a rupture. A striking feature of the case was that a Leuzenbronn official named Melchior Schmidt claimed that the cunning man had been sent to the village by Best's father, who was the pastor of Wörnitz (another of Rothenburg's rural parishes), although the visitors apparently forgot—or decided not—to investigate this potentially embarrassing allegation against one of their own clergymen.[29] The fact that at least some pastors and schoolmasters, who were the main agents of Lutheran education in the hinterland villages, dabbled in magic showed what an uphill struggle Hartmann and the Rothenburg councillors faced in trying to change the behaviour of rural parishioners.[30]

The ordinance of 1666 was reissued in the wake of the 1668 visitations.[31] The councillors' policy of repeatedly reissuing ordinances that attempted to discipline all aspects of their subjects' behaviour, with an introductory lamentation to the effect that nothing much had improved since the last edict had been issued, continued until the end of the eighteenth century. Use of magic, and in particular the activities of cunning folk, remained a concern in these ordinances.[32] Reading the future from coffee-grounds was added to the list of 'superstitious' practices condemned by the council in 1763, an interesting detail that showed how fortune-tellers moved with the times by incorporating

---

[27] Ibid., fo. 2r.

[28] Ibid., fo. 5r. For the edict, see RStA Rats-Edicta und Ordnungen A366b fos. 196r–7r.

[29] For reports on the 1668 rural visitations, see StAN Rothenburg Repertorium Konsistorialakten 200/III, vol. 2097 fos.1r–33r. For the Best case, see ibid., fos. 5r–6r. The pastor of Wörnitz from 1661–76 (and Ohrenbach from 1676–97) was Johann Georg Best (b. 1636, d. 1697), see Dannheimer, *Verzeichnis*, 44.

[30] See the earlier example given by Hartmann of the schoolmaster who chalked the name of Saint Nicasius on his school building, above, n. 16.

[31] RStA Rats-Edicta und Ordnungen A365 fos. 282r–5v.

[32] For example, RStA Rats-Edicta und Ordnungen A366a fos. 185v–198v (1685); A366b fos. 149r–150r (1689); AA122a fos. 459r–478r (1698); AA122a fos. 479r–497r (1721); AA122a fos. 523r–530r (1763).

new consumer goods into their repertoires.[33] The ordinance of 1685 constituted a slight innovation in the context of this repetitive legislation. In it the council condemned superstition as a sin against the First and Second Commandments in unusual detail and included a lengthy list of the different white magic experts to whom its subjects supposedly resorted on the slightest pretext: sorcerers, speakers of blessings, conjurors of spirits, gypsies, practitioners of divination, and those who used the stars, crystals, or sieves in order to see hidden things or predict the future. A clearer list of punishments for the purveying and use of magic was also specified: cunning folk were either to be imprisoned, set in the pillory, flogged, beheaded or burned at the stake, while their customers were to suffer a fine for a first offence, church penance for a second, and a corporal or capital sentence for a third, a system of punishments that stayed in force (at least on paper) throughout the eighteenth century. This was also the first such ordinance to mention use of the mandrake root, suggesting that Hartmann's focus on this practice in *Greuel* had left its mark in the minds of the Rothenburg councillors.[34]

The authorities' aim of eradicating the practice of magic in the city and its hinterland remained unfulfilled, however. The municipal account books list a steady trickle of cunning folk arrested by the council in the late-seventeenth and eighteenth century, although the fact that banishment continued to be the most common fate of such individuals, rather than the far more draconian punishments listed in the 1685 ordinance, showed the size of the gap between the councillors' rhetorical savagery and pragmatic practice. They included Hans Georg Kilian of Mittelstetten and Matthes Zehemeister of Nortenberg, both doctors of some sort (banished for working magic in 1681); Anna Maria Olethin of Bamberg (banished for speaking blessings to find lost goods in 1684); day-labourer Christoph Vogel of Bettwar (banished for working magic in 1688); musketeer Andres Killingstein (flogged and banished for theft and speaking blessings in 1692); Hans Christoph Brau, pursemaker, and Jobst Los, miller of Öhringen (banished for treasure-seeking in 1702); Apollonia Fetzer, miller's wife of Kirnberg, and Georg Adam Glautner, livestock doctor of Rothenburg (heavily fined for committing adultery with one another as part of a magical ritual to cure Fetzer's infirm husband in 1731); and a Prussian deserter and his wife (punished with a shaming ritual for speaking blessings and using other forbidden arts in 1758).[35]

---

[33] Ibid., fo. 526r.

[34] RStA Rats-Edicta und Ordnungen A366a fos. 185r–198v, fos. 188v–189r for section on magic.

[35] RStA Stadtrechnungen R531 fo. 418r (Kilian and Zehemeister); ibid., fo. 503v (Olethin); ibid., fo. 662r (Vogel, also discussed in Rowlands, *Narratives of Witchcraft*, 162);

The continued importance of beliefs about the efficacy of white and threat of black magic in eighteenth-century urban society was also shown in 1760 when Rothenburg was rocked by another scandal involving one of its master craftsmen, fifty-one-year-old cooper Johann Georg Bischoff, who tried to kill himself by stabbing himself in the throat and chest. The investigation which followed showed that Bischoff's marriage had broken down: he believed that his wife, Eva Sibylla, was a witch, and she thought the same about him. Bischoff's suicide attempt had been triggered by Eva's visit to a cunning man, day-labourer Johann Schleehuber, of the hinterland village of Gebsattel, from whom she had bought three small bundles of herbs. She had put one into the straw of Bischoff's pillow, the second under the threshold of his workshop, and sewn the third into a pair of his trousers. Eva doubtless saw these bundles as a means of protecting herself against Bischoff's supposed witchcraft, Bischoff would have regarded them as further evidence of his wife's magical power over him, while Schleehuber probably intended them as a remedy for the couple's marital problems. Schleehuber, Eva, and the Bischoffs' twenty-three-year-old daughter, Sabina, who had accompanied Eva to visit the cunning man in Gebsattel, all suffered several hours imprisonment in the Rothenburg prison dungeon, Eva and Sabina for contravening the council's ordinances prohibiting superstitious practices and Schleehuber for defrauding them of money for remedies that, in the council's opinion, did not work. Eva had to submit the three bundles of herbs that she had obtained from Schleehuber to the authorities for examination.[36] They can still be seen in the Rothenburg archive, labelled by the court scribe as 'superstitious amulets' and fixed with wax onto the pages of the relevant book of court proceedings.[37]

There is also evidence to support Hartmann's claim that magical practices used by soldiers during the Thirty Years War to protect themselves against injury, known generically as 'the Passau art', had spread to the civilian population by the second half of the seventeenth century. As Hartmann explained in *Stücklein*, the name derived from events of 1611, when an enterprising executioner had established a lively trade in paper amulets, the size of a large coin and marked with strange letters, which he had manufactured and sold to the mercenary army of Prince-Bishop Leopold of Passau. The soldiers had

---

R532 fo. 73r (Killingstein); ibid., fo. 460v (Brau and Los); R536 fo. 22r (Fetzer and Glautner); R538 fo. 367v (Prussian deserter).

[36] For this case, see RStA Urgichtenbuch A981 fos. 456r–484r; RStA Ratsprotokollen B104 fo. 644r; RStA Stadtrechnungen R539 fo. 41r. Schleehuber may well have been Catholic, see below, n. 46.

[37] RStA A981 fo. 468v: 'amuleto superstitio'.

swallowed the amulets in order to render themselves magically so hard (in German, *fest*) of body that they could not be shot or stabbed by the enemy.[38] This type of magic was easily adapted into the civilian, masculine culture of fighting, particularly in and around taverns, and was thus even more strongly associated with men than the types of profit-making magic about which Hartmann was also concerned.[39] In *Greuel*, for example, Hartmann referred to a man from one of the rural parishes who had been reported to the authorities during a visitation for frequent fighting and whose explanation for his belligerence was that he knew an art by means of which he could protect himself against being shot by opponents.[40] The belief in the possibility of making oneself *fest* was so widespread in the Rothenburg hinterland by the 1680s that a man who was skilful or lucky enough to survive several tavern brawls unscathed risked being suspected of working the Passau art.[41] One case that came before the Rothenburg council involving Hans Horn, the herdsman of Gailnau, and his son (also called Hans) in 1676, after the two had been involved in a brawl outside a tavern in Harlang, during which the son had shot at his father with a gun, provides a concrete example of how knowledge of the soldiers' magic spread.[42]

After his arrest, Hans Horn senior, who must have been at least in his sixties by 1676, told the council that he had fought in his youth in the Thirty Years War under the Bavarian general Johann de Werth. On his travels he had obtained a version of the Passau amulet—a little ball of wax containing a magical piece of paper to hang round his neck—to ensure his invulnerability to wounding, but had lost it during a battle in 1646. He attributed his survival of the war to the amulet and to two prayers, one of which had to be said after midnight to make oneself *fest* for the next day:

> Today and on this holy Monday, [or whichever day of the week it
> was]
> I will step over the threshold,
> God the Father, the Son and the Holy Ghost,
> Be my companion,
> And Our Dear Lady be my protector,

[38] Hartmann, *Stücklein*, 11–12.

[39] On taverns and male violence, see B. Ann Tlusty, *Bacchus and Civic Order. The Culture of Drink in Early Modern Germany* (Charlottesville and London, 2001), 126–33.

[40] Hartmann, *Greuel*, Introduction.

[41] See the 1683 example given in Anton Müller, *Gebsattel. Chronik eines fränkischen Dorfes* (Rothenburg, 1989), 152–3.

[42] For full case details, see RStA Urgichtenbuch A911 (unpaginated), document bundle dated 13 May 1676; RStA Stadtrechnungen R531 fo. 234v.

Let the Lord our God and the Virgin Mary,
Be stronger than anyone who might attack me today,
In the name of God the Father,
God the Son and God the Holy Ghost.[43]

The second prayer had to be spoken the next day if one met someone who threatened harm. In custody Horn also admitted to having used two other blessings, one involving the five wounds of Christ (to heal wounds), and a fourth which protected his sheep against wolves:

In the name of Jesus I drive you out
Into the angel's house, into the angel's garden,
Our Dear Lady comes to help me watch
Peter comes with the keys
To lock out the the snouts of the wolves.
In the name of God the Father,
God the Son and God the Holy Ghost.[44]

The scribe present at Horn's interrogation made a valiant, if at times muddled, attempt to transcribe all four blessings as they were recited by the herdsman, thus unwittingly preserving them for posterity.

Horn senior was banished from Rothenburg and its hinterland for his use of the Passau art and the speaking of blessings. His son was also banished but put in the pillory and flogged first for what the authorities interpreted as attempted parricide. Horn junior was extremely taciturn in custody and never explained why he had taken a pot-shot at his father, missing him only narrowly. The most probable interpretation is that their brawl had been stage-managed to demonstrate the efficacy of Horn senior's protective blessings to the soldiers with whom they had been drinking in the Harlang tavern, perhaps in the hope that the soldiers would want to buy the blessing from Horn. It seems likely from the blessings that he recited in custody that Horn was (or had been) Catholic, and late seventeenth-century visitation records took note of the fact that several other hinterland villages employed herdsmen who

---

[43] 'Heüt und an diesen heiligen Montag; Tritt ich über die Tür geschwell; Gott vater sohn und heiliger geist; Seÿ mein mitgesell; Und unser liebe frau sey mein Schutzmann; Irer stärcker ist alss Gott der Herr; und die Jungfrau Maria; der greif mich heut auf diesen tag; an, in nahmen Gottes dess Vatters; dess Sohns und dess heiligen geists', RStA A911, 13 May 1676 (semi-colons show original line-breaks).

[44] Ibid., 'In Jesus nahmen treib ich auss; Ins engels haus, ins engels garten; Komt unser Liebe Frau, hilft; mir warten, Komt der Petrus; mit dem Schlüssel, sperrt dem; Wolff und der Wölfin den Rüssel; in nahmen Gottes des vatters; dess Sohns und dess heÿl. Geistes'.

were Catholic.[45] The importance of herdsmen in protecting and healing livestock meant that the profession was traditionally linked with the practice of magic: perhaps Catholic herdsmen were taken on by Lutheran communities because they were recognized as having a particularly rich repertoire of blessings at their disposal. A Catholic tradition of speaking blessings was probably also maintained in the hinterland by the inhabitants of Gebsattel, a large village situated close to the city of Rothenburg which, because of its Catholic overlord, remained predominantly Catholic throughout the early modern period.[46] The blessings identified by Hartmann in *Greuel* as Catholic would thus have been very hard to eradicate in Rothenburg and its hinterland, given the territory's continued openness to Catholic influence and customs.[47]

Troop movement during the Thirty Years War and the reintegration of ex-soldiers into civilian life in its aftermath thus helped expedite the spread of the Passau art throughout Germany, especially in Rothenburg, which was at a crossroads of troop movement during the war and which experienced a significant influx of new inhabitants, especially in the depopulated hinterland, after 1648.[48] The Thirty Years War thus added another mode of spreading knowledge of white magic to those that already existed, the most common of which were from generation to generation within families, and along the networks created by craftsmen, especially during the time they spent beyond the confines of their home towns as journeymen. The transmission of blessings in written rather than—or as well as—verbal form seems to have become increasingly important in Rothenburg in the seventeenth century. In *Greuel*, Hartmann lamented that parents passed on blessings to their offspring as if they were precious secrets or kept them, written on paper or in religious books, in chests like family treasure,[49] and he gave

---

[45] StAN Rothenburg Repertorium Konsistorialakten 200/III, vol. 2097 (visitation records from 1668) fos. 6r, 16r.

[46] 76 of the 89 households in Gebsattel belonged to Komburg, a Catholic monastery situated near Schwäbisch Hall. The Rothenburg city council had a long history of conflict with Komburg over lordship rights in Gebsattel which was exacerbated by religious divisions following the Reformation. See Rowlands, *Narratives of Witchcraft*, 107–110. The cunning man involved in the 1760 case of Johann Georg Bischoff, discussed earlier in this essay, was also from Gebsattel.

[47] See above, n. 8.

[48] On the devastating impact of the Thirty Years War on the inhabitants of Rothenburg and its rural hinterland, see Rowlands, *Narratives of Witchcraft*, 195–9.

[49] Hartmann, *Greuel*, 37. On the increasing importance of the spread of magical knowledge in written form in 17th-century Rothenburg, see Rowlands, *Narratives of Witchcraft*, 68.

examples of *Kunstbüchlein* which he had handled personally in both *Greuel* and *Stücklein*.[50] Aware that these texts were regarded as magical objects in their own right, the authorities in Rothenburg investigated their use and tried to confiscate them whenever possible.[51] The authorities had to be careful not to assist, albeit unwittingly, in the transmission of knowledge about white magic itself, however. Tracts written against superstition risked being used as *Kunstbüchlein*. Hartmann was aware of this problem, noting in *Greuel* that he intended to leave out the details of specific blessings to avoid exerting a bad influence on his readers.[52] He also knew that clerics faced difficulties in preaching against superstition without publicising the magical arts to their parishioners. His solution was to advise pastors to preach publicly only against the best-known superstitions, on the theory that everyone knew about them anyway, and to take individuals to task for novel or little-known arts in private.[53]

People's reliance on magic to cope with the exigencies of everyday life probably also increased during the Thirty Years War for reasons other than the availability of new types of soldier magic. The war brought the inhabitants of Rothenburg and its hinterland disease, death, dearth, and financial hardship on an unprecedented scale. Given that magic was used to cope with misfortune, to manage people's anxiety about their health and material survival, and to try to predict the future, it seems reasonable to suggest that the importance of magic increased during periods of warfare when misfortune and insecurity also increased. Second, organized religious life in the Rothenburg hinterland virtually collapsed during the war, and the process of trying to make the area a godly Lutheran territory suffered a severe setback as a result.[54] The post-war Superintendents—Hartmann and his predecessor Georg Zierlein, who held the office from 1621 until 1661—were forced to devote much of their time and energy to recovering lost ground.[55] The threat of war again became the defining feature of life in late seventeenth-century Rothenburg as a result of Louis XIV's military aggression between 1672 and 1678 (with the Rothenburg hinterland again affected by troop movements) and in 1688, when French troops deliberately set fire to eighteen

[50] See above, n. 18.

[51] See for example the role which books of ritual magic played in the cases of Hans Georg Hofmann in 1605 and Michael Würth in 1663, Rowlands, *Narratives of Witchcraft*, 162–8.

[52] Hartmann, *Greuel*, Introduction.

[53] Hartmann, *Stücklein*, 47.

[54] See above, n. 48.

[55] For a summary of Zierlein's biography, see Dannheimer, *Verzeichnis*, 144.

hinterland villages.[56] The Rothenburg elites (Hartmann included) interpreted the war-related disasters visited upon Germany in general and Rothenburg in particular as evidence of God's wrath with his sinful people, hence the urgency of their exhortations to their subjects to live more pious lives.[57] In this context, the appearance of comets in 1666 and 1680 was understood by the authorities as a clear sign of God's still-burning anger with the area's inhabitants: in 1666, according to Hartmann's comments at a Consistorium meeting, because the Sabbath continued to be profaned by dancing and the performance of comedies by travelling players.[58] Clearly, then, late seventeenth-century Lutheran Rothenburg was still, to borrow Bob Scribner's phrase, 'a world of highly charged sacrality', in which the lengthy seventeenth-century experience of war seems to have reinvigorated the apocalyptic tone of the early sixteenth-century Reformation.[59]

In the face of the clerical admonition that Lutheranism was fundamentally incompatible with superstition, users of magic tried ever harder to justify their activities in their own moral and theological terms. In *Greuel*, Hartmann plays 'devil's advocate' and lists the many arguments that people put forward to support the use of blessings (many of which he had doubtless heard personally in the course of his pastoral duties) in order to prove them inadmissible according to the theological logic that all magic was diabolic.[60] Some users of blessings defended their conduct by asserting that blessings could not be evil as they used words that were good, taken from the Bible; moreover, blessings were an accepted part of Lutheran practice in certain circumstances, such as when the pastor blessed his flock in church, or when a prayer was said

---

[56] Heinrich Schmidt, 'Ludwig XIV. stört den friedlichen Aufbau', *Fränkischer Feierabend* (June 1960), 46–8; (July 1960), 49–56; 'Ludwig XIV. gefährdet das Reich', *Fränkischer Feierabend* (January 1961), 1–8; (February 1961), 9–16; (March 1961), 17–24.

[57] This message formed the preface to several late seventeenth-century ordinances published by the city council, see RStA Rats-Edicta und Ordnungen A366b fos. 196r–197r (1666); fos. 153r–154r (1683); fos. 149r–150r (1689).

[58] RStA Rats-Edicta und Ordnungen A366a fo. 141r (1680); StAN Rothenburg Repertorium 200/III Konsistorialakten, vol. 2093 fo. 2r (1666). Hartmann was still complaining about the performance of profane comedies on Sundays in 1671, see ibid., fo. 114r.

[59] Robert W. Scribner, 'The Reformation, Popular Magic, and the "Disenchantment of the World"', in C. Scott Dixon (ed.), *The German Reformation. The Essential Readings* (Oxford, 1999), 262–79, esp. 269.

[60] Hartmann, *Greuel*, 243–88. Hans-Christoph Rublack also mines a range of texts written by disillusioned Lutheran pastors from 17th- and 18th-century Germany for such 'popular apologies'—attempts by Lutheran lay-people to justify what their clerics regarded as 'ungodly' behaviour, see Rublack, 'Success and Failure of the Reformation'.

at meal-time.[61] The defenders of blessings also likened the ceremony of baptism to a healing blessing: according to their logic, the child was christened in God's name to drive out the spiritual disease of sin in the same way that they might use God's name in a blessing to cure physical disease.[62] In using blessings to combat disease people argued that their actions mirrored Christ's example of healing the sick and fulfilled the Christian duty of loving one's neighbour: moreover, they understood good health as a 'noble thing', the implication being that it should be striven for with any means possible.[63] The severe line adopted by Hartmann—that it was better to let one's body suffer rather than resort to magic and thereby imperil one's soul—must have seemed impractical, if not downright cruel, to many people as they and their loved ones suffered the horrors of early modern diseases.[64] Even when Hartmann's condemnation of magical practices was echoed in other quarters, this was usually for very different reasons. For example, the master-brewers of Rothenburg demanded Hans Wilhelm von Berg's expulsion from their guild after he had admitted to employing a thief's thumb to try to improve his takings in 1672 not because they regarded him as in league with the devil, but because von Berg had sought to deprive them of their livelihoods by nefarious means and because he had dishonoured himself through contact with the gallows by touching and using the severed thumb of an executed criminal.[65]

The slow progress Hartmann experienced in trying to convince the inhabitants of Rothenburg and its hinterland of the error of their 'superstitious' ways is not surprising, considering the means he had at his disposal for so doing and the fact that few of his secular or ecclesiastical colleagues shared his fervent, single-minded zeal in the fight against sin. The impact of preaching and teaching in persuading parishioners that superstition was diabolic was shaped by the quality of the pastors conveying this message, as well as by the receptiveness to it of the parish audience. Hartmann obviously regarded the mid-seventeenth-century pastors of the Rothenburg hinterland as mediocre, as he introduced an annual pastors' synod in 1666, at which rural pastors were to appear to dispute theological points, as a way of raising standards.[66]

---

[61] Ibid., 247–8, 249, 255.

[62] Ibid., 252–3.

[63] Ibid., 243, 257, 277.

[64] Ibid., 259.

[65] RStA Urgichtenbuch A908 (unpaginated), von Berg case document-bundle (dated 27 June 1672–3 March 1673), document dated 3 March 1673. Von Berg moved from Rothenburg to Anfelden in 1679, see Bürgerrechtbuch B42 fo. 142r.

[66] StAN Rothenburg Repertorium Konsistroialakten 200/III, vol. 2093, fo. 5r. Hartmann was further hampered by the fact that he had no authority over the pastors of 7 hinterland

Hartmann's original hope had been to hold the disputations in public in Rothenburg, but this plan was shelved when the members of the Consistorium realized that the poor responses of the pastors would have harmed rather than enhanced the reputation of the church.[67] It was also at Hartmann's instigation that regular weekly sermons (in addition to those held on Sunday) were reintroduced in all parishes.[68] Of course, what Hartmann perceived as mediocrity in preaching may simply have been a necessary compromise on the part of a rural pastor to establish and maintain a harmonious relationship with the villagers with whom he and his family had to live on a daily basis, and who did not enjoy being berated once or twice a week from the pulpit.[69] That zealous preaching might be used—and resented—as a weapon in conflicts between pastors and their flocks is hinted at in the case of Wettringen pastor, Nicolaus Rosenbach. During a visitation in 1672 Rosenbach reported to the authorities that he had preached against the speaking of blessings in weekly sermons but one wonders how seriously his words were taken, given that his flock had reported him to the visitors in 1668 for drunkenness and violence.[70] Parishioners doubtless had a 'pick and mix' approach to sermons, ignoring, resenting or forgetting what they did not want to hear, or striving to make it fit with their own view of what made a 'good Lutheran'. Hartmann's books were likewise probably of limited contemporary impact, appealing mainly to pastors (for whom they offered material for sermons) and those who already believed in the sinfulness of 'superstition' (and were, of course, literate).

Eradicating the use of magic through punitive means was likewise problematic. Cunning folk and their customers had first to be identified and, as the Rothenburg council lamented in an edict of 1763, no-one seemed willing to tell them about such sinners: this edict established a system of rewards for informers to encourage people to overcome their reluctance to tell tales on their neighbours.[71] Only on the rare occasion when customers were deeply

---

parishes (Östheim, Reubach, Brettheim, Insingen, Hausen, Bettenfeld and Lohr) where the appointment rights belonged to the Margrave of Brandenburg-Ansbach.

[67] Ibid., fo. 7r.

[68] Ibid., fo. 13r. Hartmann also published several books of instruction to aid parish pastors, see Schattenmann, 'Dr. Ludwig Hartmann', 73–4.

[69] 'If a parson always preached in a punitive way, the laity simply switched off, demanded a different preacher or just stayed away', Ulinka Rublack, *Reformation Europe* (Cambridge, 2005), 170.

[70] StAN Rothenburg Repertorium Konsistorialakten 200/III, vol. 2097 fos. 20r–21r (1668); 77r–78r (1672).

[71] RStA Rats-Edicta und Ordnungen AA122a fos. 523r–530r.

dissatisfied with the services they had received from a cunning man or woman might they risk bringing this individual to the authorities' attention. Most of the cunning folk listed earlier as having been punished for magical crimes in late seventeenth- and early eighteenth-century Rothenburg either fell into this category, or were itinerant cunning folk who were more vulnerable to arrest, or had come to the council's attention initially for other reasons (theft, brawling, and so on).[72] Users of magic also tended to elicit official investigation as a result of bad luck, rather than as the result of any systematic process of surveillance: Hans Wilhelm von Berg's use of the thief's thumb only became public knowledge in 1672 because his 'supplier', Hans Martin Crantz, was arrested and interrogated in Marktbergel on suspicion of theft.[73] When they were held, visitations might, of course, uncover purveyors and users of magic, but only insofar as parish pastors and officials were willing to run the risk of social discord within their communities by incriminating neighbours. Individual sinners identified during visitations or called before the Consistorium or the Superintendent between visitations tended just to be exhorted to desist from their sins in future. This was in line with the idea— that was a key feature of the Rothenburg Church Ordinance—that sinners should be given every chance to improve their behaviour. The other weapon that the Consistorium had at its disposal—that of excommunication—was too drastic a measure with which to punish every sinner it identified.[74] Perhaps in recognition of this, Hartmann was successful in calling in September 1666 for the introduction of the sanction of church penance in Rothenburg, as was the practice elsewhere and because of the high level of sin, as he put it.[75] Philip Kneip was the first individual to suffer this sanction, doing penance for incest and adultery in Rothenburg on 31 May 1668.[76] More research is needed, especially for the eighteenth century, to ascertain whether church penance became a significant weapon in the fight against 'superstition'. What can be said at present is that the enthusiasm with which clerics could impose public penance remained closely controlled by the city councillors, who made all final decisions on punishments in criminal cases in the purely secular context of the city's criminal court, and who were also able

---

[72] See above, n. 35. The Rothenburg council had never had a particularly punitive or systematic approach to the policing of cunning folk: see Rowlands, *Narratives of Witchcraft*, 72–5, for discussion of the issue for the 16th and early 17th century.

[73] See above, n. 21.

[74] On the limited effect of visitations and the Consistorium in policing sin, see Rowlands, *Narratives of Witchcraft*, 71–2.

[75] StAN Rothenburg Repertorium Konsistorialakten 200/III, vol. 2093 fo. 7r.

[76] Ibid., fo. 39r.

to strongly influence the proceedings of the Consistorium (usually in favour of pragmatism rather than zeal) through their membership of it.[77]

It was not, of course, the case that nothing had changed with regard to people's belief in and practice of magic in Rothenburg and its hinterland since the formal adoption of Lutheranism by the city council in 1544. As happened in other German Protestant territories, the sacred objects that had often been appropriated from the Church for use in magical ritual in the pre-Reformation period—blessed bread, salt, holy water, palms and so on—had disappeared by the seventeenth century, to leave a range of practices (such as the speaking of blessings) that, with their emphasis on the power of holy words, 'had come to constitute what was, in effect, a Protestant form of magic'.[78] Moreover, despite its imperfections, the post-Reformation system of trying to police sin in Rothenburg, in which councillors and Superintendent endeavoured to coordinate their efforts through visitations, Consistorium meetings, and the promulgation of ordinances, at least encouraged the inhabitants of the city and its hinterland to become warier and more secretive in their employment of magic. This was why they resorted to ever more inventive excuses to justify their actions, while cunning folk who fell foul of the authorities insisted that their remedies were natural and effected without the use of blessings. Such habits of popular dissembling in the face of increased clerical admonition were also evident in other German Protestant territories from the sixteenth through to the eighteenth centuries and were testimony to the impressive ability of Lutheran lay-people to shape religious life to suit their own needs and priorities.[79] Central to this process of adaptation was the continued popular belief in and use of magic, which in Rothenburg (and doubtless elsewhere in Germany) was given a huge boost by the protracted warfare of the seventeenth century which helped create both the material and psychological conditions that encouraged recourse to magic and the

---

[77] On the working of the city's criminal court, see Rowlands, *Narratives of Witchcraft*, 7. Although the Rothenburg Consistorium had three clerical and three secular members, the secular (3 senior city councillors, including one of the ruling mayors) far outweighed the former in influence, see Schattenmann, *Einführung*, 124. For examples of their pragmatic approach under Hartmann's chairmanship, see StAN Rothenburg Repertorium Konsistorialakten 200/III, vol. 2093 fos. 2r, 7r, 114r.

[78] Scribner, 'The Reformation, Popular Magic, and the "Disenchantment of the World"', 275.

[79] On these points, see Rublack, 'Success and Failure of the Reformation', esp. 160–5; C. Scott Dixon, *The Reformation and Rural Society. The Parishes of Brandenburg-Ansbach-Kulmbach, 1528–1603* (Cambridge, 1996), esp. 143–207.

networks of transmission that helped spread ideas about new magical practices.[80] What we can discern through the filter of Hartmann's clerical polemic in *Greuel* and *Stücklein*, then, is a vibrant, robust and arguably increasingly masculine culture of popular magic in late-seventeenth-century Rothenburg and its hinterland, and one that was shaped more by the experience of war than by the efforts of reforming clerics.

---

[80] On the continuity of magical practices in this area, see e.g. Eberhard Wagner, 'Hexenglaube in Franken heute', *Jahrbuch für fränkische Landesforschung* (1970), 343–56; Fritz Heeger, 'Fränkische Segensprüche aus drei Jahrhunderten', *Bayerisches Jahrbuch für Volkskunde* (1960), 163–74.

Recording Superstition in Early Modern Britain: The Origins of Folklore

Alexandra Walsham

In Victorian and Edwardian Britain, the task of recording 'superstitions' was nothing less than an intellectual and cultural obsession. Scholars, ministers, and educated gentlemen and women dedicated themselves to collecting quaint remnants of a way of life they were convinced was fading rapidly into oblivion. The many anthologies of popular 'antiquities' prepared and published in this period are a monument to their determination to preserve these precious artefacts of a remote and primitive past for the benefit of posterity. Drawing on both literary and oral sources, such works were eclectic miscellanies which typically incorporated a combination of the following phenomena: pastimes associated with the seasonal cycle and ecclesiastical calendar; curious customs connected with birth, marriage, and death; charms, spells, and magical cures; ceremonies linked with megaliths and holy wells; omens, portents, and auguries; second sight and divinatory rituals designed to foretell the future; landscape legends and historical myths; local proverbs, rhymes, and sayings about the weather; rural assumptions concerning animals, plants, insects, and birds; and assorted beliefs about witches, ghosts, fairies, familiar spirits, diabolical apparitions, and other manifestations of the supernatural. Detecting in these 'druidical' opinions and practices clear traces of the pagan religions that had once held sway in these islands, they described them as 'the debris of ancient mythologies', living relics and heirlooms of the mental world inhabited by their pre-Christian forebears. Deliberately tolerated or unwittingly accommodated by the medieval Church, such traditions had been transmitted from generation to generation by word of mouth. Defined in contradistinction to the culture of books and learning, the natural habitat of superstition, such writers argued, was the realm of speech.[1]

---

[1] Quotation from John Harland and T. T. Wilkinson, *Lancashire Folk-Lore: Illustrative of the Superstitious Beliefs and Practices, Local Customs and Usages of the People of the County Palatine* (London, 1882), 153 and iii.

Past and Present (2008), Supplement 3

Following in the footsteps of W. J. Thoms, who had coined the Anglo-Saxon neologism 'Folk-Lore' in 1846 and initiated the first systematic attempts to assemble and analyse this scattered material, figures like William Henderson, Charles Hardwick, Edwin Sidney Hartland, George Laurence Gomme, Edward B. Tylor and Charlotte Burne laid the foundations of the new field he had christened. The formal establishment of the Folklore Society in 1878 added academic respectability to this branch of activity and the ensuing fifty years were the heyday of the scientific study of superstition and of the elaborate theory of survivalism that came to underpin it. Fascinated by the parallels they observed between the 'animistic' and 'irrational' culture of the peasantry in the outlying districts and sleepy villages of England, Scotland, and Wales and that of 'backward' and 'savage' tribes in 'uncivilised' parts of the globe, these self-styled ethnologists supposed they had also found a key to unlocking the psychology and philosophy of aboriginal man.[2] Guided in the technique of oral history by Gomme's *Handbook of Folklore* (1890), many engaged in tours of undisturbed corners of the countryside in pursuit of popular superstitions.[3] '[A]lthough composed of such flimsy materials, and dependent upon the fancies of the multitude for their very existence', these had 'nevertheless survived shocks by which kingdoms have been overthrown, and . . . preserved their characteristic traits from the earliest times down to the present'.[4]

A profound ambivalence, it may be argued, lay at the very heart of the early folklorist enterprise. The motives of the Victorians and Edwardians who collected and recorded popular 'antiquities' and 'superstitions' were very mixed. On the one hand, we can discern a clear element of nostalgia and regret for the passing of customs and beliefs that embodied a rose-coloured and romanticized vision of traditional rural life—a vision of simplicity, innocence, and harmony the folklorists created even in the very process of 'empirically' reporting it. Time and again such anthologies lament the decline

[2] W. J. Thoms, 'Folk-Lore', *The Athenaeum*, no. 982 (22 August 1846), in Richard M. Dorson (ed.), *Peasant Customs and Savage Myths: Selections from the British Folklorists*, 2 vols. (London, 1968), i. 52–4. On the development of the Folklore movement, see Richard M. Dorson, *The British Folklorists: A History* (London, 1968); and, on a European scale, Giuseppe Cocchiara, *The History of Folklore in Europe*, trans. John N. McDaniel (Philadelphia, 1981; first publ. in Italian 1952).

[3] George Laurence Gomme, *Handbook of Folk-Lore* (London, 1890); rev. edn by Charlotte Sophia Burne (London, 1914).

[4] Harland and Wilkinson, *Lancashire Folk-Lore*, 2. This closely echoes a passage in the preface to John Brand's *Observations on Popular Antiquities: Including the Whole of Mr Bourne's Antiquitates Vulgares* (Newcastle, 1777), p. iii, for which see below.

of an outlook under serious threat from the advance of education, literacy, industrialization, technological innovation, emigration and urban expansion. They seek to rescue an enchanted world which railways, factories, collieries, national schooling, and the mass media are quickly ushering into extinction. In 'the age of the steam engine, and the electric battery, and the many other practical adaptations of the triumphs of physical science', sighed one compiler, 'such "waifs and strays" from the mythical lore of the dim and distant Past' were in danger of being permanently effaced.[5] Silently editing out their more disreputable and unruly features, the folklorists sentimentally treasured the 'superstitions' of the common people.

At the same time, such collections must also be seen as panegyrics to the intellectual progress of the British nation and its liberation from the 'vulgar', 'barbarous', 'pernicious' and 'degrading' errors that had benighted and blemished its earlier phases. The subtext of much of this literature is undeniably one of self-congratulation. By recording the 'puerile superstitions' of former generations that are fast disappearing in the face of the spread of 'correct information', its authors throw into sharp relief the 'rational' ethos of their own superior and 'enlightened' era.[6] Even as they savour them, they celebrate the demise of fallacies which 'begat cruelty and injustice' and were a disgraceful blot on the history of England, Scotland and Wales, not to say 'a stain on the human soul'.[7] Their loss, wrote John H. L'Amy in *Jersey Folk Lore* (1927), 'is the toll demanded by civilisation—and it will be paid'.[8] Accompanying the folklorists' efforts to register them for posterity there is thus more than a hint of embarrassment about and apology for publishing such 'despicable rubbish'.[9] 'Many', A. W. Moore anticipated in his anthology on the Isle of Man, 'will doubtless think that the attempt to perpetuate these figments of an ignorant and superstitious past is a mistaken one'.[10] Underlying these

[5] Charles Hardwick, *Traditions, Superstitions, and Folk-Lore, (Chiefly of Lancashire and the North of England): Their Affinity to Others in Widely-Distributed Localities; their Eastern Origin and Mythical Significance* (Manchester, 1872), p. vii. See also William Henderson, *Notes on the Folk-Lore of the Northern Counties of England and the Borders* (London, 1879), pp. vii-ix and 1; Edgar MacCulloch, *Guernsey Folk Lore*, ed. Edith F. Carey (London, 1903), author's preface.

[6] MacCulloch, *Guernsey Folk Lore*, author's preface; John Harland and T. T. Wilkinson, *Lancashire Legends, Traditions, Pageants, Sports &c* (London, 1873), p. v.

[7] Harland and Wilkinson, *Lancashire Folk-Lore*, 182; Carveth Read, *Man and his Superstitions* (Cambridge, 1925 edn), 44.

[8] John H. L'Amy, *Jersey Folk Lore* (Jersey, 1927), 15.

[9] Hardwick, *Traditions, Superstitions, and Folk-Lore*, p. vii.

[10] A. W. Moore, *The Folk-Lore of the Isle of Man, being an Account of its Myths, Legends, Superstitions, Customs, and Proverbs* (London, 1891), p. vi.

collections is a subconscious desire to suppress and snuff out the very beliefs and customs they so lovingly seek to preserve in the protective aspic of writing and print.

This essay focuses on the fundamental tension between curiosity and censure upon which the modern discipline of folklore was built. Disentangling these apparently contradictory impulses, it offers a partial and tentative reassessment of its complex cultural and intellectual genealogy and roots. The folklorists, it will be suggested, were the inheritors of two different, but never wholly separate and often interacting strands of discourse and activity: one essentially antiquarian in character and the other polemical.

I

The first of these skeins of discourse on 'superstition' was the by-product of reforming Protestant zeal. Early anti-Catholic controversialists like William Tyndale launched a vehement assault upon medieval Catholicism as a false and idolatrous religion. They adopted one strand of the standard scholastic definition of superstition as a form of unauthorized devotion or service to God and applied it to the rituals and doctrines of the Roman Catholic Church in their entirety. These, they insisted, were based not on the truths about salvation Jesus had preached to his disciples and faithfully enshrined in the canon of Scripture, but on a set of 'human traditions' invented and then cunningly manipulated by the papacy and priesthood to keep the laity in awe and subjugation. Intent upon exposing the conspiracy perpetrated by Antichrist in their own times, Protestant polemicists like Thomas Becon compiled catalogues of *The Reliques of Rome* (1563), ranging from theological 'fictions' such as purgatory and transubstantiation to a welter of impious, 'unsavory', and 'croked customes', including the hallowing of water, the blessing of candles, and creeping to the cross.[11] Translated from the Lutheran Thomas Naogeorgus's *Regnum Papisticum*, Barnabe Googe's *Popish Kingdom* (1570) was a similar unmasking of the flimsy and unbiblical foundations of the Catholic religion, which rested on nothing more solid than the whims and 'dreames of men'. Designed to reveal the crafty methods by which these 'blinde and wicked guides . . . leade men into thickets, or wildernesses' of ignorance and superstition, it too described traditional customs in graphic detail to the end that 'the truth and the brightness of the Gospell may the better shine out'.[12] In a comparable vein, a tract entitled *The Beehive of the*

---

[11] Thomas Becon, *The Reliques of Rome* (London, 1563), fo.>2v and chs. 43–57.

[12] *The Popish Kingdome, or Reigne of Antichrist, Written in Latin Verse by Thomas Naeogeorgus*, trans. Barnabe Googe (London, 1570), sig. B3r and epistle *passim*. In the same tradition, the Lutheran Magdeburg Centuriators listed the ceremonial inventions

Romishe Churche published in 1579 listed Easter eggs alongside the ringing of sacring bells and the licking of relics among the vast mass of idolatrous liturgical practices, 'peeces and patches of mens devises', this institution had engendered for political purposes. These and many other popish traditions were laid open so 'that very babes & sucklings may behold their abominations', though its editor hoped that no reader would 'play . . . the part of a Spider, which out of sweet and odiferous flowers sucketh deadly poyson'.[13] The miracle tales embedded in the legends of the saints were likewise superstitions manufactured by the clergy to give their cults spurious legitimacy and fill their coffers and pockets with money. These too were recorded by Tudor controversialists from John Bale onwards to show the impartial reader the desperate lengths to which the Romanists had been prepared to go to keep their ramshackle cause afloat.[14]

It is necessary to emphasize three aspects of the concept of superstition embodied in these texts. Firstly, superstition was conceived of as a heinous sin, part of a grand diabolical design to seduce mankind to damnation. In fabricating such precepts and practices, it was implied, the Church of Rome had contracted an alliance and pact with Satan himself. Therein lay the basis of the polemical commonplace that popery was no more than a species of magic and sorcery. In equating the Catholic economy of the sacred with witchcraft, Protestant writers were invoking a further aspect of the pre-Reformation conception of superstition—the idea that there was no power inherent in words, signs, symbols, or inanimate things to effect marvellous transformations in natural objects—and using it to dismiss not just illicit popular misappropriations of ecclesiastical rituals and artefacts but the official system of sacraments and sacramentals itself. For them this rested on a misplaced and indeed diabolically inspired trust in the capacity of human actions to access and harness supernatural grace: this flowed from and through God alone.[15]

---

that had submerged true doctrine: [Matthias Flaccius Illyricus et al], *Ecclesiastica Historia*, 13 vols. (Basel, 1560–74).

[13] [Phillips van Marnix van St Aldegonde], *The Beehive of the Romishe Churche*, trans. George Gilpin (London, 1636 edn; first publ. 1579), fos. 14v–15v and sigs. *4r and *5r.

[14] John Bale, *The Actes of the Englysh Votaryes* (Wesel [Antwerp], 1546). John Gee's *The Foot out of the Snare* (London, 1624) is a later example in a similar vein.

[15] See Stuart Clark, *Thinking with Demons: The Idea of Witchcraft in Early Modern Europe* (Oxford, 1997), ch. 32 and 532–7; Euan Cameron, 'For Reasoned Faith or Embattled Creed? Religion for the People in Early Modern Europe', *Transactions of the Royal Historical Society*, 6th ser. viii (1998). See also Keith Thomas, *Religion and the Decline of Magic* (Harmondsworth, 1973), 32–9, 55–6, and ch. 2; Helen Parish and

Secondly, we should note the frequency with which Protestant denunciations of 'superstition' emphasized its oral character. It was arguably from the reformers' tirade against the 'unwritten traditions' which the papists privileged above the Holy Bible that the notion that folklore was conveyed through the medium of the spoken word originally emerged. The equation of 'superstition' with verbal transmission was, of course, a trope that was centuries old, but after the Reformation, at least in Britain, it acquired a distinctly anti-Catholic tinge.[16]

Thirdly, the authors of these and other texts systematically conflated popery with paganism. Some writers engaged in elaborate attempts to demonstrate the parallels between heathenism and Romanism, including the Scottish divine Thomas Morison in a Latin work entitled *Papatus, seu depravatae religionis origo et incrementum* printed in 1594 and the York rector Joshua Stopford in his *Pagano-Papismus* of 1675. The latter was once again designed to fortify Protestants against the allurements of Rome, 'to expose unto publick View such dismal pieces of their Catholick Doctrine and Worship', and to show how the priesthood kept the common people 'in ignorance of their Sacred Mysteries', a 'piece of Policy they seem to have learn'd of the old Pagans'.[17] This argument had humanist precedents, especially in the Italian scholar Polydore Vergil's *De Rerum Inventoribus*, which likewise traced many religious rites to pagan origins, including Candlemas tapers, New Year's gifts, and midsummer bonfires, once again with the

---

William G. Naphy (eds), *Religion and Superstition in Reformation Europe* (Manchester, 2002), 'Introduction'. For superstition conceived as idolatry and impiety, see John Calvin, *Institutes of the Christian Religion*, trans. H. Beveridge, 2 vols. (1845), i. 46–9.

[16] See Peter Marshall, 'The Debate over "Unwritten Verities" in Early Reformation England', in Bruce Gordon (ed.), *Protestant History and Identity in Sixteenth-Century Europe*, 2 vols. (Aldershot, 1996), i. 6–77; Nicholas Hudson, ' "Oral Tradition": The Evolution of an Eighteenth-Century Concept', in Alvaro Ribiero and James G. Basker (eds), *Tradition in Transition: Woman Writers, Marginal Texts, and the Eighteenth-Century Canon* (Oxford, 1996); Alexandra Walsham, 'Reformed Folklore? Cautionary Tales and Oral Tradition in Early Modern England', in Adam Fox and Daniel Woolf (eds), *The Spoken Word: Oral Culture in Britain, 1500–1850* (Manchester, 2002), esp. 174–80.

[17] Thomas Morison, *Papatus, seu depravatae religionis origo et incrementum* (Edinburgh, 1594); Joshua Stopford, *Pagano-Papismus: or, an Exact Parallel between Rome-Pagan and Rome-Christian in their Doctrines and Ceremonies* (London, 1675), 'The epistle to the reader'.

underlying aim of reforming these products of papal whim and heathenism.[18] Post-Reformation writers took up this theme with enthusiasm and turned it to serve the ends of anti-Catholic propaganda. Their works helped to entrench in contemporary thinking the notion that Rome was a repository of 'ethnic superstitions' and that many Catholic rites, including the mass, were merely thinly concealed versions of sacrificial ceremonies performed to honour or appease pre-Christian deities. In arguing that holy water was the Roman *aqua lustralis* in disguise, that Shrove Tuesday celebrations were *saturnalia*, rogation processions *ambarvalia*, and so forth, these propagandists were not just pointing to the imperfect eradication of pagan culture that had followed the imposition of the Christian faith. They were also alleging that this insidious process of accommodation had been condoned by the Church itself.

Setting their sights on customs and rituals that the English Reformation had failed to remove at the outset, second and third generation Protestants of the hotter sort revived these arguments in their efforts to purge the Church of England of remaining popish ceremonies and persuade society at large to abandon immoral pastimes of heathen origin. Thus Philip Stubbes's *Anatomie of Abuses* (1583) denounced the maypole as a 'stinking Idoll' and church ales and parish wakes as relics of the ancient feast of *bacchanalia*, while in his voluminous *Histrio-mastix* (1633) William Prynne sought to document in exhaustive detail that a direct line of succession could be traced from Roman spectacles consecrated to the gods to the modern theatre.[19] The puritan campaign to abolish Christmas in the 1640s was couched in similar terms and in his *Funebriae Florae* (1660) the West Midlands minister Thomas Hall renewed the claim that May-games were remnants of pagan fertility rites with particular vigour. First invented by the Romans, these 'prophane revels' were later adopted by the Catholic Antichrist as 'a prime prop' of the Pope's 'tottering Kingdome', as well as by the devil as a 'bellows to blow up the fire of lust and uncleanness'. Hall thought that there was no better way 'to debauch

---

[18] Polydore Vergil, *De Rerum Inventoribus* (1502), trans. as *An Abridgement of the Notable Worke of Polidore Vergile conteygnyng the Devisers and First Finders out aswell of Artes, Ministeries, Feactes [and] Civill Ordinaunces, as of Rites, [and] Ceremonies, Commonly Used in the Churche*, trans. Thomas Langley (London, 1546). See Ronald Hutton, *The Rise and Fall of Merry England: The Ritual Year 1400–1700* (Oxford, 1994), 144–5.

[19] Philip Stubbes, *The Anatomie of Abuses* (London, 1583), sigs. M3v–7v; William Prynne, *Histrio-Mastix: The Players Scourge, or Actors Tragaedie . . . Wherein it is Largely Evidenced . . . that Popular Stage-playes (the very Pompes of the Divell . . .) are Sinfull, Heathenish, Lewde, Ungodly Spectacles* (London, 1633).

a people, and draw them from God and his worship to superstition and Idolatry' than to introduce this kind of abomination.[20] Constructed around an opposition between 'custom' and 'veritie', the literature of moral complaint against popular recreations was one manifestation of the growing clerical conviction that, despite the efforts of Protestant evangelists, too many laypeople remained wedded to the old superstitions in which they had been nurtured by the Church of Rome.[21] An impulse to record traces of the 'popish dung' that still stuck between their teeth also inspired some of the most memorable descriptions of the religion of 'the common sort of Christians' produced in this period. The aim of the Essex minister George Gifford's much quoted account of *Countrie Divinitie* (1582), for instance, was to confute it through an edifying dialogue and to convince those in high places that through 'the want of a sincere ministerie of the woorde . . . a flood of ignorance and darknes [was] overflowing the most part of the land'.[22] Other godly divines provided equally revealing portraits of the superstitious beliefs and practices that lingered on in different parts of rural Britain: William Perkins prefaced a catechism with a list of thirty-two proverbial sayings he had encountered in Cambridgeshire. Elsewhere he outlined the 'vain' and groundless opinions his parishioners harboured about hares crossing their paths and other tokens of bad luck and the illicit divinatory practices in which they engaged in an effort to find out their future fortunes, once again in order to condemn these rivals to the Protestant doctrine of divine providence.[23] Such practices were wrong and idolatrous because they involved people putting undue trust in material objects or particular gestures and formulae.

This technique reached an extreme in the Kentish gentleman Reginald Scot's *The Discoverie of Witchcraft* (1584), a trenchant exposure of the 'fables' that were stirring up hatred and carrying innocent victims of popular fears to their deaths at the hands of the state. He spared no detail of the silly tales they heard from 'doting old women', 'mothers maids' and

[20] Thomas Hall, *Funebriae Florae, The Downfall of May-Games* (London, 1661 edn), 13–16.

[21] A good example is Thomas Lovell, *A Dialogue between Custom and Veritie Concerning the Use and Abuse of Dauncing and Minstrelsie* (London, [1581]).

[22] George Gifford, *A Briefe Discourse of Certaine Points of the Religion, which is among the Common Sort of Christians, which may be Termed the Countrie Divinitie* (London, 1582), sig. >3r–v and 22. Gifford's *Dialogue concerning Witches and Witchcraftes* (London, 1593) should be seen in the same light.

[23] William Perkins, *The Foundation of Christian Religion Gathered into Six Principles* (London, 1595 edn), sig. A2r–v and *The Damned Art of Witchcraft* (London, 1610 edn), 66–73.

'masse preests', and 'eventually swallowed up through tract of time, or through their owne timorous nature or ignorant conceipt'; of the 'fond observations', enchantments, amulets, and charms they employed to keep a hostile environment at bay; or of tales about elves, fairies, dwarfs, giants, and ghosts parents told their children to scare them into obedience and submission. Animated by the heterodox opinion that spirits had no corporeal reality, Scot's corrosive scepticism was both ill-received and unrepresentative. Yet at the same time his book was merely the logical extension of the savage anti-Catholicism that animated other contemporary critiques and catalogues of 'superstition'. Like them it pointed up the parallels with heathenism and embodied a tendency to trace vestigial popery to female credulity, utilizing the phrase 'old wives tales' as a synonym for resistance to the Protestant Reformation and identifying the nursery as the seedbed of many mistaken opinions. As we have seen, the same assumptions were still leaving their mark on the collections compiled by members of the Folklore Society three hundred years later.[24]

This diverse body of polemic has one other feature which deserves special mention. And that is that it has ironically provided scholars and historians with incomparable evidence of the very customs and beliefs it was so anxious to erase. Even as they sought to defuse and undermine these remnants of 'popish and pagan superstition' by displaying them in the clear light of day, the authors of such texts were paradoxically preserving an important and colourful record of them. Indeed some seem to have been positively captivated by what they were intent upon eradicating. The rhetoric of hyperbolic outrage they frequently employed to describe 'superstition' disguises a distinct fascination with it. Protestant outrage was thus one major stimulus to quasi-ethnographic analysis of the residually Catholic and heathen opinions and practices that had survived the Reformation. It engendered what might be called a form of polemical anthropology.[25]

---

[24] Reginald Scot, *The Discoverie of Witchcraft* (London, 1594), esp. bk 1, ch. 2; bk 7, ch. 15; bk 9, ch. 3; bk 11, ch. 15; bk 16, chs 1–2. For varying assessments of the source of Scot's scepticism, see L. L. Estes, 'Reginald Scot and his *Discoverie of Witchcraft*: Religion and Science in the Opposition to the European Witch Craze', *Church History*, 52 (1983), 444–56; David Wootton, 'Reginald Scot / Abraham Fleming / The Family of Love', in Stuart Clark (ed.), *Languages of Witchcraft: Narrative, Ideology and Meaning in Early Modern Culture* (Basingstoke, 2001), 119–38.

[25] The anthropological dimension of much polemic has also been pointed out by, for example, Alan Macfarlane, 'A Tudor Anthropologist: George Gifford's *Discourse* and *Dialogue*', in Sydney Anglo (ed.), *The Damned Art: Essays in the Literature of Witchcraft* (London, 1977); Georg Modestin, 'Le gentleman, la sorcière et le diable: Reginald Scot, un anthropologue social avant la lettre?', *Médiévales*, 44 (2003), 141–53.

II

The second strand of intellectual activity that may be identified as one of the progenitors of the modern discipline of folklore is antiquarianism, though it is often impossible to disentangle this from the sphere of religious complaint and controversy completely. In the course of the sixteenth and seventeenth centuries, the pursuit of 'antiquities' became a consuming passion not merely of scholars but of the leisured and educated gentry at large. From the beginning, the antiquarian drive to unearth and recover such 'trophies of time' involved both sedentary library research and active work in the field, and extended from written texts and physical artefacts to the living relics of memory, recollection, received wisdom, and local legend. It also converged with an emerging Baconian-inspired programme of empirical observation and classification of natural phenomena, which, after the Restoration, found expression in the energetic investigations of members of the Royal Society.[26]

Learned practitioners in these overlapping fields found themselves encountering beliefs and practices which they could not help but label 'vulgar errors' and 'heathenish' and 'popish superstitions'. As Daniel Woolf has noted, many Protestant antiquaries experienced a tension between their scholarly determination to rescue historical remnants from disintegration and their pious conviction that these were the residues of false and idolatrous religions which deserved to be utterly obliterated.[27] They were torn between intellectual instincts that taught them that they could afford to discard no surviving trace of the British past and religious prejudices which persuaded them that the decay or destruction of these vestiges of ignorance and ungodliness by the hand of divine providence, working in concert with Protestant reformers and iconoclasts, should be a cause for joyful celebration. Some were not prepared to take the risk of perpetuating such foolish traditions by fixing them in print. Thus, in the preface to his *Collection of English Proverbs* (1670), John Ray declared that 'All superstitious and groundless Observations of Augury, days, hours and the like, I have purposely omitted, because I wish that they were quite erased out of peoples memories, and should be loath to be any way instrumental in transmitting them to posterity'.[28]

Others, by contrast, seem to have thought that publishing accounts of Catholic customs and 'ethnic' assumptions was the best method of exploding these silly superstitions. William Lambarde, for instance, devoted much space in his *Perambulation of Kent* (1576) to exposing the 'unwritten vanities' about

---

[26] See Daniel Woolf, *The Social Circulation of the Past: English Historical Consciousness 1500–1730* (Oxford, 2003), esp. ch. 5.

[27] Ibid., 187.

[28] John Ray, *A Collection of English Proverbs* (Cambridge, 1670), sig. A3r–v.

relics and saints such as Thomas Becket that had been fabricated by 'popishe parasites' and 'monkishe counselors' to delude the gullible medieval laity. The story of a green swathe of grass that marked the path allegedly taken by an apparition of Our Lady at Chetham (once 'faithfully credited of the vulgar sort' and still remembered by older folk) was one such 'popish illusion' which he recounted in full, insisting that this was 'profitable to the keeping under of fained and superstitious religion, to renew to minde, the Priestly practises of olde time'. The alternative explanation perpetuated by 'olde wives, and super-stitious people' that this was one of 'the dauncing places of night Spirites, whiche they call Fayries' deserved no less disdain.[29] Together with the crum-bling ruins of Kentish monasteries, such opinions prompted him 'highly to prayse God, that hath thus mercifully in our age delivered us' from the seduction of Satan and his Antichristian accomplices.[30] Nor did he pass up opportunities to draw damning comparisons between popery and paganism. A miracle associated with St Augustine was 'a Canterbury tale . . . forged A rabula Romano', evocative of a story about the god Apollo; wonders re-ported of St Eanswide were likened to stories told about Saturn, Hercules, Romulus and other deities; and offerings and gifts left for St Edith at Kemsing inspired no less animated reflections on the similarity between pagan sacri-fices and Catholic ceremonies, together with other nonsense piled up 'in ye whole heape and dunghill of theire filthie and superstitious Idolatries'.[31]

In a similar vein, in his Survey of Cornwall (1602) Richard Carew displayed a robust Protestant contempt for the therapeutic and divinatory rituals con-nected with former holy wells he recorded in ethnographic detail, comment-ing that 'in our forefathers' days, devotion as much exceeded knowledge, as knowledge now cometh short of devotion'. He also briskly dismissed 'the prejudice of over-credulous people' who supposed a dragon lurked in Halgavor Moor near Bodmin.[32] William Camden was no less critical of the 'abundance of superstitious customs' practised by the Irish he documented in his great work Britannia, from bowing to the new moon to hanging crooked horseshoe nails around the necks of sick children, declaring these a testament to the 'rudeness' and 'barbarousness' of the Gaelic people.[33] Anti-popery and

---

[29] William Lambarde, A Perambulation of Kent (London, 1576), 135, 80, and 286–8.

[30] Ibid., 236.

[31] Ibid., 247–8, 137, 373.

[32] Richard Carew, The Survey of Cornwall (London, 1602), fos. 122v–123r, 126v.

[33] Camden's Britannia, ed. Edmund Gibson (London, 1695; first publ. in Latin 1586; trans. 1610.), 1041–6. The section on Irish manners and customs was derived from a manu-script account by the English Jesuit William Good, who ran a school in Limerick and was a celebrated preacher in Youghal. See Oxford Dictionary of National Biography.

racial distaste also intermix in Barnaby Rich's *New Description of Ireland* (1610), in which the 'superstitious conceits' of the native populace concerning sacred springs are explicitly recorded 'to make manifest the light beleefe of obstinate Papistes, that . . . are [more] ready to give credit to ydle lies and fantasies, then they are to beleeve the testimony of the word of God'.[34] According to Richard Gough, writing at the end of the century, the 'idle' legend that Divlin Wood near the Shropshire village of Myddle had been so called because it was 'haunted by some airyall spiritts' had also been contrived by 'superstitious monkes and fryers': 'Butt truth and knowledge have, in these dayes, dispersed such clouds of ignorance and error'.[35] Many such writers clearly experienced difficulty in suppressing the latent polemicist and preacher within them.

In other cases, though, antiquarian enquiry into discredited traditions was less an excuse for outbursts of anti-Catholic fury against popish and pagan 'superstition' than a reaction to it. Margaret Aston has argued that the visible scars left by the Protestant assault upon idolatrous churches and monasteries were a major fillip to historical nostalgia about the medieval past.[36] It may be suggested that the same sense of loss extended to other less tangible relics of pre-Reformation belief and practice that had been the victims of repeated spasms of godly zeal. As in the case of John Stow, whose *Survey of London* (1598) is suffused by sadness and regret at the passing of old urban customs and pious assumptions, this sense of loss could have its roots in crypto-Catholicism or religious conservatism.[37] In other instances, it springs rather from Laudian and Anglican resentment of the extremes to which a puritan minority had carried their all-encompassing crusade against lingering traces of Romanism and heathenism. In these antiquarian works, a healthy Protestant contempt for such 'monkery' is counterbalanced by a distinct tone of lament. The balance between curiosity and censure tips towards the former.

This combination of sentiments finds particularly striking expression in the work of John Aubrey, whose *Remaines of Gentilisme and Judaisme*, compiled between 1686 and 1689, was an extended exploration of the links between pagan and Christian superstition. This eclectic and chaotic

---

[34] Barnaby Rich, *A New Description of Ireland* (London, 1610), 55–7.

[35] Richard Gough, *The History of Myddle*, ed. David Hey (Harmondsworth, 1981), 69.

[36] Margaret Aston, 'English Ruins and English History: The Dissolution and the Sense of the Past', *Journal of the Warburg and Courtauld Institutes*, 36 (1973).

[37] John Stow, *A Survey of London* (London, 1598) and see Patrick Collinson, 'John Stow and Nostalgic Antiquarianism', in J. F. Merritt (ed.), *Imagining Early Modern London: Perceptions and Portrayals of the City from Stow to Strype, 1598–1720* (Cambridge, 2001).

collection containing material on festivals, rites of passage, garlands, groves, fountains, omens, portents, and magical recipes and charms was the fruit of research in classical authors, from Virgil and Homer to Ovid and Pliny, designed to uncover the origins of rites and beliefs he had found lingering in his native county of Wiltshire.[38] Here and elsewhere Aubrey could employ the familiar rhetoric of anti-Catholic controversy: 'fabulous stories' about sprites and ghosts walking the night were 'derived downe from mother to Daughter &c: from the Monkish Ballance, which upheld Holy church'. He could also echo the first-century Roman writer Quintus Curtius's claim that '*Nulla res efficacius multitudinem regit quam superstitio*' ('Nothing rules the mob more efficiently than superstition').[39]

But Aubrey's commonplace conviction that many features of heathenism had been expediently adapted by the Catholic priesthood did not prevent him from simultaneously deploring their disappearance against the backdrop of changes in technology, the growth of literacy, and above all the ravages of the Civil Wars of the 1640s and '50s. He bewailed the damage done by 'barbarous soldiers' to local landmarks like the famous flowering thorn of Glastonbury and the demise of traditional rituals due to 'the fanatique rage of the late times'.[40] There was perhaps more regret than relief in his observation that the military conflicts of the period had put the practice of watching in the church porch on Midsummer Eve for visions of those who would die in the course of the following year 'quite out of fashion'. 'Warres not only extinguish Religion and Lawes', he commented, 'but Superstition: and no suffimen is a greater fugator of Phantosmes, than Gun-powder'.[41] The same mixed feelings underpinned his famous statement that books and letters had expelled 'the old Fables out of dores: and the divine art of Printing and Gunpowder have frighted away Robin-good-fellow and the Fayries'.[42] His condescending rejection of 'old-wives-tales' and 'childish customs' of the country people coexists with a conviction that out of these 'grosse things' something of use might be elicited, a suspicion that 'some sparke of Trueth might be pick't out in this Mist'. From '*Fabulae Aniles*', he wrote, one might gauge 'the measure

---

[38] John Aubrey, *Remaines of Gentilisme and Judaisme*, in *Three Prose Works*, ed. John Buchanan-Brown (Fontwell, Sussex, 1972). The *Remaines* was not published until the nineteenth century.

[39] See Aubrey, *Remaines*, in Buchanan Brown (ed.), *Three Prose Works*, 289; Bodleian Library, Oxford, Aubrey MS 3, fo. 81v; and Michael Hunter, *John Aubrey and the Realm of Learning* (London, 1975), 220, 209–10.

[40] Hunter, *John Aubrey*, 166.

[41] Aubrey, *Remaines*, in Buchanan Brown (ed.), *Three Prose Works*, 207.

[42] Ibid., 290.

of those daies'.[43] He knew that there were those who would 'nauseate these old Fables', but he defended them as 'most considerable pieces of Antiquity' that should 'be registered for posterity, to let them understand the Encroachment of Ignorance on Mankind: and to learne, what strange Absurdities Man can by Custome & education be brought to believe'.[44]

Contempt and curiosity also compete for dominance in Sir Thomas Browne's celebrated *Pseudodoxia Epidemica* (1646), which lovingly catalogued 'commonly presumed truths' about salamanders, ostriches, mandrakes, unicorns, together with popular customs and taboos such as saluting after a sneeze, throwing spilt salt over one's shoulder, and making difficult decisions with the aid of a staff and a book. Browne traced the source of these credulous opinions and practices to 'the Priests of Elder Time, [who] have put upon [the people] many incredible conceites' and the machinations of that 'invisible Agent' and 'first contriver of Error', Satan. Yet even as he underlined the 'Egyptian genealogy' of these vulgar relics of 'ancient superstition', he could not help but betray his fascination with them. His book reflects and fosters 'a qualified despondency because fabulous yet enchanting beliefs must be sacrificed on the altar of demanding truth'.[45]

In the writings of Browne and Aubrey, the word 'superstition' is used more neutrally than in the works of rabid Protestant reformers. More intrigued than outraged by the parallels they observe between Christianity and paganism, they do not seem to regard the traditions assaulted by the moralists and iconoclasts as inherently tainted by their roots in the dark and distant heathen and Catholic past. 'Superstition' is not a quality intrinsic to rites bequeathed from antiquity; it is something they degenerate into and which is also detachable from and parasitic upon them. Old-fashioned practices can be 'mere customs' and innocent whims: in technical terms, they can be things indifferent, matters on which Scripture is silent and neutral. The same fine theological distinction underpinned the sixteenth- and seventeenth-century literature that sought to defend ceremonies and pastimes against the puritan drive to purge them from the Church and society. It was implicit in the apologetic works John Whitgift, Richard Hooker, and Laudian divines wrote to vindicate controversial aspects of the Elizabethan liturgy against allegations that it contained too many remnants of 'Antichristian superstition'. It was

---

[43] Ibid., 132; Hunter, *John Aubrey*, 185, 155.

[44] Hunter, *John Aubrey*, 167–8.

[45] Thomas Browne, *Pseudodoxia Epidemica: Or, Enquiries into very many Received Tenets, and Commonly Presumed Truths* (London, 1646), 11, 37. C. A. Patrides, ' "Above Atlas his Shoulders": An Introduction to Sir Thomas Browne', in idem (ed.), *Sir Thomas Browne: The Major Works* (Harmondsworth, 1977), 37.

also a critical element in the debates about May-games, church ales, and other recreations that followed the two proclamations of the Books of Sports in 1617 and 1633. These, insisted those who defended royal policy, were not essentially or necessarily 'superstitious' and sinful and they could be lawfully employed as an instrument of ecclesiastical and civil order in a Christian commonwealth.[46] The Royalist divine Thomas Warmstry put the case clearly in a tract of 1648 defending Christmas festivities such as the singing of carols and the burning of Yule logs against the argument that they were pagan abominations: 'New Yeare's Gifts, if performed without superstition . . . may be harmles provocations to Christian love, and mutuall testimonies thereof to good purpose, and never the worse because the Heathens have them at the like times'. It mattered not that Christmas

> doth comply with the time of the Heathens *Saturnalia*, This leaves no charge of impiety upon it; for since things are best cured by their contraries, it was both wisdome and piety in the ancient Christians (whose work it was to convert the Heathens from such as well as other superstitions and miscarriages) to vindicate such times from the service of the Devill, by appoynting them to the more solemne and especiall service of God.[47]

Castigating the loose and inclusive puritan use of the term to calumniate all those things of which they disapproved, some writers turned the tables and accused the godly of being no less superstitious than the papists themselves. Aubrey thought the 'Genevists' 'as superstitious as the Romans'[48] and,

---

[46] For the background, see Leah S. Marcus, *The Politics of Mirth: Jonson, Herrick, Milton, Marvell and the Defense of the Old Holiday Pastimes* (Chicago, 1986), ch. 1; Hutton, *Rise and Fall of Merry England*, ch. 5. See Richard Hooker, *Of the Lawes of Ecclesiastical Politie* (London, 1594–7), V. 1–4 (1–10). A similar distinction between harmless and unacceptable survivals was drawn on the other side of the confessional divide by Diego Duran, a Dominican missionary in late sixteenth-century Mexico: Ronald Hutton, *The Stations of the Sun: A History of the Ritual Year in Britain* (Oxford, 1996), 418. Philippe Buc also traces the relocation of the religious ceremonies and rituals moderate Protestants (Lutherans and Anglicans) were prepared to defend and retain into the domain of the political in his *The Dangers of Ritual: Between Medieval Texts and Social Scientific Theory* (Princeton, 2001), ch. 5, esp. 164–76.

[47] Thomas Warmstry, *The Vindication of the Solemnity of Christ* (London, 1648), 24.

[48] Hunter, *John Aubrey*, 56. This trope also had longstanding roots in 'Anglican' polemic: see, for instance, Hooker, *Lawes of Ecclesiastical Politie*, V. 3, 7–9 ('Superstition is, when things are either abhord or observed, with a zealous or fearefull, but erroneous relation to God') and Samuel Harsnett, *A Discovery of the Fraudulent Practises of John Darrel* (London, 1599) and *A Declaration of Egregious Popish Impostures* (London, 1604).

echoing Francis Bacon's famous dictum that 'There is a superstition in avoiding superstition',[49] in a tract of 1645 Henry Hammond, chaplain to Charles I, declared that it was 'as . . . Superstitious to place piety in the Negative, as the affirmative'.[50]

If the Protestant campaign to remove all traces of popery and paganism promoted the recording of 'superstition' in early modern Britain, then it also fostered a determination to preserve and defend beliefs and practices that were the target of attack, helping in the process to relativize and destabilize this capacious category yet further.

III

The boundary between antiquarianism and polemic, curiosity and censure, thus remained both permeable and blurred throughout the sixteenth and seventeenth centuries. Nor is it any easier to draw in a work that is always regarded as one of the most notable forerunners of the modern discipline of folklore, the Newcastle clergyman Henry Bourne's *Antiquitates Vulgares: or the Antiquities of the Common People* (1725). Written by an author who fused the roles of reformer and antiquarian recorder, it is at once a denunciation and a defence of tradition and custom, at once a successor to the literature of evangelical complaint and a form of Anglican apologetic. Bourne's stated objective was to distinguish between those opinions and practices that should be quashed because they were sinful and wicked and those which could be retained as benign and even advantageous once they had been restored to their 'primitive Purity'. He sought to chart a path between necessary amendment and the excessive zeal and 'too great Reformation' of nonconformists who were contemptuous of antiquity and regarded it as religious 'to have no Ceremonies at all'. The ambiguity at the heart of Bourne's project is neatly summed up in his address to the reader: 'I would not be thought a Reviver of old Rites and Ceremonies to the Burdening of the People, nor an Abolisher of Innocent Customs, which are their Pleasures and Recreations.'[51]

[49] Francis Bacon, *The Essays or Counsels, Civill and Morall* (London, 1906), 53.

[50] [Henry Hammond], *Of Superstition* (Oxford, 1645), 12.

[51] Henry Bourne, *Antiquitates Vulgares: or, the Antiquities of the Common People. Giving an Account of Several of their Opinions and Ceremonies. With Proper Reflections upon each of them; Shewing which may be Retain'd, and which Ought to be Laid Aside* (Newcastle, 1725), pp. ix–xii, 5–6. On Bourne, see also Dorson, *British Folklorists*, 10–13; Rosemary Sweet, *Antiquaries: The Discovery of the Past in Eighteenth-Century Britain* (London, 2004), 335. Compare my argument here with Ronald Hutton's suggestion that Bourne 'stands at once at the end of the line of evangelical clergyman who complained of popular pastimes

Bourne shared the orthodox Protestant view that popular beliefs were 'generally either the produce of Heathenism; or the Inventions of indolent Monks, who having nothing else to do, were the Forgers of many silly and wicked Opinions, to keep the World in Awe and Ignorance'. He cited the tale of St Dunstan taking the devil by the nose with a pair of tongs as an example of the follies with which their brains were filled.[52] He endorsed the widespread suggestion that the 'legendary stories of nurses and old Women' were the cause of many unnecessary fears. Prognosticating the future by crowing cocks, chattering magpies and deathwatch beetles made men 'the Slaves of Supersition and Sin' and the vassals of Satan.[53] Foretelling the weather by observing its complexion on St Paul's and St Swithin's Days was equally pernicious, irrational and 'ridiculous', another 'Monkish Dream' 'copy'd after the Heathens'.[54] Deducing 'the Original of this Timorousness' from pagan antiquity, he also scorned the vulgar presupposition that churchyards were swarming with apparitions and thanked God that now 'we live not in the Darkness, but in the Light of Truth'.[55]

Yet Bourne's contempt for the blindness that had prevailed during the 'benighted Ages of Popery'[56] did not preclude recognition of the utility and even virtue of some customs and rituals inherited from the Catholic and pre-Christian past. He could not approve of any practice that was accompanied by 'orgy', 'debauchery', 'intemperance', 'rioting and gorging', 'chambering and wantonness', or any other kind of moral lewdness, but he thought many festive rites could be accepted as 'comely', 'decent', 'laudable' and 'harmless'—including accompanying corpses to their graves, adorning churches with garlands, decorating the windows of private houses with laurel branches at Christmas, rising early on Easter morning, tolling the soul-bell, and watching with the dead. 'Now intirely stript of any Superstition', carrying palm crosses on Palm Sunday was simply an innocent 'Emblem of the Season', as was the kindling of fires on Midsummer Eve as 'Tokens of Joy'.[57] Even though it was an unmistakable remnant of the heathen worship of water and springs, the custom of visiting former holy wells on a summer's evening 'to drink the Water of the Fountain, and enjoy the pleasing Prospect of Shade and Stream'

---

and near the beginning of the succession of scholarly observers who systematically recorded them and gave birth to the discipline of folklore': *Stations of the Sun*, 418.

[52] Ibid., p. xi, 85–6,

[53] Ibid., 41, 74–5 and ch. 9 *passim*.

[54] Ibid., 161, 163 and ch. 18 *passim*.

[55] Ibid., 59–64.

[56] Ibid., 84.

[57] Ibid., 186 and ch. 22 *passim*; 215 and ch. 27 *passim*.

was 'at this Time of Day, very commendable', shorn of its former connotations.[58] May-Day revels did not need to be laid aside because they were a
'Relick' of paganism, but rather because too many were still under the impression that the observation of such ceremonies was 'a Procurer of the Success of
the Fruits of the Earth', which was 'intirely a Piece of Superstition'.[59]

Distinguishing carefully between practices that had been cleansed of their
'superstitious' overtones and those which retained them, Bourne's *Antiquitates Vulgares* was simultaneously a measured defence of many aspects of the
legacy medieval Catholicism had left to the Church of England and a diatribe
against the lingering residues of popery and heathenism that remained
among the rural people nearly two hundred years after the onset of the Reformation. It reflects the continuing interweaving of polemic and anthropological description.

If we look ahead to the later years of the eighteenth century to those who
followed Bourne in compiling collections of popular antiquities, we find
many similarities but also some striking differences. In 1777 another
Newcastle minister John Brand published his *Observations on the Popular
Antiquities*, a haphazardly updated and expanded version of Bourne's
book, throughout which runs a vein of virulent anti-popery that is at times
sharper in tone than that of his predecessor. Brand vigorously restated
Bourne's thesis about the Catholic and pagan origins of the beliefs and practices he catalogued, accusing the popish priesthood of creating 'a profusion
of childish Rites, Pageants and Ceremonies' to divert the people from consideration of their dismal state of thraldom and keep 'them in love with their
slavish Modes of Worship'.[60] Exorcisms inspired an outburst of rhetorical
violence against 'Impious and antichristian Rome' for prejudicing 'the Cause
of manly and rational Religion', while the legend explaining the white spots
that mark the leaves of Lady's Thistle as drops of the Virgin's blood was
'an ingenious little invention of the dark ages, . . . which no doubt has been
of service to the cause of superstition'.[61] Speculating about how such silly tales
had survived the Reformation, he cemented the link between 'superstition'

---

[58] Ibid., 66 and ch. 8 *passim*.

[59] Ibid., 202.

[60] Brand, *Observations*, p. viii. Brand continued to augment the book with the intention of
publishing a second edition; this appeared, revised and organized by Sir Henry Ellis, as
*Observations on the Popular Anquities of Great Britain: Chiefly Illustrating the Origins of
our Vulgar and Provincial Customs, Ceremonies and Superstitions*, 2 vols. (London, 1813).
A further expanded edition appeared in 3 vols. in 1890. For Brand, see Dorson, *British
Folklorists*, 13–24; Sweet, *Antiquaries*, 335–8.

[61] Brand, *Observations* (1777 edn), 144, 409.

and verbal diffusion, arguing that 'though Erazed by public Authority from the written Word', they were 'committed as a venerable Deposit to the keeping of oral Tradition ... after having been snatched from the smoking Ruins of Popery'.[62]

Even so it is probably fair to say that Brand seems to have been less exercised by the superstitions he recorded than absorbed by them. His intellectual interest in extracting historical wisdom from these 'antiquities' 'by the chemical Process of Philosophy' eclipsed the reformist and didactic agenda that had marked the work of his precursor.[63] Designed to tap the growing fascination of the polite reading public with the manners and customs of their rural social inferiors, his book was above all a commercial concern. In what was meant to be an entertaining and informative anthology of British beliefs and customs that were gradually sliding into extinction, there was now no place for Bourne's stern moral reflections, 'serious Animadversions of this Sort' being 'by no Means pleasing to the refined Taste of our Age'.[64]

Two further important changes which had taken place between Bourne and Brand merit our attention. The first is that the latter book perhaps exhibits a greater sense of alienation from the culture of the common people than had previously been the case. Earlier collections were tacitly patronizing to the lower orders, but Brand's *Observations* seems to reflect a underlying fear about the anarchic potential of the labouring classes, a sentiment probably sharpened by the revolutionary turmoil that engulfed France in the 1790s. Defending innocent customs and pastimes against the cavils of 'the morose and bigoted Part of Mankind' (that is, nonconformists and puritans), he declared that it was 'of the highest political Utility' to encourage them, as well as a valuable antidote to the corrupting effects of luxury and dissipation.[65] 'Superstition', it may be suggested, was acquiring a more pronounced sociological dimension than it had manifested in the sixteenth and seventeenth centuries.[66]

Secondly, we find a fundamental redefinition of what fell inside this category. In the interval between 1725 and 1777 the label 'superstition' has been extended to a range of beliefs that had hitherto been part of the orthodox

[62] Ibid., p. iv.
[63] Ibid., p. ix.
[64] Ibid., 19.
[65] Ibid., pp. v–vi. See also the comments of Sweet, *Antiquaries*, 338–9.
[66] See Burke, *Popular Culture*, esp. 281–6; D. R. Woolf, 'The "Common Voice": History, Folklore and Oral Tradition in Early Modern England', *Past and Present*, cxx (1988), esp. 47; idem, *Social Circulation of the Past*, ch. 10. though both, I think, see this split occurring at an earlier date, about mid-way through the seventeenth century.

Protestant mainstream, namely those associated with witchcraft and the supernatural. Henry Bourne could not deny that evil apparitions sometimes troubled men and that 'Midnight Spirits' did indeed wander the earth. He was in no doubt that angels guided human beings through 'the Mazes of the Wilderness of Life' and could not quite bring himself to reject the notion that each person had a particular celestial guardian.[67] After all such things were amply attested in the pages of Scripture. But by the time that Brand was writing a sea change in learned opinion had occurred that had pushed many such phenomena beyond the pale. Scientific developments, the rising tide of 'rational religion', and Enlightenment philosophy were eroding the idea that God and the devil intervened arbitrarily and unpredictably in human affairs, with the consequence that certain assumptions about the operations of the occult increasingly lost credibility. This occurred on both sides of the Reformation divide and it entailed a silent revolution in the concept of superstition itself. Whereas demonology had once been a revered and sophisticated branch of natural philosophy, in the terms of the time it now became an irrational ideology. Witchcraft was no longer believed to have either reality or efficacy and the whole notion of people being able to make a pact with the devil was dismissed as a grotesque and fatuous myth. Stories of providential judgement, prodigies and ghostly visions that had once fostered sober reflection at every social level were overtly rejected as no less ignorant and ridiculous. In the process, as Peter Burke and Stuart Clark have remarked, 'superstition' began to acquire its modern sense of misplaced assumptions about the causality of events rooted in an erroneous understanding of the workings of nature. It ceased to mean a false or idolatrous religion and became more exclusively a synonym for foolish and senseless fears, though this conception of superstition can also be found in classical culture. As a result it largely shed the soul-destroying connotations it had carried for the root-and-branch Protestant reformers of an earlier era. Discarding its original theological frame of reference in favour of a secular one, superstition began to be defined in binary opposition not to religion but rather to science. At least in relation to witchcraft, Clark reminds us, this was more a change of degree than of kind: some beliefs that fell under this heading had long been condemned as 'superstitious', but the language of rejection established by medieval and early modern scholars and divines was now applied to demonology in its entirety. Moreover, these Catholic and Protestant churchmen were dismissed as superstitious themselves.[68]

---

[67] Bourne, *Antiquitates Vulgares*, 39, 47, 77, 220–1.

[68] Clark, *Thinking with Demons*, 485–7 and Peter Burke, *Popular Culture in Early Modern Europe* (Aldershot, 1978), 241–2; idem, *The Historical Anthropology of Early Modern*

A further symptom of these shifts is the fact that some of the seventeenth-century antiquaries and intellectuals who had pioneered the recording of custom, tradition and 'superstition' also came to seem 'exceedingly credulous' to later commentators. John Aubrey may have disparaged 'old wives tales' in his *Remaines of Gentilisme and Judaisme*, but his attitude towards the preter- and supernatural was in keeping with the dominant providentialism of his age, which itself was a central thread in and incentive to scientific investigation. Thus his 'Natural History of Wiltshire' had included sections on witchcraft, apparitions, dreams, omens, second sight, and converse with angels and spirits, material he later removed and inserted in his *Miscellanies* (1696), a text he tellingly described as 'A collection of Hermetic Philosophy'. Reflecting his serious interest in astrology and cabbalistic and sympathetic magic, this book incorporated recipes and charms for divining future marriage partners and curing disease which Aubrey copied out not so much as curiosities but with an open mind to the possibility that they might actually work in practice. He reproduced the triangular pentacle 'Abracadabra' in full, noting that 'With this Spell, one of Wells hath cured above an Hundred of the Ague'.[69] Although he exercised discrimination and rejected many examples passed on to him as impostures, it is important to stress that these were not topics that Aubrey necessarily regarded as signs of 'vulgar error'. Rather such phenomena were evidence of the existence of an invisible spirit world, which learned adepts might hope to access and even manipulate to reach a state of mystical transcendence over nature. It is a measure of how far the goalposts had moved by the later eighteenth century that the *Miscellanies* (1696) ironically became a source from which collectors extracted past superstitions and/or was mistakenly heralded as a forerunner in the task of exposing irrational suppositions.[70] At the same time the views of radical sceptical writers like

---

Italy: Essays on Perception and Communication (Cambridge, 1987), 218. See also William Monter, *Ritual, Myth and Magic in Early Modern Europe* (Brighton, 1983), ch. 7. It is interesting to note that in classical culture too, the charge of superstition had not been connected with any rejection of the supernatural: Dale B. Martin, *Inventing Superstition: From the Hippocratics to the Christians* (Cambridge, MA, 2004).

[69] John Aubrey, *Miscellanies* (London, 1696), at 141. See Hunter, *John Aubrey*, 58, 102–6, 121–47, and 212 for imputations that he was 'superstitious' and 'credulous'.

[70] For mistaken identification of the *Miscellanies* as a forerunner of 'folk-lore', see Dorson, *British Folklorists*, 25–6; Bob Bushaway, *By Rite: Custom, Ceremony and Community in England 1700–1880* (London, 1982), 280. On Aubrey's changing reputation, see Michael Hunter, 'Magic, Science and Reputation: Robert Boyle, the Royal Society and the Occult in the late Seventeenth Century', in his *Robert Boyle, 1627–91: Scrupulosity and Science* (Woodbridge, 2000), 223–44, at 234–6.

Reginald Scot, which had been out of step with the assumptions of their contemporaries, were now coming to be relabelled 'enlightened'.

Recent work by Jonathan Barry, Owen Davies and others has qualified earlier claims about the sweeping change in elite attitudes towards witchcraft, magic and related phenomena that took place in this period, offering a picture of more subtle alteration. Such things may have retreated from the sphere of public discourse but there is much to suggest that they remained a subject of private study, debate, and speculation by educated gentlemen. For many they were useful ammunition against the arguments of atheists that God did not exist, not least John Wesley and the Methodists, who at least initially nourished such beliefs by publishing examples of divine and demonic intervention in the *Arminian Magazine*. The rise of semi-respectable forms of occultism such as phrenology and mesmerism in refined circles also suggests that the intellectual revolution that expelled the supernatural out of the mainstream and onto the sidelines was neither uncontested nor universal.[71]

Nevertheless the works of Brand and other antiquaries of the late eighteenth and nineteenth centuries do seem to reflect the migration in the meaning of 'superstition' and the reconstitution of the category described above. In such texts belief in preternatural phenomena is now identified as a gross residue of credulity and ignorance, along with the assorted rituals and traditions criticized by Bourne and his predecessors. A selective nostalgia about the eclipse of fascinating remnants of a romantic past coexists with satisfaction that the barbarity begotten by 'irrational' assumptions has now been set aside. For Brand the whole fantasy of witchcraft, through the influence of which 'great Numbers of innocent Persons, distressed with Poverty and Age, were brought to violent and unseemly ends' was 'a disgrace of Humanity', as was the delay in repealing the laws permitting this in England until 1736. The views of James I, as embodied in his *Daemonologie* (1597), were now 'narrow and bigotted', while the royal practice of touching for the King's Evil (widely practised by the Stuart monarchs) evinced 'that no order of Men escaped the antient contagion of Superstition'. For Brand, in short, the early modern period was itself a time of 'Egyptian Darknes'.[72] Francis Grose's *Provincial Glossary; with a Collection of Local Proverbs, and Popular*

---

[71] Owen Davies, *Witchcraft, Magic and Culture 1736–1951* (Manchester, 1999), 7–39, 75–8 and *passim*; Owen Davies and Willem de Blécourt (eds), *Beyond the Witch Trials: Witchcraft and Magic in Enlightenment Europe* (Manchester, 2004), esp. Jonathan Barry, 'Public Infidelity and Private Belief? The Discourse of Spirits in Enlightenment Bristol, 1640–1714'. See also Ian Bostridge, *Witchcraft and its Transformations c.1650–c.1750* (Oxford, 1997).

[72] Brand, *Observations* (1777 edn), 318–19; (1890 edn), iii. 302.

Superstitions of 1787 similarly reflected on the 'terrible', 'inconvenient' and 'horrid consequences' of belief in ghosts and witches. 'No one', he wrote, could read of the hundreds 'who fell victims to this ridiculous opinion' 'without a mixture of shame, remorse and indignation'.[73] Half a century later in 1846, Thomas Wright declared that the execution of so many people for this 'imaginary crime' stood as 'a permanent and substantial testimony to what superstition can do'. Thankfully, these noxious notions had been swept aside within his lifetime by the unlikely alliance of 'schoolmasters and steam engines'.[74] The same sentiments were frequently echoed by the Victorian folklorists, who likewise lamented the long hangover of this superstitious fiction in 'the most Enlightened Christian countries' and saluted those who had done their best to undermine these 'pernicious' opinions and their 'attendant mischiefs'.[75]

What deserves particular emphasis is the manner in which these antiquaries and folklorists were applying a critique of 'superstition' inherited from the early reformers to beliefs and practices which Protestantism itself had actively sustained. They were appropriating anti-Catholic commonplaces that had their roots in the theological polemic of the mid-sixteenth century (and before that in the pronouncements of reform-minded medieval churchmen) and redeploying them to discredit and denounce assumptions about the supernatural which had been reinforced rather than undercut by Protestant theology. The Reformation may have presented itself as a movement that had liberated the laity from 'superstition' and ignorance and expelled the magic from religion, but, as recent research has shown, in neither theory nor practice did it precipitate a seismic shift in attitudes towards the intrusion of God and the devil in the earthly realm.[76] Nor, at least in England, had it broken

---

[73] Francis Grose, *A Provincial Glossary, with a Collection of Local Proverbs, and Popular Superstitions* (London, 1787; 2nd edn, 1790), 2–3.

[74] Thomas Wright, *Essays on Subjects Connected with the Literature, Popular Superstitions, and History of England in the Middle Ages*, 2 vols. (London, 1846), ii. 33–4.

[75] See, for example, William Brockie, *Legends and Superstitions of the County of Durham* (Sunderland, 1886), 1; Harland and Wilkinson, *Lancashire Folk-Lore*, 182–4; John Symonds Udal, *Dorsetshire Folk-Lore* (Hertford, 1922), 203; L'Amy, *Jersey Folk Lore*, 14.

[76] See, among others, R. W. Scribner, 'The Reformation, Popular Magic, and the "Disenchantment of the World"', *Journal of Interdisciplinary History*, xxiii (1993); Alexandra Walsham, *Providence in Early Modern England* (Oxford, 1999) and 'The Reformation and the Disenchantment of the World Reassessed', *Historical Journal*, 51 (2008); P. G. Maxwell-Stuart, 'Rational Superstition: The Writings of Protestant Demonologists', in Parish and Naphy (eds), *Religion and Superstition*; Ulinka Rublack, *Reformation Europe* (Cambridge, 2005), ch. 4.

completely with the ceremonial legacy left by the medieval Church: through a combination of inertia, pragmatism, and caution, at the Elizabethan Settlement many pre-Reformation liturgical practices were retained in a modified form. These were points that some of these writers recognized or alluded to in passing. Assimilating the charge of pragmatic adaptation of pagan ritual laid at the door of the first Christian missionaries, Brand observed with some acuity that 'in the infancy of Protestantism' many traditional ceremonies had been 'connived at by the State'.[77] William Henderson, commenting on the folklore of the north, was also conscious that the Reformation, especially on the Continent and in Scotland, had done little to check 'the old superstition'. He suggested that the curtailing of the cult of saints had only served to fasten men's minds 'the more readily upon a supernatural system of another order'.[78] Charlotte Burne realized that the study of the Bible in post-Reformation times had done as much to keep alive as to extinguish the folklore she had 'gleaned' from Shropshire. For William Brockie, author of *Legends and Superstitions of the County of Durham* (1886) the words of 'a consistent Hyper-Calvinist' lady of his acquaintance were indicative of the persistence of erroneous beliefs in 'civilised' no less than 'savage countries': she had told him flatly 'that if she were forced to give up her belief in the existence of witches, she would consider that one of the sure foundations of her faith was taken away'.[79] Anglicans keen to grind an axe against the Nonconformists were quick to take up the theme of Elizabethan and early Stuart apologists of the Church of England and stress the credulity of the hotter sort of sixteenth- and seventeenth-century Protestants (not to mention contemporary Methodists). 'The Puritans who succeeded the Papists', remarked Thomas Wright, 'were by no means less superstitious than their predecessors—their devils were but a repetition of those of the monks of earlier times.'[80]

The less perceptive silently elided the 'superstitions' to which they saw nineteenth-century Protestants clinging with the residues of popery and paganism. In deploring the 'relics of heathenism' that persisted in their society and articulating their distress that 'the thick shades of superstition which had clouded the world for ages' had not yet been fully 'dispersed by the

---

[77] Brand, *Observations* (1777 edn), p. iv.

[78] Henderson, *Notes*, 6–7.

[79] Charlotte Burne, *Shropshire Folk-Lore: A Sheaf of Gleanings . . . Edited from the Collections of Georgina F. Jackson* (London, 1883), pp. x–xi; Brockie, *Legends and Superstitions*, 1–2. See also MacCulloch, *Guernsey Folk Lore*, author's preface.

[80] Wright, *Essays*, ii. 34.

speeding effulgence of the gospel',[81] they perpetuated the pious Reformation myth that these were survivals from the Catholic and pre-Christian past. The reader who congratulated William Hone, editor of the *Every-Day* and *Table-Book* of customs for exposing 'with a masterly hand the superstitions and monkery of the olden time'[82] may well reflect the elastic expansion of the latter as well as the former term—the expansion of the term 'monkery' to encompass forms of belief and practice that self-respecting Protestants found it hard to admit had been espoused by their own Reformed forbears.

Others, though, had no difficulty in carrying the polemical tropes embedded in early Protestant controversy through to their logical conclusions and using them to unmask Christianity as one vast system of superstition itself. Presaged by early deists and atheists, the Enlightenment critique of 'superstition' as the enemy of reason that found its *locus classicus* in Voltaire's *Philosophical Dictionary* (1764) applied the label to all denominations equally. It saw this as an instrument by which the pillars of 'priestcraft' in general were upheld and (in anticipation of Karl Marx) presented religion as an opium of the people.[83] The figure who best embodied this tendency within the folkore movement in Britain was the outspoken freethinker Edward Clodd, elected president of the Society in 1895. Unhampered by confessional loyalties to any particular creed, Clodd used his first two presidential addresses to extend the attack on heathen and Romanist 'superstition' as a technique of enslavement to cover all forms of Christian dogma. The higher mission of the folklorist, as he saw it, was 'to contribute to the freedom of the spirit, to deliver those who, being children of superstition, are therefore the prisoners of fear'. A few thought his second lecture 'a landmark in the intellectual emancipation of our time', but for the committed Christian majority this radical extension of Protestantism's original crusade against false and idolatrous religion to religion per se could not be countenanced.[84]

IV

The impulse to record 'superstition' in early modern Britain, then, sprang from two complex roots, which were themselves composed of several tangled

---

[81] Quotation from William Vowles, vicar of Tiverton in 1814, in Davies, *Witchcraft, Magic and Culture*, 48.

[82] Quoted in Dorson, *British Folklorists*, 39.

[83] See Monter, *Ritual, Myth and Magic*, ch. 7 and 125–6.

[84] Dorson, *British Folklorists*, 248–57. Following Clodd's address, William Gladstone, former Prime Minister, felt himself duty-bound to resign his membership of the Folk-Lore Society.

and intertwined threads: religious polemic and antiquarianism. Before closing it is important to draw attention to two ironies that have emerged in the course of the foregoing analysis. These reflect the extent to which the assumptions that have pervaded the literature under discussion have continued to shape and distort historical understanding of the long term cultural repercussions of the Protestant Reformation.

The first is the critical role that Protestant controversialists, antiquarians, and folklorists played in preserving for posterity beliefs and practices of which they overtly or implicitly disapproved. No less curious is the fact that they did this through the very media that the theological rhetoric of the sixteenth and seventeenth centuries, reinforced by Enlightenment discourse, had exalted as vehicles of liberation and enlightenment from ignorance and error: writing and print. Setting Scripture in opposition to 'unwritten tradition', Reformed writers and later philosophers had tended to envisage the book as a natural extinguisher of 'popish' and 'ethnic superstition' and literacy as the antithesis and nemesis of the 'old wives tales', 'vulgar errors', and 'nursery fables' which had floated down from generation to generation by word of mouth. And yet in recording the proverbs, customs, stories, legends and misguided assumptions they encountered in the course of their pastoral and scholarly endeavours, the collectors analysed here may have simultaneously helped to nurture, prolong and reanimate them. Some, like John Ray, were keenly aware of this dilemma and danger, but most failed to recognize the paradox buried at the heart of their enterprise. The graphic and extravagant detail in which they described popular festive rituals kept the memory of such traditions alive at a time when they were declining and provided an important source for those who later sought to reinvent them.[85] The matter-of-fact style in which they reported 'superstitious' spells and magical charms could also be oddly counterproductive, serving inadvertently to disseminate the very lore they were supposed to defuse. Plundered for information by readers eager to gain divinatory knowledge, such texts had the potential to become self-help manuals. In this way, to echo the words of an astute Norfolk gentleman in a letter written in 1857, such works may have helped to 'manure the weed they would eradicate'.[86] The fears of these elites may have been exaggerated, but it would be wrong to dismiss them as completely unfounded: feedback is a cultural force of more than minor significance.

[85] Eric Hobsbawm and Terence Ranger (eds), *The Invention of Tradition* (Cambridge, 1983) and Bushaway, *By Rite*, ch. 7.

[86] Davies, *Witchcraft, Magic and Culture*, 166 and see 159–66 *passim*. See also Sabine Doering-Manteuffel, 'The supernatural and the development of print culture', in Davies and Blécourt (eds), *Beyond the Witchtrials*.

Adding a further twist to this intriguing process, the remnants of popery and paganism that filled the pages of antiquarian and folklore collections were themselves the hybrid products of centuries of cross-fertilisation between oral and literate culture. Some of the hagiographical tales of local saints that remained in circulation had indeed originally been monastic forgeries and fabrications, while printed pamphlets and ballads about supernatural happenings of the Tudor and Stuart period likewise helped to replenish and reinvigorate the vernacular repertoire.[87] In turn the learned legends, stories, and sayings that had successfully been absorbed into the realm of speech were gathered by later collectors and conserved once more in textual form, to be pillaged by subsequent writers who incorporated them into their own anthologies. Those folklorists, like the Scottish minister John Gregorson Campbell, who later turned completely against literary authorities and derived their information solely from oral sources, were working on the fundamentally mistaken assumption that verbal transmission was a guarantee of the authenticity of the traditions that were the objects of their scrutiny.[88] Far from pure and undiluted, these had been permanently tainted and contaminated by contact with letters and books. And, despite the extraordinary and scrupulous care the folklorists took in recording popular beliefs and customs, their own efforts to preserve such 'superstitions' in writing and print inevitably and irreversibly transformed and corrupted them once more.[89]

The second point concerns the incidental insight folklore collections yield into the impact of the Reformation—a movement which Protestant propagandists and historians likewise celebrated as an agent of what Max Weber (in more than a faint echo of this confessional trope) would call 'the disenchantment of the world'.[90] The lens of survivalism through which their authors and editors viewed the 'antiquities' they sought to rescue and record blinded them to the meanings they acquired for later generations. It prevented all but a few from recognizing the part Protestantism itself had played in shaping and sustaining such 'superstitions'.

Following the lead of Ronald Hutton, if we look closely at the 'vestiges' and 'residues' assembled in folklore collections we find that they have much to tell

---

[87] Adam Fox, *Oral and Literate Culture in England 1500–1700* (Oxford, 2000), esp. 6–8, 50, 234–5, 242–51, 258, 410–11.

[88] John Gregorson Campbell, *Superstitions of the Highlands and Islands of Scotland Collected Entirely from Oral Sources* (Glasgow, 1900), pp. vii–x: 'what is to be found in print on this subject is not trustworthy'.

[89] See the careful guidelines laid down in Burne, *Handbook of Folklore*, 6–19.

[90] Max Weber, *The Protestant Ethic and the Spirit of Capitalism*, trans. Talcott Parsons (New York, 1958), 105.

us about the processes by which people responded to the Reformation and by which Protestantism implanted and entrenched itself in British culture. The reproduction of proscribed Catholic rites in private contexts and the gradual migration of liturgical ceremonies into the realm of popular pastimes, he argues, should be read less as evidence of resistance to the theological and ecclesiastical changes imposed by the Tudor state than of how its subjects negotiated and digested the dramatic upheavals of the era.[91] Many other traditions and practices recorded by the folklorists that at first sight seem anomalous in a Protestant context might fruitfully be reassessed in similar terms. The use of the Bible as a tool of divination or for medicinal cure and the miracles allegedly worked by incombustible portraits of Martin Luther may superficially smack of the Catholic cult of relics and sacramentals and bespeak a reluctance to embrace an ideology that fiercely repudiated the localization of the holy, but they too attest to the ingenious adjustments and compromises that accompanied and eased this moment of rupture. The emergence of these and other distinctively Protestant forms of magic looks less like a measure of the failure of the Reformation to transform collective mentalities than an index of how both were subtly transposed in the course of the ensuing centuries.[92] Rather than see the persistence of belief in fairies and second sight in the eighteenth- and nineteenth-century Scottish Highlands as proof of Calvinism's inability to conquer indigenous culture, with Jane Dawson we might draw attention to the flexibility, creativity, and indeed success with which the Protestant missionaries evangelized this rugged, inaccessible and Gaelic-speaking region.[93] Instead of dismissing landscape legends that connect topographical features with the exploits of Protestant heroes like John Wyclif, George Fox, John Wesley, and various Marian martyrs as forms of 'popery' and 'heathenism' in thin disguise we ought rather to focus on what they reveal about the Reformation (and later developments)

---

[91] Ronald Hutton, 'The English Reformation and the Evidence of Folklore', *Past and Present*, cxlviii (1995); idem, *Stations of the Sun*, 415–19.

[92] R. W. Scribner, 'Reformation, Popular Magic, and the "Disenchantment of the World" '; idem, 'Incombustible Luther: The Image of the Reformer in Early Modern Germany', *Past and Present*, cx (1986); idem, 'Magic and the Formation of Protestant Popular Culture in Germany', in his *Religion and Culture in Germany (1400–1800)*, ed. Lyndal Roper (Leiden, 2001), 323–45.

[93] Jane Dawson, 'Calvinism and the Gaidhealtachd in Scotland', in Andrew Pettegree, Alastair Duke and Gillian Lewis (eds), *Calvinism in Europe 1540–1620* (Cambridge, 1994), 231–53, at 250–3.

as a midwife no less than a grim reaper of historical myths.[94] Finally, in interpreting the tales of witches, ghosts, portents, and other supernatural phenomena that are such a prominent feature of folklore collections it is vital to emphasize that these were elements of a world-view that Protestants shared with their medieval Catholic predecessors. The resurgent providentialism of the reformers strongly reinforced the idea of a moralized universe in which God and the devil intervened to punish sin and try the faith of the godly.

In short, the distorting paradigm of popish and pagan survivalism that was the legacy of anti-Catholic polemic, antiquarianism and folklore has served for too long to eclipse the fact that Protestantism, both because of and in spite of itself, engendered a prolific body of what, from the perspective of the twenty-first century, it is all too tempting to label 'superstition'. The difficulty we face in assessing the evidence provided by these texts and sources has been compounded by the mutation that has taken place in the meaning of this very word and concept. If historians have been slow to discard the notion that the Reformation and the printing press were the enemies and antidotes of 'superstitious' belief and practice, this may be because we are too much the heirs of the traditions of discourse I have been examining to be able to transcend them.

---

[94] See Alexandra Walsham, *The Reformation of the Landscape: Religion, Identity and Memory in Early Modern Britain and Ireland* (Oxford, forthcoming). See also Fox, *Oral and Literate Culture*, 251–8.

Superstition in Imperial Russia

Simon Dixon

SUPERSTITION, (*Metaphys. & Philos.*) every kind of excess of religion in general, following the ancient word, paganism; one must be pious in order to guard against falling into *superstition* [. . .] Indeed, *superstition* is a cult of false, badly directed religion, full of sham dreads, contrary to reason and to the sound ideas one ought to have of the supreme being. Or, if you prefer, *superstition* is that sort of enchantment or magical power which fear exercises over our soul; the wretched daughter of the imagination, who attacks it with ghosts, dreams, and visions [. . .] It crushes the mind, mainly with illness or adversity; it transforms good discipline & venerable customs into mummery & superficial ceremonies. Once it has put down deep roots in whatever religion it might be, good or bad, it is capable of extinguishing natural enlightenment (*les lumières naturelles*), & of troubling the soundest minds. In short, this is humanity's most terrible scourge. Even atheism destroys no natural sentiments, casts no slur on the laws, or on popular morals; but *superstition* is a despotic tyrant who makes everything surrender to its flights of fancy. Its prejudices are superior to all other prejudices. An atheist has an interest in the public tranquillity through a love of his own peace of mind; but fanatical *superstition*, born of a troubled imagination, overthrows empires [. . .]

Ignorance and barbarity usher in *superstition*, hypocrisy maintains it with useless ceremonies, false zeal propagates it, & self-interest perpetuates it.

The hand of the monarch is unsure how to put the monster of *superstition* in chains, & it is from this monster, still more than from irreligion (inexcusable as it is) that the throne should fear for its authority [. . .]

Superstition, put into action, properly constitutes fanaticism, see FANATICISM; this is one of the finest and best articles in the *Encyclopédie*. (*D[e].J[aucourt]*.)

(*Encyclopédie*, vol. 15, Sen-Tch, 669–70.)

I

'Superstition' is a word that appears but rarely in the vocabulary of recent students of the Russian peasantry. When forced to resort to it, they hold their noses in memory of the distasteful anachronisms perpetrated by an earlier generation of scholars who, rather than respond to the challenge of explaining peasant beliefs as an imaginative psychological response to the ever-present menace of disaster, elected instead to condemn them as ignorant, backward, and irrational.[1] By contrast, historians now aim to release Russian peasants from the straitjacket imposed by populist and Marxist-Leninist preconceptions in order to understand them on their own terms. And the underlying target of this scholarly project is the Enlightenment's contrast between an ignorant humanity, held captive by fear and prejudice, and modern man released by the exercise of his own reason into an era of self-confident happiness.

Whether the human species has ever made any such transition, in Russia or anywhere else, remains the subject of intense, and necessarily inconclusive, debate. Yet I have begun by quoting the *Encyclopédie* in order to suggest that the Enlightenment's conception of superstition may offer at least as promising a subject to the historian as to the anthropologist. While the nature of peasant belief remains a fascinating if ultimately elusive quarry, attempts to reshape it respond more readily to historical investigation, not least because it is usually easier to understand how and why they changed over time. Deviance lies everywhere in the eyes of the beholder. And in this case, it is striking that de Jaucourt's article should focus not only on the psychological power of superstition, but also on the perils of social and political subversion. No royal measure would be too strong to tame such a dangerous 'monster'. Even allowing for the fact that the *philosophes* sought to raise the spectre of

---

[1] For a sense of current concerns, see Christine D. Worobec, 'Lived Orthodoxy in Imperial Russia', *Kritika*, 7:2 (2006), 329–50, esp. 342. Sensitive to anachronism in others, Worobec nevertheless concludes her own richly documented study of *klikushestvo* by suggesting that the act of shrieking as if possessed 'empowered some of its victims' by 'providing a spiritual and cultural outlet for women whose emotional burdens needed release': see her *Possessed: Women, Witches and Demons in Imperial Russia* (DeKalb, IL, 2001), 205.

superstition as a way of diverting attacks on their radical atheism, there can be little doubt that they conceived superstition as an essentially political problem.[2] There was nothing in de Jaucourt's article to surprise any Russian tsar from the time of Peter I (r.1682–1725). All of them were uncomfortably aware that superstition was associated in Europe with the barbarous image they were trying to escape. All of them would have been willing to adopt a similarly capacious definition of superstition as 'any form of religious excess'. All of them hoped that ignorance could ultimately be overcome by education, though they differed over the nature of the curriculum required to achieve their aim. All of them believed that religious fanaticism in the form of the schismatic Old Belief—like Jansenism in France, the product of a politicized struggle over doctrinal reform—represented a potential threat to the stability of their regime. (Radishchev echoed de Jaucourt by asserting in his *Journey from St Petersburg to Moscow* (1790) that the Old Believers had 'done more harm in Russia' than the atheists. 'There are few such people among us, because not many of us are as yet concerned about metaphysics. The atheist errs in metaphysics; the apostate in crossing himself with three fingers.')[3] And whatever their personal religious convictions—the spectrum here was as wide as the variety of their responses to the schism—it is hard to think of a Russian ruler who did not ultimately conceive of belief in instrumental rather than transcendental terms, because all of them regarded individual moral virtue (laudable as it may have seemed as an aim in itself) primarily as a means to civic tranquillity and national security.

Though Peter I himself worshipped frequently, he remained distrustful of a providential world-view that discouraged the tireless human commitment required to drive his new empire towards European great-power status. Catherine II (r.1762–96) was a secularized Protestant, sceptical of the supernatural in all its forms. Yet, sensitized by Montesquieu to the restraining power of custom, she remained cautious about the potentially destabilizing effect of any attempt to suppress unorthodox belief. 'One must be very circumspect,' she warned in her *Instruction* to the Legislative Commission of 1767, 'in the investigation of cases concerning Magic and Heresy. If the laws

[2] On superstition as 'an enemy to civil liberty', see David Hume, 'Of Superstition and Enthusiasm', in Eugene F. Miller (ed.), *Essays Moral, Political and Literary* (Indianapolis, IN, 1987), 78–9.

[3] 'Why not allow every aberration to be out in the open? The more open it is, the quicker it will break down . . . That which is forbidden is also desirable. We are all children of Eve': A. N. Radishchev, *Puteshestvie iz Peterburga v Moskvu. Vol'nost'*, ed. V. A. Zapadov, Nauka (St Petersburg, 1992), 81 ('Torzhok').

do nothing to limit them, charges of these two crimes can seriously disturb the citizens' peace, liberty and happiness, and also be the source of an infinite number of tyrannies.'[4] Although the Romantics saw the superstitious *narod* as a repository of popular virtue, the overall trend of post-Petrine Westernization was reversed only by the self-conscious Muscovite revival sponsored by the last two tsars.[5] Only the last two tsars, proponents of a self-conscious Muscovite revival designed to reverse the trend of post-Petrine Westernization, are the exceptions who prove the rule. And it is to the vain attempts of Nicholas II (r.1894–1917) to use modern methods to stimulate a return to medieval piety—actively patronizing superstition in the increasingly desperate hope of uniting the Russian nation behind his failing dynasty—that I shall return at the end of this chapter.

Since the *philosophes* were salon-based wits, divorced, unlike their contemporaries in the German *Aufklärung*, from any role in government, their ideas have often been dismissed as impractical. Yet even such a committed believer in the reforming power of the monarchy as Voltaire never supposed that it would be easy for kings to overturn centuries of popular ignorance. 'How far does public policy permit the destruction of superstition?' he mused in his *Philosophical Dictionary*. 'It is a very thorny question. It is like asking how far one should go on tapping a dropsical man, who may die during the operation. This depends on the doctor's prudence.' Since prudence lay beyond the reach of most Russian governments, Voltaire's question proved especially prickly in the tsarist empire, where it turned out to be unusually 'difficult to fix the limits of superstition'.[6] I shall try to show why that was so by pursuing two subsidiary inquiries of my own. What were the principal influences driving attempts by Church and state to reshape Russian popular belief in the eighteenth and nineteenth centuries? And what were the circumstances inhibiting Russian public policy on the suppression of superstition? But before we examine the official response, it is natural to begin with some consideration of the nature, variety, and social diffusion of the beliefs that were so often condemned as superstitious.

---

[4] N. D. Chechulin (ed.), *Nakaz Imperatritsy Ekateriny II, dannyi kommissii o sochinenii proekta novago ulozheniia*, Tipografiia Imperatorskoi Akademii Nauk (St Petersburg, 1907), 135, article 497.

[5] E.A. Baratynskii, 'Predrassudok', in *Stikhotvoreniia, Poemy*, ed. L.G. Frizman, Nauka (Moscow, 1982), p. 277. I owe this reference to Andrei Zorin.

[6] Voltaire, *Philosophical Dictionary*, ed. and trans. Theodore Besterman (Harmondsworth, 1972), 'Superstition', 385, 384.

II

Powerful evidence of the popular faith in miracle-working icons comes from those who inflicted punishment on images that had unaccountably failed to work the wonders expected of them. Peter Henry Bruce recorded the fate of a 'poor, superstitious man' who:

> seeing the [great Moscow] fire [of 1713] advancing to consume his all, took a picture of St Nicholas and holding it between him and the fire, prayed fervently for that saint's protection, but in vain for the flames soon seized his house, for which he became so enraged at the saint, that he threw him into the fire, saying, since he would not save him, he might now save himself: this coming to the ears of the clergy, the poor man was sentenced to be burnt alive.

Pious Russian merchants were similarly inclined to reward or punish their icons according to the success of their businesses. In fact, icons were open to reproach from all manner of resentful supplicants who had prayed in vain for relief from everything from poverty to sexual impotence.[7]

To keep the devil at bay, Russian peasants were just as likely to rely on incantations, many of which took the form of simple prayers, recited by magicians (*kolduny*) and traditional healers (*znakhari*).[8] There is space here to quote only a handful of the hundreds of examples collected by Will Ryan in his magisterial study of Russian magic to demonstrate that such sorcerers often operated alongside churchmen (whether in competition or in collaboration it is not always easy to be certain).[9] The abbé Chappe d'Autéroche described a Siberian wedding in the 1760s attended by a *koldun* who was present at the liturgy to ward off malefic magic from rival magicians and led the procession to the nuptial chamber. An eighteenth-century prayer against fever that identified twelve diseases by name as daughters of Herod

---

[7] See W. F. Ryan, *The Bathhouse and Midnight: Magic in Russia* (Stroud, 1999), 199, 235, 240.

[8] B. M. Firsov and I. G. Kiseleva (eds), *Byt velikorusskikh krest'ian-zemlepashchev: Opisanie materialov etnograficheskogo biuro kniazia V. N. Tenishcheva (na primere Vladimirskoi gubernii)*, Izdatel'stvo Evropeiskogo Doma (St Petersburg, 1993), 129–32, suggests a distinction in some peasant minds between magicians, who were thought to have recourse to evil spirits, and healers, who were not. But Worobec, *Possessed*, 89–91, sensibly warns against any rigid division. See also, Samuel C. Ramer, 'Traditional Healers and Peasant Culture in Russia, 1861–1917', in Esther Kingston-Mann and Timothy Mixter (eds), *Peasant Economy, Culture, and Politics of European Russia 1800–1921* (Princeton, NJ, 1991), 207–34.

[9] Ryan, *Bathhouse at Midnight*, 75, 194.

specifically emphasized that it had to be accompanied by the generally accepted magical practice of drinking water in which a cross had been immersed. The lexicologist, Vladimir Dahl, recorded in the mid-nineteenth century that in Western Russia a gun which always hit its target was christened a *iordanka* after a spell had been cast over it at the Jordan, the hole cut in the ice to permit the consecration of the waters at Epiphany.

By the end of the nineteenth century, the vision of a Russian peasantry 'wallowing in superstitions' seduced not only non-Russians like the Finns, proud to have reached a more advanced stage of socio-economic development, but also a critical Russian intelligentsia. 'There is hardly a nation in Christendom which has a demonology—a remnant of ancient paganism—so well elaborated and so deeply rooted as is that of the Russian peasants', complained the revolutionary émigré, Stepniak (S.M. Kravchinskii, 1852–95).[10] The jurist A. A. Levenstim was particularly appalled by the case of a seventy-year-old peasant woman from Minsk province, buried alive with a group of cholera victims in 1855 on the advice of a local medical attendant (*feld'sher*). Cases of human sacrifice had recurred in all three major cholera epidemics—in 1831, 1855, and 1872—and Levenstim, writing in 1897, saw no reason to suppose that they would be the last. Commenting that such facts would 'deeply disturb any educated person', he ranked them as part of a legacy from the distant past 'with which the general progress of culture' had 'yet to come to terms'.[11]

Russian writers had first been drawn to investigate the potentially subversive counter-culture in their midst by the revolt of the Cossack Emel'ian Pugachev (1773–5) which prompted a flurry of interest in the peasantry. Although the *ABC of Russian Superstitions, Idolatrous Sacrificies, Folk Wedding Rituals, Sorcery, Shamanism, etc.* (1782, second edition 1786), compiled by the actor turned comic dramatist Mikhail Chulkov, remained the sole eighteenth-century reference work on Russian folk belief, his material was repeated in many subsequent fortune-telling books, themselves derived overwhelmingly from publications imported from the West.[12] A. O. Ablesimov's comic opera, *The Miller-Sorcerer, Cheat and Matchmaker*, based on

---

[10] Stepniak, *The Russian Peasantry: Their Agrarian Condition, Social Life and Religion* (London, 1905), 355–6.

[11] A. Levenstim, *Sueverie i ugolovnoe pravo*, Izdanie Ia. Kantorovicha (St Petersburg, 1897), 9–11. For this case, see 'Delo o krest'ianakh Andree Korsakeviche i drugikh, sudimykh za pokhoronenie zhivoi krest'ianki Man'kovoi', *Zhurnal Ministerstva Iustitsii*, 6 (1864), 707–13: the *feld'sher* was flogged and sentenced to twelve years' hard labour in Siberia.

[12] Faith Wigzell, *Reading Russian fortunes: Print Culture, Gender and Divination in Russia from 1765* (Cambridge, 1998), 51, 53–5.

Rousseau's *Le devin du village*, became the most popular Russian piece in the repertoire after opening in Moscow in 1779; Matvei Komarov's adventure story, *The Factual and True History of a Russian Swindler*, went through seven editions between 1779 and 1794.[13] Despite the gently humorous tone of such works, published in a period when the peasantry were portrayed as childlike and virtuous by sentimentalist writers such as Radishchev, there could be no doubting the underlying note of anxiety in elite circles as a new sense of the subversive nature of a predominantly superstitious peasantry slowly dawned. That anxiety became more insistent still after the emancipation of the serfs in 1861. By then, the study of superstition, enshrined in Dahl's well-known reference work,[14] had been further enhanced by research sponsored initially by the Imperial Russian Geographic Society (in whose creation Dahl had been a moving force) and culminating in 1897 with the publication of material by the Tenishev Ethnographic Bureau. The information gathered in this way was voluminous: N. Ia. Nikiforovskii's study of superstition in Vitebsk province alone ran to some 2307 entries.[15] And as F. A. Shcherbina discovered, when making the first detailed investigation of the Russian peasant economy on the basis of inquiries in Voronezh province in the 1880s and 1890s, the very process of data collection was interpreted by peasants as 'evil signs' that indicated 'if not the anti-Christ, then, in any case, unclean forces'. To repel malefic spirits, peasants tried to place crosses in the drawers of Shcherbina's researchers' desks and even marked the spines or soles of their boots with crosses.[16]

A few foreigners were prepared to admit that there was nothing exceptional about Russian popular beliefs. Lestrelin, for example, conceded in 1861 that 'All peoples, even in civilized countries, are superstitious to some extent; there are still certain provinces in France which offer us deplorable examples.'[17] Catherine II had made his point for him almost a century earlier. There was 'without doubt, a great deal of superstition, as well as of ignorance' among

---

[13] Gary Marker, *Publishing, Printing, and the Origins of Intellectual Life in Russia, 1700–1800* (Princeton, NJ, 1985), 204.

[14] V. I. Dal', *O poveriiakh, sueveriiakh i predrazsudkakh russkago naroda*, 2nd edn (St Petersburg, 1880).

[15] N. Ia. Nikiforovskii, *Prostonarodnyia primety i pover'ia, suevernye obriady i obychai, legendarnye skazaniia o litsakh i mestakh, sobral v Vitebskoi Belorussii*, Gubernskaia Tipo-Litografiia (Vitebsk, 1897).

[16] Quoted in Chris J. Chulos, *Converging Worlds: Religion and Community in Peasant Russia, 1861–1917* (De Kalb, IL, 2003), 18.

[17] Achille Lestrelin, *Les paysans russes: leurs usages, moeurs, caractère, religion, superstitions, et les droits des nobles sur leurs serfs*, E. Dentu (Paris, 1861), 212. For confirmation, see Judith Devlin, *The Superstitious Mind* (New Haven and London, 1987).

Russia's sectarians, the empress acknowledged in her riposte to Chappe's charges, and Orthodox peasants might be credulous, too. But 'name me the nation, among which the old and foolish are free from superstition', she insisted, reminding the abbé that 'for many centuries' the queens of France 'could not be brought to bed without an astrologer being placed in the wardrobe to foretell the good or ill fortune of the new-born child'.[18]

For many Western visitors, however, it was the permeation of superstitious attitudes to the apex of the social pyramid that distinguished Russia from the rest of Europe, at least until the middle of the nineteenth century. Indeed, for those foreigners who hoped to be absorbed into cosmopolitan court circles, a condescending view of Russian elite credulity served as a way of compensating for their own relatively humble social status. Martha Wilmot, of proud but comparatively obscure Anglo-Irish gentry stock, was characteristically anxious to record 'the excessive Superstition & Credulity of the Russians *in general*' during her long period of residence as a guest of Princess Dashkova in the early years of the nineteenth century:

> 'tis almost boundless. The lower orders believe rigidly in the power & influence of Fairys, Witches, &c. &c. &c. &c. The Higher Orders to a Man to a Woman play la bonne aventure on the Cards & are happy or miserable according to the good or bad Omens of the fortune telling Cards. Myriads of Nobles would not Sleep in a room alone, nor remain five minutes in the dark for worlds.[19]

It is true that a higher proportion of nobles faced prosecution for witchcraft in Russia than in the West. On the other hand, Russian writers could be more tolerant of elite superstitions, portraying them as an integral component of Russian national identity. Compare, for example, Miss Wilmot's strictures with Turgenev's sympathetic vignette of 'a real Russian noblewoman' in *Fathers and Sons* (1861). A devout throwback to Muscovite times, Arina Vlasevna 'believed in all manner of omens, soothsayings, incantations and premonitory dreams':

> She believed that, if on Easter Sunday the candles did not go out at the midnight service, there would be a good buck-wheat harvest,

---

[18] *The Antidote: or an enquiry into the merits of a book, entitled A Journey into Siberia, made in MDCCLXI* (London, 1772), 70, 7, 76.

[19] The Marchioness of Londonderry and H. M. Hyde (eds), *The Russian Journals of Martha and Catherine Wilmot 1803–1808* (London, 1935), 286, Martha's journal, 13 February 1807, emphasis added.

and that if a human eye should see a mushroom it would cease growing. She believed that every devil always liked to be near water and that every Jew had a blood-red birthmark on his chest . . . She did not eat veal, pigeon, crayfish, cheese, asparagus, artichokes or melon, because a severed melon resembled the severed head of John the Baptist.

Such ladies were already 'few and far between', Turgenev observed. 'God knows whether one should be glad of that fact!'[20]

Until recently, claims for the uniqueness of Russian popular spirituality often rested on a supposed system of 'dual faith' (*dvoeverie*), a term first employed in medieval sermons to describe the transposition of Christian rituals onto existing pagan practices, and subsequently defined in contradictory ways to signify either the coexistence of Christian and pagan belief systems or a synthesis of the two.[21] *Dvoeverie* remained an attractive concept to those in late imperial Russia who believed that animism continued to impede the progress of canonical Orthodoxy. As Chulos has noted, 'ethnographic jargon elaborated this distinction by using the ambiguous *pover'e* to refer to folk piety, and the imprecise *verovanie* to describe church religion, thus creating an artificial gap between two contradictory, yet compatible, elements of peasant Orthodoxy'.[22] Yet *dvoeverie* is now suspect as a binary theory that distorts more than it reveals, not least because many comparable overlaps between institutionalized and popular religion can be traced in Western Christian denominations.[23]

Insofar as there was anything distinctive about the Russian experience, it lay neither in the nature of popular beliefs nor in the rationalist responses they provoked among the positivist intelligentsia. What set the Russians apart, as Janet Hartley has suggested, was the 'relative freedom' with which they were allowed to pursue their magical 'practices without effective restrictions from either the Church or the government'.[24] It was not that the authorities were indifferent to such practices: far from it. But even when they sought

---

[20] Ivan Turgenev, *Fathers and Sons*, trans. Richard Freeborn (Oxford, 1991), 145–6.

[21] Stella Rock, 'What's in a word? A historical study of the concept *dvoeverie*', *Canadian-American Slavic Studies*, 35:1 (2001), 19–28.

[22] Chulos, *Converging Worlds*, 7.

[23] For the attack on *dvoeverie*, see Eve Levin, 'Dvoeverie and popular religion', in Stephen K. Batalden (ed.), *Seeking God: The Recovery of Religious Identity in Orthodox Russia, Ukraine and Georgia* (DeKalb, IL, 1993), 31–52. Ryan, *Bathhouse at Midnight*, 2–3, 14, offers a salutary warning against binary models, *tout court*.

[24] Janet M. Hartley, *A Social History of the Russian Empire 1650–1825* (London, 1999), 246.

to suppress them, in ways which we are about to examine, the state's notoriously over-stretched bureaucracy lacked the necessary supervisory power, and its efforts were not helped by a Church which had traditionally interpreted Orthodoxy in terms of the appreciation of 'right imagery' rather than by the propagation of strictly defined doctrine. However, students of Russian religion have for too long relied on such essentially timeless and ahistorical explanations when what is needed is a dynamic account of the unintended consequences of deliberate actions on the part of both Church and state. Let me now sketch a broad outline of Russian public policy on superstition, highlighting some key flashpoints in the triangular relationship between Church, state and believers.

III

The very notion of superstition was new to Muscovy in the late seventeenth century. One of the first known usages of '*sueverie*'—a term signifying 'empty' or 'vain' faith—has been traced to a sermon by Simeon Polotskii dating from 1681. But whereas Simeon used the word to describe demonic intervention, it rapidly acquired two different meanings in the Petrine era, when it was simultaneously adopted as a synonym for heresy and condemned as a refuge for swindlers.[25] Peter the Great's Ecclesiastical Regulation (1721) outlawed 'whatever may be called by the term "superstitious" ', a word he took to encompass all that was 'superfluous, not essential to salvation, devised by hypocrites only for their own interest, beguiling the simple people, and like snowdrifts, hindering the passage along the right path of truth'. So defined, Peter noted, superstition could 'be found in all classes', and he and his immediate successors made a vigorous, if erratic, effort to stamp it out.[26] A variety of anecdotes celebrating the tsar's 'zealous determination to expose cheating and destroy superstition' highlighted his suspicion of false miracles. Though no iconoclast—a dissident priest who chopped up some icons with an axe was burned alive 'as a Heretick and Violator of Images'—Peter was mistrustful of wonder-working icons. On hearing of an image of the Virgin that wept real

[25] Elena Smilianskaia, ' "Sueveriia" i narodnaia religioznost' v Rossii veka Prosveshcheniia", *Canadian-American Slavic Studies*, 38:1–2 (2004), 123–5.

[26] Alexander V. Muller (trans. and ed.), *The Spiritual Regulation of Peter the Great* (Seattle and London, 1972), 15–16. The key studies of what turned out to be erratic persecution are A. S. Lavrov, *Koldovstvo i religiia v Rossii. 1700–1740*, Drevlekhranilishche (Moscow, 2000), and E. B. Smilianskaia, *Volshebniki, bogokhul'niki, eretiki: Narodnaia religioznost' i 'dukhovnye prestupleniia' v Rossii XVIII v.*, Indrik (Moscow, 2003), though see also Ryan, *Bathhouse at Midnight*, 418–25.

tears—allegedly as a sign of displeasure with the tsar's reforms—Peter himself inspected it, confiscating it and placing it in his Cabinet of Curiosities when it was discovered that the oily 'tears' were in fact generated from a receptacle hidden in the frame.[27] For all Peter's efforts, the phenomenon of fraudulent images persisted—the bishop of Kishinev investigated two more 'weeping' icons in 1822, eventually accepting that in this case the 'tears' had somehow dripped onto the icons accidentally—constituting one of the most serious problems facing the Orthodox church in its attempts to regularize the practice of popular religion.[28]

Peter's attempts to protect his ignorant subjects from charlatanry in the name of good sense and the 'common good' foundered when it emerged that many of the judges he appointed were no less committed to unorthodox beliefs than the unfortunates brought before their courts.[29] (In this sense, the campaign against superstition offers a parallel to the tsar's equally inauspicious attempts to stamp out corruption.) No less unexpected were obstacles encountered by the Orthodox attack on superstition as a form of doctrinal deviance. Having been deprived of many of its administrative powers by the tsar, the Church embarked on a crusade against popular belief as a means of restoring its spiritual authority. But in this Christianizing enterprise, as in so many others, the clergy proved a weak reed. Many rural priests were scarcely less ignorant than their flock and efforts to improve clerical education yielded results only in the long term. Burdened by a myriad of other responsibilities, the clergy showed little enthusiasm for pastoral zeal that risked provoking resentment among the very parishioners who paid for their livelihood.[30] Conscious of clerical inadequacy, Timofei Tekut'ev, a captain in the Preobrazhenskii guards, was among those nobles who took matters into their own hands in the mid-eighteenth century by drawing up detailed

[27] E. K. Nikanora, *Istoricheskii anekdot v russkoi literature XVIII veka*, Sibirskii khronograf (Novosibirsk, 2001), 208–11; Lindsey Hughes, *Russia in the Age of Peter the Great* (New Haven and London, 1998), 293 (quoting the Hanoverian envoy, F.-C. Weber), 350.

[28] Gregory L. Freeze, 'Institutionalizing Piety: The Church and Popular Religion, 1750–1850', in Jane Burbank and David L. Ransel (eds), *Imperial Russia: New Histories for the Empire* (Bloomington, IN, 1998), 218–21.

[29] E. B. Smilianskaia, ' "Sueverie" i ratsionalizm vlastei i poddannykh v Rossii XVIII v.', in *Evropeiskoe Prosveshchenie i tsivilizatsiia Rossii*, Nauka (Moscow, 2004), 206–7.

[30] Gregory L. Freeze, *The Russian Levites: Parish Clergy in the Eighteenth Century*, (Cambridge, MA, 1977), 173–9; idem, 'The Rechristianization of Russia: The Church and Popular Religion, 1750–1850', *Studia Slavica Finlandensia*, 7 (1990), 101–35.

instructions for the regulation of popular belief among their serfs.[31] However, as priests well knew, landowners were just as likely to promote superstition as to restrict it: as late as 1832, bailiffs on the Gagarin estate at Petrovskoe had peasants flogged for failing to pray for rain.[32] Harsh was the fate awaiting the cleric who aroused the wrath of a noble landowner, who might denounce him to the bishop or inflict some more brutal punishment of his own. Among the exiles encountered in Tobol'sk by John Parkinson in 1793 was Samuil Choglokov, whose 'many offences' included 'the beating of a Priest for refusing to baptize a cat'.[33]

Since Westernization is often erroneously equated with modernization in Russian history, it is worth stressing that some eighteenth-century Russian superstitions were not only confined to the Westernized elite but dependent on Western innovations. Coffee-cup reading is but one example of a new fashion prompted by the traditional fascination with divination. First imported in the time of Peter I, coffee was consumed in greater quantities from the 1740s. By 1772, divination from coffee grounds had become sufficiently widespread among the nobility for N. I. Novikov to publish in his journal *The Painter* a critique which subsequently inspired a comic opera—*The Reader of Coffee Grounds* (1786)—by the fabulist I. A. Krylov. Having opposed 'superstitious curiosity' to 'natural human reason', Novikov went on to emphasize the harm caused by such activities. Had the coffee-cup reader been guilty of nothing more than cheating willing customers of their money, the damage she did would have been limited (so far as is known, all these fortune-tellers were female). But when her prophecy cast a 'curse' on her superstitious clients—for example by seeming to confirm a husband's false suspicion of infidelity on the part of his wife—then the ruinous consequences for the marriage were nothing less than 'satanic'.[34] Novikov's warnings were, however, in vain. The coffee-cup reader and other forms of divination remained fashionable in elite circles well into the first half of the nineteenth century.

---

[31] E. B. Smilianskaia, *Dvorianskoe gnezdo seredine XVIII veka: Timofei Tekut'ev i ego 'Instruktsiia o domashnikh poriadkakh'*, Nauka (Moscow, 1998).

[32] Steven L. Hoch, *Serfdom and Social Control* (Chicago, 1986), 176, describes this as a 'rather unusual instance'.

[33] John Parkinson, *A Tour of Russia, Siberia and the Crimea 1792–1794*, ed. William Collier (London, 1971), 136, 2 May 1793. Choglokov had been exiled as a fourteen-year-old in 1767 having allegedly sworn to assassinate Catherine II, who had grown up at the court of Empress Elizabeth under the baleful eye of his mother, Mariia Choglokova.

[34] P. N. Berkov (ed.), *Satiricheskie zhurnaly N. I. Novikova*, Izdatel'stvo Akademii Nauk SSSR (Moscow and Leningrad, 1951), 348–52; Wigzell, *Reading Russian Fortunes*, 42–3, 133, 134, 138 and passim.

By then, Novikov had himself experienced a change of heart. Complaining in 1813 that 'the current enlightened age rejects all miracles, [which] modern philosophers call superstition', he expressed the wish 'that some grammarian of the etymology of the word superstition would show them that the superstitious ones are not those who believe in miracles, but those who do not believe in them'.[35] Faith in the miraculous power of relics had always been central to Russian rulership myths. The Kremlin's Cathedral of the Dormition (*Uspenskii sobor*), where coronations were staged from the time of Ivan IV (1547), held among its most treasured possessions a nail from the True Cross, donated by the king of Georgia in 1688, and part of a finger of St John the Baptist, brought to Kiev in the twelfth century.[36] To symbolize their legitimate descent, eighteenth-century tsars made sure that the new chapels royal in St Petersburg were similarly equipped. Voltaire's German-born disciple, Catherine II, worshipped in the baroque Great Chapel of Rastrelli's Winter Palace, which housed a cross incorporating a fragment of the Life-Giving Cross of Our Lord, an image of the Filermskaia Mother of God, said to be the work of St Luke, and part of the right hand of St John the Baptist.[37] Like most of her subjects, the Empress Elizabeth, who slept with a casket of relics beside her bed, saw no contradiction between conspicuous piety and recourse to witchcraft at times of illness. 'It would be difficult to reconcile devotions and witchcraft', confided the sceptical Catherine to her mentor, Sir Charles Hanbury Williams 'if thirteen years of experience [at the Russian Court] had not convinced me that to twisted minds the same thing can simultaneously seem black and white'.[38] So long as the imperial family itself remained implicated in the overlap between magic and institutionalized religion, it was hard to define the boundaries of the culpable—and the Russian old regime, like the French, found it convenient to leave them blurred: as late as 1841, the Statute of Diocesan Consistories was content to echo Peter I's instruction to clergymen to deter their flock from 'all sorts of

---

[35] A. I. Serkov (ed.), *Pis'ma N.I. Novikova*, Izdatel'stvo imeni N. I. Novikova (St Petersburg, 1994), 165, Novikov to Kh.A. Chebotarev, 22 June 1813.

[36] A. M. Lidov (ed.), *Khristianskie relikvii v Moskovskom Kremle/Christian relics in the Moscow Kremlin*, (Moscow, 2000), nos. 18, 21.

[37] *Istoriko-statisticheskiia svedeniia o S.-Peterburgskoi Eparkhii*, vol. 3, V. Golovin, (St Petersburg, 187?), 359.

[38] A. N. Pypin (ed.), *Sochineniia Imperatritsy Ekateriny II*, vol. 12, Tipografiia Imperatorskoi Akademii Nauk (St Petersburg, 1907), 318; Serge Goriaïnow (ed.), *Correspondance de Catherine Alexéievna, Grande-Duchesse de Russie, et de Sir Charles H. Williams, Ambassadeur d'Angleterre 1756 et 1757*, Tipografiia G. Lissnera i D. Sovko (Moscow, 1909), 19, 8 August 1756.

superstitions and superstitious rituals' without entering into further detail about either term.[39]

By the same token, punishment alone could hardly suffice as a remedy for such complex misunderstandings: whereas guilt could be tackled by force, ignorance had to be overcome by means of education. So much was apparent as early as the Petrine era,[40] and it became clearer still as the Russians developed their concept of rational 'enlightenment' (*prosveshchenie*) in explicit opposition to unthinking 'superstition'.[41] At first, the dominant tone was optimistic. 'When superstition and ignorance—the main enemies of enlightenment—have disappeared', declared Elizabeth's favourite, Ivan Shuvalov, who corresponded with Voltaire in the years around 1760, 'one can look forward to undoubted successes'.[42] By 1834, when Polikarp Puzin published a study of superstition through the ages, expectations were somewhat lower. Acknowledging that it was 'impossible and even harmful suddenly to eradicate all popular superstitions', Puzin strove instead 'to destroy, little by little, the ancient building' that they inhabited. But he had not lost sight of his goal: 'When beneficial enlightenment illuminates the huge boundaries of Russia, and spreads its generous gifts to every social estate, then everyone will be convinced that all the evils in the world have derived from insufficient moral education, and all the good flows from true enlightenment, based on the principles of our gentle, meek and divine faith'.[43] The positivist Levenstim was just as insistent in 1897 on the need for education as the only remedy for superstitious ignorance, though noticeably less sanguine about its chances of success.[44] In the light of growing peasant demands for land, the question was far from academic. As Dimitrii Filosofov put it in 1900, 'it won't be the educated citizen of the future who receives free Russian land, but the ignorant contemporary peasant, capable of both enlightened and unenlightened actions – the peasant who according to some is religious, and to others superstitious. If our Westernizers are right to think that he is merely

[39] Vera Shevzov, *Russian Orthodoxy on the Eve of Revolution* (New York, 2004), 121–2. Cf. Arlette Farge, *Subversive Words: Public Opinion in Eighteenth-Century France*, trans. R. Morris (Cambridge, 1994), 81–9, esp. 85.

[40] James Cracraft, *The Church Reform of Peter the Great* (London, 1971), 290–3.

[41] E.g, Nikolai Novikov, *Opyt istoricheskago slovaria o rossiiskikh pisateliakh* (St Petersburg, 1772), 10, referred to Metropolitan Arsenii (Mogilianskii)'s 'enlightened intelligence' to signal that his mind was 'alien to superstition and hypocrisy'.

[42] Quoted by E. V. Anisimov, *Rossiia v seredine XVIII veka: Bor'ba za nasledie Petra*, Mysl' (Moscow, 1986), 204.

[43] Polikarp Puzin, *Vzgliad na sueverie i predrazsudki*, Tipografiia Imperatorskoi Rossiiskoi Akademii (St Petersburg, 1834), I, 335–6.

[44] Levenstim, *Sueverie*, 156–7, 172–3.

superstitious, then it is all the more necessary to pay attention to his religious life. Superstition is all the more dangerous because the only escape from it is a long path of education.[45] Having initially supposed that the challenge of their denominational and sectarian rivals would melt away under the light of the one true faith, the Orthodox instead found them sufficiently vigorous not only to retain their own adherents, but also to attract converts even while they were forbidden from proselytizing. Fears of apostasy prompted first an intellectual, then a pastoral response from the established church that were to have fateful consequences for its treatment of superstitious belief.[46] Turning to the Early Church in search of authentic Christianity, Orthodox scholars found not only a range of Patristic strictures, but also a much wider range of disciplinary regulations relating to liturgy and ritual. However, there was a paradoxical price to pay for the nineteenth century's attempt to tighten Orthodox confessional discipline. The more complicated and punitive churchmen made Orthodoxy seem, the less attractive it became to simple believers.

Conscious that by enforcing canonical standards they risked driving their flock into apostasy or neglect, some Orthodox priests sought a compromise with popular belief. Whereas once they might have blessed village wells as a way of placating peasants who paid their fees, now they felt obliged to do so in defence of their very faith. Noting that every Orthodox peasant considered it his 'holy duty' to pray for his livestock on St George's day (23 April), a study of popular customs in Vladimir province in 1902 recorded the sanctification services performed in the fields before favoured icons: 'Almost every cow is led to pasture by a man carrying a willow branch, taken from the Palm Sunday service and secreted from that time behind the icons'.[47] Such time-honoured practices fell somewhere between the allegedly harmless superstitions based on observation and experience which the Church was prepared to tolerate (an edificatory pamphlet published in 1907 included in this category the belief that a hen standing on one leg signified the onset of a severe frost) and more embarrassing delusions, such as the notion, derived from a belief in the power of the holy, that it was unlucky to meet a priest.[48] But this was a difficult

[45] D. V. Filosofov, *Zagadki russkoi kul'tury*, Intelvak (Moscow, 2004), p. 165.

[46] See Simon Dixon, 'The Russian Orthodox Church in Imperial Russia, 1721–1917', in Michael Angold (ed.), *The Cambridge History of Christianity, Vol. 5: Eastern Christianity* (Cambridge, 2006), 330–7.

[47] Timofei Pozdniakov, *Narodnye obychai v Aleksandrovskom uezde Vladimirskoi gubernii*, Tipo-Litografiia Gubernskago Pravleniia (Vladimir, 1902), 2–3. Cf. Ryan, *Bathhouse at Midnight*, 195–6.

[48] *Sueveriia i predrazsudki russkago naroda*, Sinodal'naia Tipografiia (Moscow, 1907), 9, 48.

balance to hold and, whatever their motivation, clergy who tried to reach an accommodation between religion and magic left themselves open to charges that they had merely helped to perpetuate the superstitions that they should have been striving to overcome.[49]

Not that those who sought to purge Orthodoxy of its popular imperfections found their task any easier. Contributors to the ecclesiastical periodicals that proliferated after 1860 were swift to adopt the vocabulary of modern medicine, stigmatizing both superstition and sectarianism as contagious infections, psychopathic disorders or cancerous growths in the body of the Church.[50] Some religious writers belatedly came to accept a view long shared by their educated parishioners: that the remedies prescribed by doctors and priests were complementary rather than incompatible.[51] By ranking physicians on a par with priestly 'spiritual doctors',[52] the new breed of secular diocesan missionaries who emerged in the late 1880s could not only assuage persistent insecurities about their own lowly social status, but also forge a professional dual alliance against an ignorant common enemy: the znakhar. It was 'offensive', churchmen complained, for Christians to trust a peasant healer rather than put their faith in 'the heavenly Doctor' himself.[53]

Most clergy, however, continued to think Christianity superior to science, while the controversial claims of Western psychopathology prompted at least one qualified medic to declare that the popular belief in miracles 'stood on more logical, more rational, and more solid ground' than 'scientific fantasies'

---

[49] For examples of such charges, see Levenstim, Sueverie, 11, 157–8.

[50] Daniel Beer, 'The Medicalization of Religious Deviance in the Russian Orthodox Church (1880–1905)', Kritika, 5:3 (2004), esp. 460–74.

[51] E. I., Chudesnoe iztselenie, ili puteshestvie k vodam Spasitelia v selo Rai-Semenovskoe, prinadlezhashchee G. Tainomu-Sovetniku, deistvitel'nomu Kamergeru i Kavaleru A.P. Nashchokinu, Tipografiia V. Plavil'shchikova (St Petersburg, 1817), 3–4, 31–2, 36–9, 43–50, 63–4, and passim, gives the case of a retired courtier who cured his rheumatism by taking the waters on his doctor's advice, attending the consecration service at the beginning of the Dormition Fast on 1 August (after which the people bathed themselves and their livestock in the 'holy water' of the River Nara), and praying before a renowned miracle-working icon.

[52] For example, N[ikolai] S[lednikov], 'O neobkhodimosti v bolezni pol'zovat'sia pomosh-ch'iu vrachei', Pribavleniia k Vologodskim eparkhial'nym vedomostiam, 1905, no. 8–9, 237–41. Sosnin, O sviatykh chudotvornykh ikonakh, 68, gives an earlier medical metaphor. For the part played by doctors in the evaluation of miracles, see Worobec, Possessed, 54–62.

[53] Sueveriia i predrazsudki russkago naroda, 35. For an earlier attack on the znakhar, see N. Zavarin, 'O sueveriiakh i predrazsudkakh sushchestvuiushchikh v Vologodskoi eparkhii', Pribavleniia k Vologodskim Eparkhial'nym Vedomostiam, 3 (1870), 91–7.

such as 'the magical, material forces and energies of the brain' discussed by the York physician Daniel Hack Tuke in his *Illustrations of the influence of the mind upon the body in health and disease designed to elucidate the action of the imagination* (London, 1872).[54] On 23 July 1888, the year in which Tuke's book was translated into Russian under the title *The Spirit and the Body*, a series of events at the Imperial Glassworks in St Petersburg seemed to offer a classic case in point. Although all its other images were destroyed by fire after lightning struck the factory's small wooden chapel, an icon of 'The Joy of all Grieving' Mother of God survived with a number of copper coins, donated by the poor, stuck to its surface.[55] A collection promptly began for a new stone chapel on the site. By 1890, however, donations had declined so precipitously that construction had to be suspended. Interest was rekindled only when Kolia Grachev, a fourteen-year-old epileptic whom doctors had abandoned as incurable, made a miraculous recovery before the icon in 1891. The story spread, pilgrims flocked back, and by 1898 a new stone church, designed in the Muscovite style for 1,200 worshippers, had been completed at a total cost in the region of 200,000 roubles.[56] Trumpeted as an 'exposure' of the sceptical approach to miracles espoused by evangelical followers of Colonel V. A. Pashkov, Kolia's cure soon generated a thriving cult.[57] By the time Father Kapiton Rakhmanin's pamphlet on the icon reached its ninth edition in 1902, some 80,000 copies had already been sold and the principal organ of Orthodox evangelism in the capital, the Society for the Propagation of Religious and Moral Enlightenment in the Spirit of the Orthodox Church, still found a ready market for its own sixty-eight-page brochure on the subject in the middle of the First World War.[58]

[54] [Dr] N. Peskovskii, 'Sueverie v srede uchenykh', *Strannik* (September 1896), 67, reviewing *Dukh i telo: Deistvie psikhiki i voobrazheniia na fizicheskuiu prirodu cheloveka Khek T'iuka*, trans. P. Viktorov, Tipografiia V. F. Rikhter (Moscow, 1888). See also, [Deacon] A. Lebedev, 'Razgovor sviashchennika s doktorom o chudesiakh', *Strannik* (1860), 291.

[55] *Sobytie 23 iiulia 1888 goda s ikonoiu Bozhiei materi Vsekh Skorbiashchikh radosti nakhodiashcheisia v chasovne, postroennoi bliz Stekliannago zavoda v S. Peterburge*, Tipografiia P. Voshchinskoi (St Petersburg, 1889).

[56] *Sankt-Peterburgskii dukhovnyi vestnik*, 31 July 1898, 525–31; V. V. Antonov and A. V. Kobak, *Sviatyni Sankt-Peterburga: Istoriko-tserkovnaia entsiklopediia*, vol. 1, Izdatel'stvo Chernysheva (St Petersburg, 1997), 153–6.

[57] [General E. V. Bogdanovich], *Golosa iz Rossii protiv Pashkovskago lzheucheniia po povodu nedavnago priskorbnago sluchaia*, Tipografiia Tovarishchestva 'Obshchestvennaia Pol'za' (St Petersburg, 1891), V, 43–50.

[58] [Sv. Kapiton Rakhmanin], *Chudotvornaia ikona presviatyia bogoroditsy 'Vsekh Skorbiashchikh Radosti' (s monetami) v selenii Imperatorskago Stekliannago Zavoda g. S.-Peterburga*, 9th edn, Tipografiia A. L. Trunova (St Petersburg, 1902); *Chudotvornaia*

Confronted with the mobilizing power of such wonder-working images and relics, the Church had initially responded with caution. On the one hand, as German theologians questioned the authenticity of miracles in the years around 1800, Orthodox scholars promoted them as a means of preserving the faith in an age of doubt, arguing that miraculous cures and the survival of uncorrupted relics constituted proof of the Creator's unique power to vary the otherwise immutable laws of nature. On the other hand, as one such scholar insisted, 'miracles ought not to be too frequent' lest their proliferation devalue their currency or tempt the unwary into the sort of fatalism that the Church sought to combat in the cause of responsible free will. So the authorities remained alert to the potential for false miracles resulting from 'vanity', 'cupidity', or 'blind and ignorant zeal' on the part of the faithful.[59]

The fate of the relics of Ieromonakh Platon, discovered in a hidden grave at the Archangel monastery in Velikii Ustiug in 1819, offers a revealing example. Though accounts of their discovery varied—a local teacher testified that he had inspected the relics with the aim of disproving some 'superstitious nonsense' about uncorrupted remains regaled to him by local women; Bishop Onisifor claimed that the drunken teacher had inadvertently revealed the tomb after overturning a nearby barrel of pitch—the essence of their testimony was identical. A long-serving priest confirmed that Platon had been buried during the eclipse of the sun in 1762 and this was believed to be one reason why his relics had miraculously survived intact. So quickly did the story of their curative powers spread that by 1822 some fifty sick pilgrims claimed to have been healed at his grave. Yet, after lengthy investigations and appeals, the Synod concluded in 1825 that the 'miracles' at Velikii Ustiug were attributable to nothing more than 'popular rumour' and could not be authenticated.[60]

Similarly intensive efforts were made to investigate hundreds of miracle-working icons reported all over nineteenth-century Russia. Those found in

ikona presviatyia bogoroditsy Vsekh Skorbiashchikh Radosti (s monetami) . . . *i opisanie chudes ot nei*, Tipografiia Obshchestva rasprostranenii religiozno-nravstvennago pros-veshcheniia v dukhe Pravoslavnoi Tserkvi (Petrograd, 1916).

[59] Dmitrii Sosnin, *O netlenii sviatykh moshchei v tserkvi khristianskoi*, 3rd edn, Universitetskaia Tipografiia (Moscow, 1849),10 and passim; idem, *O sviatykh chudot-vornykh ikonakh v tserkvi khristianskoi*, 2nd edn, Universitetskaia Tipografiia, (Moscow, 1849), 5, 29–35, 41–5, 51–2, 62–70, quoted at 62, 29.

[60] Andrei Titov, 'Delo o velikoustiuzhskom ieromonakhe Platone (ego moshchi)', *Russkii arkhiv*, 1911, no. 6, 275–92, esp. 277–8 (the teacher, Veresniagov), 279–81 (Onisifor), 291 (Synod resolution). The Transit of Venus—the reason for Chappe's visit to Russia—in fact took place in 1761.

Moscow—such as the image of the 'Old Korsunskaia Mother of God' from Vladimir province that attracted 'a multitude of people of various callings with hysteria and afflictions' when displayed in the house of a Moscow merchant in 1825—were usually sent for examination at the Kremlin's Monastery of Miracles.[61] Lacking such an authoritative repository of authentication, diocesan authorities elsewhere were drawn by their reliance on imprecise eighteenth-century legislation into seemingly arbitrary distinctions which were understandably greeted at local level with incomprehension bordering on resentment. It was far from irrational for bewildered villagers in Riazan province to express sadness in 1892 that their prayers before a respected icon of the Mother of God had been dismissed as 'inauthentic and superstitious' by ecclesiastical authorities who apparently considered that they had 'begun to venerate someone whom Orthodox Christians should not even think about'.[62]

Repression, however, was not the only ecclesiastical option. Since two centuries of struggle had done little to reshape popular belief, churchmen were increasingly inclined, from the 1880s, to seek to sponsor practices they had once excoriated. While many defended miracles in opposition to Count Leo Tolstoy, who made no secret of his belief that no sane modern person could believe in them, what the Church needed most was a figure of comparable stature among the people.[63] It found him in Father John of Kronstadt, a charismatic priest whose powers ranged from exorcism to cures. 'Seeing him', Vasilii Rozanov wrote in 1905, 'the Russian people gives way to its wonder; they run after him in crowds; they kiss the hem of his clothing; they kiss the ground on which he walked; they rip apart any handkerchief, towel, or any object that he held in his hands and treasure these particles as "relics" '.[64] Such reactions were by no means confined to the uneducated. On hearing of one of Father John's visits to Moscow to pray for a sick aristocrat in 1884, Metropolitan Isidor (Nikol'skii) remarked acidly that his intercession would have been just as effective had it been said in St Petersburg (a jibe aimed as much at noble ignorance as at the pretensions of the Kronstadt holy

---

[61] Oleg Tarasov, *Icon and Devotion*, trans. Robin Milner-Gulland (London, 2002), 89–90.

[62] Vera Shevzov, 'Miracle-working icons, laity and authority in the Russian Orthodox Church, 1861–1917', *Russian Review*, 58:1, (1999), 40.

[63] R. F. Christian (trans. and ed.), *Tolstoy's Letters*, vol. 2 (London, 1978), 474; Sv. Ioann Orfanitskii, 'Chto takoe chudo?', *Vera i tserkov'*, 1901, no. 1, 65–97.

[64] Quoted in Nadieszda Kizenko, *A Prodigal Saint: Father John of Kronstadt and the Russian People* (Pennsylvania, 2000),161.

man).[65] At his death in 1908, Father John's apartment in St Petersburg was besieged by well-to-do female admirers on a ghoulish quest for some 'holy' item of clothing he had worn, and he continued to work wonders from beyond the grave.[66]

The adoration of Father John flourished in the context of a politically motivated rejection of Western values under the last two tsars. Whereas public discussion of earlier miracles had been conducted largely by means of antiquarian scholarship,[67] the imperial family's survival in the tragic railway accident at Borki on 17 October 1888 signalled a more immediate approach, closer to popular values. Pamphlets showing the exact position of the derailed carriages presented the miracle as proof of God's grace for tsar and people. The 'Joy of all Grieving' cult in St Petersburg was also officially supported (Father John himself was brought in to consecrate a chapel at the new Glassworks church).[68] So, on a national scale, was the opening of the remains of St Feodosii Uglitskii at Chernigov in September 1896: their authentication was as much a political as a religious act.[69] Seven years later, Nicholas II personally sponsored the canonization of Serafim of Sarov (1759–1833), a critic of Western rationalism who had complained that the Russians had 'lost the simplicity of the early Christians' and plunged themselves back 'into dark ignorance' by their quest for 'so-called enlightenment'.[70]

The most fanatical opponent of Western ways in early twentieth-century Russia was Iliodor (Trufanov), a young ascetic lost in a state of spiritual

---

[65] Rossiiskii Gosudarstvennyi Istoricheskii Arkhiv, f. 796, op. 205, d. 452, l. 436, Isidor's diary, 6 June 1884.

[66] *Chudesnye znameniia po molitvam o. Ioanna Kronshtadtskago*, issue 2, Tipo-Litografiia M. P. Frolovoi (St Petersburg, 1912); 'Pis'mo v redaktsiiu', *Kronshtadtskii pastyr*, 1916, no. 4, 59.

[67] E.g., Vasilii Krylov, *Istoricheskaia zapiska o sele Okovtsakh i chudotvornykh ikonakh Presviatyia Bogoroditsy Odigitrii i Zhivotvoriashchago Kresta Tverskoi Eparkhii, Ostashkovskago uezda*, Tipografiia Gubernskago Pravleniia (Tver, 1862).

[68] *Chudesnoe spasenie 17 Oktiabria 1888 g.*, Tipografiia Tovarishchestva 'Obshchestvennaia Pol'za' (St Petersburg, 1888); Richard S. Wortman, *Scenarios of Power: Myth and Ceremony in the Russian Monarchy*, vol. 2: *From Alexander II to the Abdication of Nicholas II* (Princeton, NJ, 2000), 289–93.

[69] 'Opredelenie Sviateishago Sinoda o proslavlenii i otkrytiia moshchei sviatitelia Feodosiia uglitskago, arkhiepiskopa chernigovskago', *Missionerskoe Obozrenie*, (September 1896), 115–19. For local and national ceremonies, with texts of accompanying sermons, see *Pribavleniia k Tserkovnym Vedomostiam*, 1896, no. 37, 1329–37; no. 38, 1367–74.

[70] Quoted in Robert L. Nichols, 'The Friends of God: Nicholas II and Alexandra at the Canonization of St Serafim of Sarov, July 1903', in Charles E. Timberlake, *Religious and Secular Forces in Late Tsarist Russia* (Seattle and London, 1992), 207.

delusion (*prelest'*), who acquired a huge (predominantly female) following for his own brand of self-consciously medieval piety, heavily laced with superstition. Using 'all kinds of allegories to impress the people', Iliodor paraded a huge cardboard dragon—'the hydra of Revolution'—through the courtyard of his monastery in Tsaritsyn, filling the beast with children dressed as demons (on the model of the Trojan horse), and preaching 'that out of this foul mouth proceeded the devils of devastation, starvation and death'.[71] Rumours of an impending pogrom followed later in 1911 after Iliodor prophesied that 'Saturn [a symbol of death] is in the sky! Take care, you Jew and Russian fool: Rus' is on the march!'[72] Only the patronage of Rasputin himself—'a man who fits closely the traditional description of the *koldun* or Russian magician'[73]—allowed Iliodor to defy successive attempts by the Synod and Stolypin's government to remove him.

The campaign against superstitious belief had come full circle. What had once been condemned as a deviant swindle was now held up as a model of unspoilt piety. Yet each of Nicholas II's 'medievalising' projects served ultimately to discredit the monarchy. Courtiers attending the canonization of St Serafim looked self-indulgent when contrasted with the indigent peasantry, and the legitimacy of the ritual was undermined when it emerged that Serafim's remains had been inadequately preserved.[74] John of Kronstadt acquired so fervent a following that some peasants mistook the charismatic priest for God himself.[75] Since a much larger group of *Ioannity* worshipped him as Christ reincarnate, the Synod, having originally hoped to see Father John at the spearhead of its internal mission, was instead obliged to confront a flourishing sect.[76] Iliodor's fate was sadder still. His mass pilgrimage to the Sarov monastery in July 1911 caused a national scandal. While a choir of women chanted psalms on the top deck of his Volga steamer, the lower-decks thronged with thuggish acolytes of the proto-Fascist Union of Russian People, who disembarked in towns along the route to wreak havoc among the

---

[71] Iliodor, *The Mad Monk of Russia: Life, Memoirs, and Confessions of Sergei Michailovich Trufanoff* (New York, 1918), 42–3, offers a characteristic mixture of evasion, exaggeration, and in this case corroborated fact.

[72] *Utro Rossii*, 9 August 1911.

[73] Ryan, *Bathhouse at Midnight*, 24.

[74] Gregory L. Freeze, 'Subversive Piety: Religion and the Political Crisis in Late Imperial Russia', *Journal of Modern History*, 68:2 (1996), 308–50.

[75] Tsentral'nyi arkhiv goroda S.-Peterburga, f. 19, op. 97 (1905g.), d. 60, ll. 1–4.

[76] Kizenko, *A Prodigal Saint*, 197–232.

local population.[77] Consumed by ambition, Iliodor took a step too far by denouncing Rasputin in December 1911. He was imprisoned in an isolated monastery; his own was closed, though his followers in Tsaritsyn remained undimmed in their enthusiasm.

IV

Successive Russian governments might be forgiven for thinking that de Jaucourt was right to regard superstition as a beast that would be difficult to tame. Indeed, its subversive potential remained no less powerful at the beginning of the twentieth century than it had been two hundred years earlier, when Peter the Great inveighed against sorcery and witchcraft. While doctors and positivist intellectuals had come to portray superstition as 'bad science' in the second half of the nineteenth century, the tsarist regime and the Russian Orthodox Church persisted in thinking of it as 'bad religion' throughout the imperial period. That being so, the main difficulty they faced in their attempts to 'fix the limits of superstition' was the extent to which popular culture incorporated not only magical beliefs bearing no relation to canonical religion, but also a wide range of excesses relating to explicitly Orthodox phenomena such as miracle-working icons. In response to the challenges of the multi-denominational Russian empire, the nineteenth-century church attempted to promote these phenomena at the heart of a newly-confessionalized and authentically Russian faith. By doing so, however, it not only exposed Orthodoxy to charges of ignorance and barbarity from rationalist intellectuals, but also to charges of inauthentic salvation from the Protestant sectarian movements which flourished by tempting Russians into a simpler form of worship. The Muscovite revival sponsored by the last two tsars was in some part intended to redress the balance. However, hi-jacked by the radical Right after the revolution of 1905, their re-evaluation of popular piety did more to discredit the monarchy than to emasculate superstition, which proved much more durable in Russia than the tsarist regime.

---

[77] See, in particular, *Novoe Vremia*, 1 July and 30 July 1911, *Utro Rossii*, 15 July and 29 July 1911, *Russkoe Slovo*, 26 July 1911.

Superstition in Mexico: From Colonial Church to Secular State

Alan Knight

Every October thousands of pilgrims make their way to Magdalena de Kino, a small, sweltering town in the north-western Mexican state of Sonora. They queue, four-abreast, outside the church which, in an elaborate (1977) chapel, complete with Corinthian columns, red velvet drapes, and a huge crystal chandelier, houses the life-size, wood-and-plaster statue of St Francis Xavier, clad in black Jesuit robe, reclining on a white marble bier. The paint on the saint's hair and face has been worn away by the touches of pilgrims and, as the fiesta proceeds, he becomes festooned with votive offerings—'candles, flowers, jewelry, milagros, pillows, clothing, and miniature statues'.[1] Over the years, the milagros—literally, 'miracles', in fact, small metal images, depicting men, women, children, arms, legs, eyes, hearts, cows, and cars—steadily accumulate; in 1981 the local priest had two trunks full of milagros, which numbered some half a million, collected over forty years.[2] Magdalena is the

---

[1] Eileen Oktavec, *Answered Prayers. Miracles and Milagros Along the Border* (Tucson, 1995), p. xvii. Rubbing the statue transfers power to whatever is doing the rubbing; thus, smaller statues are rubbed against the big one in order to 'recharge their batteries' (ibid., 30). Toes and fingers have been broken off the statue to be used as portable miraculous devices; in 1966, the local priest recalls, 'someone took both of the hands and we had to get new ones' (ibid., 13).

[2] Ibid., p. xviii, recounts sorting and counting 43,891 milagros. Given half a million milagros accumulated over 40 years, the annual rate is about 125,000 a year, or 34 a day. In 1992 Oktavec (*Answered Prayers*, 33) observed 1,300 milagros being offered during 7 days of fiesta, i.e. 186 a day. The Church employs attendants who regularly collect up the offerings in metal buckets; one sharp-eyed old attendant watches the statue and 'whenever large amounts of money or expensive-looking milagros or jewelry were placed on the statue, he would wait until the people left and then he would reach out, grab the offering, and drop it in the large locked donation box' (ibid., 24). Milagros bear comparison with sigils, astrological charms cast in copper or tin and 'used for all the traditional magical purposes', a trunkload of which were sent by William Lilley to Elias Ashmole in 1667: Keith Thomas, *Religion and the Decline of Magic* (Harmondsworth, 1973), 759–60.

biggest centre of a cult of St Francis which spans much of north-western Mexico and spills across the border into Arizona, roughly following the ancient pattern of Jesuit and Franciscan proselytization. The cult is fluid and fungible: not only does it cross borders and attract pilgrims of different class and ethnic backgrounds, it is also religiously heterodox, since it is not clear whether the St Francis who is being venerated is St Francis of Assisi or St Francis Xavier; and, while some Catholic priests tolerate the cult as a an example of 'popular faith' which complements the 'institutional church', others 'consider milagros part of a superstitious folk ritual and refuse to bless them'.[3]

The state also takes an intermittent interest in these proceedings. The wooden statue of St Francis was carved in Guadalajara around 1940; it replaced an older—reputedly finer—statue which had been burned in 1934, at the height of the revolutionary state's anticlerical and iconoclastic campaigns, which had been particularly intense in Sonora.[4] In the eyes of radical anticlericals like the then Governor of Sonora Rodrigo Elías Calles (and of his father, ex-President, revolutionary *jefe máximo*, and celebrated *comecuras* ['priest-eater'], Plutarco Elías Calles), Catholicism was a tissue of superstitions which bemused credulous Mexicans (women especially), retarded progress, divided the nation, and obstructed the redemptive work of the Revolution. Echoing the denunciations of radical Enlightenment thinkers, revolutionary anticlericals sought not only to weaken the institutional Church—which was an old liberal/anticlerical objective dating back at least to the early nineteenth century—but also to extirpate the popular beliefs and practices associated with it, which, they claimed, were indistinguishable from superstition.

The continued vitality of the St Francis cult (and of many comparable twentieth-century Mexican cults, notably the Virgin of Guadalupe and the Christ of Chalma) strongly suggests that revolutionary anticlericalism failed, if not entirely. But the vitality of such cults was not necessarily a triumph for the Catholic Church, whose ambivalence has been noted. Furthermore, cults, and their associated fiestas, were woven into Mexican social and economic life: at Magdalena

---

[3] Ibid., 27–8, 39.

[4] Ibid., 14. US consular reports recount how, in 1937, the church, closed in accordance with the government's anticlerical policy, was allowed to reopen, though without the 'miraculous statue of San Francisco which attracted thousands of pilgrims to Magdalena': US State Department Records, Internal Affairs of Mexico, 812.00/511, June 1937. See also Adrian Bantjes, *As If Jesus Walked on Earth, Cardenismo, Sonora and the Mexican Revolution* (Wilmington, Del., 1998), 76.

during the San Francisco fiesta, all the streets near the church are transformed by the influx of thousands of pilgrims and by the smells of cooking fires, freshly brewed coffee, hot tortillas and grilled meat drifting from dozens of makeshift outdoor restaurants. Mariachi bands stroll by . . . vendors tempt people with everything from balloons, sneakers, and plastic dishpans to parrots, jewelry and fine leather jackets. Herbalists hawk dozens of varieties of dried plants and sea life said to cure everything from sore throats to cancer . . . A couple of sleight-of-hand artists and fortune tellers operate at the far ends of the plaza and photographers with Polaroid cameras stay close to the church, offering to take people's pictures as mementos of their pilgrimage.[5]

Thus, not only do we get the usual business and bustle of a popular fiesta—the Mammon piggybacking on Mariolatry which historically characterized the Basilica of Guadalupe on the outskirts of Mexico City; we also encounter quack medicine dealers, fortune tellers, and card sharps. Mexican fiestas were ever thus, and their encouragement of drinking, eating, gambling, and petty crime had been an object of both clerical and secular-criticism for generations;[6] and part of the criticism focused on the pig-ignorant superstitions which fiestas exemplified and propagated. But who, in this ebullient scenario, was fomenting superstition? The fortune-tellers 'at the far ends of the plaza'? The herbalists hawking cures for cancer? The card sharps and their victims? Or the pilgrims themselves, lining up to venerate an icon whose origins and identity were confused, whose cult some Catholic priests denounced as superstitious, and whose predecessor had been consigned to the flames by revolutionary anticlericals bent on extirpating superstition in the name of progress and enlightenment?

I

The case of San Francisco and the Magdalena fiesta both encapsulates several aspects of Mexican 'superstition' and poses the intractable question of what 'superstition' is (or was).[7] Conceptual indeterminacy is a common problem for historians and other social scientists. In some cases, there is at least an

---

[5] Ibid. 16.

[6] William B. Taylor, *Magistrates of the Sacred. Priests and Parishioners in Eighteenth-Century Mexico* (Stanford, 1996), 250–60; Fanny Calderón de la Barca, *Life in Mexico* (London, n.d.; first pub. 1843), 137–9, 202–8, 376–82.

[7] Defining superstition is an 'all-but-impossible assignment', according to Stuart A. Vyse, *Believing in Magic. The Psychology of Superstition* (Oxford, 1997), 19. The difficulty of the task is somewhat exemplified by Gustav Jahoda, *The Psychology of Superstition*

ample body of literature from which definitions may be derived; a discussion of 'the state', for example, could draw on reams of literature ranging back to Plato and Aristotle. 'Superstition', however, seems to be seriously neglected.[8] Etymological dictionaries in this instance are not a great help;[9] furthermore, etymology is particularly useless when we are dealing with cross-cultural and cross-temporal comparisons, since words and concepts cannot be trafficked across these frontiers without paying a heavy tariff, which may make them worthless (roughly, this is the problem of 'indexicality').[10] Even within cultures, words change over time (for example, 'pagan'). Perhaps within the family of Romance languages (including, for this purpose, English), words derived from the Latin *superstitio* have something in common; but whether the phenomenon which these cognate words denote is capable of translation into, for example, Swahili or Mandarin Chinese is a moot point (see Geschiere, this volume). For at this stage the question becomes both linguistic (what can be said in Swahili and Mandarin?) and also substantive (is there a superstitious syndrome in these cultures?). As Lacan might say, both the signifier and the signified are open to question. Here, we have to leave linguistics and enter the field of comparative history, anthropology, sociology (and perhaps psychology). Maybe this book, in broaching this relatively novel question, can advance some tentative answers.

My focus, of course, is necessarily more modest: superstition in Mexico.[11] Even if 'superstition' exists as a meaningful and useful concept only in loosely Romance terminology,[12] Mexico remains a valid test-case amid several (we could compare, inter alia, the UK, the US, France, Italy, Spain, Portugal and the rest of Latin America). Furthermore, it might then be worth exploring whether it can transcend its 'Romance' boundaries, just as other words

---

(Harmondsworth, 1970), ch. 1 ('What is superstition?'), whose opening question hardly receives a satisfactory answer.

[8] Not least by anthropologists, who seem distinctly leery of the term (perhaps because of its ethnocentric baggage). The index to the last ten years of *Current Anthropology* contains no reference to the topic; similar absences are apparent in many book indexes, including those of canonical texts like J. G. Frazer, *The Golden Bough. A Study in Magic and Religion* (abridged edn, London, 1976; first pub. 1922).

[9] 'Superstition', from Latin *superstitio, superstare*. See Bowden, this volume.

[10] Stephen Welch, *The Concept of Political Culture* (Basingstoke, 1993), 76–7.

[11] Though modest in terms of its Mexican focus, the paper does seek to cover several centuries, and Mexico is a large and complex country. Fellow-Mexicanists may well blanch at the generalizations presented here.

[12] Including English, given that the English word is of Romance origin.

of Romance origin—such as 'state', 'revolution', 'nation'—regularly do; the signifier may vary but the signified may still exist in different cultures.[13] Though the Mexicans, ethnocentric like the rest of us, like to claim that 'como México no hay dos' ('there's only one Mexico'), there are plenty of historical processes in Mexico—state-building, revolution, industrialization, urbanization—which can be roughly defined and usefully subjected to comparative analysis, since there are clear analogues in other countries and cultures. In short, if 'superstition' works as an organizing concept amid the cactus-strewn canyons of Anáhuac, there may be grounds for believing that it works elsewhere and is amenable to comparative analysis.[14]

Before wading into the Mexican data, however, I offer a cursory discussion of the conceptual problems which surround 'superstition', at least as I see them. As historians, we often use words and terms which were used by the historical actors themselves; but we necessarily impose our own terminology too. Despite occasional assertions to the contrary, we don't and can't confine ourselves to the 'emic' words and concepts used by historical actors.[15] Of course, we seek to understand such terms and, where necessary, to explain them (especially when their meanings vary by time and/or place). But we also introduce 'etic' terms and concepts from our own vocabulary: we talk of sixteenth-century inflation, seventeenth-century depression, eighteenth-century proto-industrialization, and so on. Both practices are essential, but we should be careful to distinguish between the two.

Thus, in the case of superstition, it is necessary to examine how historical actors (let us call them 'contemporaries') used the term—and, necessarily, how they differentiated it, if they did, from kindred concepts and terms like 'magic', 'witchcraft', and 'religion'. But we cannot rest content with the mere recovery of such 'emic' usage, important though that is. The point of history, after all, is to take advantage of hindsight, which was denied contemporaries; we can also profit from modern knowledge which was likewise denied them. Useful examples would include: medicine and epidemiology; demography, statistics, and Cliometrics; and neoclassical, Marxist, and development economics. Less useful examples (which have been used nonetheless) would

---

[13] On the bewildering cross-cultural variability and subjectivity of 'superstition', note the observations of Voltaire, cited in Jahoda, *The Psychology of Superstition*, 1.

[14] 'Anáhuac', a Nahuatl term, denoting the central Mexican heartland of the Aztec empire, sometimes used as a generic label for the country (compare 'Albion', 'Hibernia', 'Iberia').

[15] Marvin Harris, 'History and Significance of the Emic/Etic Distinction', *Annual Review of Anthropology*, 5, (1976), 329–50.

include structural-functionalism, game theory, and psycho-analysis.[16] While hindsight roughly correlates with time, the heuristic benefits conferred by such branches of modern knowledge also vary from case to case; such benefits are a product of the fruitfulness of the approach (demography good, psycho-analysis not so good) and of its suitability for the matter in hand (demography good for studying medieval agrarian history, not so good for explaining the industrial revolution). For these two reasons, the gulf separating emic and etic concepts—or, to put it differently, the 'value-added' provided by etic (that is, *ex post*, hindsight-enhanced, theoretically-informed) approaches—varies, depending on both time and perspective. The Spanish conquest of Mexico and the ensuing demographic collapse of the Indian population were seen at the time (thus, 'emically') as the work of Providence. God wanted it to happen this way. Modern historians, while taking account of this important emic (contemporary) perspective, avoid such providential explanations in favour of more secular and scientific (etic) interpretations.[17] Two hundred years after the Conquest, when a nun at the convent of Jesús María in Mexico City, consumed 'by anger and rage', scourged a crucifix, spat out the host, and tried 'to stab it and fry it in oil', the question of diabolical possession immediately arose; later historians, however, might regard this as 'a straightforward case of neurotic delusion'.[18]

Of course, the (emic) perception of diabolism remains—'phenomenologically'—important as a historical factor; such perceptions coloured contemporaries' judgements and affected their behaviour; and such perceptions also changed over time, being, of course, socially constructed.[19] In prehistoric times, for example, schizophrenics may have been hailed, not as victims of the devil, but as inspired shamans, prophets, and rulers.[20] The emic/etic distinction is more clear-cut when we are dealing with phenomena, such as

---

[16] Freudian explanations of superstition and ritual, for example, illustrate the poverty of the psychoanalytical approach. Thus, we have spilt salt triggering an 'unconscious fear of ejaculatio praecox' (Thomas, *Religion and the Decline of Magic*, 749, citing Ernest Jones) and fiesta fireworks 'reiterat[ing] . . the male sexual role of penetration and explosion' (Taylor, *Magistrates of the Sacred*, 256, quoting Stanley Brandes). See also Jahoda, *The Psychology of Superstition*, ch. 4 ('Superstition and the Unconscious') and 111–17, on Jung.

[17] Anyone who disagrees will no doubt disagree with most of what follows.

[18] Fernando Cervantes, *The Devil in the New World. The Impact of Diabolism in New Spain* (New Haven, 1994), 102–3.

[19] The social construction of such perceptions — and, indeed, of all culturally transmitted ideas and practices — is obvious and does not need to be laboured (still less proclaimed with a chorus of 'eurekas').

[20] David Horrobin, *The Madness of Adam and Eve: How Schizophrenia Shaped Humanity* (London, 2001).

disease, mortality, and schizophrenia, which at least in part invite 'natural scientific' rather than 'social-scientific' explanations, since (*pace* Kuhn or, at least, some Kuhnians) science provides more solid, testable, and cumulative knowledge than the social sciences, history included.[21] Future analysts, possessed of greater hindsight and superior knowledge, may look back to our times and consign psychoanalysis to the theoretical dustbin along with notions of diabolical possession (indeed, some, like Gellner and Medawar, have done so already);[22] future analysts may even agree with Deirdre McCloskey and derogate neoclassical economics, the hegemonic social-science doctrine of today, to the status of what she calls 'apotropaic magic'.[23]

These considerations are relevant to the case of superstition. Here, the emic/etic distinction offers two important conclusions. The first, which is more clear-cut and (I think) incontestable, concerns superstitious beliefs and practices viewed in modern scientific terms; the second treats the same beliefs and practices in terms of modern social science (including history). Superstition, as commonly and usefully understood, by both experts and by many lay people, involves beliefs and practices that are scientifically irrational and which obey a non-scientific, non-naturalistic, hence in some sense supernatural, rationale.[24] It is not difficult to list illustrative examples: astrology, divination, lucky numbers, numerology, love potions, charms, amulets,

---

[21] It is my impression that Kuhn's original argument—which Kuhn himself qualified—is of limited application and has almost certainly been exaggerated by ultra-Kuhnians who have painted science in excessively relativistic colours: see John D. Barrow, *The Universe That Discovered Itself* (Oxford, 2000), 374–7. The social sciences cannot aspire to the same degree of testable and cumulative knowledge, hence mini-Kuhnian paradigms abound, enabling schools of thought to spin different conclusions from similar data (compare, for example, neoclassical, Keynesian and Marxist economics). The social sciences can, however, sustain a somewhat scientific methodology, based on citations, open debate, peer review and the like.

[22] Ernest Gellner, *The Psycho-Analytic Movement. The Cunning of Unreason* (Evanstown, 1996). F. A. Hayek was explicit: 'I believe men will look back on our age as an age of superstition, chiefly connected to the names of Karl Marx and Sigmund Freud' (quoted in Gellner, *The Psycho-Analytic Movement*, 222).

[23] Donald N. McCloskey, *If You're So Smart. The Narrative of Economic Expertise* (Chicago, 1990), 99.

[24] Any definition can be measured against two criteria: how *common* it is (that is, how much it is used, thus how widely communicable it is); and, more important, how *useful* it is (that is, how far it enables us to understand certain phenomena). It may once have been common to define the moon as a lump of cheese, but such a definition would not have advanced astronomical understanding.

talismans, omens, and rituals for securing good outcomes or avoiding bad outcomes ('apotropaic magic' again).[25] Such a list would include beliefs (about toads and black cats, for example), practices (seances, psychokinesis, wearing your underwear back to front for good luck), and artefacts (wax dolls, magic magnets, rabbits' feet, badgers' claws and dessicated humming-birds).[26] We can, at the outset of our analysis, toss into the cauldron whatever ingredients we reasonably think belong there (not forgetting 'eye of toad and toe of frog, wool of bat and tongue of dog').[27] The task, as we proceed, is to find out if the selection makes sense and what criteria lie behind it.

This, the superstitious syndrome, varies from place to place and from time to time. It includes, as I said, both beliefs and practices; more specifically, it involves a set of techniques, designed to achieve certain goals;[28] and, in a good many cases, where superstition flourishes, it implies a broader rationale or theory. A good example would be astrology; or, in 'traditional' Mesoamerican medicine, the pervasive quasi-humoral theory of 'hot' and 'cold' foods, ill-nesses, conditions, and remedies.[29] Magic, James Frazer believed, obeyed the twin principles of similarity and contiguity and, even if he overcalled his hand, he identified two recurrent elements in both magic and superstition.[30] Thus, a form of 'bounded rationality' may exist within the domain of magic or superstition, especially, perhaps, when that domain is extensive

---

[25] For such common-sense lists, see Jahoda, *The Psychology of Superstition*, 10, and Vyse, *Believing in Magic*, 6, 18, 28, 184, 213–14.

[26] Marcela Olavarrieta Marenco, *La Magia en los Tuxtlas, Veracruz* (Mexico, 1977), 114–20, 124, 134–6. Compare Thomas, *Religion and the Decline of Magic*, 746–7. Toads, in particular, seem to have paid a heavy price for human superstitiousness: Olavarrieta Marenco, *La Magia en los Tuxtlas*, 117, 142.

[27] William Shakespeare, *Macbeth*, Act IV, Scene I, l. 14–15.

[28] The goals may be positive or negative, associated with 'good' or 'bad' outcomes, from which (roughly) we get the widespread distinction between 'white' and 'black' magic.

[29] Luz María Hernández Sáenz and George M. Foster, 'Curers and Their Cures in Colonial New Spain and Guatemala', in Brad R. Huber and Alan R. Sandstrom, (eds), *Mesoamerican Healers* (Austin, 2001), 19–21, 42–5. Additional (more recent) examples are given below, n. 43. This is the best example of a widespread, 'superstitious theory' (i.e., a conceptual schema which embraces a range of phenomena). Other notions which inform a good deal of Mexican magic and superstition are: *mal ojo* (the evil eye), *aire* ('air', usually *mal aire*, bad air), *naguales* (roughly, 'familiars'), *susto* and *espanto* (shock, fear). For a good analysis, see Michael Kearney, *The Winds of Ixtepeji. World View and Society in a Zapotec Town* (New York, 1972), 46–58; note also Robert Redfield, *Tepoztlan. A Mexican Village* (Chicago, 1930), 162–4.

[30] Frazer, *The Golden Bough*, 14–59.

and 'hegemonic'.[31] Conversely, in modern secular societies, such 'bounded rationality' is less evident and superstition is therefore more demonstrably irrational. To believe in alchemy today is more irrational than to have believed in it in the Middle Ages.[32] Now that we know that constellations are cosmically meaningless, it requires heroic irrationality to believe in astrology. (However, as I note in conclusion, modernity and secularism are not as pervasive as often assumed and heroic irrationality lives on lustily).

The key point is that the entire syndrome, its beliefs and practices, techniques and theories, lack any scientific foundation: there is no experimental justification for believing in them, they are not 'falsifiable', they are not subject to critical analysis. 'The Azande', as Evans-Pritchard put it, 'are not experimentally inclined'.[33] Superstition, like magic, but unlike science, is therefore a closed system and, by and large, it is not cumulative.[34] It would be hard to prove that the superstitions of the twentieth century (UFO abductions or the Puerto Rican *chupacabras*, for example) are intellectually superior to nineteenth-century seances or eighteenth-century old wives' tales, or that sportsmen who develop idiosyncratic 'new' superstitions (like eating chicken every day) perform better than those who rely on traditional 'old' ones (like making the sign of the cross on entering the field of play).[35] The non-scientific status of superstition remains even when its practitioners allow for scientific and naturalistic explanations of some aspects of the world; indeed, I shall argue that such cognitive and behavioural eclecticism is less the exception than the rule.

That is not to say that superstitious technique never achieves its goals. As Montaigne—and many since—have pointed out, astrological predictions are bound to get it right occasionally.[36] Magic spells and cures may 'work' because

---

[31] Where a system of supernatural beliefs is extensive and hegemonic, general principles may exist which govern *both* these beliefs and their associated practices (as in an established church); the result may therefore be a domain in which a form of shared ('bounded') rationality exists, making sense of what goes on. Outside that domain, of course, the rationality breaks down.

[32] Vyse, *Believing in Magic*, 19.

[33] Cited in Thomas, *Religion and the Decline of Magic*, 772.

[34] On the distinction between superstition and magic on the one hand, and science, on the other, note: Olavarrieta Marenco, *La Magia en los Tuxtlas*, 31, 52–3; Thomas, *Religion and the Decline of Magic*, 767, 793; and Jahoda, *The Psychology of Superstition*, 108, citing Robin Horton.

[35] Vyse, *Believing in Magic*, 3–4, 27–9, 118–19.

[36] 'Nobody keeps a record of their erroneous prophecies since they are infinite and everyday; right predictions are prized precisely because they are rare, unbelievable and marvellous': Michel de Montaigne, *The Complete Essays* (Harmondsworth, 2003), 44. On 'selective forgetting' (of failed predictions), see Jahoda, *The Psychology of Superstition*,

of the placebo effect, both positive and negative: sick people may recover faster if treated by a shaman, wizard, or healer, just as victims of a curse or spell may suffer psychosomatic illness.[37] Magic and superstition may also serve as a kind of therapeutic counselling, alleviating anxiety, if only by creating the illusion that, when times are hard, problems are manageable and purposive action is possible.[38] Divination, both positive and negative, may prove to be self-fulfilling: more accidents may occur on Friday the Thirteenth because drivers are more anxious (of course, if drivers are therefore more careful, the superstition confounds itself; but it still has a phenomenological effect).[39] There may even be some instances in which a naturalistic scientific explanation may underlie a superstitious or magical practice—for example, the use of herbs or potions possessing genuine pharmacological powers (though I suspect that these cases are offset by the vast number where the 'cure' is either irrelevant or downright harmful).[40] Finally, and obviously, there are forms of (disguised)

38, citing Alfred Lehmann; and Vyse, *Believing in Magic*, 95–130, on the part played by faulty 'mathematics of cognition'.

[37] On the placebo effect: Olavarrieta Marenco, *La Magia en los Tuxtlas*, 93; Vyse, *Believing in Magic*, 135–7; Daniel C. Dennett, *Breaking the Spell. Religion as a Natural Phenomenon* (New York, 2006), 136–8; and Steven Lukes, *Emile Durkheim: His Life and Work* (Harmondsworth, 1975) 473, quoting Durkheim: '(the) Arunta who has been properly rubbed with his churinga feels himself stronger; he is stronger'. (The Arunta are an Australian 'tribe'; the churinga is a stone or wooden talisman).

[38] See Thomas, *Religion and the Decline of Magic*, 775, following Malinowski, on the 'valuable side-effects' of magic; Vyse, *Believing in Magic*, 28–9, 201–2, notes how 'pregame rituals and [baseball] dugout superstitions' can relieve tension at critical times when purposive action is impossible. However, as Isaac Asimov pointed out (Vyse, *Believing in Magic*, 196), justification on the grounds of 'solace and comfort' could also be applied to drink, drugs, and violence. And, as I mention below, random benefits must be set against systemic failures. For a critique of the consolation argument, applied to religion in general, see Richard Dawkins, *The God Delusion* (London, 2006), 195–6, 396.

[39] Jahoda, *The Psychology of Superstition*, 8; Thomas, *Religion and the Decline of Magic*, 747–8, on self-fulfilling prophecies.

[40] Olavarrieta Marenco, *La Magia en los Tuxtlas*, 115–16, gives the example of *toloache* (*datura*), which has genuine physiological effects. When, in the 1940s, snake bites caused a spate of fatalities among construction workers in the Papaloapan River basin, not far away, *culebreros* (snake-charmers) were apparently able to effect cures, when conventional doctors had failed: Calixta Guiteras Holmes, *Sayula. Un pueblo de Veracruz* (Havana, 1990), 120. In contrast, the hot-cold dichotomy (see n. 43 below) seems to have generated some pretty horrendous medical treatments: Salvador Aguilar, *Veinte años de medicina rural* (Mexico, 1994), 46, 48; June Nash, *In the Eyes of the Ancestors. Belief and Behavior in a Maya Community* (New Haven, 1970), 148–9. I therefore find Jahoda's

prudential advice which may make sense: people who do not walk under ladders may be marginally less likely to be hit on the head by falling objects (though they may trip on the kerb or collide with passing cyclists. Like proverbs, many superstitious aphorisms cut both ways).[41] By virtue of the placebo effect, counselling, common sense, or some genuine pharmacological causality, magic and superstition may develop a kind of useful 'technology', involving both curing and therapy. However, this is not science; it is hit-and-miss; it lacks the 'controlled experiment and innovation' of science;[42] and, in many cases, it possesses it own quite distinct and erroneous non-scientific rationale (like the 'hot' and 'cold' dualism of Mesoamerica).[43]

In the past, things were different; indeed, we could put it simply and say that, prior to the scientific revolution of the seventeenth century, the test of scientific validation was largely absent.[44] Beliefs depended on trial and error, or, more usually, on the authority of Church and state (or, earlier still, the authority of shamans, patriarchs, and prophets). This would, of course, be true of revealed religion such as Catholicism.[45] As the Magdalena case illustrates,

---

argument (*The Psychology of Superstition*, 145, 147) that, in evolutionary terms, superstition may be an 'adaptive mechanism', possessing 'positive survival value', pretty unconvincing. The evolutionary function of religion is the subject of lively current debate: Dennett, *Breaking the Spell*; Dawkins, *The God Delusion*; and (in my amateur opinion, the best study) Scott Atran, *In Gods We Trust. The Evolutionary Landscape of Religion* (Oxford, 2002).

[41] On 'prudential injunctions', see Thomas, *Religion and the Decline of Magic*, 746. Terry Rugely, *Of Wonders and Wise Men. Religion and Popular Cultures in Southeast Mexico, 1800–1976* (Austin, 2001), 26–8, gives examples of folk tales and supernatural stories which, in nineteenth-century Yucatán, inculcated positive values and warned people against 'such destabilizing faults as pride, excess, jealousy and cruelty'. Of course, if the advice is blindingly obvious—'do not put your hands in the fire'—it loses any arcane or superstitious quality (example taken from Frazer, *The Golden Bough*, 25–6).

[42] Thomas, *Religion and the Decline of Magic*, 793. In a 'closed system' of this kind, systematic testing and peer review are absent; furthermore, failures can readily be attributed to imperfect ritual rather than fundamentally misconceived remedies.

[43] For examples of the 'hot/cold' syndrome, see Olavarrieta Marenco, *La Magia en los Tuxtlas*, 208–11; Guiteras Holmes, *Sayula*, 128–9; Robert Redfield, *The Folk Culture of Yucatan* (Chicago, 1941), 128–9, 306–7.

[44] On the seventeenth-century watershed: Thomas, *Religion and the Decline of Magic*, 773; Jahoda, *The Psychology of Superstition*, 123.

[45] Though not deism. The key point is whether a deist God started the Universe, laying down inexorable laws of Nature, and then letting things develop of their own volition; or whether She continued to interfere, theistically, thus introducing other-wordly causation which, in the case of miracles, transgressed the laws of Nature.

Catholicism allowed for miracles, for healing effected by divine or saintly intervention; Catholics were encouraged to seek benefits of this kind, involving both avoidance of bad outcomes (apotropaic religion) and the securing of good ones. Catholic practice regularly contravened the laws of nature (miracles, exorcism, transubstantiation). Colonial Catholic authorities, while combating magic, diabolism, and witchcraft, gave credence to these phenomena, which inhabited the same broad mental landscape: belief in diabolical possession, the Franciscan Mateo Bonilla argued, 'is as much a matter of faith as belief in the most Holy Sacrament'.[46] Religion, magic, witchcraft and superstition thus shared a common, contested terrain, across which there occurred constant cultural commerce, borrowing, pilfering and even grand larceny.

Nevertheless, these borders had to be defined and policed, especially by the institutional Church, in this case, the Catholic Church. While critics readily denounced the 'superstitious' beliefs and practices of the Catholic Church, the Church itself maintained a key distinction between religion on the one hand and superstition and magic on the other.[47] While, from a modern, scientific, etic standpoint, revealed religion, superstition and magic substantially overlap and may even be indistinguishable, the Church had to maintain this scientifically spurious distinction. Etic (modern, scientific) analysis is therefore capable of identifying superstition, but necessarily lumps it along with a host of other phenomena (magic, witchcraft, revealed religion) which, in the (emic) eyes of most contemporaries were radically different.

At this point, therefore, the sharp scientific perspective must yield to the blurred vision of the social sciences.[48] Superstition, magic, diabolism, and revealed religion may all be self-deluding attempts to understand and control important but apparently capricious phenomena—the weather, ill-health, sex, agriculture, animal husbandry—on the basis of misconceived theory and practice. When it comes to storms, smallpox, miscarriages, potato blight, and cattle murrain the (etic) explanations provided by modern science serve better than the (emic) 'explanations' offered by superstition, magic, or religion. But, as historians and social scientists, we also need (our own) *etic* explanations of these *emic* (that is, contemporary) explanations. Why, for example, is speaking with tongues regarded as divine or diabolical behaviour in one context, as schizophrenia in another? Schizophrenia may be a global

---

[46] Cervantes, *The Devil in the New World*, 122; see also 60.

[47] On Popish 'superstitions': Thomas, *Religion and the Decline of Magic*, 78–9; Walsham, this volume; and n. 51 below. As I mention later, twentieth-century Mexican anticlericals stridently echoed these sentiments.

[48] Thus, what follows may be accepted by readers who may have disagreed with the argument so far; and vice versa.

phenomenon which occurs pretty regularly throughout human society, but it is explained and treated very differently according to time, place, and circumstances.[49] Why are schizophrenics sometimes revered, sometimes persecuted; sometimes walled up in Bedlam, sometimes consigned to 'care in the community'? Here, broad questions of power, politics, and patriarchy enter in; and we are ineluctably drawn into a Durkheimian search for the 'social function' of superstition.[50] If, for example, religion is the opium of the people, is superstition a comparable soft drug (the marijuana of the masses?), which, as Hume suggests, deadens resentment and makes a hard life more tolerable?[51] Or is it a form of deviance and even resistance, a potential solvent of hierarchy and authority? Believers do not, of course, have to be aware of such social functions for their beliefs to be efficacious; indeed, it is probable that sincerely held beliefs are more efficacious as levers to move—or to maintain—the social and political order; if religion is the opium of the people, or if superstition is the marijuana of the masses, it may be best administered by those who are genuine addicts themselves.

In the Mexican context the social role of superstition, viewed etically, displays several patterned characteristics. First, religion, magic, diabolism, and superstition all inhabit common ground and feed on each other. Hence the interminable scholarly debates concerning their relationship, in particular, the old chicken-and-egg question of whether magic spawned religion or vice versa (a question I avoid).[52] Even when religion condemns magic, diabolism, or superstition, it grants them a certain legitimacy (they may be evil and/or misguided, but they work, they are not nonsense).[53] 'Believers' therefore

---

[49] Horrobin, *The Madness of Adam and Eve*; Vyse, *Believing in Magic*, 180–3.

[50] Vyse, *Believing in Magic*, 9; Lukes, *Emile Durkheim*, 470–7.

[51] 'Superstition . . . steals in gradually and insensibly; renders men tame and submissive; is acceptable to the magistrate and seems inoffensive to the people': David Hume, *Essays Moral Political and Literary* (Oxford, 1963), 79. Hume is here contrasting bland, insidious superstition with red-blooded 'enthusiasm'; superstition, he argues, 'is a considerable ingredient in almost all religions' (77), but it is a particular speciality of 'the Romish church' (79).

[52] On the 'endless "dialectic" of magic and religion' see the useful resumé in Olavarrieta Marenco, *La Magia en los Tuxtlas*, 25–57; Frazer, *The Golden Bough*, 63–79; and, for a more ambitious synthesis, Daniel Lawrence O'Keefe, *Stolen Lightning. The Social Theory of Magic* (New York, 1983), 148–50, 231–50. O'Keefe's conclusions are complex (and diagrammatic: see 238–9, 250); but the central conclusion is, very roughly: 'religion is the institution that models magic for society' (244). That fits quite comfortably with my argument about superstition (as well as magic and religion).

[53] On the kinship and permeability of religion, magic and superstition: Cervantes, *The Devil in the New World*, 58–60; and Thomas, *Religion and the Decline of Magic*, 55–7, which

confront a wide repertoire of beliefs and practices from which they can choose, especially as they set about making sense of a puzzling and often threatening world. Superstition, like religion and magic, offers both understanding and help. Like Marx's ineffectual philosophers, superstition explains the world; but, like Marx, it also seeks to change it. It may therefore become particularly relevant in difficult times, when both explaining what is going wrong and putting it right become crucial: thus, when ill-health, failed harvests, warfare or bad weather threaten hapless individuals, families, and communities. However, within this great melange of (etic) irrationalism, an (emic) hierarchy exists, premised not on scientific proof but rather on power and ideological persuasion.[54] Organized religion—in this case, the Catholic Church—possesses a structure of command, reasonably effective means of recruitment, communication, and repression, and a roughly agreed canon or theory.[55] It can therefore lay down what is right and wrong: miracles wrought by the supernatural power (or, strictly, mediation) of the saints are valid; but supernatural outcomes achieved by means of witchcraft (*brujería*), diabolism, or freelance healers (*curanderos*) are not. Indeed, they may be positively evil and should be stamped out.[56]

Of course, like other 'religions of the book', Catholicism is not just about invoking supernatural assistance to cope with the challenges of life. It offers a grand cosmology, from the Creation to the Last Judgement; and its ethical teachings—the Ten Commandments, the Beatitudes—offer moral precepts in a way that competing supernatural systems (magic, diabolism, superstition) usually do not. Magic and superstition do not enjoin moral behaviour;

---

includes the telling comment of the Elizabethan Reginald Scot: the Pope 'canonizeth the rich for saints and banneth the poor for witches'. A slew of additional witchcraft references could, of course, be appended to this footnote.

[54] Again, we might deploy a Gramscian notion of hegemony: the Church calls the shots by virtue not only of church courts and *autos da fe*, but also of eloquent sermons and seductive ritual. Indeed, I would hazard the opinion that the Mexican Catholic Church has been one of the mightiest engines of 'hegemony' that the world has seen.

[55] The Mexican Catholic Church has also been, since its sixteenth-century foundation, relatively stable and orthodox: it suffered no Reformation and no major schisms; even the late twentieth-century challenge of Liberation Theology has been successfully blunted (for which Pope John Paul II can take a good deal of credit, or blame). The cohesion of the hierarchy thus militated against serious popular heterodoxy.

[56] In cracking down on *curanderos*, the Church found an ally in Spanish physicians, who were out to stifle the competition; however, demand always outstripped supply, guaranteeing the *curanderos* a steady clientele: Carlos Viesca Treviño, '*Curanderismo* in Mexico and Guatemala', in Huber and Sandstrom (eds), *Mesoamerican Healers*, 54–5.

hence they are often seen as a form of technique (even, rather misleadingly, as 'proto-science');[57] they are ways to get things done, not ways to live the good life or to achieve salvation. In Vyse's words, religion is 'celestial', superstition is 'terrestrial'.[58] Similarly, religion espouses 'ideal' goals, magic concentrates on 'real' ones.[59] The rival appeals of—and the functional division of labour between—religion and superstition thus depend in large measure on the goals or concerns which are at issue: if they are cosmological and moral, religion trumps superstition and magic; but if they are earthly and practical, religion has to compete with its rivals; and, in doing so, it comes to resemble them.[60] Thus, the more religion seeks to offer practical solutions (and not just vague solace), the more it has to mix with its rivals in the marketplace

---

[57] On the presumed kinship of magic and science, see Olavarrieta Marenco, *La Magia en los Tuxtlas*, 27, 30–1; and Thomas, *Religion and the Decline of Magic*, 769–70. As the latter notes, however, 'the union of magic and science was short-lived'. Indeed, if we follow Wolpert's useful distinction between science (which, pursuing a given methodology, 'produces ideas') and 'technology' (which 'results in the production of usable objects'), it would be more accurate to see magic as 'proto-technology'—i.e., as a means to affect the world in a predictable and useful way by following certain known procedures (procedures whose rationale often remains unfathomable and is certainly unscientific): see Lewis Wolpert, *The Unnatural Nature of Science* (London, 1993), esp.ch. 2 (quotes from 25). Indeed, we could generalize that magic and superstition offer *pseudo-technologies* to deal with intractable but pressing problems; as James Dow puts it, glossing Malinowski, 'magic in general is an extension of human effort beyond the point where ordinary technology fails': 'Central and North Mexican Shamans', in Huber and Sandstrom (eds), *Mesoamerican Healers*, 72. Thus, apes use sticks to extract honey from hives; and pre-industrial, pre-scientific men devised levers, blocks, tackles, and pulleys to raise megaliths and pyramids. But when it comes to health, fertility, weather, and the harvest, patterns of causation are obscure and the scope of technology is more limited, hence magic and superstition are brought to bear.

[58] Vyse, *Believing in Magic*, 40.

[59] See the neat formulation in Olavarrieta Marenco, *La Magia en los Tuxtlas*, 48: religion uses symbolic means to achieve 'ideal' goals; magic uses symbolic means to achieve 'real' goals; and applied science uses real means to achieve real goals. But see the qualification in n. 60 below.

[60] Thus, Mexican Catholicism, especially the cult of the saints, addresses very 'real' goals (hence the piles of milagros at San Francisco Magdalena); and, in this respect, religion and magic become indistinguishable, according to Olavarrieta Marenco's schema (n. 59 above). Religion addresses 'fundamental issues of human existence' as well: morality, the meaning of life, and life after death (Thomas, *Religion and the Decline of Magic*, 761, citing Malinowski). But, depending on the time, the place, and the cult, religion also offers more mundane, practical and concrete benefits (symbolic means to achieve 'real' goals). Hume (n. 51 above) would no doubt have agreed.

of 'mana';[61] and we may speculate that the outcome will depend a good deal on the choices of the customers. Are they looking for the meaning of life? For moral guidance? Or for help in curing cancer, bringing rain, or making unrequited love requited?

Customer choice aside—thus, shifting the focus from 'subaltern agency' to 'structural power'—the social and political role of organized religion is also crucial. By virtue of being rich and established, the Catholic Church wields substantial 'cultural' power, which is reinforced by elaborate and costly ritual. Mexican organized religion is overt and ostentatious, while magic and superstition are to a degree covert and discreet. Catholicism has its grand cathedrals and teeming shrines; magic and superstition retreat to murky caves and remote hilltops.[62] For similar reasons, religion is collective—much of it is public and addresses 'public' issues (hence, Te Deums for the accession of kings)[63]—whereas magic and superstition are more individual, deployed for private benefits.[64] Prayers tend to be general and supplicatory: God can be petitioned, but not commanded; and there are many desirable outcomes— finding buried treasure, making an enemy sick, improving your love life— which it would be unseemly (and, presumably, futile) to solicit from God. Spells, in contrast, have a certain automaticity to them: if done properly, by an accomplished *brujo* (wizard), they should work.[65] Religion too has a canon— a set of texts and rules—and these, although they may be hotly debated, afford the basis for ideological control and enforcement. Churches therefore have courts, judges, trials, and *autos da fe*. Magic and superstition have no equivalent institutions (there is no 'Church of magic', as Durkheim noted; wizards have clients, not church-goers);[66] they can rarely coerce and their 'canon' is shifting, largely unwritten, and dependent on oral communication. Mexican healers disagree among themselves regarding the appropriate days on which

---

[61] I use (Melanesian) 'mana' as shorthand for sacred, supernatural, or numinous (as against profane, natural, or mundane): Olavarrieta Marenco, *La Magia en los Tuxtlas*, 54–5; Vyse, *Believing in Magic*, 3, citing Levi-Strauss; Lukes, *Emile Durkheim*, 464, 468, 513.

[62] On the Indians' initial 'hiding of the gods' following the Conquest, see Serge Gruzinski, *Images at War. Mexico From Columbus to Blade Runner (1492–2019)* (Durham, 2001), 52–6. And, for colonial, nineteenth- and twentieth-century clandestinity: Taylor, *Magistrates of the Sacred*, 65, 268; Cervantes, *The Devil in the New World*, 49–50, 91–3; Calderon de la Barca, *Life in Mexico*, 312; Dow, 'Central and North Mexican Shamans', 80; Olavarrieta Marenco, *La Magia en los Tuxtlas*, 133, 156.

[63] Cheryl English Martin, *Governance and Society in Colonial Mexico. Chihuahua in the Eighteenth Century* (Stanford, 1996), 107–9.

[64] Olavarrieta Marenco, *La Magia en los Tuxtlas*, 40, following William Howells.

[65] Cf. Thomas, *Religion and the Decline of Magic*, 46.

[66] Vyse, *Believing in Magic*, 10; Olavarrieta Marenco, *La Magia en los Tuxtlas*, 32–3.

rituals should be conducted; and there is no way of convening a Council of Nicaea or Synod of Whitby to rule on the matter and come up with the 'right' answer.[67] While the established Church, we might say, runs a religious command economy, staffed by appointed commissars and loyal party members, magic and superstition more closely resemble a decentralized market, where consumers shop around, where freelance (including fraudulent) specialists seek to meet their needs (often on the basis of individual inspiration and improvisation), and there is also a good deal of amateur 'do-it-yourself'.[68]

Magic and superstition, apart from being more individualized and instrumental, are therefore more popular and demotic; they well up within society and, as we shall see, they are stubbornly resistant to top-down control. For this reason, superstition is often regarded as 'vulgar', 'crude', or 'ignorant',[69] even if, viewed scientifically, its beliefs are often no more intrinsically irrational than those of organized religion and, from a sociological perspective, superstitious practices are by no means confined to 'ignorant' plebeians. Finally, by virtue of its canon, its authority, and its 'ideological apparatus', the church gets to draw the boundary lines within the sprawling terrain of the supernatural. It is the Church which decides where revealed religion stops and forms of deviance start (and which, along with the secular arm, in this case the Spanish Crown, decides what to do with deviants). Here, a rough pattern emerges, as I argue below: deviance which appears to threaten the very basis of

---

[67] Olavarrieta Marenco, *La Magia en los Tuxtlas*, 131 on *brujo* divergence. Councils and synods may not be able to enforce complete uniformity; but at least they try, and have some success.

[68] Hence, we get 'personal' superstitions, devised by individuals for their own benefit. However, these superstitions usually follow well-known patterns, such as lucky numbers, colours, or garments: Vyse, *Believing in Magic*, 22. The collective culture provides the template, the individual takes his or her pick. Again, there are parallels with the cult of the saints. For a good autobiographical account of a scam seance in the city of Oaxaca in the 1920s, see Carlos Velasco Pérez, *Oaxaca de mis recuerdos* (Oaxaca [?], 1995, pub. by the author).

[69] Thomas, *Religion and the Decline of Magic*, 773; Jahoda, *The Psychology of Superstition*, 3, 11, which describes a 'religious core' shading into peripheral superstition. Thomas, *Religion and the Decline of Magic*, 44, also refers to 'sub-superstitions'—demotic spin-offs from the official cult which claim 'a crudely material efficacy' (compare Cervantes, *The Devil in the New World*, 58). It is not clear to me what, apart from the authority of the Church, differentiates a great many official religious beliefs from unofficial 'superstitious' ones: in colonial Mexico, for example, 'priests . . . had no intention of compromising on fundamental matters of doctrine such as monotheism and the Trinity, the temptations of Satan and transubstantiation in the mass; but in other respects they tolerated . . . superstition': Taylor, *Magistrates of the Sacred*, 51.

the established Church is, understandably, regarded with greatest hostility. Thus, heresy (the denial of the Catholic Church in favour of a rival) is anathema. Diabolism which resembles heresy—that is, which seems to offer devil-worship as an alternative Church/religion—is also anathema (but it is also very rare).[70] Magic is less seriously threatening: it is certainly deviant and misconceived; it often serves illicit goals (such as making money or inflaming passion); and by definition it does so by illicit means (spells, charms, invocations). Black magic, which seeks evil outcomes is, of course, worse than white magic, which may seek good outcomes by bad means.[71] White magic shades into superstition, which I take to be the most minor, venial, and demotic of such forms of deviance.[72] Unlike diabolism or heresy, superstition does not challenge the Church; it coexists, often quite harmlessly, with the Church;[73] it boasts no rival hierarchy or canon; and it may often resort to religious formulae and artefacts (thus giving indirect legitimacy to orthodox religion). Furthermore, many clerics, like many members of the literate elite, entertain their own superstitions. The Church can therefore take a more relaxed view of superstition than of magic, and of magic than diabolism or heresy.[74] However, it is the Church—sometimes in cahoots with the state—which ultimately decides where the boundaries are to be drawn: where, in other words,

[70] In Mexico, 'whole-hearted demonic devotion was rare': Cervantes, *The Devil in the New World*, 83. In this respect Mexico resembled Europe: Thomas, *Religion and the Decline of Magic*, 614–16, rebutting Margaret Murray. Recent anthropological research seems to confirm as much: Olavarrieta Marenco, *La Magia en los Tuxtlas*, 154–64.

[71] 'Black' magic substantially overlaps with witchcraft and sorcery. Belief in the latter is pervasive—'practically universal in central and north Mexico'—but recorded cases are rare and, following a kind of professional ethic, 'most shamans discourage vengeance sorcery': Dow, 'Central and North Mexican Shamans', 87–90.

[72] Jahoda, *The Psychology of Superstition*, 3, differs: stressing its 'ignorant' and 'unreasoning' connotations, he concludes that 'the term "superstition" has a strongly pejorative flavour'. Even if true for today (which I doubt: see below), such a conclusion is surely historically misleading (Jahoda, to be fair, is a psychologist, not a historian). In Mexico, as elsewhere, 'superstition' was no mark of status or intellect; but it was both pervasive and tolerated, at all levels of society. If superstition had a 'strongly pejorative' reputation, how would witchcraft, black magic and diabolism be described?

[73] Cf. Thomas, *Religion and the Decline of Magic*, 762, which depicts the clergy and their competitors—the 'cunning folk and astrologers'—as 'deadly rivals'. While such cross-cultural comparisons are difficult, I argue (below) that, at least from *c.*1600, Mexico witnessed less 'deadly rivalry' than cautious coexistence. Of course, clerical attitudes to heresy and diabolism were much more antagonistic.

[74] Mainstream opinion today takes a similarly relaxed view of superstition: Vyse, *Believing in Magic*, 175.

harmless superstition becomes a more worrisome magic; and where magic involves the yet greater dangers of diabolism and even heresy. In the rest of this chapter, I offer some examples of such clerical beating-the-bounds. These rough definitions thus combine both emic and etic qualities. They are emic in that it is contemporary actors—the Church hierarchy in particular—who decide which is which, where the fuzzy lines of demarcation are to be drawn. But there is a rationale to their decision-making, even if the decision-makers are unaware of it (hence, it is an etic rationale that we, sharp-eyed social scientists, on the look-out for Durkheimian social functions, can detect with the benefit of hindsight). Take, for example, the supposed Marian apparition which occurred at Juquila, Oaxaca, Mexico, in 1928.[75] What should the Catholic Church, in the form of the parish priest, Ausencio Canseco, make of the story told by an eight-year-old Chatino Indian girl and endorsed by her mentor, the devout spinster Matilde de Narváez? The Church has to decide if this is a purely natural phenomenon—fraud, self-delusion, mental illness—or one requiring a supernatural explanation. If it opts for the latter, in defiance of etic scientific claims, it has to decide if the event was a miracle (the result of divine intercession, which may eventually lead to further miracles, a new cult, even canonization) or a diabolical manifestation (designed to ensnare gullible souls, thus requiring urgent clerical investigation and counter-measures). After some initial prevarication, cura Canseco opted for diabolism and conducted an exorcism. The Church set its face against the new cult, which gradually withered away. Patriarchy also played its part: the cult was begun by women and never won the allegiance of male *cofradías* [sodalities]. Matilde de Narváez, excommunicated, remained a believer until her death some twenty years later. At least she outlived her clerical nemesis, since in 1933 cura Canseco was swept from his horse during a flood and drowned.

In the case of other cults, the Church was more credulous and supportive.[76] Or, where fraud or self-delusion was diagnosed, it was sceptical and hostile. Where cults were concerned, the stakes were potentially high: they involved miracles, sainthood, and eternal souls, as well as important mundane considerations (money, trade, clerical preferment, and local politics). But roughly similar questions were posed by less important issues, such as

---

[75] Edward Wright-Ríos, 'Envisioning Mexico's Catholic Resurgence: The Virgin of Solitude and the Talking Christ of Tlaxcoxcalco,1908–1924', *Past and Present*, 195 (May 2007).

[76] The most obvious being the Virgin of Guadalupe: see Taylor, *Magistrates of the Sacred*, 277–300. But here, too, the Church did not espouse the cult from the outset; and, very recently, clerical experts have cast doubt upon the literal story of the Virgin's apparition in 1531 (thus incurring the wrath of Mariolatrists).

popular superstitions and 'syncretic' religious practices.[77] Should they be tolerated (even, in some cases, welcomed as signs of popular religiosity)? Or should they be condemned, and proportionately repressed, as either ignorant errors, cynical frauds, or diabolical or heretical challenges?[78] Faced with the Juquila story, natural scientists, adopting their own etic perspective and, therefore, accepting Hume's refutation of miracles, would regard all supernatural explanations as untenable;[79] they would settle for fraud or self-delusion or mental illness. Similarly, 'miraculous', 'magical', and 'superstitious' restorations of health would be attributed to the patient's antibodies, perhaps encouraged by the placebo effect or even the natural effects of a supernatural/superstitious remedy. Social scientists (including historians) might well agree with this diagnosis, but would look for a second-order etic explanation of the social phenomenon: why the patient was treated in this way and how the treatment was conceptualized, by the patient, the local community, and the authorities. Or, in the case of Juquila, why the apparition happened when and where it did;[80] why the various actors assumed the roles they did; and why the Church's veto prevailed over the abiding faith of old Matilde Narváez.

II

The question now becomes how these emic distinctions were made and maintained. The Mexican Catholic Church, I argue, maintained a kind of tripartite distinction. Revealed religion, magic, witchcraft, and superstition all involved belief in supernatural, otherwordly, and thus inexplicable powers.[81] God moved in a mysterious way; but so did devils, *naguales*, *brujos/brujas*, and

[77] For a good resumé of 'syncretism', see Taylor, *Magistrates of the Sacred*, 53–9.

[78] Some good examples, drawn from nineteenth-century Yucatán, are given by Rugely, *Of Wonders and Wise Men*, 127–38. For an analysis of similar dilemmas in Spain, see William A. Christian Jr, *Local Religion in Sixteenth-Century Spain* (Princeton, 1989), and the same author's *Visionaries. The Spanish Republic and the Reign of Christ* (Berkeley, 1996).

[79] Hume, *Essays*, 517–46, the nub of the argument being on 526.

[80] During the 1920s, Oaxaca, like the rest of Mexico, was recovering from the ravages of the Mexican Revolution; the attendant upheaval was exacerbated by a violent conflict between Church and state, which peaked in 1926–9; and Oaxaca itself witnessed several natural disasters, including serious earthquakes in 1928 and 1931. Rugely, *Of Wonders and Wise Men*, 18, makes a similar point about nineteenth-century Yucatán: 'misery' (dearth, drought, plague and rebellion) 'was all around . . . (and) misery entailed agency'; that is, it drove people to seek both causes (such as witchcraft) and solutions (white magic, the intercession of the saints, superstition). Atran, *In Gods We Trust*, 59–61, argues that the search for agency 'may be a crucial part of our evolutionary heritage'.

[81] The kinship of these belief systems is well illustrated by Olavarrieta Marenco, *La Magia en los Tuxtlas*, 48. Note also Thomas, *Religion and the Decline of Magic*, 755, 761.

curanderos/curanderas (spirits, wizards/witches, and healers).[82] By 'inexplicable' and 'mysterious' I do not mean arbitrary and entirely uncontrollable (compare, perhaps, the arbitrarily capricious deities of the Aztecs). God and his saints could be moved by prayer and sacrifice, correctly done;[83] the devil's aid could be purchased by means of permanent pacts or, much more commonly, short-term deals; wizards and witches could, in effect, be hired; and there were recognized ways to ward off their spells. Forms of divination, such as astrology, followed elaborate rules and procedures; magic often evinced Frazerian principles of similarity and contiguity—which the cult of the saints sometimes replicated;[84] and folk cures, building on ancient Mesoamerican tradition, often obeyed a kind of 'theory', based on hot/cold dualism.[85] Thus, magical and superstitious practice reflected a crude kind of theory; but such practice said little about cosmology, the transcendent meaning of life, or ethical behaviour.

No-one—not even the Church hierarchy—could explain how these practices achieved their desired outcomes.[86] By and large, religion, magic, and superstition depended on faith and authority. Hence the Catholic Church's rough tripartite categorization: revealed religion (very good); heresy, black magic, idolatry and diabolism (very bad); white magic, shading into superstition (trivially bad but relatively harmless).[87] I suspect that a similar tripartite

---

[82] *Naguales* (cf. n. 29) are animal spirits, resembling 'familiars', who play a large part in Mexican magical beliefs: see Kearney, *Winds of Ixtepeji*, 51–3; Olavarrieta Marenco, *La Magia en los Tuxtlas*, 165–6.

[83] God could be appealed to, but only for positive and religiously correct outcomes (such as long life or good health), and His response could not be counted on; maybe, in His omniscience, He knew better than to concede the favour.

[84] Thus, Santa Lucia helped people with bad eyes: Nash, *In the Eyes of the Ancestors*, 206. It is worth noting the local (Amatenango del Valle, Chiapas) version of how Santa Lucia lost her sight: enamoured of St Thomas, she gave him her eyes, which he, to her chagrin, rejected. If the former is an example of Frazer's 'sympathetic' magic, the rubbing of San Francisco's statue at Magdalena exemplifies Frazer's 'Law (*sic*) of Contact or Contagion': Frazer, *The Golden Bough*, 14.

[85] See n. 43 above.

[86] Hence they were poles apart from science, as described by Wolpert, *The Unnatural Nature of Science*.

[87] As with most social or cultural typologies, these categories blur at the edges (even in the eyes of the Catholic Church, which tends to like sharp boundaries, e.g. Heaven, Hell, Purgatory). The white magic/superstition boundary is, I suspect, chiefly professional: white magic is the preserve of specialists, born with and/or trained in esoteric powers; superstition is a lower common denominator, accessible to lay people, perhaps purloined in the past from the specialists. Such a division of labour still pertains in parts of Mexico.

categorization may be evident in other Churches and cultures. Meanwhile, particular beliefs and practices shuttled to and fro across these somewhat arbitrary emic boundaries. One key frontier area was the cult of the saints, which is crucial to any analysis of Mexican or Spanish-American Catholicism. For, as the case of San Francisco de Magdalena suggests, while the saints were (*de jure*) paid-up members of the official Church, they were also (*de facto*) purveyors of magical and superstitious services, who were often treated like local shamans or wizards. Below, I offer a tentative diagrammatic explanation, based on two axes: [i] organization, hierarchy, and structure versus local, popular, and decentralized; and [ii] good versus bad—in the eyes of the Catholic Church:

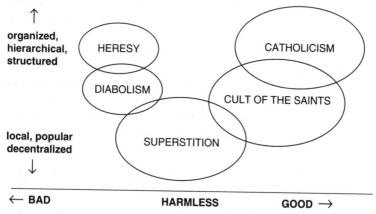

Given the underlying kinship between these several forms, they existed in tense symbiosis (and, with the scientific revolution and the Enlightenment, they came under common attack). Whatever the relationship of religion and magic,[88] the two fed upon each other, even when they were in outright conflict. So, too, religion and witchcraft (the relationship of magic to witchcraft is, of course, another moot question). In defining its enemies and combating them, the Church adopted a reasonably coherent and evolving strategy. Heresy—in this case, Protestantism—was exceptionally dangerous, since it posed a fundamental threat to the established Church and even to the rule of the Most Catholic Kings. Heresy-hunts and *autos da fe* peaked during the late

---

In modern Britain, the specialist 'white magicians' are few and far between, but the superstitious residue remains.

[88] See n. 52 above.

sixteenth- and early seventeenth-centuries when the union of the Spanish and Portuguese crowns provoked fears of *converso* heresy.[89] However, heresy was not a massive problem, in the way that it was in Europe. More serious was Indian religious dissent and backsliding, which, in its more serious manifestations, took the form not of heresy (deliberate perversions of Christianity) but of paganism and diabolism—the two being closely linked. After the optimistic humanism of the early Conquest dissipated, Spanish repression of Indian religious beliefs and practices became violent and intense (*c.*1550-1650). However, it was also pretty successful. The huge collapse in Indian population removed old believers *en masse* and made the survivors vulnerable to the prudential appeal of Christianity. The old priestly elites were eliminated, sacred texts were systematically destroyed, and pre-Conquest religion was relegated to the peripheries (Chiapas and the Yucatán hinterland, as well as the sparsely settled north) and down into the lower reaches of Indian society, where its carriers were no longer blood-spattered priests brazenly standing atop great pyramids, but local wise men, *curanderos*, *brujos*, and occasional 'man-gods' (local prophets), who usually did their work discreetly, even clandestinely, in murky caves or on remote hilltops.[90] During this second phase, roughly 1550–1650, diabolism became a major concern—a 'growing obsession'—of the Church.[91] Indians were turning, not to Protestantism, but to the devil; and the equation of the devil with old pre-Conquest gods—especially Huitzilopochtli—made this association more plausible and dangerous. Thus, the Church both defined and inadvertently propagated diabolism: the Indians were warned of the power of the devil, and the devil's association with the old gods; not surprisingly, some decided it made sense to seek the devil's aid.[92] Thanks to demographic collapse and mendicant proselytization there was never any danger of a mass-based Indian religious revivalism, nor of any institutional rival arising to challenge the Catholic Church. But local and individual backsliding was common and the devil was often to blame.

This phase of supposed diabolism and repression lasted until around the mid-seventeenth century. Thereafter, although diabolism never disappeared entirely, it waned in significance; that is to say, the Church began to take

[89] Solange Alberro, *Inquisición y sociedad en México, 1571–1700* (Mexico, 1988), 77–8, 172–7, 215.

[90] Serge Gruzinski, *Man-Gods in the Mexican Highlands: Indian Power and Colonial Society, 1529–1800* (Stanford, 1989).

[91] Cervantes, *The Devil in the New World*, 8, 15–16, 25–39, 47 (quote).

[92] Ibid., 36, 56, 125–6; Taylor, *Magistrates of the Sacred*, 66–7.

a more relaxed view of Indian—and Spanish or caste—idolatry.[93] When, in the 1690s, the Franciscans reported horrendous tales of diabolical possession in a Querétaro nunnery, these were roundly dismissed by a 'sceptical' Holy Office, which considered them to be frauds, fantasies, and 'nonsense', perpetrated by perverse friars on deluded women.[94] Later cases were also dismissed as 'matter(s) of no substance'.[95] The authorities' more calm and considered response did not mean that the phenomena had themselves disappeared, but rather that their importance was now downplayed; diabolism, we might say, shifted down the league table of deviance, approximating more and more to a form of ignorant superstition which was to be regretted and countered, but not ruthlessly repressed. When, in 1704, a mulato claimed to be a witch who communed with the devil, the Inquisition commissary wearily recorded that 'such vices and superstitions are very widespread among the common folk'.[96] William Taylor thus notes how, by the end of the seventeenth century, Spanish concern for diabolism and idolatry had waned: 'practices that had been taken as manifestations of idolatry—magical invocations to natural forces, auguries, love potions, medicinal magic and devotion to animal figurines and other effigies, became relatively harmless superstitions'.[97] Late colonial pastoral visitations therefore involved occasional reprimands for 'superstitious acts', which might be 'evidence of Satan's power', but genuine idolatry was rarely suspected or imputed.[98]

Superstition was thus construed as the lowest, least threatening stratum of popular religious deviance, below heresy, diabolism, and idolatry. The Church did not condone superstition—by definition, it was naive and wayward—but it was not seen as a serious challenge. Here, I think, we touch upon some key attributes of superstition which can be generalized from the (Mexican colonial) case I am now describing: superstition was wrong, but not egregiously, heretically, or diabolically wrong; it could therefore be tolerated and/or gently counteracted; a full-scale assault would be risky and even counterproductive (for it might drive the superstitious into the arms of heresy or diabolism). Furthermore, while clerics might have been confident in their ability to distinguish religion from superstition, the overlap between the two was substantial; 'official orthodox remedies' and the cures and spells of

[93] Cervantes, *The Devil in the New World*, 125–6.

[94] Ibid., 115–26.

[95] Ibid., 137, describing a 1724 case from Parral, which involved the devil being kept locked up in a Jew's pantry.

[96] Cervantes, *The Devil in the New World*, 137.

[97] Taylor, *Magistrates of the Sacred*, 66–7.

[98] Ibid., 67.

curanderos coexisted in 'a 'symbiotic relationship';[99] the healer Antonio Pérez, while admitting to using herbs and charms, pleaded his Catholic orthodoxy ('I put my trust first in God and only then in herbs') and cited a Dominican friar as his former mentor, who 'taught me cures for everything'.[100] In the eyes of many, religion, magic, and superstition complemented rather than challenged each other (in which respect, *vox populi* was arguably more rational than censorious clerics who tried to draw a line down the middle of this loose melange of related beliefs and practices). Antonio Pérez, we have seen, resorted to God before he tried herbs. Spaniards pleaded that they appealed to the Devil only when God had failed them.[101] 'God is very good', declared a man from Tamazula (Jalisco), 'but the devil isn't so bad, since he helps men'.[102] The devil was seen as a kind of maverick saint, not the radical antithesis of God. Deals with the devil did not necessarily involve selling one's soul for eternity: they were often short-term contracts serving specific needs. 'Wholehearted demonic devotion' was extremely rare and, as already mentioned, eclectic diabolism was, in part, a backhanded tribute to the persuasive powers of the Church, which had invested a good deal of effort in telling people that the Devil was a force to be reckoned with.[103] Such casual eclecticism—which appears to contrast with the English experience—continued down through the twentieth century.[104]

Superstition (as defined by the Church) was therefore heterodox and pragmatic. Compared to Catholicism, it also tended to be local and popular.

---

[99] Cervantes, *The Devil in the New World*, 58–9.

[100] Ibid., 72–3.

[101] Ibid., 73, 83. As I note in conclusion, this pragmatic, 'playing-the-field' approach to supernatural solicitation has continued down to the present in Mexico.

[102] Taylor, *Magistrates of the Sacred*, 263.

[103] Cervantes, *The Devil in the New World*, 78, 83. There is also some evidence that, as Michael Taussig has argued for Bolivia, the devil—a victim of authority, turned subversive trouble-maker—may have appealed to exploited underdogs, like Indians, slaves and mulattos: Cervantes, *The Devil in the New World*, 78–80.

[104] Thomas, *Religion and the Decline of Magic*, 762–3, seems to suggest a greater degree of compartmentalization, on the part not only of clerics and authorities (as might be expected), but also of the common people: 'at a popular level it was usual. . .to see witchcraft, prophecies, fairies or ghosts as explanations of misfortune which were essentially different from those offered by the clergy'. Of course, we cannot pontificate about the perceptions of long dead plebeians who left no testimony of their own; however, it seems that Mexicans more readily elided the official categories—religion, diabolism, magic, witchcraft—than did their English counterparts. This elision, as I suggest in what follows, reflected both the weight of pre-Conquest beliefs and the (relative) weakness of clerical control.

No hierarchy pronounced on the finer points of superstition: the 'experts' were local, usually illiterate, autodidacts, or, at most, apprentices of older 'experts'. Many superstitions existed in the public domain, required no training or innate gift, and were therefore thoroughly demotic and amateur. Superstition, we might say, was the lowest stratum of a Little Tradition that owed obedience to no presiding Great Tradition (thus, we cannot simply equate superstition with popular or 'folk' Catholicism which, however heterodox, did).[105] Nevertheless, superstition was pervasive: it was by no means a dwindling vestige of defunct pre-Columbian beliefs (though it certainly embodied many of those beliefs, as I note below); it drew heavily on Catholic notions and rituals, including Christian 'white magic'; and it incorporated all ethnic groups, Spaniards and castes as well as Indians. Indeed, Spaniards and castes often felt they had a lot to learn from the Indians who, after all, knew the lie of the land—both figuratively and literally—better than recent immigrants. The records of the Inquisition show how 'a large number of people opted to defer to the Indians' superior knowledge of their world and its spiritual forces'.[106]

Superstition and magic were pervasive for three principal reasons. First, in Mexico as in early Christian Europe, superstition was a sink in which the detritus of older religions accumulated.[107] In the Mexican case, superstition combined elements of ancient pre-Columbian religions; it involved sacred caves, hills, and streams; sacred objects, such as bundles, amulets, stones, maize pith, copal resin; and old religious rites, now transferred from the control of hieratic elites and perforce entrusted to lowly plebeians.[108] Such 'disjointed residues' were extensive and durable,[109] in part because, in the wake of the Conquest, an ancient monistic world-view had to be squeezed into a new and alien Catholic dualism. The Christian dichotomy of radical good and evil was alien to Mesoamerican religion (hence, a morally complex deity like

---

[105] Robert Redfield, 'On Folk Society', *American Journal of Sociology*, 52 (1947), 293–308.

[106] Cervantes, *The Devil in the New World*, 60.

[107] Thomas, *Religion and the Decline of Magic*, 750, depicts the English spiritual landscape as strewn with 'the cultural debris of many different ways of thinking, Christian and pagan, Teutonic and classical'. However, in England the battle against paganism had been going on for a thousand years (Judith Herrin, *The Formation of Christendom* (London, 2001), 171–2); in Mexico it had begun with the relatively recent Spanish Conquest in the sixteenth century.

[108] Taylor, *Magistrates of the Sacred*, 49, 268–9; Cervantes, *The Devil in the New World*, 91, 93; Serge Gruzinski, *La colonización de lo imaginario. Sociedades indígenas y occidentalización en el México español. Siglos XVI-XVIII* (Mexico, 1991), 156, 173, 195, 231.

[109] Cervantes, *The Devil in the New World*, 68.

Huitzilopochtli could be identified with both Jesus and, more commonly, the Devil).[110] As is well known, some old gods transmuted into new Catholic saints, lending Mexican Catholicism a polytheistic veneer.[111] The cult of the saints thus embodied a good many older beliefs, which combined quite comfortably with Catholic 'white magic'; among the Mixtecs of Oaxaca the *brujos* (wizards) even acquired their own patron saint.[112] Thus, while the Church repressed some older beliefs and practices, it incorporated and Christianized others. Some remained beyond the pale: not all the shrines and holy places of the past could be converted into Catholic religious sites (for one thing, the Church did not have the institutional power to map and police all the sprawling and inhospitable territory of New Spain). As a result, much of the old religious topography, especially in more remote and mountainous regions, fell into the domain of magic and superstition.[113]

Second, superstition survived because it was tolerated, in ways that heresy and diabolism were not.[114] In a sense, this formulation is tautological: precisely because it was tolerated, superstition was superstition; it did not pose a fundamental threat to the greater ecclesiastical and political order; it did not subvert the Great Tradition of Catholicism. The Church regarded superstition as a wayward but relatively harmless popular failing; like a lot of popular failings, it could be excused on the grounds that the common people drank

---

[110] Ibid., 15; Enrique Marroquín, *La cruz mesiánica. Una aproximación al sincretismo católico indígena* (Oaxaca, 1989), 64.

[111] Taylor, *Magistrates of the Sacred*, 53; Gruzinski, *La colonización de lo imaginario*, 163, 181; and Marroquín, *La cruz mesiánica*, 11–12, 65–9, which also illustrates the mutability of saints over time.

[112] Marroquín, *La cruz mesiánica*, 65.

[113] Such as Oaxaca and the Otomí highlands around Tututepec (both of which had resisted integration into the Aztec empire): Gruzinski, *La colonización de lo imaginario*, 183–4. We could compare Julio Caro Baroja's depiction of the mountainous interior of the Basque country where, well into the twentieth century, 'witchcraft and magic were still very much realities': *The World of the Witches* (London, 2001; first edn, 1964), p. ix. Such a topographical explanation holds so long as the authorities, clerical and secular, are based in the cities and lowlands (as they usually are) and are bent on the extirpation of dangerous deviance; however, as I note in conclusion, magic and superstition can also flourish in big modern cities, so long as the authorities and public opinion remain indifferent, or even benign.

[114] The same was generally true of magic, so long as it was not classified as diabolism. If a 'magic' balloon were added to my diagram above, it would float just above 'superstition', overlapping with the latter and with the 'cult of the saints' balloon.

too much.[115] Sobriety was the best antidote to superstition. Frequently, the Church was called upon to adjudicate particular cases: was Fulano de Tal, for example, a relatively harmless *curandero* (healer), a diabolist, or a heretic? Over time, as we have seen, the Church tended to take a more relaxed view. It did so, first, because the colonial regime proved remarkably stable, at least until the later eighteenth century; popular protest was sporadic, limited, and rarely fuelled by religious deviance.[116] In the absence of a Protestant Reformation, no major heretical option presented itself; and, by the same token, the hegemonic Catholic Church still commanded a reassuring repertoire of supernatural remedies, notably those provided by Mexico's ubiquitous and versatile saints.[117] The European Church's 'battle with magic'—which 'always had something of the air of a trades union closed shop about it'[118]—was not replicated in Mexico, where the Church, especially the cult of the saints, had cornered most of the market. Furthermore, the Church had limited manpower and, by and large, adopted a cautious and legalistic approach to such matters.[119] So the category of *curandero* grew at the expense of the others ('man-gods', devil-worshippers, idolaters); superstition absorbed the diabolism and heresy of previous generations. Returning to the diagram above, we could say that, with time, the two balloons in the top left quadrant (heresy and diabolism) deflated, while the others expanded (and overlapped). The net result was a shift from left to right, from 'bad' to 'good' beliefs and practices.

Third, in Mexico as elsewhere, superstition answered practical needs: it was chiefly concerned with 'health, safety, fertility and prosperity'.[120] The devil, in particular, was less an evil demiurge than 'a friend whose help could be

---

[115] Taylor, *Magistrates of the Sacred*, 65–6. Drugs, such as peyote, also played an important part in popular fiestas and rituals, provoking the censure of elites and authorities: ibid., 71–2.

[116] William B. Taylor, *Drinking, Homicide and Rebellion in Colonial Mexican Villages* (Stanford, 1979), shows that local rebellions, though quite frequent, were limited in scope and modest in their objectives; they targeted abusive local officials and rarely challenged the fundamentals of the colonial regime. Exceptions were to be found largely in the extreme northern and south-eastern peripheries of the colony (see Taylor, *Magistrates of the Sacred*, 68). For a more general analysis of colonial legitimacy and stability, see Alan Knight, *Mexico: The Colonial Era* (Cambridge, 2002), 102–50.

[117] The absence of the Reformation clearly sets Mexico apart from European cases, such as England: Thomas, *Religion and the Decline of Magic*, 763–4.

[118] Diarmaid MacCulloch, *Reformation. Europe's House Divided, 1490–1700* (London, 2004), 564.

[119] For example, Taylor, *Magistrates of the Sacred*, 67. On the insecurity of clerical authority, ibid., 202–6; and Gruzinski, *La colonización de lo imaginario*, 247.

[120] Taylor, *Magistrates of the Sacred*, 66.

invoked' in times of need.[121] In a poor agrarian society, where bad harvests occurred about every eleven years, bringing dearth and sometimes famine, people required reassurance, consolation, and means to control a fickle natural world.[122] Specific occupations, which similarly involved apparently random vicissitudes, seem to have been prone to diabolism and, we might hypothesize, superstition: miners, stockraisers, gamblers, bullfighters, and bandits.[123] Perhaps, too, these were individualistic occupations, cut off from the collective life and ritual of peasant communities, for whom the patron saint was the first port of call in times of need.[124] Of course, the Catholic Church and, especially, the cult of the saints, catered to similar needs (as we have seen in the case of St Francis at Magdalena). In the Mixtec highlands of Oaxaca the very term for 'saint' translates as *hágame el favor*, do me the favour.[125] But the institutional Church could not monopolize these public goods: it was too stretched, especially in the sweeping northern prairies and sierras, or amid the dense, semi-autonomous Indian villages of the south, where lay associations (*cofradías*) ran local cults and parish priests were too 'scarce or indolent' to assume close control.[126] Where the Church was weak, official religion, with its cult of the saints and charitable works, was outbid—or commandeered—by unofficial, freelance healers, wizards, and wise women.[127] In addition, perhaps particularly in the towns and

---

[121] Cervantes, *The Devil in the New World*, 56.

[122] Enrique Florescano, *Precios del maíz y crisis agrícolas en México (1708-1810)* (Mexico, 1969), charts climatic fluctuations and harvest failures.

[123] Cervantes, *The Devil in the New World*, 80, 88–90. Twentieth-century analyses identify similar 'superstitious' occupations: 'gamblers, sailors, soldiers, miners, financial investors and. . .college students': Vyse, *Believing in Magic*, 26; cf. Jahoda, *The Psychology of Superstition*, 128, 135. On the remarkable vitality and complexity of saints' cults in a modern Mexican mine, see Elizabeth Emma Ferry, *Not Ours Alone. Patrimony, Value, and Collectivity in Contemporary Mexico* (New York, 2005), 110–12.

[124] A significant proportion of diabolistic accusations concerned blacks and mulattos (Cervantes, *The Devil in the New World*, 85, 87, 88, 93, 97, 137). While this probably did reflect their occupational profiles and spatial mobility, it is also a function of the Inquisition records, which, by and large, neglect Indians. On patron saints, see Gruzinski, *La colonización de lo imaginario*, 240.

[125] Marroquín, *La cruz mesiánica*, 63.

[126] Cervantes, *The Devil in the New World*, 67 (quote); Gruzinski, *La colonización de lo imaginario*, 247; Taylor, *Magistrates of the Sacred*, 202–6.

[127] When 'commandeered' by local laymen, the cult of the saints became highly pragmatic: icons wrought cures and miracles, were fought over, and suffered chastisement when they failed to deliver. The Church therefore frowned on some cults, regarding them as wayward, superstitious, and even fraudulent, while seeking to regain control over others.

more mobile society of northern Mexico, white magic and superstition served self-interested ends for which the Catholic Church was less suitable. The devil, for example, could bring wealth and prosperity; he could satisfy sexual cravings (even those of a precocious six-year-old); in contrast to the sombre killjoys of the Counter-Reformation Church, he offered a fun-loving life, 'flying through the air in idle pleasure'.[128] Superstition, likewise, involved love charms and spells to find buried treasure; in short, it offered self-gratification and individual advancement, as well as relief from hardship. These were hardly benefits which the devout could openly solicit from the severe authorities of Baroque Catholicism. Either way - whether it was a question of the Church's limited reach or its refusal to entertain profane desires—magic and superstition answered to popular needs which the Church (not to mention the state) could not satisfy; so the Great Tradition (of Catholicism) ceded an ample zone of self-government to the Little Tradition (of superstition).

III

In the early nineteenth century, Mexico achieved independence. The colony collapsed and the Church emerged, somewhat chastened, but no longer constrained by its entangling alliance with the Spanish Crown. Echoes of the Enlightenment and the 'Atlantic Revolution' reverberated throughout New Spain, soon to be the republic of Mexico. Subjects became citizens; liberal discourse caught on; and the political regime was genuinely transformed. But Mexican society and economy changed more sluggishly and there is little evidence that popular—superstitious, magical, or religious—beliefs were similarly transformed. Indeed, the insecurities of life, enhanced by the savage wars of independence and the vicissitudes of the new nation state, probably made the consolations of both religion and superstition all the more coveted. Thus, while the new notions of liberalism, nationalism, and even democracy gained ground, they proved compatible with older beliefs.[129]

The Juquila story thus had numerous colonial precedents. See Taylor, *Magistrates of the Sacred*, 266–9; Gruzinski, *La colonización de lo imaginario*, 244–6.

[128] Cervantes, *The Devil in the New World*, 85, 87.

[129] There is considerable debate concerning the impact of these new notions; however, even those who argue, with some cogency, for a fairly rapid process of ideological diffusion, do not see liberalism and nationalism as incompatible with more 'traditional' forms of religious belief: see Peter Guardino, *Peasants, Politics and the Formation of Mexico's National State: Guerrero, 1800–1857* (Stanford, 1996). A provocative recent study of nineteenth-century Mexican liberalism goes even further, over-stressing its essentially religious foundations: Pamela Voekel, *Alone Before God. The Religious Origins of Modernity in Mexico* (Durham, 2002).

Nineteenth-century liberalism, even when it sought to clip the wings of the institutional church, denying it legal privileges and landed wealth, did not challenge the basic premises of revealed religion; nor did liberals have the will, the capacity, or (in many cases) the desire to tamper with popular superstition. Both Church and state, released from their tight colonial embrace, and fumbling their way in the new, confused, postcolonial world, conceded considerable latitude to popular beliefs and practices.

In the late nineteenth century, this began to change. The Mexican Church took advantage of the Pax Porfiriana (1876–1911) and of the new organizational and ideological currents propelling Catholicism into the twentieth century and set about reforming, reorganizing and reasserting its ideological power. The Church's institutional reach was extended (especially in central and centre-west Mexico); new technologies such as railways, telegraphs, and the print media were readily adopted; and a new form of Catholic 'mass politics' developed, incipiently during the later Porfiriato, more dramatically in the wake of the Revolution of 1910. One aspect of this Catholic revival was a crackdown on popular superstition, not least by new regular orders who regarded Mexican popular Catholicism as 'ignorant', 'naive', and 'superstitious'.[130]

Meanwhile, the state followed a roughly similar trajectory: a form of authoritarian state-building under Porfirio Díaz (1876–1911) gave way to the mass-based, reformist project of the Revolution, which culminated in the regime of the 1920s and '30s. Now, Church-state, Catholic-anticlerical, conflict was renewed, but in a more profound fashion, since what was at stake was not simply legal privileges or property rights, but mass allegiances, the hearts and minds of the Mexican people, men, women, and children. The state, too, took advantage of new technologies, such as radio, and new practices, such as sport; while the 'massification' of politics brought on by the Revolution gave the infant state unprecedented scope for potential social engineering, by means of schools, trades unions, *ejidos* (agrarian reform communities), the official press, public radio, film, architecture, and art (notably the didactic murals of Rivera, Siqueiros and Orozco). Church and state came to see themselves as engaged in a quasi-Manichaean battle for the soul of Mexico, a battle which generated serious violence, especially during the Cristero War (1926–9).

Two aspects of this complicated story deserve attention here. First, the revolutionaries' ambitious efforts to change hearts and minds involved

---

[130] Marroquín, *La cruz mesiánica*, 25–6, deals with (Indian) Oaxaca; but censorious priests were also at work in 'orthodox', mestizo Mexico too: Luis González y González, *Pueblo en vilo. Microhistoria de San José de Gracia* (Mexico, 1972), 96–7.

sustained campaigns against popular credulity. They battled against what they saw as the deadweight of superstition; but, even more important, the radical anticlericals among thm certainly included Catholicism in the same indictment. Thus, when, in 1934, Plutarco Elías Calles, ex-president and *jefe máximo* of the regime, called for a 'psychological revolution' that would 'banish prejudices' from Mexican minds, there was no doubt that the old clerophobe had the Catholic Church in mind.[131] Apart from limiting the number of priests and compelling priests to register with the state, revolutionary leaders advocated aggressive policies of 'defanatization', which they saw as the latest and most radical episode in the historic struggle between Religion and Science.[132] To this end, the state introduced a form of 'socialist education', which sought to inculcate a 'rational and exact notion of the universe and of social life'.[133] The 'truth of science', it was hoped, would sweep away the cobwebs of religion and irrationality.[134] Mexicans would learn that they were subject to 'natural laws', not the caprice of God and his saints; peasants would therefore cease imploring the saints for rain and, instead, invest in irrigation systems; children were taught that 'the saints do not exist and those made of wood are good only for burning'.[135] In order to break the power of Catholic 'fetiches' ('symbols of bourgeois hierarchy'), the state encouraged aggressive campaigns of iconoclasm.[136] Jerky newsreels from Tabasco—a notoriously jacobin state—show a diverse crowd of local iconoclasts, including flapper girls and bearded peasant patriarchs, hacking to bits a hefty wooden crucifix.[137] In the same state, it was said, iconoclasts

---

[131] Carlos Martínez Assad, *El laboratorio de la revolución. El Tabasco garridista* (Mexico, 1979), 83.

[132] Alan Knight, 'Popular Cuture and the Revolutionary State in Mexico, 1910–40', *Hispanic American Historical Review*, 74:3 (1994), 393–444; Martínez Assad, *El laboratorio*, and Bantjes, *As If Jesus Walked on Earth*, ch. 1, offer good case studies, of Tabasco and Sonora respectively.

[133] Victoria Lerner, *Historia de la Revolución Mexicana. Periodo 1934-40. La educación socialista* (Mexico, 1979), 74–5, 82.

[134] Marcela Tostado Gutiérrez, *El intento para liberar a un pubelo. Educación y magisterio tabasqueño con Garrido Canabal, 1924–35* (Mexico, 1991), 49.

[135] Dawson, Veracruz, to State Department, 2 Sept. 1931, SD 812.00/Veracruz/26; Daniels, Mexico City, to State Department, 5 Nov. 1935, SD 812.42/303 (citing Calles' opinions).

[136] Elpidio López, Federal Education 'Plan de Trabajo' for Sonora, 1934–5, 1 Sept. 1934, in Secretaría de Educación Pública (SEP) archive, caja 1093/106. Adrian Bantjes (University of Wyoming) is currently preparing a monograph on Mexican iconoclasm in the 1930s.

[137] Jaime Soler Frost and Mónica Zacarías Najjar, (eds), *Los pinceles de la historia. La arqueología del régimen, 1910–55* (Mexico, 2003), 40–1.

played baseball with the wooden heads of decapitated religious icons.[138] In neighbouring Veracruz the effigy of Santa Teodora was smashed and put on display, so that the people of Jalapa could see that it was just cotton and wax, not 'flesh and blood, miraculously preserved'.[139] In Sonora, as we have seen, the statue of San Francisco—along with other religious icons—was seized and destroyed.[140] As the Santa Teodora case shows, this was not mindless vandalism, but didactic iconoclasm: 'the destruction of fetishes will serve as scientific instruction'.[141] If icons were the chief targets, revolutionary anticlericals also made off with church bells; while, in Oaxaca, they banned and burned the sacred mescal—agave liquor—which was the necessary accompaniment of many religious and magical rituals.[142] At the same time, the revolutionaries took positive steps to 'defanaticize' the population: they expanded rural and primary education, imposing the new 'socialist' curriculum; they organized evening and weekend events at which orators declaimed against the Church, the confessional, the sacraments, and the myth of miracles; for a time, they even experimented with secular rites of passage—'socialist' baptisms and marriages—which would break the ideological thralldom of Catholicism. Needless to say, a good many of these audacious jacobins came to a sad end: they suffered violent Catholic reprisals; or, the devout noted, they suffered God's retribution. The massive Paricutin volcano reared its head in a Michoacan cornfield because of the sins of the local people.[143]

The 1930s thus witnessed a sustained effort by the state to mould hearts and minds, extirpating both Catholicism and superstition; indeed, unlike their more moderate liberal predecessors, the anticlerical *enragés* of the revolutionary period equated Catholicism with magic and superstition, just as they equated socialism with science. Their attitudes were frankly elitist; they deplored the primitive mentality of Mexicans—even the erstwhile 'revolutionary' Zapatistas of Morelos - which remained cluttered with pagan superstitions.[144] Anticlericalism tended to be a patriarchal ideology: women were especially vulnerable to clerical wiles and, in a good many families, Catholic

[138] Martínez Assad, *El laboratorio*, 198. Tabasco also boasted a baseball team called the 'Macuspana Atheists'.
[139] Dawson, Veracruz, to State Department, 2 Sept. 1931, SD 812.00/Veracruz/26.
[140] Bantjes, *As If Jesus Walked On Earth*, 6–7, 10–15.
[141] Elpidio López, Federal Education 'Plan de Trabajo' for Sonora, 1934–5, 1 Sept. 1934, in SEP archive, caja 1093/106.
[142] Marroquín, *La cruz mesiánica*, 26.
[143] Pedro Carrasco, *El catolicismo popular de los tarascos* (Mexico, 1976), 136–40.
[144] Report of Donaciano Murguía, Cuernavaca, 20 Aug. 1935, SEP 202/6.

wives and mothers had to contend with anticlerical husbands and sons.[145] Anticlericalism also emerged most strongly on the Mexican peripheries, for example, Sonora in the north and Tabasco on the Gulf coast, where the institutional church was weakest and where, perhaps, an ideology of hard work and rugged individualism exerted particular appeal. To some extent, therefore, it became a vehicle for 'modernizing' and nationalizing elites who, having emerged—like Calles—from the periphery, sought to fasten their power on the benighted and backward Mexican heartland.[146] In my view, they were usually genuine in their beliefs, which they proudly traced back through the glorious tradition of Mexican liberalism to the seminal inspiration of the Enlightenment.[147]

Yet, at the same time, the Catholic Church not only denied its 'superstitious' status, but continued to campaign against what it saw as the superstitious deviance of the common people. Thus, when popular cults sprang up, as they did quite regularly, a few were welcomed into the bosom of the Church, where they could be clasped close and controlled. Their popularity and their profits would thus redound to the benefit of the institutional Church. Many cults, however, were spurned; the faithful were warned off; and die-hard devotees were reduced to a 'superstitious' rump.[148] Quite often, official Catholic discourse seemed to echo that of the Church's sworn enemy, the anticlerical state: in Morelos, a Catholic activist lamented, 'the reigning atmosphere . . . . is one of paganism and indifference'; calls to Catholic action fell on deaf ears; and, in consequence, Morelos 'advances rapidly toward moral ruin'.[149] For all its hierarchy and authoritarianism, therefore, the Church was far from being all-powerful or monolithic. Indeed, the Church tended to divide, very roughly, between 'traditionalists', who clung to heterodox, local, popular cults, often controlled by lay sodalities, and 'militants', who followed the lead of the clergy, advocated more strictly orthodox

---

[145] Thus, 'put crudely, anticlericalism was a program developed by men and aimed at women and chldren': Patience A. Schell, *Church and State Education in Revolutionary Mexico City* (Tucson, 2003), 181.

[146] There may be tenuous parallels with Napoleon and Stalin.

[147] Some have argued, I think usually wrongly, that revolutionary jacobinism was a smokescreen designed to distract the people from socio-economic grievances (such as unemployment) or the failings of the Revolution (the slow pace of agrarian reform): for example, Carleton Beals, cited in Hugh G. Campbell, *La derecha radical en México, 1929–49* (Mexico, 1976), 27.

[148] As in Juquila in the 1920s (see above).

[149] Jocelyn H. Olcott, 'Las hijas de Malinche: Women's Organizing and State Formation in Postrevolutionary Mexico, 1934–40', Yale University Ph. D. diss., 2000, 113.

practices, and tended to support clerical-conservative political movements.[150] The militants and their clerical leaders, despite their bitter hatred of the revolutionary state, found themselves in agreement with the jacobin thesis that the Mexican people were prone to superstition, and that the country would be better off—would be more sober, enlightened, civilized, and productive—if superstition were extirpated.

However, the state, with unprecedented boldness, now included the Catholic religion within the dark penumbra of superstition: it sought a secular, even 'socialist', citizenry, devoted to the *patria* and loyal to the revolutionary regime. The Church, while battling the state (and denying charges of benighted, superstitious, medieval backwardness), at the same time kept up a rearguard action against popular religious deviance, especially in the deep (Indian) south and the sprawling (mestizo, Americanized) north. In the south, old Indian practices survived and new Catholic—especially Marian—cults sprang up (stimulated, perhaps, by the upheaval of the Revolution and aided, in part, by better communications); the Church appropriated some for its own spiritual and pecuniary purposes, vetoed others (again, alleging superstition), while turning a blind eye to a good many more.[151] In the north, Protestantism, spiritualism, and indifference were identified as threats—and were probably exaggerated; but the north also harboured heterodox cults which tended to break the Catholic mould (the institutional Church being weaker in the north): Santa Teresa de Cabora, El Niño Fidencio, Juan Soldado, Jesús Malverde.[152] In terms of cultic etiology, the north perhaps resembled other American frontier zones where the institutional Church was weak and individuals and communities, seeking to survive in a dynamic, fluid, frontier society, resorted to forms of spiritual self-help, often in pragmatic, eclectic fashion.[153] Not surprisingly, the Catholic hierarchy was alarmed and reacted much as it had in the past. Serious ('heretical') threats, such as Protestantism, were aggressively combatted; superstitious deviance was treated more indulgently and condescendingly. The Church therefore drew its usual squiggly line down the middle of spiritual and supernatural

---

[150] Carrasco, *El catolicismo popular*, 142.

[151] Wright-Ríos, 'Envisioning Mexico's Catholic Resurgence', and the same author's work in progress.

[152] Paul J. Vanderwood, *Juan Soldado: Rapist, Murderer, Martyr, Saint* (Durham, 2004), which, 211–16, also includes discussion of Jesús Malverde (now the patron saint of drug traffickers) and El Niño Fidencio.

[153] For example, the Brazilian north-east and, perhaps, the North American frontier.

practices, while the state sought to lump almost all such activities in the camp of obscurantism and irrationality.[154]

The Mexican people, no less wayward and recalcitrant for being (supposedly) increasingly 'modern', did not readily yield to these rival 'top-down' projects.[155] The State's defanatization policy experienced very limited success. It worked, to a degree, where the State came bringing genuine gifts: land, schools, credit, roads, jobs, trades unions. Communities went along with 'socialism' and secularization where there were concomitant benefits; it was in part a question of calculated cost-benefit analysis (if Paris had been worth a mass to Henry IV, dirt-poor peasant farmers were prepared to trade the mass for a school or a cornfield).[156] Perhaps, too, the state's provision of some minimal security, thus of enhanced control over a capricious environment, diminished the appeal of religious—and superstitious—solace.[157] But the state's doctrinaire onslaught on the Church was shortlived. President Lázaro Cárdenas (1934–40), committed to radical social reform, backed away from anticlericalism and 'defanatization', which, it became clear, were provocative policies that compromised other revolutionary goals (such as

---

[154] Yet, even at the height of revolutionary anticlericalism, there was some strange backsliding, as jacobin *enragés* began to flirt with faith-healing and spiritualism (which then enjoyed a certain vogue in Mexico); Plutarco Elías Calles—a notorious *comecuras* ('priest-eater'), but also a chronic invalid—sought the services of El Niño Fidencio in 1928: Vanderwood, *Juan Soldado*, 216.

[155] I put 'modern' in quotation marks, since it is a notoriously indeterminate adjective, sometimes a lazy synonym for 'recent', more often suggesting literacy, mobility, urbanism, secularism, which do not necessarily coexist. If, resorting to a more precise and historical interpretation, we equate 'modernity' with Enlightenment ideals of rationality, secularism and scepticism (cf. Jonathan I. Israel, *Radical Enlightenment. Philosophy and the Making of Modernity* (Oxford, 2001), p. vi, 4–12), then we must conclude that 'modernity' is patchy, capable of reversal, and by no means guaranteed by urbanization, industrialization or social mobility.

[156] Some were not prepared to make the trade; hence the revolutionary regime faced strenuous opposition from die-hard Catholic communities in centre-west Mexico (Guanajuato, Jalisco, Michoacan), for whom the very notion of a 'socialist' school or an official land grant (an ejido) was anathema. But most Mexican peasants were less clericalist and more calculating.

[157] The logic of the argument seems persuasive: religion, magic and superstition throve on insecurity (Thomas, *Religion and the Decline of Magic*, 777–83); by the same token (perhaps) the recent decline of religion in Western Europe coincided with post-war stability and welfarism. The Mexican state (*c.*1930–*c.*1970) could not claim as much; but it did preside over an increasingly peaceful society, unacquainted with major wars; it provided some of the peasantry with both material and 'psychic' benefits (land, credit, roads, education); and it witnessed increasing life expectancy.

education and land reform) and even threatened civil war (Spain provided a timely warning). From the mid-1930s, such policies were wound down; by the 1940s the 'revolutionary' state—now a good deal less revolutionary—had reached a rough *modus vivendi* with the Catholic Church. Socialism and secularism yielded to a bland aggregative nationalism (which contained an important religious element: the Virgin of Guadalupe); and the task of moulding hearts and minds increasingly fell to business, the mass media, and the market.

These powerful forces, boosted by the wartime boom, happily coexisted with popular superstition, magic, and the cult of the saints; indeed, it may be that the increased mobility, migration, and urbanization of post-1940s Mexico reinforced such beliefs. After all, the swelling cities lacked the stable collective religious organization of peasant villages; as yet, they also lacked extensive social insurance; and they teemed with the threats which magic and superstition claimed to counter (illness, job loss, marital breakdown, sexual betrayal, crime, and violence). So the migrants who flocked to Mexico City in the 1940s and '50s soon put up their family altars, consulted astrologers and *curanderos*, and experimented eclectically with charms and patent medicines.[158] As one woman, a convert to spiritualism put it: 'here in Mexico City there is more witchcraft than in the villages'.[159] The same was probably true of post-war provincial towns.[160] As in the past, personal crises, or the simple desire to survive and prosper in a cut-throat economy, led people to experiment, to explore pragmatically the whole repertoire of

[158] Oscar Lewis, *Five Families. Mexican Case Studies in the Culture of Poverty* (New York, 1959), 38, 62 (evil spirits); 46, 71, 90, 173, 175, 194–5 (sorcery and bewitchment); 69 (charms); 149 (healers); 72, 129–30, 142 (saints); 205, 253 (ghosts).

[159] Lewis, *Five Families*, 152. I have not found much quantitative data dealing with superstition in Mexico. One survey, conducted by the Catholic Church, suggests that in Mexico City in the early 1990s 64% of respondents believed in the saints (but 80% in the Virgin of Guadalupe), while 38% believed in the devil and 18% in *brujería* (witchcraft). There was no significant difference based on sex; but belief (of all kinds) tended to correlate with age; young people (15–24 years old) were in general more sceptical, especially regarding the devil; but 16% still believed in *brujería*: Luis Leñero Otero, *Perfil de la religiosidad en la arquidiócesis de México, D.F.* (Mexico, 1994).

[160] Olavarrieta Marenco, *La Magia en los Tuxtlas*, 77 (spiritualism),114 (love potions), 125–6, 132 (deals with the devil); Isabel Lagarrida Attias, *Medicina tradicional y espiritismo* (Mexico, 1975), which deals with Jalapa (Veracruz). We might contrast these Veracruz (i.e., Gulf coast) towns with San José de Gracia, Michoacan, a fervently Catholic small town, where, post-1945, the Church ruled and 'superstition lost ground'—'it was enough to look at people's necks and see the scant number of amulets to be found hanging there': González, *Pueblo en vilo*, 265–6.

natural and supernatural services on offer. If aspirin failed, the sick consulted a spiritualist *curandero*, who specialized in trances and patent medicines.[161] Shops sold magic magnets alongside Catholic images.[162] Coins were taken from church collections to be used in casting domestic spells.[163] Black and white magic still coexisted; and the devil—again, a somewhat ambiguous figure, by no means all bad—continued to offer his services, especially to those who sought to get rich quick.[164] Healers and wizards, both urban and rural, remained influential and sometimes notably prosperous.[165] They were also alive to innovation.[166] A traditional healer in Veracruz, a specialist in 'sucking the pulse' in order to remove 'fear' (*espanto*), claimed to have imported a state-of-the-art *extractor de espanto* from the US.[167] Some wizards began to tap into the gullible tourist market.[168] As in the past, the cult of the

---

[161] Olavarrieta Marenco, *La Magia en los Tuxtlas*, 77; see also 108–9.

[162] Ibid., 124. Similarly, the Christian calendar was important when it came to casting spells or initiating new *brujos* (wizards): ibid., 130–1. In the 1940s, the *curanderos* ('healers') of Sayula (Veracruz), some of whom had 'talked with the Devil', learned their trade by ascending three hilltops, home of the 'chief wizards', where they collected plants 'which come out at night'. However, all this had to be preceded by ritual devotion to the Virgin of Catemaco; the expedition had to occur on the first Friday in March; and subsequent healings/spells were accompanied by frequent invocations of Christ, the Virgin Mary, and Easter Thursday (sic): Guiteras Holmes, *Sayula*, 121–2.

[163] Olavarrieta Marenco, *La Magia en los Tuxtlas*, 125.

[164] Again, a deal with the devil might be an enduring pact, or a one-off transaction: Olavarrieta Marenco, *La Magia en los Tuxtlas*, 155–9, 162–3.

[165] Ibid., *La Magia en los Tuxtlas*, 190–1, which gives the example of a poor boy from Catemaco who made good as a *brujo*. One important source of income was rich clients: 'it is not unusual to see luxury cars, whose plates indicate they have come from far away, parked outside the modest house or "consulting room" of some local specialist'.

[166] Compare Thomas, *Religion and the Decline of Magic*, 786: 'magic was conservative in its subject-matter, as well as in its techniques. The village wizards of our period had little in their repertoire to distinguish them from their medieval or, possibly, even their Anglo-Saxon predecessors'. Of course, twentieth-century Mexican wizards were living through a time of unusually rapid economic and technological change; so, more than their early-modern English counterparts, perhaps, they had to adapt and innovate. Furthermore, magic benefited from rising real incomes: in Zinacantan (Chiapas), 'the increase in wealth is an important factor in the proliferation of both shamanistic rites and cross shrines': Evon Vogt, *Tortillas for the Gods. A Symbolic Analysis of Zinacantan Ritual* (Cambridge, Mass., 1976), 197. Geschiere, this volume, also notes the happy marriage of magic and 'modernity'.

[167] Olavarrieta Marenco, *La Magia en los Tuxtlas*, 112.

[168] Ibid., 160. We also find a Popoloca shaman running a mail order sorcery business: Dow, 'Central and North Mexican Shamans', 89.

saints was also sensitive to changing needs, even in defiance of Church authority. The drug boom in Sinaloa greatly enhanced the status of Jesús Malverde, who acquired shrines, altars, offerings, and *ex-votos* from grateful *narcos* and *pistoleros*.[169] Thus, economic 'modernity'—at any rate, dynamic urban industrial capitalism—in no sense required mental 'modernity' (that is, the secular rationalism advocated by Enlightenment thinkers and vainly espoused by the anticlerical reformers of the1930s).[170] As close neighbours of the United States, the Mexicans should not have been surprised by this ostensible contradiction.[171]

Somewhat paradoxically, critiques of superstition now emanated less from the state than from the Catholic Church which, in the post-war period, emancipated from the fear of official anticlericalism and riding another wave of organizational reform, set about combatting the 'superstitious' deviations within popular Catholicism. The line of demarcation was therefore redrawn yet again. In Oaxaca, severe reformers like the Salesians cracked down on the cult of the saints which, with good reason, they saw as verging on superstition and syncretism.[172] They snooped censoriously around the caves of the Mixteca Alta where, for centuries, sacrifices had been conducted; some advocated dynamiting the caves in order to put an end to such practices.[173] And more than one young parish priest lost his job by intruding too

---

[169] Elijah Wald, *Narcocorrido* (New York, 2001), 60–8.

[170] Cf. Thomas, *Religion and the Decline of Magic*, 788–91.

[171] On the prevalence and, perhaps, resurgence of superstition, magic, and related beliefs in the United States, see Vyse, *Believing in Magic*, 15, 17–18, 24–5, 37–8; Jahoda, *The Psychology of Superstition*, 24–5, 28–32, 129–30; and Michael Shermer, *Why People Believe Weird Things* (New York, 1997). Jahoda, writing in the UK in the 1960s, averred, 3, that 'few people care to admit that they are superstitious', while Vyse, writing thirty years later in the United States, rather sheepishly admits, 219–20, that he has no superstitions and that 'our culture is one that values belief and faith and, to some, the non-superstitious person seems somewhat cold and lacking in imagination'.

[172] Etzuko Kuroda, *Bajo el Zempoaltepetl. La sociedad mixe de las tierras altas y sus rituales* (Oaxaca, 1993), 144–5, 179, 259. Also in Oaxaca, Italian missionaries, Bible in hand, declaimed against Indian (Mazatec) witchcraft and healing, invoking dire images of Sodom and Gomorrah: Eckart Boege, *Los mazatecos ante la nación* (Mexico, 1988), 252. Similar clashes between popular custom and clerical moralizing occurred in Michoacan: Carrasco, *El catolicismo popular*, 88–9.

[173] Not for the first time, clerical opinion was divided: the offending caves contained images of St Peter, St Paul and the Holy Cross, put there by the bishop, c.1965, in order to wean the Indians away from pagan sacrifice; some priests regarded this as a capitulation to syncretism, and some therefore favoured blowing the caves up: Kuroda, *Bajo el Zempoaltepetl*, 283.

officiously into the activities of lay *cofradías*.[174] Sometimes, the saints them-selves displayed their displeasure at such clerical meddling.[175]

Like the revolutionary anticlericals before them, Catholic reformers had limited success. The old practices lingered, both in Mexico City and in the countryside. Saints continued to be used in instrumental fashion (to locate lost animals, to combat disease, to help find marriage partners); saints who failed to deliver were punished; families raised household shrines, which, in suitably eclectic fashion, might be blessed either by the parish priest or by the local wizard (*brujo*).[176] Even when they succeeded—even when they managed to purge popular Catholicism of its syncretic and superstitious accretions—reformist clerics courted another form of failure. Human nature, we might say, abhors a spiritual vacuum.[177] As Catholicism adopted more rigorous, disciplined and intrusive controls on popular beliefs, so rivals sprang up.

---

[174] Marroquín, *La cruz mesiánica*, 73; Boege, *Los mazatecos*, 252 and Kuroda, *Bajo el Zempoaltepetl*, 146–7 give further examples of *cura-pueblo* conflict. Nash, *In the Eyes of the Ancestors*, 228, notes how a reformist *cura* banned Holy Week Judas-burnings 'on the grounds that it was a pagan ritual' (which also stigmatized Jews and Ladinos [*mestizos*] as Christ-killers). However, as soon as the *cura* had left town, the Indians, follow-ing their subaltern textbook, 'took Judas on his customary rounds'. A similar story is told by Lola Romanucci-Ross, *Conflict, Violence and Morality in a Mexican Village* (Chicago, 1986), 161–6.

[175] Marroquín, *La cruz mesiánica*, 68. So did irate *brujos*: Boege, *Los mazatecos*, 253.

[176] Carrasco, *El catolicismo popular*, 60–2; Marroquín, *La cruz mesiánica*, 72–3. For an inter-esting discussion of saint-sanctioning, see Ambassador Galsworthy to Foreign Secretary Crosland, 22 Dec. 1976, FCO7/3143, National Archives, Kew Gardens, describing how the Chamula Indians of Chiapas subject their saints to what he calls 'positive vetting': 'the Stakhanovite who has produced a bumper harvest will get a new embroidered robe . . . but those who have failed . . . are removed from the Church and placed in a dark corner . . . with their heads enveloped in cloth bags. Should they be given a second chance and fail again, back they go to limbo, but not before their left arm has been severed. This is the Chamula version of a cabinet reshuffle'.

[177] Some would go further and see some form of supernatural belief as 'hard-wired' into the human psyche: thus, Andrew M. Greeley, *Unsecular Man. The Persistence of Religion* (New York, 1972), adopts a broadly sociological (and North American) perspective; Steven Mithen, *The Prehistory of Mind* (London, 1996), 198–202, relates the origins of religion to fundamental changes in the human brain, *c.*50,000 years ago. Paul R. Ehrlich, *Human Natures* (New York, 2000), 213–21, offers a good synthesis. It remains to be seen whether recent secularization in Europe is a mere blip in human history, or, as Dawkins, *The God Delusion*, hopes, the beginnings of a sustained and systematic trend—'secular' in both senses of the word.

In particular, Protestantism, which had historically been seen as a heresy of an aspiring middle-class minority in the north and the big cities, now won mass converts among the poor Indians of southern Mexico (and of Guatemala and points south). While the success of evangelical Protestantism is the subject of much debate, it seems clear that it offered grass-roots autonomy and mobility, allowing new sects, churches and local lay leaders to proliferate; it encouraged a brand of charismatic Christianity, rich in ritual and raw emotion; and it promised material rewards, both directly and indirectly.[178] To the Catholic hierarchy, this was superstition mutating into heresy; to the historian (this historian, at least) it was yet another case of a more cerebral, rational, and hieratic religion (late twentieth-century Catholicism) yielding to a more earthy, populist, and practical alternative.

For it was ever thus. Superstition, like religion and magic, supplied answers and catered to needs, perhaps especially the needs of hard-pressed people struggling for survival in a harsh world. Such people, careless of theological niceties and the canon of the Catholic Great Tradition, played the field; indeed, we might say that they shared a sensible awareness that revealed religion, magic, and superstition were closely akin; the cult of the saints, as exemplified by the fiesta of San Francisco at Magdalena, comprised elements of all three, to the point where the lines of demarcation cannot be drawn— save by clerical authoritarians, speaking *ex cathedra*, in support of their 'closed shop'. Now, as in the past, the Catholic Church claimed to distinguish the true religion from serious deviations (like Protestantism) and more venial failings (like superstition). Protestantism was more serious because it posed a relatively new, official, institutional challenge (hence, in part, the violence directed against Protestants, notably in Chiapas);[179] superstition, in contrast, was more ancient, unofficial, and private—it lacked a church, a canon, and a clerisy. But it possessed both an established praxis and, in some measure, a related theory; and, by meeting some evident needs, it continued to exert an enduring appeal, having successfully defied the strictures of both the

---

[178] David Stoll, *Is Latin America Turning Protestant?* (Berkeley, 1990); David Martin, *Tongues of Fire: The Explosion of Protestantism in Latin America* (Oxford, 1990). For a good example of how a censorious 'modern mestizo-Catholic clergy', critical of the rowdy rituals of a 'folk-Catholic' Indian community, can offend local people and unwittingly promote the evangelical Protestant cause, see David Yetman, *Scattered Round Stones. A Mayo Village in Sonora, Mexico* (Albuquerque, 1998), 72–6.

[179] George A. Collier with Elizabeth Lowery Quaratiello, *Basta! Land the Zapatista Rebellion in Chiapas* (Oakland, 1994), 55–66.

revolutionary state and the religious establishment. In conclusion, we might misquote Gibbon: all the diverse paraphernalia of supernaturalism—revealed religion, magic, and superstition—seemed to the jacobin state equally false, to the hard-pressed Mexican people equally useful, and to the Catholic Church equally subject to the arbitrary diktat of the clergy.[180]

---

[180] Edward Gibbon, *The History of the Decline and Fall of the Roman Empire*, (London, 1776), ch.. 2: 'the various modes of worship, which prevailed in the Roman world, were all considered by the people as equally true, by the philosopher as equally false; and by the magistrate, as equally useful'.

Mokoagne moni: Sorcery and New Forms of Wealth in Cameroon[1]

Basile Ndjio

Since the mid-1990s, *feymen*, as young successful urban tricksters and professional swindlers are commonly known in Cameroon, have become the iconic
figures of what many Cameroonians conceive as prosperity, success, and
good life.[2] They have also become the embodiment of a successful monetary
quest which is the main concern of many marginalized youths in this country.[3] Through the economy of fraud, swindle, and deception, these young
people, who mostly come from underprivileged social backgrounds, manage
to accumulate huge fortunes enabling some of them to wear flashy clothes,
drive fancy cars, live in impressive mansions in gentrified residential areas of
Douala (the economic capital) and Yaounde (the political capital), or to
patronize music bands or football clubs in their home town. More importantly, *feymen* have become the living icons of what Jean and John Comaroff
aptly call 'occult economies',[4] one of the most noticeable manifestations of
millennial capitalism in contemporary Africa. These 'occult economies'
explain the process of wealth creation by appeal to techniques that 'transgress
conventional, rational and moral principles as well as challenge common
knowledge'.[5] The 'occult economies' also express the fantastic ways of enrichment which have been characterized in Cameroon as *feymania*.[6]

[1] Much of the material in this chapter is drawn from my PhD dissertation which was
sponsored by WROTO (Netherlands Foundation for the Advancement of Topical
Research) and ASSR (Amsterdam School of Social Science Research). I would particularly like to thank the anonymous reviewers whose insightful comments and valuable
suggestions helped me to improve the form and content of this chapter. As usual, Peter
Geschiere, and Jean and John Comaroff have been a great source of inspiration.

[2] D. Malaquais, 'Arts de feyre au Cameroun', *Politique Africaine*, 82 (2001), 101–18.
[3] G. Séraphin, *Vivre à Douala: L'Imaginaire et l'Action dans une Ville africaine en Crise*, (Paris, 2000).
[4] J. Comaroff and J. L. Comaroff (eds), *Millennial Capitalism and the Culture of Neoliberalism*, (Durham, N.C., 2000).
[5] J. Comaroff and J. L. Comaroff, 'Occult economies and the violence of abstraction: Notes from the South African postcolony', *American Ethnologist*, 26:3 (1999), 279–301.
[6] For a detailed study of this practice, especially on how young Cameroonian confidence

In popular understanding, this concept (*feymania*) refers not only to wealth acquired through swindling, business frauds, and financial deceptions, but also to riches obtained by occult means. Thus, as a fantastic way of generating instantaneous wealth from nothing, and yielding incomes without production and values without effort, *feymania* exemplifies the magical dimension of present-day neoliberal capitalism. That is why from the beginning, *feymania*-related activities and the 'magic money' they yield, have fuelled all sorts of collective fantasies and superstitious beliefs which generally associate these unusual modes of wealth creation with occult-related practices, or with what many Cameroonians now refer to as *mokoagne moni* (magic money or wealth obtained by occult means).[7]

This popular interpretation of the new forms of wealth in terms of occultism or sorcery is a reminder that the latest modernist age, often presented as an age of logical and rational principles, has not yet freed so-called (post)-modern subjects from an essentially magical view of the world, or from what could be seen as 'superstition,' 'irrationality', and 'backwardness', as Karl Marx and Max Weber confidently assumed. It is proof that this latest phase of modernity rather inflates the re-enchantment and mythologization of the world. Symptomatic of this magicalization of our present time is the growing tendency among socially and economically marginalized Cameroonians to believe that the deployment of occult powers is an efficient way of creating wealth, especially in times of uncertainty and anxiety.[8]

In other respects, this popular 'mystification' of new forms of wealth updates the anthropological discussion on the modernity of witchcraft in sub-Saharan Africa.[9] In addition, the popular reflection on 'magic money'

---

tricksters manage to defraud their victims of their assets, see Malaquais, 'Arts de feyre', 101–18; B. Ndjio, '*Feymania*: Magic Money, New Wealth and Power in Contemporary Cameroon,' PhD thesis, University of Amsterdam, 2006, notably ch. IV.

[7] This expression which derives from Badenkop, one of the several Bamileke languages, was popularized in the mid-1990s by a group of young comedians from Douala (*Les Guignols de Douala*), whose satiric sketches were mostly directed against *feymen* they derisively called *mokoagne men* (rich sorcerers).

[8] See J. Comaroff and J. L. Comaroff (eds), *Modernity and its Malcontents: Ritual and Power in Postcolonial Africa*, (Chicago, 1993).

[9] On the modernity of witchcraft discourses in postcolonial Africa, see C. F. Fisiy and P. Geschiere, 'Sorcellerie et Accumulation', in P. Geschiere and P. Konings (eds), *Les Itinéraires d'accumulation au Cameroun/Pathways to Accumulation in Cameroon*, (Paris and Leiden, 1993), 99–131; D. Ciekaway and P. Geschiere, 'Containing Witchcraft: Conflicting Scenarios in Postcolonial Africa,' *African Studies Review*, 41:3 (1998), 1–14; P. Geschiere, *The Modernity of Witchcraft, Politics and the Occult in Postcolonial*

testifies to the capacity of witchcraft discourses to adapt to modern changes, and especially to appropriate the vocabulary and logics of the monetized market economy.[10] For local populations interpret today the 'sorcery of wealth' (*mokoagne*) in terms of global transactions of human bodies and an international market of sorcery where 'rich sorcerers' (*mokoagne men*) can buy and sell human flesh from and to one another.[11] In Cameroon for instance, rich sorcerers now allegedly team up with the Mafia, organizing a worldwide zombie traffic in which the country, like many African countries, is only a local relay of global occult transactions dominated by the West.[12] Just as important is the fact that the resort to occultism to explain how successful urban tricksters come up with their fabulous riches is a reminder of the role of superstitious beliefs, mythological thought and irrational principles in helping ordinary people understand the neo-liberal economic system, a system which, as Jean Comaroff and John Comaroff have rightly observed, 'offers up almost instantaneous wealth to a handful of individuals or groups who master its "spectral technology", and simultaneously marginalizes the vast majority of the population.'[13]

Thus this paper discusses what I will call a superstitious interpretation of the so-called *feymen*'s 'magic money' by socially and economically marginalized Cameroonians. By 'superstitious interpretation', I do not simply mean a mystical understanding of these new forms of enrichment that defies common sense. Nor do I limit my definition to the production of tall stories, fairy tales, and alarming rumours through which people voice their astonishment at the spectacular social promotion of these young professional swindlers. In this paper, this expression also makes reference to the folk belief that invisible forces are the real sources of their extraordinary economic success, and that it is thanks to their involvement in occult-related practices that these young, successful, urban tricksters manage to amass considerable fortunes in a span of little time.

Focusing on the all-compassing notion of *mokoagne moni* or 'magic money' which exemplifies this superstitious understanding of the new

---

Africa, (Charlottesville, VA, 1997); P. Geschiere, 'Sorcellerie et modernité: retour sur une étrange complicité', *Politique Afrique*, 79 (2000), 17–32.

[10] Fisiy & Geschiere, 'Sorcellerie et Accumulation', 99–131; B. Meyer, 'The Power of Money: Politics, Occult Forces, and Pentecostalism in Ghana', *African Studies Review*, 41:3 (1998), 15–37.

[11] See also Comaroff and Comaroff (eds), *Millennial Capitalism*; R. Pool, *Dialogue and Interpretation of Illness: Conversations in a Cameroonian Village*, (Oxford, 1994).

[12] See *La Nouvelle Expression*, 1236 (16 January 2001), 5–6.

[13] Comaroff and Comaroff (eds), *Millennial Capitalism*, 291–343.

forms of accumulation in Cameroon, this study seeks to understand why many Cameroonians tend more and more to associate the novel forms of wealth with witchcraft-related practices; and more precisely, to comprehend why, since the emergence in the mid-1990s of a group of wealthy young confidence tricksters and international swindlers, the idiom of witchcraft/ sorcery has become in Cameroon a key concept for explaining the exceptional social promotion of these former underprivileged youths some of whom are able today to compete with the politico-bureaucratic elites in terms of display of wealth, lavish lifestyle and ostentatious consumption of western commodities; and finally, why the upsurge of this new class of nouveaux riches was followed by an unprecedented proliferation of alarming rumours linking their economic success to the sorcery of wealth, or to what we have referred to earlier as 'magic money?'

The main argument of the study is that popular witchcraft beliefs and collective fantasies about *feymen*'s fabulous wealth are informed by a moralizing criticism of asocial modes of wealth accumulation and consumption that contravene established conventional principles, or do not comply with dominant social norms. In other words, the pervasive concept of 'magic money' accounts for the 'non-standard money'—as one informant put it— which can be spent carelessly because it does not originate from hard work, effort and savings. Through the case-study of witchcraft accusations that Tonga villagers in the western region of Cameroon instigated in January 1996 against Tom Dollar[14] (a member of the wealthy elite from that village, and one of the most notorious *feymen* in Cameroon), the paper will show that frightening rumours about *feymen*'s involvement in witchcraft-related practices or about the occult sources of their fabulous wealth do not necessarily reflect people's magical view of the world. Nor do they illustrate their inability to understand the 'magical' production and consumption of wealth under the present conditions of neoliberal capitalism. On the contrary, the spread of alarming rumours that demonize the new forms of wealth as a dangerous 'magic money' is above all part of individual or collective strategies to control or fix the flow of the ever more evanescent 'magic money' which is diverted from their locality in favour of 'foreigners' and 'strangers.'

Mokoagne moni: the unsanctioned wealth

Before getting to the heart of the matter, it is necessary to underline that the new forms of wealth creation which are now associated with the so-called 'magic money' first drew public attention in the mid-1990s when Cameroon,

---

[14] I have deliberately used this pseudonym to avoid naming this powerful *feyman* who now enjoys good connections with government officials and barons of the ruling CPDM party.

like most sub-Saharan African countries, was experiencing an unprecedented economic depression which compelled its government to endorse willy-nilly drastic structural adjustment policies imposed by international institutions such as the World Bank and IMF. The effects of these programmes were catastrophic for many people, especially the underprivileged youths whose social and economic conditions dramatically changed for the worse.[15] Indeed, these draconian measures drastically narrowed their chances of finding a permanent job in the formal sector, because most of the state-owned companies were closed down or privatized as a result of mismanagement. Even state agents who were lucky enough to retain their jobs in a context dominated by the massive lay-offs, saw their salaries being reduced by more than 65% between 1993 and 1994.[16]

In other respects, the economic depression, which started in the late 1980s, helped to dramatize the disagreement between the politico-bureaucratic elites and the masses who were no longer willing to accept the status quo that maintained them in a desperate and hopeless condition. No wonder that many disenfranchised Cameroonians welcomed the restoration of the multiparty system of the early 1990s with excitement which sometimes bordered on fanaticism.[17] But the failure of the opposition coalition to unseat the current President (Paul Biya) during the controversial presidential election of October 1992, coupled with the assimilation[18] of many of its leaders in the matrix of what people now derisively call 'democracy of personal profits' (*démocratie du gombo*) finally wiped out the expectations of change raised by the brief interlude of the democratization process. This political compromise among political elites over the sharing of national resources was

---

[15] Some statistics on the socio-economic conditions in Cameroon: GNI per capita (current US$): 960.00 in 1990, 730.00 in 1992, 660.00 in 1995, 640.00 in 2000; life expectancy at birth, total (in years): 52.2 in 1990, 48.7 in 1997 and 46.7 in 2005; school enrolment, secondary (% gross): 52.2 in 1990 and 29.0 in 2000; unemployment rate: 15% in 1990 and 28% in 1995; labour lorce: 6.68 million in 2004; national poverty rate: 40%; urban poverty: 44.4% in 1995; % of population living with less than $2 a day: 64.44 in 1995. Sources: Development Data Group, The World Bank, March 2002, World Development Indicators Database, April 2006.

[16] See N. B. Jua, 'Differential Responses to Disappearing Pathways: Redefining Possibility among Cameroon Youths', *African Studies Review*, 46:2 (2003), 13–36; *La Nouvelle Expression*, 1056 (31 July 2000), 4.

[17] See B. Ndjio, 'Millennial Democracy and Spectral Reality in Postcolonial Africa', *Africa Development*, forthcoming.

[18] On the fusion and reciprocal assimilation of the politico-administrative elites, see J.-F. Bayart, *The State in Africa: the Politics of the Belly*, trans. M. Harper, (London and New York, 1993), 150–79.

made at the expense of the populace, particularly the youths. The latter's reaction to their social exclusion was to invent their own survival strategies, which in many respects gave preference to 'alternative modes of accumulation'[19] that not only circumvented the role of the corrupt and clientelist state in the production of riches, but also challenged the officially sanctioned modes of wealth creation and distribution in Cameroon.

While some youths, turned hawkers or peddlers, found in the growing informal economy a means of securing a sustainable livelihood, others rather opted for *feymania* as a means of achieving their dreams of modernity.[20] As a result of the remarkable social promotion of some cunning urban tricksters, the practice of *feymania* became one of the new forms of enchantment that offered the underprivileged and marginalized youth the hope of getting access to instantaneous riches. Moreover, *feymania* captivated people's attention because it proposed a new form of enrichment that allowed them to command respect and consideration from other people, and also to challenge the hegemonic position of the postcolonial politico-bureaucratic elites in society. That is why right from the beginning, *feymania* appeared as what James Scott would have called a 'hidden transcript of resistance'[21] that was essentially directed against the dominant groups, since most of the local victims[22] of *feymen*'s confidence tricks were either the politico-bureaucratic elites or wealthy businessmen who were connected with the ruling CPDM (Cameroon People's Democratic Movement) regime.

If one acknowledges the pervasiveness of the notion of 'magic money' when it comes to explaining the *feymen*'s stunning economic success, it is very tempting to assert that witchcraft or sorcery has become in Cameroon an all-purpose concept for explaining the extraordinary social promotion of these formerly marginalized urban youths who have managed to turn their former miserable existence into a success. For example, one day in Douala,

---

[19] Geschiere & Konings, *Les Itineraires d'Accumulation*.

[20] Jua, 'Differential Responses', 13–36; P. Konings, '"Bendskin" drivers in Douala's New Bell Neighbourhood: Master of the Road', in P. Konings and D. Foecken (eds), *Crisis and Creativity: Exploring the Wealth of the African Neighbourhood*, (Leiden & Boston, 2006), 46–65.

[21] J. Scott, *Domination and the Arts of Resistance. Hidden Transcripts*, (New Haven, 1990). See also J. Scott, *Weapons of the Weak: Everyday Forms of Peasant Resistance*, (New Haven, 1985).

[22] But unlike the older generation of *feymen*, the new generation of young international swindlers, who emerged in the late 1990s, are now more and more inclined to carry out their swindling operations abroad, especially in western countries and the Persian Gulf. In addition, they tend to prey on White foreigners and well-off Arab businessmen who are the main targets of their confidence tricks. See Ndjio, *Feymania*, esp. ch. IV and VI.

I was engaged with friends in a passionate discussion about the story that one local newspaper had reported the previous day about the extraordinary feats of some Cameroonian swindlers in Europe.[23] An old man with whom we were sharing a table in the bar interrupted our discussion to say that he was less convinced by the reporter's explanation. He rather thought that these 'cunning and audacious young men' as the newspaper described them, had a mystical power permitting them to perform such unusual exploits. He questioned whether 'a *simple man*' (he meant someone who was not a sorcerer) would be able to cheat 'all these White people in their own countries and come back home unscathed'.

The man's argument was so riveting that it encouraged a group of middle-aged men who were drinking next to us to intervene in our conversation. All of them observed along the same lines that the *feymen's* occult powers were behind their extraordinary prowess and their remarkable rise in fortune. As one of my interlocutors asked: 'Can you explain how a formerly under-privileged young man can become overnight extremely rich without resorting to magic?' 'You *longs crayons* (educated elites or intellectuals) always find rational explanations for everything, even when it is beyond common sense,' the oldest man among the group added.

What our interlocutors' statements express is a general opinion that prevails today in Cameroon about the *feymen's* sensational rise to fortune. This widespread belief maintains that these nouveaux riches are involved in occult-related practices, and that their stunning economic success rests not so much on their cunning spirit and devilish intelligence, as some analysts uphold, but rather on their magical power.[24] For these men, as for many of my informants, only those who are endowed with a supernatural power can accumulate a fabulous fortune outside the state framework which remains the main centre of production and distribution of riches in this country. That is why some famous Cameroonian *feymen* who succeeded in cheating many African heads of state between 1993 and 1995, were seen as great sorcerers.[25]

---

[23] See *Le Messager*, 1074, 16 November 1996, 11.

[24] See B. Hibou (ed.), *Privatising the State*, trans. J. Derrick, (London & CERI, 2004); J.-F. Bayart, S. Ellis, and B. Hibou, *Criminalization of the State in Africa*, (Oxford, 1999); Malaquais, 'Arts de feyre'.

[25] In Africa people generally associate political power with occult forces. That is why heads of state or chiefs are told to be the most powerful sorcerers in their country or chiefdom. Thus, succeeding in swindling these powerful people means that the author of the offence is not a 'simple man,' as the man in the bar explained. See also Geschiere, *The Modernity of Witchcraft*.

They allegedly possessed powerful talismans[26] enabling them to delude their victims or to evade police controls.[27] Likewise, in the popular literature the fortune of these former car washers, touts, cart pullers, bouncers, or hawkers turned nouveaux riches was described as 'magic money'.[28]

As these examples show, the concept of sorcery, or more precisely what the popular imagination in Cameroon refers to as *mokoagne moni* provides a comprehensive answer to people's perplexity at the ability of some marginalized urban youths who have little connection with the politico-bureaucratic elites, to accumulate a considerable wealth at times of economic depression and austerity. But to understand why *feymen's* extraordinary enrichment is believed to be 'magic money', it is necessary to bear in mind that the social imagination in Cameroon only sanctions wealth acquired through the legitimate production and conservation of value. That is why the older generation of affluent merchants and prosperous entrepreneurs whose wealth allegedly derived from the sweat of their brow; that is, from hard-work, effort, patience, and thriftiness, were (and are still) appreciated as self-made men.[29] And the fact that they have been able to pass their fortune down to their heirs, confirms people in their beliefs that their wealth is 'good money;' at least is not 'ill-gotten money' that allegedly blows out like a candle. Conversely, capital that is not accumulated through constant effort, self-control, and frugality is illegitimated or devalued because it is an asocial form of wealth: what we have referred to earlier as 'non-standard money'. But this expression of 'non-standard money' accounts less for riches engendered through activities that transgress socially accepted ways of accumulation, than for fortune produced in the emergent realm of the 'occult economies'. This social imagination of wealth can explain why people, who become rich all of sudden, are immediately suspected of having come up with their riches through illicit means including witchcraft-related practices.

Thus *feymen's* extraordinary wealth is believed to be 'magic money', not only because it derives from unconventional forms of wealth creation (*feymania*) that are generally seen as morally illegitimate, but also because it allegedly uses the human body as a commodity that one can exchange

---

[26] Some people relate these talismans to the heavy golden necklaces that successful *feymen* usually wear.

[27] See also Malaquais, 'Arts de feyre', 101–18.

[28] See *Le Messager Popoli*, 134 (November 1995), 3–4; *Mami Wata*, 37 (19 January 1996), 4.

[29] The frugal and ascetic behaviour of a large number of these older generations of businessmen, who mostly came from the Western region of Cameroon, has contributed to forge what some analysts call, the 'Bamileke parsimonious spirit.' See Geschiere & Konings, *Les Itinéraires*; J-P. Warnier, *L'Esprit d'Entreprise au Cameroun*, (Paris, 1993).

for money. Indeed, it is widely believed in Cameroon that to succeed in *feymania*-related activities one has to enter into a partnership with a mystical organisation, most notably a sorcery society, to which one sells one's vital force or offers up one's relatives as sacrificial victims, in return for an immense fortune. The setbacks of a number of *feymen* who have fallen on evil days, and especially those who have died in the prime of life, have urged many Cameroonians to believe that the sorcery society only allows its members to enjoy a short-lived happiness.

Mokoagne moni: cursed or barren money

Mokoagne moni explains not only the mysterious source of the *feymen's* sudden fortune, but also their extravagant lifestyle and spendthrift behaviour. For example, on 20 July 2003, the Biyem-assi Acacia quarter, the most populated residential area in Yaounde, was shaken by an exciting witchcraft story that gripped later the whole district: a young *feyman* who had just come back from a successful swindling operation in Switzerland where he reportedly swindled more than $US 500,000 from a Swiss banker, had collapsed and then lost consciousness in a café where he was having fun with his friends. A few hours after this dramatic but nonetheless ordinary incident, fear and panic ensued not only among the victim's companions, but also amongst the residents of Biyem-assi Acacia neighbourhood, who had received a present from the open-handed young man. Indeed, the day before the incident the *feyman* had offered drink, food, and money to almost all the young men from that neighbourhood.[30] The cause of people's anxiety was a widespread speculation that associated the young man with a get-rich-quick organization. In other respects, it was largely stated that his affliction was the consequence of his transgression of the secret pact that linked him to this alleged worldwide occult society. As days went by, and despite the doctor's diagnosis that the patient was suffering from a malign epilepsy and severe insomnia, people became more and more concerned about their lives. Their anguish was exacerbated by another tenacious rumour that announced the mysterious death of two young men from the neighbourhood to whom the *feyman* had reportedly offered two tailored suits and FCFA 300,000 (almost $ US 600). In addition, this alarming news predicted the same misfortune to those who had consumed or accepted from the young man what some folks now described as 'cursed gifts' or 'magic money.' Hearing all these frightening rumours, people started throwing away or destroying the presents they had received

---

[30] This tragic incident was of particular importance for me not only because I knew the victim whose family was my close neighbour, but more because my own relatives were devastated for having profited from the man's generous gifts.

from the generous nouveau riche, not without cursing the man they thought was the cause of their distress.

Some analysts may portray the behaviour of the residents of Biyem-Assi Acacia as little more than collective fantasies, or a thinly disguised hysteria of superstitious folks.[31] But, when the criticisms have been conceded, what emerges most strongly from this account is the sense of a community confronted today with the emergence of new forms of accumulation (appropriation) and new modes of consumption (destruction) of wealth that flout accepted patterns of social norms. As a result of the alleged connections of the nouveaux riches with occult forces, 'magic money' is used as a key metaphor for explaining their 'ethos of munificence'.[32] By this expression, I mean not only the *feymen*'s practice of non-productive investments, but also their pathological propensity to fritter away their capital through extravagant consumption, parties, and lavish lifestyle. This hedonistic behaviour is generally interpreted as an indication of a deal that they have made with demonic forces which allegedly compel them to squander their wealth carelessly. Ironically, one of the very characteristics that stimulate the *feymen*'s notoriety with the youngsters—extravagant behaviour, spendthrift practices, and above all their unusual prodigality—is also one of the main causes of the association of their riches with 'magic money'. Indeed, these nouveaux riches enjoy an astonishing popularity with the marginalized urban youth, either because they are carefree people or merry-makers who live in the fast lane or know how to turn life into a party.

However, their excessive generosity and munificence often stir up suspicion, and even panic among beneficiaries of their largesse. This is justified by the common fear that the unusual kindness of the nouveaux riches might be a mischievous plan of luring their innocent victims into their alleged demonic sects. For, according to a popular belief, beneficiaries of the so-called 'poisoned gifts' supposedly become indebted to the *feymen*'s mystical sect, and have to pay back their debt with their lives.[33]

Yet, what makes people distrust *feymen*'s excessive prodigality and munificence, or suspect them of hiding devilish motives, is the fact that the large majority of successful urban tricksters and professional swindlers come from

---

[31] See S. D. Arata, 'The Occidental Tourist: Dracula and the Anxiety of Reverse Colonialism,' *Victorian Studies*, 33:4 (1990), 621–45; D. Glover, *Vampires, Mummies, and Liberals: Bram Stoker and the Politics of Popular Fiction*, (Durham, N.C., 1996).

[32] I have borrowed this expression from Warnier, *L'Esprit d'Entreprise*, 23–37.

[33] P. Mbunwe-Samba, *Witchcraft, Magic and Divination. A Personal testimony*. Bamenda: Leiden, 1996; E. Bongmba Kifon, *African Witchcraft and Otherness: A Philosophical and Theological Critique of Intersubjective Relations*, (New York, 2001).

the Bamileke ethnic group (populations from the Grassfields region of Cameroon): a community well-known for promoting the virtue of production and accumulation above the pleasure of consumption and spending. Indeed, Grassfields populations are reputed for their excessive attention to financial matters, and also for their thrifty and cautious spirit.[34] For many Cameroonians, especially people from other ethnic groups, Bamileke fellows are not only the most penny-pinching among Cameroonians. They are also 'people who do not play with their money', as people usually say. Saying that someone behaves like a 'Bamileke'—it is a common joke in Cameroon—means that he/she is both a cunning and mean person.

Thus, confronted with such unusual conduct on the part of people who come from a community where heavy investments are generally placed in self-discipline and thrift, both the older generations of Bamileke and non-Bamileke use the metaphor of sorcery or witchcraft to render intelligible the 'incomprehensible' largesse of young Bamileke *feymen*. Indeed, many people have come to believe that, if these young Grassfields fellows spend their fortune carelessly or are unusually prodigious with their destitute friends and neighbourhood fellows, it is because their wealth is a cursed money which ends up possessing its holder. As reflected in these popular beliefs, only those who are under the influence of some mystical forces or have capitalised 'magic money' can play at ducks and drakes with their money at this time of economic crisis and austerity when people should rather spend their money wisely. This reflection reminds me of Filip de Boeck's comments about young diamond smugglers from the former Zaire, who reportedly 'eat' (spend) their money 'like idiots' because they have no control over their alleged ill-gotten fortune.[35] Because of the propensity of these young men to squander their diamond money on women, beer, and clothes—as Cameroonian *feymen* generally do—their wealth is widely believed to be a 'bitter' money which is generally viewed as dangerous. Like 'bitter' money, 'occult wealth' or 'magic money' is also treacherous because it refuses to stay in its holder's hands. One of my informants even compared it to a basket with a big hole underneath. As the elderly man explained: 'Like a damaged basket that never keeps anything, *mokoagne moni* hardly stays in the hands of its owner;

[34] See L. Dongmo, 'Le Dynamisme Bamileke (Cameroon)', CEPER, vol. 2, (Yaoundé, 1981); M. Rowlands and J-P. Warnier, 'Sorcery, Power, and the Modern State in Cameroon', *Man*, 23 (1988), 118–32; Warnier, *L'Esprit d'Entreprise*.

[35] F. de Boeck, 'Domesticating Diamonds and Dollars: Identity, Expenditure and Sharing in Southwestern Zaire (1984–1997)', in B. Meyer and P. Geschiere (eds), *Development and Change*, special issue on 'Globalization and Identity: Dialectics of Flows and Closures,' 29:4 (1998), 777–809.

it always rolls through his fingers or burns a hole in his pocket. It seems as if the holder of this magic money was driven by a mystical force which always compels him to unwillingly fritter away his resources.'[36]

However, the above comments should not mislead us into believing that the folks associate any form of 'non-standard money' with 'magic money', or that they lack rationality when it comes to explaining the stunning economic success of their fellows. Though people generally believe that most of the nouveaux riches are 'rich sorcerers', or that they have recourse to occult means in their accumulative project, they make a clear distinction between rich sorcerers and what Cameroonians disdainfully call 'fiddlers' (*magouilleurs*), or 'embezzlers of public funds' (*détourneurs des fonds publics*) who generally make use of both the patrimonial and criminal character of the Cameroon state. In other respects, if the local populations strongly believe that *feymen's* fantastic rise to fortune is morally illegitimate, it is less because these young nouveaux riches are involved in unlawful activities than because they have allegedly acquired their wealth by devilish means. We have seen that fortune produced in the obscure world of sorcery and witchcraft was perceived as dangerous because it often implied the commodification of human bodies to some demoniac sects, or the zombification of the alleged *feymen's* victims who are forced to do slave work for their masters. This is another way of saying that the local populations vilify the nouveaux riches not because they are law-breakers, but rather because they are evil-doers or malevolent sorcerers who allegedly prosper at others' expense. In addition the popular discourse on 'magic money' concerns not wealth acquired by the means of corruption or embezzlement, but rather fortune earned by occult means. While the former is generally criminalized as 'dirty money,' the latter is generally demonized as 'blood money'.

From cursed money to blessed money

In this last section, I will discuss the case of Tom Dollar, a notorious Yaounde-based *feyman* who has succeeded in turning his alleged 'occult wealth' into what his village fellows now perceive as 'good money,' because it helps them better their living conditions or promote the development of their locality. This example reveals a contradiction in people's perception of the so-called 'magic money'. This suggests that the symbolism of sorcery is only a metaphorical expression of social and economic marginalization of destitute folks by their wealthy elites. More importantly, this example shows that that rumours about *feymen's* alleged 'occult money' can be a hidden transcript of people's interests in the new forms of wealth which are so alluring, especially

[36] Conversation: 25/06/03

for those who are excluded from the state clientelist networks and the global economy. During the campaign for the municipal elections of 6 January 1996, I witnessed in Tonga a witchcraft episode that involved the notorious *feyman* who was accused by his village fellows of using his 'occult wealth' to corrupt them.[37] Rumours about Tom Dollar's association with a sorcery sect were triggered by the affliction of two young men from the village, who for unknown reasons began to behave strangely as if some mystical forces had possessed them.[38] Words had it that the famous *feyman* wanted to offer them to the sorcery sect in order to win the elections for which he stood on the ruling CPDM (Cameroon People's Democratic Movement) party ticket. As a result of suspicions that Tom Dollar was a dangerous, rich sorcerer, the locals massively voted for his opponent, a young farmer, who was finally elected mayor of Tonga on behalf of the SDF (Social Democratic Front), the main opposition party in Cameroon. The comments made by a young prince from the Bandounga chiefdom (21km away from Tonga) expressed to a certain degree the way in which local populations perceived their wealthy elite. As he stated:

> Many people (from Tonga) think that Tom Dollar is a *mokoagne man* (rich sorcerer), because he uses his financial power to weaken the very existence of those (his village fellows) he is supposed to protect. He is not like other Bamileke elites who devote their fortune above all to the development of their village, or who financially support their young 'brothers.' He always gives his preference to Beti fellows at the expense of his village kinsmen, as if he were a Beti. That is why I say that his wealth is useless.

Like my informant, many people from Tonga considered the fortune of their successful elite as 'useless' or not profitable to them and their community, because it rather served the interests of Beti people with whom Tom Dollar had built up political, economic, and social alliances.[39] It is not surprising that

---

[37] Tonga is a small town of about 25,000 inhabitants. It is located in the south-east of the Western province of Cameroon, and precisely in the Nde Division.

[38] Surprisingly, the young men who were enjoying themselves together with their friends in a popular bar began to scream with pain, tear apart their clothes, and to wrap themselves up in the dust.

[39] He had good connections with some elite Betis who were high government officials, was married to a Beti girl, and was a high profile member of the ruling CPDM party which is generally associated with the Beti from the forest region of Cameroon.

many of his disappointed kinsmen often referred to him as traitor to his own community or a renegade.

But when in June 2003 I returned to Tonga just a few years after the passionate witchcraft episode, I was really surprised to see the same *feyman* being celebrated like a national hero by those who formerly accused him of harming his kin-group with his alleged 'occult wealth'. This was during the opening of seven new classrooms at the Tonga government school, and the inauguration of a computer centre both financed by the affluent local elite. This popular event which mobilized the locals and their elites from the cities was interesting above all because it endorsed the significant change in the folks' attitude towards their wealthy elite. For example, during the opening ceremony, Tom Dollar was received with honours reserved for heads of state. This fervent and enthusiastic welcome the local populations were giving to their successful elite, made it hard to believe that not long ago, the same man was exposed to public contempt, or was called all the names under the sun.

Yet, this popular acclamation of Tom Dollar was just the confirmation of his amazing regaining of popularity in his region of origin. This comeback started less than two years after the witchcraft drama that led to his bitter defeat during the local elections of January 1996. Unlike what many people had predicted, Tom Dollar did not stay away from his native village after the election that undermined his political ambition. Instead, he managed to search for new ways not only of consolidating his role as the political leader in his native region, but also of reasserting his social prestige and popularity among his village kinsmen. In practice, he resorted to different strategies that enabled him to build in little time an image of a good man, and to turn his formerly dubious 'cursed money' into what is now seen by many of his village kinsmen as 'good money.'

Indeed, after the humiliation he had endured during the local elections of January 1996, Tom Dollar became an active member of the Tonga Development Committee. Since then, the *feyman* has become the main fundraiser for this local Development Committee which has already achieved several development projects in the region. More importantly, since 1998, he has been playing like many Bamileke urban elites who are eager to get a political position in their native land, a defining role in the organization of the famous *Rice festivity* in Tonga. The (declared) objective of this popular event that generally mobilizes local populations as well as their expatriate elites from the cities, is to maintain strong ethnic solidarity and cultural identity among all the sons of soil, regardless of their age, gender, and political affiliation. The enthusiastic and massive participation of the local population in the *Rice festival* organized in July 1999, even from those who in times past opposed the *feyman* during the witchcraft accusation, thus gave him an opportunity to clear his former negative image as sorcerer. Moreover, his sponsorship of this *Rice festival* permitted him to reconcile himself with his village fellows who no longer viewed him as working against the village's interests, or as a 'man who caught a game and shared it only with "strangers," while his own people were hungry,' as one elderly man from Tonga pointed out during the witchcraft allegations levelled at him.

Thus, even before the holding of the general elections of June 2002 which witnessed the *retour en force* of the former 'sorcerer,' there was already a significant transformation in the way in which many Tonga villagers perceived their affluent elite: from the formerly despised fellow, called 'traitor' (*fingon*) or 'sorcerer' (*swenga*), Tom Dollar had become the adored 'protector of the community' (*deulah*) and 'father of the community' (*talah*). Moreover, many of his village kinsmen now considered him an 'illustrious and prodigal son' who was the village's pride. As an elderly man from the Bandounga chiefdom said, 'he was the village's "White man"(*mekat*)', which meant that he was the person who brought prosperity, happiness, welfare and enjoyment in the community. Even the presents the *feyman* offered to the local population during the election campaign for the June 2002 general elections were no longer considered 'cursed gifts.' Nor did people behold them as his underhand plan to lure innocent villagers into a sorcery sect.

When questioned about the local population's abrupt change of heart towards their affluent village kinsman, many of my informants (even Tom Dollar's former political opponents) stressed the fact that making up for his previous mistakes and wrongdoings, the man had changed positively. According to an elderly man from Tonga I interviewed during the *Rice Feast* in July 2003, 'he was no longer the fiend fellow who only marginalized and victimized his village kinsmen, as he used to do in the past.' Some people mentioned the fact that Tom Dollar had made a considerable effort to get fully integrated within his community. As my informant metaphorically explained, the 'lost son had come back home and did no longer neglect his own "brothers" for the benefit of "foreigners" [the Beti people]. Yet, what was significant in all these explanations, was above all the shift in people's perception of Tom Dollar's wealth: his fortune was no longer viewed as dangerous 'magic money'. But instead, it was perceived as a blessed fortune that a 'successful son brings back home for the development of his village and people,' to quote the paramount chief of Bandounga.

Reflecting on this flexibility in people's perception of the *feymen's* fortune, one could say that what is at the core of the stigmatization of the 'magic money' or 'occult wealth' is less the *feymania*, the extraordinary mode of enrichment per se; it is not the occult sources of this wealth, but its bad use or redistribution. More explicitly, the folks tend to criminalize all riches they considered non-profitable to them, that is, wealth 'captured' by one of their fellows, but which is wasted in an ostentatious consumption that does not correspond to accepted patterns of social norms. Most of all they tend to stigmatize riches that do not flow towards their community; either because they have been misappropriated or monopolized by 'strangers' or 'outsiders,' or because of a discriminative redistribution that 'does an injustice to the legal claimants who think they have first claim on this fortune', as one informant from Bandounga village once said. In this respect, the figure of the selfish and extravagant *feyman* who inverts the communal principle of solidarity into the destructive selective mechanisms of redistribution, or who allegedly uses his fortune to alienate his village kinsmen embodies the image of a villain sorcerer who thrives at his fellows' expense.

Yet, the native population's claims on the wealth of their village or homeland fellow should be appreciated with regard to the Cameroonian context marked by poverty and scarcity, and most of all dominated by the prevailing ethno-politics which encourages on the one hand the new emphasis on ethnic withdrawals and parochial solidarities, and on the other hand the exclusion of allochthon populations or 'outsiders' from access to national or local resources.[40] Moreover, these popular claims should be understood in the light of the accepted belief that the emergence of a nouveau riche person from a particular region or locality must benefit first and foremost his kin-group or homeland fellows. It means on the part of the successful elite both the obligation to share with his 'brothers' what is commonly perceived as a 'spoil,' and the commitment to using his wealth only for enhancing the development of his homeland and the welfare of his people. Therefore, failing to comply with this traditional moral obligation vis-à-vis one's own community is comparable to an act of treachery.

In this respect, the 'rich sorcerer' personifies the image of a bad hunter who practises a 'destructive hunting'.[41] By this expression, we mean when the act of hunting does not 'feed or enhance the well-being of the hunter's kin-group,' or when the hunter's catch does not make his community grow and multiply, as expected by his kinsmen. Thus, by selfishly and ostentatiously spending the benefits of his 'hunting' or by marginalizing his own people,

---

[40] On ethno-politics in Cameroon, see P. Geschiere and F. B. Nyamnjoh, 'Capitalism and Autochthony: The Seesaw of Mobility and Belonging,' in *Public Culture*, 12:2, (2000), 423–52; A. Socpa, 'Ethnicity and politics in Cameroon: A New Kind of Uncertainty in the 1990s', in B. Berner and P. Trulsson (eds), *Manoeuvring in an Environment of Uncertainty: Structural Change and Social Action in Sub-Saharan Africa*, (Aldershot, 2000), 91–108; Ndjio, *Feymania*, 66-87.

[41] de Boeck, 'Domesticating Diamonds', 777–809.

the 'rich sorcerer' undermines the social order. His anti-social behaviour also flouts the logic of solidarity and the ethics of sharing.

Therefore, one can say that by superseding the former economy of retention by an economy of flow; that is, by 'capturing' and bringing back home the magical wealth, Tom Dollar has succeeded in legitimizing his fortune. Moreover, he has been successful in turning his formerly alleged 'occult wealth' into what local people now call 'money for the community' (*nkap ngo'o*). By this expression, people mean a wealth that helps to strengthen the community and not to weaken it. That is why the 'money for the community' suggests above all the idea of (re)gain, unlike the former ('magic money') which embodies, as we saw, the general feeling of loss and failure. But it sustains as well people's position as legal claimants of their 'brother's' fortune, as much as it denies 'outsiders' or 'intruders' the right to make the most of this wealth too.

Conclusion

This paper has revealed a contradiction in people's understanding of the new forms of wealth, and precisely what is commonly known in Cameroon as *mokoagne moni* which has become over time the embodiment of the 'occult economies' and 'millennial capitalism' in this country, like in many African countries. Indeed, since the outbreak of economic and financial crisis in the late 1980s and early 1990s, many Cameroonians have tended to vilify as dangerous 'magic money' or 'occult wealth' all new acquisition of riches that does not correspond to socially accepted modes of accumulation and consumption of wealth. At the same time, there is a growing tendency among underprivileged Cameroonians to valorize as good or blessed money, any wealth that serves their interests and those of their community, no matter if this fortune is obtained through occult means or not. This contradiction indicates that the pervasive notion of *mokoagne moni*, used today for explaining economic success and extravagant behaviour under the present conditions of economic crisis and poverty, not only reflects people's disappointment with both the local and globally dominant system that only exacerbates their social, economic, and political marginalization, but also expresses people's concern with new forms of dazzling wealth that can enable them to achieve their 'expectations of modernity'.[42] What is symptomatic is the present propensity of many Cameroonian youngsters to idealize *feymen's*

---

[42] J. Ferguson, *Expectations of Modernity: Myths and Meanings of Urban Life on the Zambian Copperbelt*, (Berkeley, 1999).

stunning social promotion and their hedonistic lifestyle, generally viewed as a marker of success, prosperity, good life, and power.[43]

However, the changing attitude of Tonga villagers towards their successful fellow, as well as their ambivalent perception of his wealth firstly as a cursed or bad money (*mokoagne moni*), and later as a good or blessed money (*nkap ngoh moni*) shows that the popular stigmatization of the new forms of wealth as dangerous 'occult wealth' takes a dramatic turn only under specific circumstances, that is, especially when a successful local man practises either the 'economy of retention' (non-sharing and egoism) or the 'economy of ejaculation' (lavishness and wastefulness).

As the case study discussed in this chapter has shown, the popular perception of *feymen* either as 'dangerous sorcerer' or as 'protector of the community,' as well as the evaluation of their wealth either as 'bad wealth' or 'good money' depends above all on their opposition to or endorsement of the autochthony discourse and the politics of belonging promoted at the national level by state officials, and at the local level by traditional rulers. In other words, only the nouveaux riches who allow themselves to be encapsulated in the political fence and ethnic enclosure can enjoy social recognition from their kinsmen, and political protection from the ruling CPDM regime. For example, Tom Dollar's social prestige and popularity with his village fellows came only when he made a *retour au village*, that is, when he accepted the need, not only to supersede his former national ambition by a communal or regional project, but also to 'localize' or 'ethnicize' his wealth.

Conversely, the nouveaux riches who refuse to play the ethnic or political game are not only viewed as a threat to their community; they also challenge the hegemonic project of the Cameroon government which, since the mid-1990s, has been making use of the 'autochthony governmentality'[44] to limit the ambition of this newly emerging class of affluent *feymen* who tend to emphasize their cosmopolitan and national identity over ethnic and regional identity. Moreover, since their emergence in the mid-1990s these young subversive nouveaux riches have been striving through construction of extravagant houses, ostentatious display of wealth, conspicuous consumption and social investments to invert or reconstruct to their own advantage particular configurations of power, wealth, and hierarchy that characterize the Cameroonian post-colonial society.

In conclusion, all these examples shed light on the predicament of the nouveaux riches in contemporary Cameroon, especially at this particular

---

[43] See Ndjio, *Feymania*, 105–29.

[44] I have borrowed this expression from Geschiere and Njamnjoh, 'Capitalism and Autochthony', 423–52.

moment when there is a tension between the global capitalism that prioritizes an uncontrolled flow of wealth, and local desperate attempts to fix its flux,[45] that is, to make these resources flow towards their locality. And since the mid-1990s, the pervasive discourse on witchcraft and sorcery has become a privileged means for disappointed Cameroonians to 'localize' the new dazzling riches that have proven very deceptive for many, as they have been monopolized by selfish and non-sharing elites.[46] But the example of the young, lavish, and extravagant conman from the Biyem Assi neighbourhood in Yaounde, who was cast in the role of a villain sorcerer, also showed that the elite who fritters away his fortune, or who 'pathologically' or 'excessively' redistributes it, can endure too a social marginalization, because his lavish lifestyle and excessive prodigality flout socially sanctioned patterns of spending and redistribution.

[45] See M. Featherstone (ed.), *Global Culture: Nationalism, Globalization and Identity*, (London, 1990); S. Hall, 'The Local and the Global: Globalization and Ethnicity,' in A. D. King, (ed.). *Culture, Globalization and the World System: Contemporary Conditions for the Representations of Identity* (London, 1991), 19–39; Meyer and Geschiere, *Development and Change*; P. Geschiere and J. Gugler (eds), 'The Politics of Primary Patriotism, Africa', *Journal of the International Africa Institute*, 68:3 (1998); Geschiere and Nyamnjoh, 'Capitalism and Autochthony'; B. Ndjio, 'Intimate Strangers: Neighbourhood, Autochthony and the Politics of Belonging', in P. Konings and D. Foecken (eds), *Crisis and Creativity: Exploring the Wealth of the African Neighbourhood*, (Leiden Boston), 66–87.

[46] F. B. Nyamnjoh, 'For Many are Called but Few are Chosen: Globalisation and Popular Disenchantment in Africa', *African Sociological Review/Revue Africaine de Sociologie*, 4:2 (2000), 1–45.

Imperial Secrets: Vampires and Nationhood in Puerto Rico[1]

Lauren Derby

Rumour is the process by which a collective historical consciousness is built.

(Jan Vansina)

Secrecy lies at the very core of power.

(Elias Canetti)

In 1994, residents of a small town in Canóvanas, Puerto Rico, reported that dozens of farm animals had been discovered dead, their blood apparently sucked dry via tiny perforations in the neck and abdomen. The creature attacked small animals such as ducks, rabbits, pigs, chickens, and goats, its preference for goats soon earning it the appellation 'chupacabras' or goat-sucker in Spanish. Over the coming months the depredations continued, spreading into the Southern United States and Mexico, with over 300 animals reported dead in northern Mexico alone in the coming months, and some 2000 in total by April 1996.[2] Eyewitnesses came forth with descriptions of a grotesque creature about three feet tall, with membraned wings, a hunched

[1] I wish to thank César Ayala, Rafael Boglio, William Lockwood Benet, Juan Guisti, Jorge Giovanetti, Dain Borges, Francisco Scarano, Manuel Valdés Pizzini, Laura Briggs, Reinaldo Román, Claudio Lomnitz, Ryan Cook, Andrew Apter, and Michael Powell for their helpful comments and suggestions. Research assistance has been provided by Victor Rodríguez, Rey Phillips, Biella Coleman, Seonaid Valiant, Yarimar Bonilla and Julian Apter. This essay was presented at the Conference on Superstition in Historical and Comparative Perspective, Department of History, University of Essex; the Berkshire Conference on the History of Women, the UCLA history Dept. and the UCLA Department of Anthropology seminar on Cultures of Capitalism; thanks to Matthias Röhrig-Assunçao, Peter Geschiere, Alexandra Stern, Laura Briggs, Teo Ruiz, Tim Taylor, Pablo Alabarces, Catherine LeGrand, Steve Smith and Alan Knight for their insightful comments.

[2] Carlos Hamann, *The Globe* (El Paso, TX). The chupacabras rumours may have been a resuscitated version of the 1960s cattle mutilation reports from the US border states, which fused with UFO rumours about Roswell (Ryan Cook, pers. comm., 2002). Cook is

back, large eyes, covered with either scales or quills. It was said to resemble a kangaroo since it leapt from large back legs, and had tiny front arms, with a strikingly pungent smell. Over time the panic caused by the slaughter caused inhabitants to board up their residences, hire guards to protect their animals and supervise children on their way to school. Sheep and cattle ranchers as far afield as northern Mexico sold off their herds since they had already been hard hit by an extended drought that had had catastrophic consequences. The governments of Mexico and Puerto Rico eventually intervened in the crisis, as authorities sought to assuage fears through holding informational press conferences with prominent biologists who theorized that drought might have forced bats to look for new nutritional sources or that the deaths might have been caused by a pack of wild dogs. The President of the Puerto Rico House of Representatives Agricultural Commission called for an official investigation, and even in Miami zoo pathologists held a public necropsy to demonstrate their case that the supposed chupacabras was a puma or dog.[3]

The chupacabras quickly spread out of its local context as it was picked up by the news media and popularized by Latino television network Univisión, NBC, The New York Times and Latina talkshow hostess Cristina, who did a show on the events, websites formed on the web, and eventually it was memorialized in an X-Files episode and even a Scooby Doo cartoon. The trickster symbol held special appeal to countercultural urban Latino youth who sported its image on tee-shirts, embracing it as a figure of urban savagery akin to the tattoo and nose pierce. It was merchandised in the form of baseball caps, key-chains and Halloween costumes, and not only by large corporate chains. What is striking is how the chupacabras became a popular cultural phenomenon as individuals designed and produced tee-shirts of the beast and then consumed them in droves. At the 1994 Puerto Rican day parade in New York City, there were so many chupacabras tee-shirts that this became the focus of journalistic coverage of the event. The chupacabras became a creole totem and anti-hero, a source of laughter and gothic humour for many; since at least one image invited the public to ridicule the 'true' believers.[4]

---

writing a dissertation on this subject in the Dept. of Anthropology, University of Chicago.

[3] In Puerto Rico, the Department of Agriculture's veterinary service combined forces with the Dept. of Health and conducted vivisections and sent specimens to a specialized lab in New Jersey.

[4] Reinaldo Román; 'Of Dread and Laughter: Chupacabras and Vampires as Parodies' (paper presented at the meetings of the Caribbean Historians Association, 2003); and Ramon López, 'Las Camisetas del Chupacabras' (www.boricua53.com).

Notwithstanding its mass cultural spread, this essay seeks to disentangle the discursive threads interwoven in these accounts to uncover some of the meanings the chupacabras held, especially for the original Puerto Rican eyewitnesses, those who initially generated the reports that spread to Mexico, Chile, and elsewhere. The chupacabras craze, I will argue, had its own significance to the inhabitants of Canóvanas who were at first flattered by the international attention they received; a mood which shifted to sour betrayal upon discovering just how quickly their narratives could escape their ownership and control. They felt manipulated by an international media that first competed to collect their stories, which were then used to mock them as ignorant hicks.[5] The rumours commenced in Canóvanas, quickly spreading to the internet where they were endowed with a new set of meanings that were later re-embedded in Canóvanas. The chupacabras tales belie the presumption that superstitions are necessarily pre-modern atavisms. I will propose by contrast that the chupacabras belief was an urban legend, a popular commentary on modernity and its risks as they are perceived in Puerto Rico.[6] Along the way, I also want to explore the larger methodological problem of how to interpret popular beliefs or superstitions that are both widely held, as well as widely held to be false; thus 'ideoscapes' in which "revelation and concealment, trick and technique, faith and scepticism work in tandem".[7]

Scholars examining the link between witchcraft and politics have considered how witchcraft and sorcery accusations reflect political structures. Peter Geschiere for example, has examined how witchcraft which commenced as the 'dark side of kinship' became a language for expressing moral disdain for

---

[5] The derision is evident in the tone of Tito Armstrong, 'Chemo "Jones" Soto: Our Last Hope?', on the Chupacabras Homepage set up by a Princeton University student at the time (www.princeton.edu/~accion/chupa.html). Reinaldo Román treats the popular satirical *vacilón* component of chupacabras humour in his essay, 'Of Dread and Laughter'.

[6] Joel Best and Gerald T. Horiuchi, 'The Razor Blade in the Apple: The Social Construction of Urban Legends', *Social Problems* 32:5 (Jun. 1985), 492; and Gary Fine, 'The Kentucky Fried Rat', *Journal of the Folklore Institute* 17 (1980), 222–243.

[7] Birgit Meyer and Peter Pels, 'Introduction', *Magic and Modernity: Interfaces of Revelation and Concealment* (Stanford, 2003). 'Ideoscapes' is from Arjun Appadurai, *Modernity at Large: Cultural Dimensions of Globalization* (Minneapolis, 1996). My thinking about rumours has been sharpened through the insightful essays, S. A. Smith, 'Talking Toads and Chinless Ghosts: The Politics of "Superstitious" Rumors in the People's Republic of China, 1961–1965', *American Historical Review* 111:2 (April 2006), 405–27; and Glen A. Perice, 'Rumors and Politics in Haiti', *Anthropological Quarterly* 70:1 (Jan. 1997), 1–10.

the new forms of accumulation of state elites in postcolonial Cameroon.[8] Others have considered the way notions of sorcery or concealed power have been invoked to explain contemporary backstage state practices, especially in the Latin American arena where the theatre of politics extends into personal encounters and informal deal-making. Neoliberal economic policies of the 1980s and 1990s undercut traditional safety nets for the poor resulting in a new level of suspicion among the citizenry, many of whom were correct in accusing statesmen of earning large kickbacks as unemployment and basic commodity prices rose, creating the basis for potent new allegations of illicit wealth accumulation among statesmen and their international allies such as the IMF.[9] Fears about globalization translated into veritable sorcery accusations in many contexts as gringos were attacked under the presumption that they were stealing babies and cash undercover.[10] In contexts such as Guatemala, anxieties about the globalization of markets in a context of transnational unequal exchange were thus displaced onto a more tangible enemy. Puerto Rico, however, was protected from this particular phase of 'millennial capitalism' and the fears of sovereignty erosion that resulted from it due to its commonwealth status as US overseas territory, which artificially buoys the economy through corporate tax exemption and welfare subsidies for the poor. Yet the fact that the chupacabras was read as a sign of surreptitious power reflects Puerto Rico's own uniquely bifurcated political structure.[11]

I wish to argue that the chupacabras rumours in Puerto Rico were a reflection of how the imperial US state is seen in the political imagination of Puerto Ricans, one that expresses a set of contradictions that are very specific to being an 'unincorporated territory,' that is, 'belonging to but not being

[8] Peter Geschiere, *The Modernity of Witchcraft: Politics and the Occult in Postcolonial Africa* (Charlottesville, 1997).

[9] Michael Taussig, *Shamanism, Colonialism and the Wild Man: A Study of Terror and Healing* (Chicago, 1986); Stephan Palmié, *Wizards and Scientists: Explorations in Afro-Cuban Modernity and Tradition* (Durham, 1996).

[10] Abigail E. Adams, 'Gringas, Ghouls and Guatemala: The 1994 Attacks on North America Women Accused of Body Organ Trafficking', *Journal of Latin American Anthropology* 4:1, 112–33; Nancy Scheper-Hughes, 'Theft of Life: The Globalization of Organ Stealing Rumors', *Anthropology Today*, 12:2 (1996), 3–11.

[11] Witchcraft is defined as concealed power in Neil l. Whitehead and Robin Wright, (eds), *In Darkness and Secrecy: The Anthropology of Assault Sorcery and Witchcraft in Amazonia* (Durham, 2004); and as 'mystical power' in Isak Niehaus, *Witchcraft, Power and Politics: Exploring the Occult in the South African Lowveld* (London, 2001), 2. On Dominican anxieties about globalization, see 'Gringo Chickens with Worms', in Gilbert Joseph et al. (eds), *Close Encounters of Empire: Writing the Cultural History of U.S.-Latin American Relations* (Durham, 1998), 451–93.

a part of the United States'.[12] Governmental bureaucracy is split since much of the daily operation of Federal governmental agencies operates according to policy directives emanating in Washington. The very concealment of Federal authorities and their motivations produces a particular kind of 'state effect' as people wonder and talk about what transpires behind the mask of power at the point of origin where it does articulate with civil society.[13] The state in Puerto Rico is thus pervasive yet remote; commanding yet invisible, since much of the actual muscle of US imperial power resides on the island because the US armed forces have enormous holdings on Puerto Rican soil. It is the command centre for the South Atlantic fleet, the testing and training grounds for interventions such as Iraq. Puerto Ricans, thus, are actually intimately linked to US military power, but they remain outsiders looking in, condemned to the surfaces of the wall of secrecy, one which as Georg Simmel reminded us, often amplifies the perceived value within, as well as creates a lust for confession, as we shall see.[14]

In God we trust

One issue raised by these narratives is whether one can speak of local meanings at all when the rumours in question received so much coverage in the global media. Oral historians speak of 'interference' and 'feedback' in oral testimony, which implies that there is an original version that can be distinguished from the collective conversation within which it resides. Indeed, the fact that chupacabras tales were immediately diffused in mass media has meant that many believe that the craze was nothing more than a popular appropriation of a science fiction novel or film; just as in Mexico many maintain that the chupacabras story was planted by the government to divert attention from the crisis that developed after Carlos Salinas Gortari's fall from grace. Indeed, the chupacabras was readily compared with cartoon creatures such as Bugs Bunny's favourite adversary the Tasmanian devil, and eyewitnesses even plotted their stories of the origin of the chupacabras within a narrative structure suspiciously close to films about alien subterfuge and disguised colonization such as the film *Species*, which hit the screens at the

---

[12] Edwin Meléndez and Edgardo Meléndez, 'Introduction', *Colonial Dilemma: Critical Perspectives on Contemporary Puerto Rico* (Boston, 1993), 1.

[13] Thomas Blom Hansen and Finn Stepputat, 'Introduction', *States of Imagination: Ethnographic Explorations of the Postcolonial State* (Durham, 1991); Timothy Mitchell, 'The Limits of the State: Beyond Statist Approaches and Their Critics', *American Political Science Review* 85:1 (1991), 77–96.

[14] 'Secrecy', in Kurt H. Wolff (trans. and ed.), *The Sociology of Georg Simmel* (New York, 1950), 337–9.

commencement of the panic.[15] Indeed, visual media were seamlessly incorporated into this phenomenon from the onset, providing imagery for the tales as they emerged. The extent of media involvement in shaping popular understandings of these rumours and diffusing particular versions certainly makes it impossible to render a highly localized sociological reading in the style of early modern European witchcraft scholars for whom the vectors of accusation sketched fissures in the social order. One problem of course is that chupacabras sightings involved a manifest outsider. If early modern European witchcraft was 'an idiom of intimacy' revealing kinship tensions within families, as Luise White has said for East African vampires, the chupacabras were 'outside the social context . . . they were seen to be internationalized, professionalized, supervised and commodifying'.[16] As one observer said, 'it was something monstrous, strange, outside the natural. I don't believe it could have been human, canine or primate'.[17] Yet as quintessential other, what, then, did the chupacabras represent?

Much of the journalistic coverage sought to locate the chupacabras within the traditional folklore of shapeshifter trickster figures in the Caribbean.[18] Along these lines the chupacabras could be seen as a modern incarnation of a range of night creatures with the ability to transmogrify from one species to another. The *gallipote* in the Dominican Republic is one such nocturnal creature which can fly and suck blood, and the *garadiablo* is a frightening creature that guards lagoons and swamps. In the Puerto Rican province of Loiza, contiguous to where the chupacabras was first sighted, femininity is said to have its malevolent side; women are said to be able to change into witches, just as in Haiti lesbians are said to cause earthquakes. Nor was this the first vampiric creature to hit Puerto Rican shores. In 1975, Puerto Rico was assaulted by the *vampiro de Moca*, which had also purportedly sucked animals to death.[19] The Spanish province of Galicia which sent disproportionate numbers of immigrants to the Hispanic Caribbean in the nineteenth century

---

[15] Jorge Martín, *Vieques: Polígono del 3er. Tipo* (San Juan, 2001), 46.

[16] Luise White, *Speaking with Vampires: Rumor and History in Colonial Africa* (Berkeley, 2002), 29.

[17] Clarence Beardsley, 'Chupacabras: Vecinos comparten dudoso privilegio de haber visto al elusive criatura', *El Vocero* (21 Feb. 1996) (my translation).

[18] See 'Chupacabras: Depredaciones del enigmático monstruo fomentan un interés ya internacional', *El Vocero*, nd, (1996); and Loren Coleman and Jerome Clark, *Cryptozoology A to Z: The Encyclopedia of Loch Monsters, Sasquatch, Chupacabras, and Other Authentic Mysteries of Nature* (New York, 1999).

[19] Román, 'Of Dread and Laughter', 4.

has a deep tradition of vampire lore that may have meshed with lingering sorcery practices of the Taíno and Carib indigenes which feature corpse resurrection among other necromantic rites.[20]

But this assumes that the chupacabras should be classed as part of the animal species. Like the Andean *pishtaco*, however, there is something mechanical about the chupacabras. *Pishtaco* (aka *Kharisiri*) rumours tell tales of plump white men wearing chaps and cowboy boots and hats who suck the fat from Indian bodies and send it to industrial plants to fuel machinery.[21] Thus if the *kharisiri* is human, it works closely with technology and the depth of its vileness deprives it of all humanity. The chupacabras appears automated, almost machine-like; it was said to fly as fast as a bullet. For example, Madeline Tolentino was struck by the large blank eyes of the chupacabras that resembled 'Christmas lights,' its apparent absence of genitalia, as well as its slow and regular movements which made her think it was actually a 'robot' that was manipulated by something else. It is often claimed that it lacked certain defining features of animal life such as ears, nose or genitals. She described its putrid smell as akin to battery acid, or the medicinal Chloroseptic. As Tolentino put it, 'it was not animal or human; it was not of this world'. Nor does the chupacabras appear in sites that exemplify nature, the kind of bucolic traditional springs and hills where miraculous Virgins and Christian figures make their appearance. The chupacabras appears in a car mechanic's workshop, on the highway near K-Mart, or near the Arecibo telescope.

Of course, this is quite appropriate to Puerto Rico since, as Sidney Mintz has noted, the Caribbean is an intrinsically modern region due to its absence of any autochthonous population, and as a region of immigrants defined by the protoindustrial rhythms of sugar monoculture and slavery. In the late nineteenth century, Puerto Rico was transformed from a mixed agroexport economy with a creole *hacendado* or landholding class into a sugar monocultural economy dominated by US-owned agroexport plantations concentrated in the hands of a few large corporations. While the sugar economy was based in the coastal regions and thus did not penetrate the interior, rural inhabitants were forcibly drawn into the wage labour force through the *libreta* or passbook system in the 1870s. Unlike neighbouring Cuba and the Dominican Republic, Puerto Rico had already become a nation of dispossessed peasants by the time the US arrived in 1898, a condition which grew even more acute after US annexation with the expansion of large corporate

---

[20] Teo Ruiz and Neil Whitehead, verbal communications.

[21] See Mary Weismantel's fascinating discussion of the *pishtaco* in her *Cholas and Pishtacos: Stories of Race and Sex in the Andes* (Chicago, 2001), ch. 5.

sugar plantations.[22] As Gordon Lewis put it, the average Puerto Rican is today a proletarian, whether urban or rural.[23]

That said, the municipality of Loíza within which the birthplace of the chupacabras, Canóvanas, was located until 1971, was one of the last refuges for the survival of a *jíbaro* or mountain peasant lifestyle, one which defiantly held on to its independence even in the face of proletarianization. Loíza divided into two distinct zones: a lowland sugar plantation area surrounded by mangrove wetlands, and the Sierra de Luquillo where El Yunque rainforest is located. An itinerant subculture developed in which *jíbaros* combined seasonal wage labour in the lowland with sales of gathered products in San Juan. The existence of extensive coastal and highland forests enabled an autonomous 'protopeasantry' to exist for centuries even as the Canóvanas plantation expanded.[24] The Luquillo mountains had long served as an internal frontier, providing a sanctuary to Taíno rebels, runaway slaves, and other fugitives, a region lacking settled hamlets even when much of it was transformed into a protected US government forest in 1903. Jail escapee Toño Bicicleta became a folk hero there as late as the 1970s.[25] The deep identity divide in this whiter backlands mountain subculture, which perceived itself as very distinct from the largely black coastal sugar population below, was one of the reasons Canóvanas broke away and formed its own municipality in 1971.[26]

Today Canóvanas remains an enclave of relative autonomy for a community in which most inhabitants hold service-sector jobs as hairdressers, drivers, vendors, or car mechanics, jobs which unlike factory work provide a modicum of autonomy and control over one's time. This birthplace of the chupacabras has a rural feel, yet as is the case in Puerto Rico more generally, the only thing vaguely rural about the chupacabras is its name. Incorrectly pluralized, its name evokes the speech of the lower classes in the Hispanic

[22] César J. Ayala and Laird W. Bergad, 'Rural Puerto Rico in the Early Twentieth Century Reconsidered: Land and Society, 1899–1915', *Latin American Research Review*, 37:2 (2002), 65–97.

[23] Gordon K. Lewis, *Puerto Rico: Freedom and Power in the Caribbean* (New York, 1963), 243.

[24] Guisti estimates that three-quarters of their garden crops were market bound (Juan A. Guisti-Cordero, 'Labor, Ecology and History in a Caribbean Sugar Plantation Region: Piñones (Loíza), Puerto Rico 1770–1950' (PhD Thesis, State University of New York at Binghamton, 1994, 371). The term protopeasant is from Sidney Mintz, see his essays in Mintz and Sally Price, (eds), *Caribbean Contours* (Baltimore, 1985); although Guisti prefers a modified version of peasant-proletarian.

[25] Yarimar Bonilla first indicated this connection to me, pers. comm., 2002.

[26] See Guisti's 'Labor, Ecology and History', an extraordinarily rich regional study of Loíza microhistory, economy and ecology.

Caribbean who are prone to eliminate the "s" from everyday speech, but then tend to hypercorrect pluralization in the presence of interlocutors especially status superiors, sprinkling s's in their speech indiscriminately. However proximate and linked through trade networks to cosmopolitan San Juan it may be, however, the political and religious identity of Canóvanas is stubbornly independent. For example, the central mountain chain in which Canóvanas is nestled is a stronghold of Pentecostalism. Pentecostalism came to Puerto Rico in the 1920s via Puerto Rican evangelists and has become the basis for a very homegrown form of religious expression, one that offers a more egalitarian organizational structure than the Catholic Church since services are offered in the homes of local lay clergy on weekday evenings; they have no dress codes and have sought to appeal to youth since they incorporate popular music such as salsa, meringue, rock en español and rap in services. A populist phenomenon that proselytizes at bus stops and baseball games, it includes possession by the holy spirit and speaking in tongues and thus resembles other Creole religious practices such as Santería and Espiritismo which channel faith through bodily experience, yet evangelical Protestantism presents a whiter, more respectable visage.[27] Unlike Catholicism which has been administered largely through foreign clergy, and has a meagre formal presence in rural and suburban locales, Pentecostalism's message of humility, redemption, upward mobility, and self renewal may hold special appeal to the lower middle classes who have trouble conforming to the nuclear family standard requisite to gente decente in the face of poverty and high un- and under-employment.[28] The moralizing discourse of Pentecostalism offers respectability to lower middle-class 'marginal dons' who work with their hands but see themselves as decente, and thus clearly differentiated from

---

[27] Héctor M. Martínez, 'Religious Leaders, Religious Groups and Politics in Puerto Rico' (PhD Dissertation, University of Michigan, 2000), 132; and Sidney Mintz, Worker in the Cane: A Puerto Rican Life History (New York, 1960). Judith Bettleheim makes this point in her essay, 'Espiritismo Altars in Puerto Rico and Cuba: The Indian and the Congo', in Andrew Apter and Lauren Derby, (eds), Activating the Past: Latin America in the Black Atlantic, (forthcoming, Newcastle-on-Tyne). Nélida Agosto Cintrón argues, however, for continuities between folk Catholicism and Pentecostalism in her Religión y cambio social (Río Piedras, 1998).

[28] Virginia Garrard-Burnett and David Stoll, (eds), 'Introduction', Rethinking Protestantism in Latin America (Philadelphia, 1993). These Pentecostals should not be confused with televangelicals which preach a 'theology of prosperity', see Martínez, 'Religious Leaders'. On the family, see Oscar Lewis, La Vida: A Puerto Rican Family in the Culture of Poverty – San Juan and New York (New York, 1966).

the urban poor and their vices.[29] In recent decades the expanding informal service sector has helped swell the ranks of *Evangélicos*, enabling them to emerge as a political force in many parts of Latin America, perhaps because they aptly represent a group that lacks a fully formed class location and thus is more available to religious discourses that offer a ready social and political identity.

Indeed, this was the case in Puerto Rico where Governor Pedro Rosselló of the Partido Nuevo Progresista or New Progressive Party, the NPP, which advocates Puerto Rican statehood, was carried into office in a landslide victory in large part by his capture of Evangelical Protestant votes in both 1992 and 1996. Seeking to harness Pentecostalism to his political agenda, Rosselló carried their message into the political arena through frequent allusions to God and Christian values in his rhetoric, ecumenical breakfasts with Pentecostal groups in the Governor's palace, and populist measures such as land hand-outs to the *pueblo evangélico*, or evangelicals.[30] Rosselló had a particular connection to Canóvanas, where his PNP ally mayor Chemo Soto resides, since most Pentecostals in Puerto Rico are not statehooders but rather members of the Commonwealth Party. This special connection may have given a unique inflection to Rosselló's slogan, '*estadidad jíbara*' or creole statehood, a PNP slogan intended to reassure that even as a state Puerto Rico could maintain its language and culture, since the *jíbaro* of course hails from the heartland of Puerto Rican identity, El Yunque, contiguous to Canóvanas.[31] As a stronghold of Pentecostalism and statehooder sentiment, thus, Canóvanas is quite distinctive in the Puerto Rican context. The chupacabras appeared first not in a remote or marginalized frontier zone, but rather within a community with such a strong sense of entitlement that it feels it deserves 'the equality of citizenship within the nation whose citizens we are'.[32]

---

[29] Edward L. Cleary and Hannah W. Stewart-Gambino, 'Introduction: Pentecostals, Prominence and Politics', *Power, Politics, and Pentecostals in Latin America* (Boulder, CO, 1997), 1–24; Eileen J. Suárez Findlay, *Imposing Decency: The Politics of Sexuality and Race in Puerto Rico, 1870–1920* (Durham, 1999).

[30] Martínez, "Religious Leaders," 166. Land lots were offered to churches for $1; later he was forced to open this up to non-profit organizations.

[31] To challenge the Catholic mobilization called Nation on the March; see Martínez, 'Religious Leaders', 113, n. 156.

[32] Words of PNP leader Carlos Romero-Barceló cited by Meléndez, *Puerto Rico's Statehood Movement*, 176. A full statement of his platform can be found in *La estadidad es para los pobres* (San Juan, 1976).

Smoke and mirrors

The original theatre of the chupacabras rumours thus represented a particular political subculture or 'occult cosmology' in Puerto Rico, a small relatively homogenous island but one that is shaped by a deep political divide.[33] Most residents of Canóvanas are members of the statehood party, NPP, thus advocates of a total merger with the United States in the form of a fifty-first state. Thus the question emerges why a group that arguably sees itself as most closely identified with the US on the island would conjure up a beast that they see as a product of the predatory designs of the United States on Puerto Rico, as we shall see. The chupacabras narratives thus reveal a complex and deeply ambivalent 'cognitive map' to use Frederic Jameson's terms, one which is both deeply suspicious of power, but at the same time longs to be able to identity with it.[34]

Certainly Canovanas outsiders saw the chupacabras rumours as superstition in the sense of being religiously and morally illegitimate; and as a result many witnesses kept quiet for fear of ridicule.[35] Yet Edward Evans-Pritchard abandoned terms like superstition precisely for its derogatory connotations. As he would have it, the chupacabras rumours sought to explain the otherwise inexplicable scores of real animal deaths, and they had their own rationality.[36] Discerning their deeper logic, however, forces one to move beyond the shape of apparition itself. The assailant's description varied wildly from account to account, as did the explanations of its purported true origin. It was said to be scaly or furry or plumed; a beast, a humanoid, a robot, or a space alien; a dinosaur relic or a futuristic clone from outer space; or the very incarnation of the devil with its tell-tale sulfuric stench.[37]

If there were debates about exactly what the chupacabras looked like, however, the far more interesting discussion was over where it came from. And if analyzing the beast's appearance might locate it within the realm

---

[33] "Occult cosmology" is from Todd Sanders and Harry G. West, 'Power revealed and Concealed in the New Order', *Transparency and Conspiracy: Ethnographies of Suspicion in the New World Order* (Durham, 2003), 1–37. On Puerto Rican parties, see Nancy Morris, *Puerto Rico: Culture, Politics and Identity* (Westport, 1995).

[34] Frederic Jameson, 'Cognitive Mapping', in Cary Nelson and Lawrence Grossberg (eds), *Marxism and the Interpretation of Culture*, (Urbana, 1988), 347–57.

[35] Jorge Martín, *La conspiracion chupacabras: Evidencias del vinculo entre los ovnis/ETs y estas criaturas*, (San Juan, 1997), 39.

[36] Edward E. Evans-Pritchard, *Witchcraft, Oracles and Magic Among the Azande* (Oxford, 1937). Another factor in terms of the timing of the rumours was the prevalence of millennial and apocalyptic fears circulating in the US in the later 1990s.

[37] This version is presented by Eliezer Rivera, who is a retired police detective and a Pentecostal lay priest in Canóvanas. See Martín, *La conspiración chupacabras*, 140.

of mythic beings, its accompanying narratives of origin reveal it to be a subset of conspiratorial political lore. The UFOlogist community which quickly adopted the chupacabras as their totemic object claimed that it was the result of a military intelligence experiment the US government was conducting on Puerto Rico. In one version, the beast was an interspecies hybrid clone that had been developed in a laboratory and had escaped. In this account, the chupacabras is a kind of 'plantanimal' or 'hupig' perhaps a cross between a rabbit and a camel. At times it is said to have a strange chitinous coating that looks chameleonic and emits a smell or sound that causes nausea in onlookers, possibly created by a Chinese scientist living in Moscow who learned how to imprint genetic information onto DNA.[38] Rumour had it that a Federal Agency had created a task force to investigate where these creatures were coming from, and had set up a 'secret primate research' laboratory for further study.[39] People say that SWAT teams had been seen chasing simian-looking beasts in the forest with orange fatigues with NASA insignia.[40] In another version the DOD, the FBI and the CIA had created a mutant 'bionic' creature, half organic and half machine, that it let loose in Puerto Rico as an experiment since the population there was expendable.[41] Many of these accounts emanated from retired army personnel involved in high security communications who claimed that the US armed forces were keeping the true identity of the chupacabras a secret.[42]

If the beast itself seemed utterly alien, it chose quite traditional sacred stages for its appearances, however. Indeed, extraterrestrials in Puerto Rico have become quite seamlessly absorbed into older Catholic sacred topographies.[43] 'Manimals' have been frequently spotted in sites where miraculous

[38] This story indicates a strong Cold War connection to these narratives, a theme Joseph Masco considers in his essay, Jutta Weldes et al., (eds), 'States of Insecurity: Plutonium and Post-Cold War Anxiety in New Mexico, 1992–96', in *Cultures of Insecurity: States, Communities and the Production of Danger* (Minneapolis, 1999), 203–31.

[39] 'Nemesis: The Chupacabras at Large', A SAMIZDAT Update (Summer 1996), 1.

[40] Scott Corrales, *Chupacabras and Other Mysteries* (TN, 1997), 170.

[41] Martín, *Conspiración chupacabras*, 165. These rumours bear a close resemblance to African American rumours about US government agencies enacting nefarious plots on the black population; see Patricia A. Turner, *I Heard it Through the Grapevine: Rumor in African American Culture* (Berkeley, 1993), ch. 4.

[42] This is very apparent in Jorge Martín's two accounts, *Vieques*, and *La Conspiración Chupacabras*, although he extends his evidence to include chupacabras sited elsewhere such as Chile and Panamá, and his informants frequently are also retired US army intelligence (see e.g. *Conspiración*, 152–3).

[43] A logic similar to Andrew Canessa, 'Fear and Loathing on the *Kharisiri* Trail: Alterity and Identity in the Andes', *The Journal of the Royal Anthropological Institute* 6:4

virgins have appeared, such as the site of Blessed Virgin at Monte Santo near Lomas Verdes, which is also a place where other kinds of paranormal activity such as UFOs have been reported.[44] In the 1970s during a wave of UFO sightings, apparitions of weeping Virgin statues, and Christ appearances in churches coincided with manimals and reports of 'Men in black'.[45] At times, extraterrestial apparitions merge the alien and the sacred in uncanny ways, such as the figures seen in Laguna Cartagena who were described as tall, delicate men with long hair who could be Star Wars characters with their silver space suits, or modern day Jesus Christs.[46] UFOs are here seen as wondrous signs of the supernatural, indicative that, as Carl Jung argued, 'the theme of humanity's rescue by extraterrestrial beings is a religious myth recast in technological guise'.[47]

Many flying saucer sightings have taken place in the rain forest of El Yunque, site of the 'primeval Puerto Rico', the largest national park and 'last wilderness in Puerto Rico', a space where since the colonial period mythological night creatures, fugitives from the law and the great symbol of national identity the *jíbaro* or white backlands peasant have resided. Jungles are cast as a space of magical transformation within Taíno indigenous beliefs, and as covert hideaways were also frequently locations of African-derived religious practices which were prohibited in the colonial period. Manuel Valdés Pizzini describes El Yunque as 'the most solid emblem of national identity . . . a sacred and mysterious area' yet ironically one which excludes native habitation and is governed by the USDA Forest Service as a reserve.[48] In Puerto Rico, magic and modernity are patently not mutually

(2000), 705–21. See Reinaldo Román, *Governing Spirits: Religion, Miracles and Spectacles in Cuba and Puerto Rico, 1898–1956* (Chapel Hill, 2007).

[44] Corrales, *Chupacabras*, 171.

[45] Corrales, *Chupacabras*, 172.

[46] Jorge Martin, *Vieques: Polígono del 3er. Tipo* (San Juan, 2001), 124. For more on the blending of media and the miraculous see Román, 'Conjuring Progress and Divinity', ch. 6.

[47] James R. Lewis, 'Introduction', *The Gods Have Landed: New Religions from Other Worlds*, (Albany, 1995), xiii.

[48] Manuel Valdés Pizzini, Alfonso Latoni and Virgilio Rodríguez, 'El Yunque or the Caribbean National Forest? Meaning, Management and Culture in the Urban-Tropical Forest Interface', *Culture, Conflict and Communication in the Wildland-Urban Interface*, A. W. Ewert, D. J. Chavez and A. W. Magill, (eds), (Boulder, 1993), 222.

exclusive; if extraterrestrials have been absorbed into popular Christian folklore and sacred geography, they are not always signs of sacred benevolence, however; their awesome power can equally inspire fear and dread. At times, these narratives of origin present the chupacabras as evidence of ever more sinister designs on the part of the US government. In a collection of anecdotes presented by prominent UFOlogist Jorge Martín who hosts a popular radio program and has written several books on extraterrestrial phenomena, the chupacabras is an alien species that US defence intelligence was observing and with which they were in secret collusion. The chupacabras is thus a UFO messenger.[49] The creature is sent on feeding missions in which it sucks blood for its extraterrestrial hosts, later returning the eviscerated bodies to earth.[50] In another book, Martín presents oral testimony that the department of defence has a secret UFO marine station located below the subordinate island of Vieques where it observes and communicates with extra-terrestial beings of superior intelligence. Vieques island was taken over by the US Navy for use as a live bombing range in 1947, most of its land used for war manoeuvres and bomb storage. The station is said to emit an enormous magnetic force, created via huge metallic tubes. Residents claim to have seen two very tall men, so beautiful they resembled women, with shoulder-length hair, who are linked to this subterranean space station and who are said to be highly intelligent and beneficent. Interestingly, the image of this saintly being from below the ocean bears a strong resemblance to Jesus Christ.[51] Here, the US government is inhibiting local access to these godlike superior beings from other worlds.

While much humour implicitly accused the chupacabras' eyewitnesses of being gullible and superstitious country folk, this is a case of mystification that resulted not from being distanced from power, but rather too close to it. The rumours resulted not from a lack of education, but rather conspicuous exposure to the public display of secrets located just beyond the grasp of locals. This is thus quite unlike the South Africans in the mid-1990s who lacked the tools to decipher a 'millennial capitalism', or the 'mysteries of the market' which inspired an 'occult economy'.[52] This view presumes that political subjects fetishize state power because of its 'invisible hand', or in Arjun Appadurai's rather more Marxist cast, because a portion of the

[49] Martin, 'Nemesis', 2–3.

[50] Martín, *La conspiración chupacabras*, 137.

[51] Martín, *Vieques: Polígono del 3er. Tipo*, 124.

[52] Jean and John Comaroff, 'Occult Economies and the Violence of Abstraction: Notes from the South African Postcolony', *American Anthropologist*, 26:2 (1999), 283.

operative mechanics are so distant they are occluded from view.[53] Indeed, the chupacabras reflects a contradiction very peculiar to Puerto Rico, which is a very small island with an extraordinarily pervasive array of US military installations, most of which are classed as top secret and therefore declared off limits to locals.[54]

Stealth bombs?

Since World War II, Puerto Rico has played a key geostrategic role for the US military. As Jorge Beruff puts it, 'Puerto Rico is the central command of a vast system of military installations, and the center of naval command and the South Atlantic'. As García Muñiz continues,

> Puerto Rico is the major naval and staging base for conducting training, fleet deployments to the region, and testing weapons ranges. It also provides port, airfield, and logistics facilities to support naval operations during contingencies. Roosevelt Roads is a training ground for surrogate security forces from Central America and the Caribbean and also serves as a base for military interventions in these same regions.[55]

Until very recently Puerto Rico's adjacent islands of Culebra and Vieques were the central sites for US military exercises using live bombs, and thus provided crucial training grounds for the Atlantic fleet.[56] The military presence in Puerto Rico took a great leap forward in 1944 when the amount of GNP dedicated to military expenditure jumped from 1.3 to 41.6 per cent.[57] During the Lend Lease program, FDR built a vast system of military bases in Puerto Rico, including the air force base at Fort Buchanan, the Roosevelt Roads naval base, Ramey Base and the Borinquen Army airfield, and commenced the forced removal of inhabitants in neighbouring subordinate

---

[53] Arjun Appadurai, 'Introduction: Commodities and the Politics of Value', *The Social Life of Things: Commodities in Cultural Perspective*, ed. A. Appadurai, (Cambridge, 1988), 54.

[54] For a fascinating essay on secrecy and its effects in Los Alamos, see Joseph Masco, 'Lie Detectors: On Secrets and Hypersecurity in Los Alamos', *Public Culture* 38 (2002), 441–67.

[55] Humberto García Muñiz, 'U.S. Military Installations in Puerto Rico: Controlling the Caribbean', in Edwin Meléndez and Edgardo Meléndez, (eds), *Colonial Dilemma: Critical Perspectives on Contemporary Puerto Rico* (Boston, 1983), 65.

[56] Until 2002, when US authorities finally capitulated to protesters and agreed to withdraw from the subordinate island of Vieques.

[57] Jorge Rodríguez Beruff, *Política militar y dominación: Puerto Rico en el contexto Latinoamericano* (San Juan, 1988), 158.

islands Culebras and Vieques, which eventually cleared up to 76% of the latter island's land area for military uses. Under Eisenhower's policy of dispersing nuclear arsenal, Puerto Rico became a nuclear base for both the air force and the marines.[58] As a result, most of the Latin America military interventions of the twentieth century were staged from Puerto Rican bases, ports, and military airports, as were major excursions into other regions such as the Middle East.

This small island of about four million people houses half the military personnel in the Caribbean, and is the principal training camp and testing theatre for new military weaponry for the greatest marine power in the world. In 1978, military spending on the island was over 60 per cent of all US government spending on the island.[59] The extensive militarization of Puerto Rico is not only territorial, however; it is also demographic. Citizenship was given to Puerto Ricans in 1917 so as to enable the recruitment of Puerto Ricans to the armed forces through obligatory military service. For a time the administration of the entire island was placed under the jurisdiction of the Department of War, and the population is disproportionately represented by war veterans as well as servicemen employed in the various civilian branches of the armed forces such as the Coast Guard, the ROTC, the Civil Defense, the National Guard, and the Police.[60]

Unlike the US naval base at Guantánamo, Cuba, or the Panama Canal, the Puerto Rican installations are not localized or marginal enclaves; they are pervasive and ubiquitous. The US military presence is not only deeper and more expansive than elsewhere, it is also far more off limits since so much of it consists of military installations classed as top secret, which require what Joseph Masco describes as 'hypersecurity protocols'.[61] These codes of conduct extend to Puerto Rico due to the fact that it houses five communications facilities providing transmitters and receivers which form part of the US president's special communications network that would relay nuclear weapons commands in the event of a strike.[62] Nor are these installations the only 'public secrets' cordoned off from the gaze of locals; there are others which allow public access, but their goals are only vaguely understood by a public

---

[58] Although Ramey was eventually transferred to the Coast Guard.

[59] Humberto García Muñiz, 'U.S. Military Installations in Puerto Rico: Controlling the Caribbean', in Edwin Meléndez and Edgardo Meléndez, (eds), *Colonial Dilemma: Critical Perspectives on Contemporary Puerto Rico* (Boston, 1983), 53; Beruff, *Política militar y dominación*, 166.

[60] From 1909–1934.

[61] Masco, 'Lie Detectors', 458.

[62] García Muñiz, 'U.S. Military Installations', 61.

without the requisite techno-scientific background.[63] Administered by Cornell University and funded by the National Science Foundation and NASA, the Arecibo radio telescope, for example, is the largest single-dish radio telescope in the world, where astronomers such as Carl Sagan have led the search for evidence of extraterrestrial intelligence. Until 1969, Arecibo was under the control of the Department of Defense. Even the El Yunque rain forest has been at times declared off limits to the public for reasons not at all clear to the neighbouring population who may be local residents but who are defined very explicitly as trespassers; thus in the words of Valdés Pizzini, they are 'declared enemies, those who need education, those who need scrutiny (so they don't enter) those who are excluded, and those who are punished'.[64]

The very opacity of these symbols of US military prowess, technological wizardry and territorial domain has created a robust rumour culture about what goes on behind these closed doors. Thus a culture of secrecy has given way to what Paul Johnson calls 'secretism', 'the circulation of the reputation of secrets', forms of gossip which themselves invest the secrets with further importance.[65] For example, it is said that Roosevelt Roads is actually a nuclear arsenal warehouse, and that the FBI has an undisclosed training program for regional police forces there. Indeed, even when some information is provided, the reigning presumption is that the US government is always doing far more than it will own up to. It is commonly believed that deep in the rainforest of El Yunque there are military installations, nuclear weapons warehouses and experiments carried out by the Department of Defense; that troops engage in secret exercises such as counterinsurgency warfare in conditions of dense undergrowth, and use defoliant products such as Agent Orange.[66] As Johnson says, 'secrets die, but secrecy grows'.[67] And Puerto Ricans tell many tales about the colossal Arecibo telescope, which emits a powerful radar beam that seems to attract UFOs like flies.

---

[63] The term 'public secret' is poached from Michael Taussig, 'Viscerality, Faith, and Skepticism: Another Theory of Magic', in Birgit Meyer and Peter Pels, (eds), *Magic and Modernity: Interfaces of Revelation and Concealment* (Stanford, 2003), 297.

[64] Manuel Valdés Pizzini, 'Desmontando discursos: el nuevo orden forestal en el imaginario colonial, 1898–1925', *Los arcos de la memoria. El '98 de los pueblos puertorriqueños*, ed. S. Álvarez Curbelo, et al., (San Juan, 1998), 91.

[65] Paul Christopher Johnson, *Secrets, Gossip and Gods: The Transformation of Brazilian Candomblé* (Oxford, 2002) 18.

[66] 'El Yunque or the Caribbean National Forest?', 228; Beruff, *política militar y dominación*, 163.

[67] Johnson, *Secrets, Gossip and Gods*, 26.

If Puerto Ricans distrust the Federal Government's true motivations and objectives, there is a long history that gave rise to this presumption of guilt. In Vieques, for example, there is ample testimony that live bombing included dirty bombs containing depleted uranium and chemical munitions which have left toxic residues such as lead, cadmium, cobalt, and radiation that have given rise to high rates of skin disease, cancer and other abnormalities.[68] And within the domain of health care, during the infamous Rhoads affair the Rockefeller Foundation was said to have injected cancer cells into Puerto Ricans as part of a genocidal plot to eliminate the Puerto Rican population.[69] While as Laura Briggs relates, this particular allegation was found to be untrue, the creation of a permanent federally funded birth control program was seen by some as part of a broader effort to reduce the unwanted poor and brown Puerto Rican population, as were the later introductions of birth control products and techniques such as spermaticides, Depo-Provera, the IUD, the pill and sterilization measures. As Briggs states, ' "the relentlessly fertile" Puerto Rican woman provided the ideal testing ground for experimentation, just as the island became the jewel in the crown of US development policy'.[70] Indeed, one could argue that given this history of misunderstanding and at times outright connivance there is good reason for Puerto Ricans alongside African Americans and Native Americans to believe the worst about US government intentions.[71]

Keeping secrets

The hunger for knowledge about US covert activities has led to a vibrant market for texts that reveal secrets; such unlikely material as the memoirs and personal correspondence of Navy Admiral William Leahy, governor of Puerto Rico from 1939 to 1940, have become recreational reading.[72] While short, his regime was of great importance because he presided over the dramatic expansion of the US military presence as Puerto Rico became the

---

[68] See the papers presented at the Congreso Universitario de Investigaciones y Proyectos sobre Vieques, Universidad de Puerto Rico, Río Piedras, 16–17 April 1992, esp. those by Massol, García and Nazario (http://unescopaz.rrp.upr.edu/documentos/viequesupr/congresovieques.html).

[69] Laura Briggs, *Reproducing Empire: Race, Sex, and Science, and U.S. Imperialism in Puerto Rico* (Berkeley, 2002); and Cornelius Packard Rhoads, *The Unsolved Case of Dr. Cornelius P. Rhoads: An Indictment* (San Juan, 2004).

[70] Briggs, *Reproducing Empire*, 110–11.

[71] This position is taken by Turner, *I Heard it Through the Grapevine*; and Nancy Scheper Hughes, 'Theft of Life'.

[72] Jorge Rodríguez Beruff, (ed.), *Las memorias de Leahy: Los relatos del Almirante William D. Leahy sobre su Gobernación de Puerto Rico (1939–1940)* (San Juan, 2001).

'sentry station for the Caribbean and the Panama Canal'.[73] Another example of a surprise best-seller is the book detailing secret negotiations between the highly popular governor Luis Muñoz Marín and Robert McNamara over the proposed removal of every last inhabitant of Vieques and Culebra and even their cemeteries, a poignantly morbid detail that seems to bespeak a US desire to erase not only the human presence, but all remaining traces of its history, even if their intention was the opposite. The aptly named *Plan Drácula* resembled a classic devil's pact narrative—an exchange of untold treasure for human life—since the deal would have swapped 8,570 people and their ancestors' remains for millions of dollars from the Department of Defense.[74]

A fictional work that might also be somewhat uneasily accommodated into this genre of 'rites of exposure' that made a tremendous splash was the historical novella *Seva* by Luis Lopez Nieves, which was a runaway success with more than seven printings.[75] This book recounts the story of a previously undisclosed US intervention months before the real arrival of US troops in July 1898, when Puerto Rico was taken by force into the US imperial orbit. In this account, an earlier intervention occurred which was defeated by valiant Puerto Rican resistance, but US General Miles returns to have the entire town razed so that all traces of the event would be erased. The memory of the event, however, was protected by the sole survivor, whom the narrator eventually tracks down. In the text, Miles built Roosevelt Roads Naval Base in the very ashes of the heroic town of Seva.[76] Here we see the secrets concealed by the military materialized as a hidden history of heroic resistance that the US violently uprooted, erased, lied about and eventually bulldozed over; the US government is accused of hiding a secret of such profound importance that it would completely change the way Puerto Ricans imagine themselves, their history and US-Puerto Rican relations. This tale of US betrayal rang so true to Puerto Rican 'patterns of mistrust' that while fictional it was taken as historical fact.[77]

---

[73] Ibid, 61.

[74] Evelyn Véliz Rodríguez, *Proyecto V-C. Negociaciones secretas entre Luis Muñoz Marín y la Marina. Plan Drácula* (Río Piedras/Santo Domingo, 2002), 20–1.

[75] Taussig, 'Viscerality, Faith and Skepticism', 298.

[76] This plot-line bears some resemblance to Martín's allegation of a UFO space station under Vieques, since the ashes of the mythical Seva lie underneath Roosevelt Roads; both narratives assume that there are undisclosed secrets hidden behind the façade of the US military front.

[77] Turner, *I heard it Through the Grapevine*, 109. Luis Lopez Nieves, *Seva: Historia de la primera invasión norteamericana de la Puerto Rico ocurrida en Mayo 1898* (San Juan, 1984). The book is presented as a series of historical documents and maps which also helped give rise to its genre misrecognition.

A disproportionate number of chupacabras narratives have been generated by the inside/outsiders who have some access to the secrets of power, or who police its margins; those who are close enough to touch the walls and halls of power, the 'skin of the secrets', and yet are still denied real access.[78] Indeed, retired police officers, members of the Civil Defense force, the ROTC, the Meteorological Service, the forestry service, army veterans and police detectives are key traffickers in the currency of information about the chupacabras and UFOs, here read as clues revealing hidden truths about US military activities, thus secrets of state.[79] If secrecy forms a veil that enhances the power of the concealed object, these individuals, as Johnson puts it, help 'mill and polish' the reputation of secretism, that is, the gossip exchanged about the reputations of the secrets.[80] They also magnify the perception of the power of the concealed by what Michael Taussig calls the 'skilled revelation of skilled concealment'; reminding us that 'exposure of the trick is no less necessary to the magic of magic than is its concealment'.[81] These gatekeepers located in between the US military and Puerto Rico, the federal and local government, then play a crucial role in instantiating the boundary between these domains, as well as animating the monstrous chupacabras by their 'lust for confession'. As James Arnold reminds us, 'the monster occupies a necessary, liminal position at the edges of any culture's conceptual field where Others must be dealt with'.[82]

The spectacle of secrets

So we must now return to the question of why the particular community of Canóvanas would be responsible for the invention of the gargoyle face of the

---

[78] Taussig, 'Viscerality, Faith and Skepticism', 306.

[79] This is quite evident in Jorge Martín's books on the chupacabras and Vieques. For more on state secrecy see Micheal Taussig, *The Magic of the State* (New York, 1997). Even Canóvanas mayor José R. 'Chemo' Soto played an important role since he lent much credibility to the allegations when he led an expedition into the bush looking for the chupacabras. A fervent believer, he told me in 2000 that he is writing a book about the chupacabras as space alien.

[80] Simmel, 'Secrecy'; and Johnson, *Secrets, Gossip, and Gods*, 184.

[81] Taussig, 'Viscerality, Faith, and Skepticism', 272, 278. As Jeanne Favret-Saada reminds us of course they also augment the agency and power of the speaking subject; see her *Deadly Words: Witchcraft in the Boçage* (New York, 1980).

[82] Drawing upon Victor Turner of course; A. James Arnold, 'Introduction', in Arnold, (ed.), *Monsters, Tricksters and Sacred Cows: Animal Tales and American Identities* (Charlottesville, 1996), 9. See also Patsy Spyer, 'Introduction', in Spyer, (ed.), *Border Fetishisms: Material Objects in Unstable Spaces* (New York, 1998), 1–12. Román also links the chupacabras to US Federal secrecy, 'Of Dread and Laughter', 11–12.

chupacabras and its attendant narratives of US covert operations and men in black run amok. One possible scenario is that the chupacabras initially emerged as a figure of Satan, a frightening changeling or shape shifter that provided a moralistic explanation for the run of small farm animal deaths that had plagued this interior mountainous region; these deaths may have been read as apocalyptic signs due to turn-of-the-millennium anxieties. Indeed, one of the first informants was Elieser Rivera, a Pentecostal priest, and mayor Chemo Soto, Margaret Tolentino, and her husband of course all form part of the tightly-knit Pentecostal community of Canóvanas.[83] Evangelical churches with their strong interpersonal networks and media command have been found responsible for other rumours of remarkable spread such as the stories of satanic ritual abuse that emerged around US day-care centres in the late 1980s. Allegations that satanic cults were sacrificing children and eating their victims alive landed many day-care providers and associated parents in jail.[84] These accounts may then have then been taken up by Puerto Rican UFOlogists, who proceeded to embellish the narratives, revealing the beast to be a totemic emblem of larger sinister governmental forces including the CIA, FBI and DOD, and extraterrestrial agents of a higher order. These narratives made sense due to the culture of suspicion shared by many Puerto Ricans vis-à-vis US government motives, the widespread belief in UFOs, and a certain anxiety about where Puerto Rico really stands in relation to the US. If as Black says, the Caribbean is the US 'backyard', a place where we let our hair down and dump our garbage, Puerto Ricans indeed may have some troubling uncertainties as to whether they are located on the frontstage of the backyard, or the backstage of the frontyard.[85]

Millenarian anxieties ran rife in the years leading up to 2000 as rumours spread like wildfire that computers and other technology would crash. If these rumours indexed apocalyptic concerns about the impact of humankind on nature, in Puerto Rico these issues are intimately bound with the problem of sovereignty since the US, after all, is the machine in their garden. Long an agrarian society, today seventy per cent of the food consumed on the island is imported from the mainland US, and while people enjoy their *fastfú* (fast-food), they also worry about *transgénicos* or genetic hybrid foodstuffs and whether they are being sneaked onto the shelves of their local *bodegas* or corner markets. While Vieques with its powder-white beaches looks like an

---

[83] Caroline Walker Bynum, *Metamorphosis and Identity* (New York, 2001).

[84] Lawrence Wright, *Remembering Satan: A Tragic Case of Recovered Memory* (New York, 1994).

[85] George Black, *The Good Neighbor: How the United States Wrote the History of Central America and the Caribbean* (New York, 1988).

island paradise, it is actually riddled with thousands of tons of undetonated concrete explosives, rockets, and mines, and much of the waterfront has been declared a 'danger zone' by the US Navy. And for an island which casts its postcolonial history as pastoralism lost, the ultimate contradiction may be that the live impact area of Vieques has now been renamed a 'wilderness area', with public access prohibited due to hazardous contaminants.[86] This reversal of the very relationship between nature and culture indexes a world very much out of balance.

Michael Rogin has elucidated the curious way that during the Cold War, secrecy actually came to function as a form of spectacle in the US political theatre.[87] In the name of national security, nuclear warfare became a key component of American foreign policy-making, the actual contours of which may not be divulged but which nonetheless became a 'public secret' that served to represent US strength overseas.[88] This may explain the strange fact that in eyewitness sightings observers who encountered the beast who should be relaying how they saw the chupacabras, end up recounting the uncanny experience of actually being watched by the creature. As Miguel Molina told me, 'my wife saw it through the window and it watched her, it observed her'.[89] These testimonies bespeak an experience of exclusion, fear, and wonder which was foregrounded during the 1995 chupacabras panic, but one which is part of the background noise of everyday life for many Puerto Ricans, who feel highly vulnerable in the face of an all-powerful Federal government.

This essay has explored a popular fantasy of secrecy at the heart of US imperial statecraft, one in which the federal government is presumed to be a cipher for diabolical intentions and the state appears as a surreptitious and malevolent force. Born of a particular contradiction that is deeply Puerto Rican, one of extensive US presence which is concurrently shrouded in wonder due to its very inscrutability, the chupacabras then provides us with a glimpse of the phenomenology of US imperial power at the *fin-de-siècle* by the poor and marginal who live in its shadows. Perhaps this is why the post-Canóvanas trail of the chupacabras in Latin America followed that

---

[86] To: Jorge L. Colón, 'Memorandum: Response to Comments on Time Critical Removal Action (TCRA) of Unexploded Munitions in the Former Vieques Naval Training Range (VNTR)', From: NAVFAC, Atlantic, Mar. 28, 2006.

[87] Michael Rogin, ' "Make My Day!" Spectacle as Amnesia in Imperial Politics', *Representations* 29 (1990), 99–123.

[88] Rogin, 'Make My Day!'; and Cynthia Enloe, *Bananas, Beaches and Bases: Making Feminist Sense of International Politics* (Berkeley, 1990). See also Masco, 'States of Insecurity'.

[89] Interview in Canóvanas, 2000.

of US twentieth-century war and covert operations, from Mexico, the Dominican Republic, Guatemala, and Chile, and may even invite comparisons to the far-flung Soloman islands, where Michael Scott reports that a cargo cult with an imaginary air fleet under the water lies awaiting the return of the US Navy, where a US base was established during World War II.[90] This also helps explain why the chupacabras was ultimately embraced with some humour, since it bespoke a profound ambivalence about things American that resonates deeply with many Puerto Ricans. Canovenses were mocked by the media, but in many ways their homegrown chupacabras monster reveals not their 'paranoid delusions' so much as their resounding belief in a populist discourse of conspiracy, one that dreams of transparency even in the face of abundant evidence of the dark and sordid designs of the US on Puerto Rico and elsewhere. And given the history of the US in Puerto Rico, it bespeaks a paranoia which as George Marcus sensibly reminds us may be 'a reasonable component of rational and commonsensical thought in certain contexts'.[91] Thus the chupacabras begins to look less like an element of folkloric residue, and more a post-Cold War glimpse of the face of American imperialism as it looks from the backstage of empire, in the eyes of those who want nothing more than to be on the other side of the curtain. After all, Freud would argue that these narratives must represent longing and desire as much as they do fear and loathing.

[90] Michael Scott, Dept. of Anthropology, London School of Economics, pers. comm..

[91] The term 'paranoid delusions' is from Richard Hofstader's classic work. See George Marcus, 'The Paranoid Style Now', in Marcus (ed.), *Paranoia Within Reason: A Casebook on Conspiracy as Explanation* (Chicago, 1999), 2; George Marcus and Michael Powell, 'From Conspiracy Theories to the Incipient New World Order of the 1990s to Regimes of Transparency Now', *Anthropological Quarterly*, 76:2 (2003), 323–4; Mark Fenster, *Conspiracy Theories: Secrecy and Power in American Culture*, (Minneapolis, 1999); and Susan Harding and Kathleen Stewart, 'Anxieties of Influence: Conspiracy Theory and Therapeutic Culture in Millennial America', in *Transparency and Conspiracy*, 258–87.

Witchcraft and the State: Cameroon and South Africa

Ambiguities of 'Reality' and 'Superstition'

Peter Geschiere

Introduction[1]

One of the more problematic aspects of recent developments in many parts of the African continent is the great popular unrest about a supposed proliferation of new forms of 'witchcraft', against which the older sanctions would no longer be of any avail. Such convictions trigger an often desperate search for new sanctions against such novel, occult threats. The fear of a proliferation of the occult leads to increasing popular pressure on the state to do something about this, and throughout the continent governments feel obliged to try out new approaches in order to contain popular worries.[2] This chapter compares

[1] This chapter is an extended version of a paper first presented at the May 2003 Radcliffe / Harvard conference organized in honour of Jean and John Comaroff, and published in the conference volume, J. Comaroff and J. L. Comaroff (eds), *Law and Disorder in the Post-Colony*, (Chicago, 2006). Many thanks to the participants at the Radcliffe conference, notably Adam Ashforth, Arjun Appadurai, Jean and John Comaroff, Rosalind Morris, Janet Roitman and Nancy Scheper-Hughes, and to Barbara Oomen, Isak Niehaus, and Tlou Makhura for their valuable criticisms and suggestions on this earlier version. For the present version I further profited from attending a truly seminal conference on *Justice et Sorcellerie* by Eric de Rosny (Catholic University of Central Africa), in Yaounde, March 2005. Finally I want to thank Steve Smith and Alan Knight for their stimulating comments during the 2005 Essex conference on 'Superstition'.

[2] It is a moot point whether witchcraft is increasing (how is it possible to quantify such hidden threats?). But it is clear that, since the end of the 1980s, witchcraft is much more in the open in many parts of Africa. In the 1960s and 1970s it was, for instance, not done in Cameroon to talk too much about these hidden forms of aggression. This was seen as putting Africa back in time. Over the last decades, however, witchcraft has become a hot issue which is constantly debated in public, and in the modern media (newspapers, radio, TV). The popular concern about a proliferation of new forms of witchcraft is clearly linked with the general disappointment in the development discourse that dominated expectations of rapid modernization in the preceding decades. Under neoliberalism the impact, ever more direct, of the capitalist market economy—the rapid enrichment of the few and the aggravating misery of the many—adds to a general feeling of crisis. It is

two recent judicial initiatives by state officials in the struggle against 'witch-craft'. In Cameroon, around 1980, judges in the East Province—generally considered as one of the most backward parts of the country and infested with witchcraft—began to condemn 'witches' with heavy sentences (up to ten years in jail and high fines).[3] This was a striking reversal of contemporary jurisprudence, especially since the judges were now ready to accept the testimony of *nganga* ('traditional healers') as conclusive proof. Until then it was rather the *nganga* who risked persecution (for defamation and disturbance of the peace). In the 1980s they became, on the contrary, crucial witnesses for the prosecution.

In the 1990s, the new ANC regime in South Africa also came under heavy pressure to intervene against 'witchcraft'. Towards the end of apartheid, the northern parts of the country especially became the scene of violent witch-hunts, in which gangs of young people—often associated with the ANC[4]— played a leading role, supported by *inyanga* (local experts in magic that can be compared to the Cameroonian *nganga*). In 1995 the ANC government of the Northern Province (later re-baptized Limpopo Province) instituted a commission, named the Ralushai commission after its chairman, to look into the causes of these disturbances. In 1996 the report of this commission advised a change in the law so that not only *inyanga* and other specialists, but also a person 'who does any act which creates a reasonable suspicion that he is engaged in the practice of witchcraft' could be prosecuted (p. 55).[5] One may wonder how the latter recommendation—which can be read as confirming the reality of witchcraft as a crime—is to be to reconciled with the general

---

striking, moreover, that in many respects witchcraft discourse seems to be of direct relevance for interpreting and understanding the chaotic impact of capitalist forces (see further P. Geschiere, *The Modernity of Witchcraft, Politics and the Occult in Postcolonial Africa* (Charlotsville, 1997).

[3] See C. Fisiy and P. Geschiere, 'Judges and Witches, or How is the State to Deal with Witchcraft? Examples from Southeastern Cameroon', *Cahiers d'Etudes africaines* 118 (1990), 135–56 and Geschiere, *Modenrity of Witchcraft*, ch. 6.

[4] The Ralushai report (1996: 270 and 273) refers to 'revolutionary forces' which—towards the end of the 1980s, sought to 'politicise the rural communities' and therefore 'chose witchcraft and ritual killing to destablize these communities'.

[5] Ralushai Commission, Report of the Commission of Inquiry into Witchcraft Violence and Ritual Murders in the Northern Province of South Africa (1996), 55. Moreover, for this offence the Ralushai report proposes the heaviest punishment of the three categories it distinguishes. The name of the new law proposed by the Ralushai commission seems characteristic: 'Witchcraft *Control* Act' which is supposed to replace the old 'Witchcraft *Suppression* Act' of 1957 (my italics).

trend of legislation under the post-apartheid regime, notably with the much celebrated 'modernist' tenor of the new Constitution. In the mean time the witch-hunts in Limpopo and in neighbouring Mpumalanga seem to have abated somewhat. According to Isak Niehaus this is mainly due to the restoration of the authority of 'traditional' chiefs in these areas.[6]

However, it is clear as well that the ANC government—like the Cameroonian regime—continues to be under heavy popular pressure to deal one way or another with witchcraft. The general panic about a supposed proliferation of witchcraft is certainly not limited to the rural regions. In several recent publications, Adam Ashforth (1998a, 2000 and 2005) showed, for instance, that witchcraft panics are becoming ever stronger even in Soweto, the largest township in the country. He concludes that witches have replaced the former apartheid regime as an explanation for people's sufferings; and he even adds that it might seriously affect the ANC regime's credibility if it cannot show itself capable of dealing with this threat. Indeed, in December 2004 the South African Parliament voted with great enthusiasm—clearly inspired by President Mbeki's call for an 'African Renaissance' which implies proper respect for 'African knowledge'—for a new law that formalizes further possibilities for state officials to work together with *inyanga*. It is as yet not clear what the practical implications of this law will be.

The aim of this chapter is to compare these two efforts to combat the rising fear of witchcraft. My question is whether one can expect the law—and I mean here state law—to contain the rising fear of witchcraft, that so many see now as a most threatening form of disorder? The comparison between Cameroon and South Africa shows how quite different initiatives on the part of the government became entangled in the ambiguities and circularities of witchcraft thinking—notably because the *nganga/inyanga* had to be involved in one way or another in the state's interventions. In practice, these local experts turned out to act as a kind of 'Trojan horse': by collaborating with them, state officials became involved in all the ambiguities that characterize the field of witchcraft and thus their interventions risked becoming counterproductive.

---

[6] Isak Niehaus (with Eliazaar Mohlala and Kally Shokane), *Witchcraft, Power, and Politics—Exploring the Occult in the South African Lowveld* (London, 2001). There is a striking contrast here with the Ralushai report (1996) which tends to emphasize the involvement of chiefs with witch-hunts. There might be regional differences: Niehaus writes especially about the Lowveld/Mpumalanga while the Ralushai report is mainly based on findings from the Limpopo, notably Vendaland. Even though full-scale witch-hunts became much less frequent, general panics about zombie practices, *muti*-murders and such, hardly abated in the 'new' South Africa.

This comparison might be of interest to debates on 'superstition' in various respects. To many—also to sceptics in Africa—witchcraft is the arch-form of 'superstition'—a relict of 'traditional' ways of thinking that inevitably will be unmasked as an illusion with ongoing 'modernization'. However, the strong pressure in many parts of present-day Africa on the state to intervene in this marshy field shows that it is hard to deny that witchcraft has retained at least some sort of enduring 'reality'. Moreover, the ways in which state initiatives become bogged down in all the ambiguities of witchcraft thinking indicate how much force these representations still retain, including to people who in many respects participate in 'modern' forms of life.[7] Such resilience, despite all the modern changes, might suggest some caution before downplaying these ways of thinking as just another form of 'superstition'. The problem with the latter term might be that it seems to have taken on a new kind of meaning with the European Enlightenment. It is striking that in the rich enumeration of various forms of 'superstition' in the call for papers for this conference, older examples seem to have a different tenor compared to the more recent ones. Since the Enlightenment, the term seems to have taken on connotations of something outdated: representations that are clearly based on some sort of misunderstanding (or even a 'false consciousness'); once *aufgeklärt* ('enlightened') by the impact of modern ideas, people will leave behind such traditional relicts. In the older examples 'superstition' was certainly not something that would more or less automatically disappear with new developments. It referred to ideas that might be unacceptable, but were not thought to be unreal—on the contrary, heretical forms of 'superstition', or even the Devil himself, were experienced as extremely dangerous threats to the survival of 'true' beliefs.

---

[7] These modern dynamics of 'witchcraft' in Africa form not only an urgent, but also a dangerous topic. Attention to such aspects risks exoticizing or even primitivizing the continent (as caught in ancient traditions and incapable of modernizing itself). The terminological problems are manifold and in many respects characteristic. Western terms—like 'witchcraft', 'magic' sorcellerie etc.—offer an unfortunate distorting translation of African terms with a much broader array of meanings. Some Africanists refuse, therefore, to use these notions in academic publications. But these Western terms have been generally appropriated by African populations: public debates in the media and elsewhere are waged in these terms and so it seems quite futile to refuse to use them. Refusing to address the topic as such because it is politically incorrect seems to be not very helpful either. The challenge is rather to show that Africa is not so exceptional in its obsession with occult forms of aggression—it seems to be an undercurrent throughout the 'modern' world.

Both connotations might be quite unhelpful if one wants to understand the resilience of 'witchcraft'—or 'magic', or whatever term one prefers—throughout the 'modern' world. The omnipresence of witchcraft in many parts of present-day Africa, as a haunting everyday concern, represents a particularly challenging case for exploring the role a notion like 'superstition' can play in our analysis. Yet, it is important to emphasize that Africa is certainly not exceptional in this respect. As many anthropologists have recently emphasized, 'modernity' seems to be everywhere marked by its own forms of magic, and in many respects it might be better to speak of modernity's 'enchantment' rather than assuming a basic trend towards 'disenchantment'.[8] Such views seem to be closely related to the implosion of 'modernization' as a confident meta-narrative. Fortunately, it is no longer self-evident that one can categorize a wide-ranging array of phenomena according to a simple dichotomy of 'traditional' versus 'modern'. The problem is that things that used to be classified as 'traditional' exhibit a quite disturbing capacity to graft themselves onto the 'modern'—in Africa, but also, for instance, in the modern West (think of the return of religion or the even more disturbing re-emergence of all sorts of 'parochial' identities). One does not have to be a 'postmodernist' to be no longer at ease with the modern-traditional opposition, that despite all criticism still tends to pervade so much of Western thinking.

This has had quite decisive consequences for the attitude of many anthropologists when faced with the resilience of representations that used to be classified as 'traditional'. Indeed, the quite surprising 'modernity of witchcraft' (the title of my book on politics and the occult in postcolonial Africa) is one of the most challenging examples of this. Most colleagues would hesitate now to repeat Evans-Pritchard's classic formula on witchcraft being an 'imaginary offence because it is impossible'.[9] On the contrary, they feel that

[8] See B. Meyer and P. Pels (eds) *Magic and Modernity—Interfaces of Revelation and Concealment* (Stanford, 2003). See also Jean and John Comaroff, 'Occult Economies and the Violence of Abstraction: Notes from the South African Postcolony', *American Ethnologist* 26 (1991), 279–301; and, 'Millennial Capitalism: First Thoughts on a Second Coming', *Public Culture*, 12:2 (2000), 291–344 (special issue on *Millennial Capitalism and the Culture of Neoliberalism*, ed. Jean and John Comaroff) on 'millennial capitalism'as being marked throughout the present-day world by a wide array of 'occult economies'; and Peter Geschiere 'On Witch Doctors and Spin Doctors, The Role of "Experts" in African and American Politics', in B. Meyer and P. Pels (eds), *Magic and Modernity*, (2003), 159–83, on striking parallels between the roles of 'witch-doctors' in African politics and of 'spin-doctors' in American politics.
[9] E. E. Evans-Pritchard, *Witchcraft, Oracles and Magic among the Azande* (Oxford 1937), 418. Of course Evans-Pritchard could only be so categorical because he created strict

classifying these ideas as simply 'unreal' is not very helpful if one wants to understand the continuing hold they have over people's minds.[10] In such a context the notion of 'superstition' with its modern connotations of 'dated' and 'backward' may raise problems. The challenge seems to taking, in one way or another, such magical ways of thinking more seriously if one wants to understand their amazing dynamics and resilience in grafting themselves upon modern developments that used to be seen as their very antithesis. For historians such a challenge might seem to be less pressing—after all they mostly study 'witchcraft' and similar ideas in historical contexts that only indirectly relate to present-day issues. Yet, a possible point of discussion for them also might be to what extent notions like 'superstition' might serve to keep a safe, academic distance from the shocking representations they study. The question is whether this does not form an obstacle to historical studies as well if one wants to gain a deeper understanding of the compelling force such representations had for the people concerned? I will return to this question in the conclusion.

Comparing recent state interventions in the field of witchcraft in Cameroon and South Africa might be relevant for such broader issues, precisely because these interventions are clearly inspired by a feeling of urgency: the pressure on the state to do something about the supposed proliferation of witchcraft is apparently all too real. The central question in my comparison is to what extent the state in both cases is, indeed, equipped to deal with this tricky issue. There seem to be good reasons to focus on the limits of the law in this context.[11] The Cameroonian example shows that a state offensive against witchcraft can be quite counterproductive. In practice it seems to have reaffirmed the popular obsession with witchcraft as an omnipresent danger. Moreover, the sanctions imposed proved to have completely opposite effects

---

opposition between 'witchcraft' (as purely imaginary) and 'sorcery' (which is all too real). This opposition has been criticized by generations of anthropologists after him (yet it still keeps coming up in introductions and manuals).

[10] See Michael Taussig, *Shamanism, Colonialism and the Wild Man: A Study of Terror and Healing*, (Chicago, 1987), 7; J. Favret-Saada, *Les mots, la mort, les sorts* (Paris, 1977) (= *Deadly Words, Witchcraft in the Bocage*, 1980) 7; see also for a more extensive discussion of this 'reality' issue Peter Geschiere, 'Sorcellerie et modernité: Retour sur une étrange complicité', *Politique africaine* 79 (2000) (special issue on *Pouvoirs sorciers*, ed. Florence Bernault and Joseph Tonda) 48–66.

[11] My title is a form of academic piracy from the title of one of the main research programmes of WISER (the new research institute at Univ. of Witwatersrand), 'The Limits of the State'. Clearly the latter title relates very well to present-day predicaments in South Africa (and elsewhere).

to those intended: what is the use of locking up a supposed witch for several years in jail, when everybody is convinced that by the time (s)he comes out, (s)he will have become an even more dangerous witch? However, such criticisms may seem to be gratuitous in view of the pressure on the government to do something. The question is, can South Africa do better? Two crucial issues, or stumbling blocks, seem to stand out. The first of these is the circular and subversive character of witchcraft discourse. A precondition for any form of legislation—just as for our endeavours as academics— seems to be the creation of clarity and unequivocal distinctions. However as soon as the legislator has to deal with witchcraft, (s)he (again just like we academics) becomes entangled in a minefield of ambiguities and shifting meanings, that seem to block any effort towards control. Secondly, and in direct relation to the first issue, is the key role of the local expert (*nganga, inyanga, sangoma*, healer, diviner, witch-doctor, or whatever term one prefers) as an intermediary. Can judges ever establish proof in this occult domain without using their expertise? But, if so, doesn't that mean legitimating the same forces as those attributed to the witches? And, concerning sanctions, are local experts' forms of 'healing' not more effective than the state's sanctions? In practice, it is precisely these indispensable intermediaries that entangle judges and legislators in all the ambiguities of witchcraft discourse. Clearly, there are good reasons to take the ongoing cogency of these representations seriously, rather than relegating them to the order of outdated superstitions.

However, first a brief excursion might be helpful on how to place 'witchcraft' in the context of the everyday social order of the societies concerned.

Witchcraft as disorder?

In general, interventions by the law into the field of witchcraft, be it in present-day Africa or early-modern Europe, are based on the assumption that witchcraft constitutes a direct attack on the social order. During the heyday of anthropological witchcraft studies in the 1940s and 1950s, anthropologists tended to agree with this view. Max Gluckman, the guru of the so-called Manchester school, which produced a series of monographs on British 'Central Africa', that deeply influenced anthropological views on witchcraft,[12] typically saw it as a very effective form of social control, precisely because it constituted a threatening anti-thesis to the social order itself.

---

[12] See notably M. Marwick, *Sorcery in Its Social Setting: A Study of the Northern Rhodesian Cewa* (Manchester, 1965) and also V. W. Turner, *Schism and Continuity in an African Society: A Study of Ndembu Village Life* (Manchester, 1954).

He compared the morality ingrained in witchcraft representations to that of an Anglican anthem and deemed it even more effective:

> ... beliefs in the malice of witchcraft ... do more than ask [to love your neighbour] as an act of grace; they affirm that if you do not love one another fervently, misfortune will come.[13]

It was this threat that, in his view, made witchcraft so effective in obliging 'men and women ... to observe the social virtues'.[14] From this peaceful view it is, indeed, a far cry to the horrors depicted (both in writing and in photographs) in the Ralushai report. Or to Peter Delius' shocking descriptions of how in 1986, the 'comrades' in two villages in Sekhukhuneland (present-day Limpopo province) called in the help of a local diviner, a certain Ramaredi Shaba, who no longer threw bones but instead had developed a more modern divining technique, called 'African television'. On her oversized screen the figures of the 'witches' would appear, who were then to be 'necklaced' by the comrades.[15] No doubt, Gluckman would have characterized such horrors as symptomatic of a period of transition. But then we may have to see the entire postcolonial period as one great transition. Indeed, since people increasingly feel that the whole world is in constant transition, the term seems to lose its meaning.

It might be more relevant to question Gluckman's (and many other anthropologists') view of witchcraft as the opposite of the social order, serving to keep this order in shape. My informants in East Cameroon, just like several people quoted in the Ralushai report, rather seem to see it as an integral part of the social order: it may be an extremely evil force, yet it can bring also—more or less directly—riches, luck, and power. Laburthe-Tolra concluded that among the Beti of Central Cameroon, *evu* (now always translated as *sorcellerie*) is seen as the dark side of power, extremely dangerous, yet at the same time necessary for maintaining the social order.[16] In these societies, the link between witchcraft and power rather seems to express the deep

---

[13] M. Gluckman, *Custom and Conflict in Africa* (Oxford, 1955), 94.

[14] See also M. Douglas, 'Introduction: Thirty Years after "Witchcraft, Oracles and Magic"', in Mary Douglas (ed.), *Witchcraft Confessions and Accusations*, (London, 1970), pp. xiii–xxxviii and her ironical comment that for some time anthropologists managed to depict witchcraft as 'domesticated' and 'not running amuck'—this in stark contrast to historians.

[15] P. Delius, *A Lion amongst the Cattle: Reconstruction and Resistance in the Northern Transvaal* (Johannesburg, 1996) 195.

[16] P. Laburthe-Tolra, *Minlaaba: Histoire et société traditionnelle chez les Bëti du Sud Cameroun* (Paris, 1977).

conviction that any form of power, even if it is necessary, is highly dangerous. And, again, it is striking that in the Ralushai report so many quotes from informants, especially those concerning the position of Venda chiefs, seem to echo this idea.

This view, relativizing the distinction of good versus evil in witchcraft discourse, that was so strongly conveyed to me by my informants from the Cameroonian forest area, has been strongly criticized by several colleagues.[17] In a recent contribution, the French-Togolese political scientist, Comi Toulabor, reproaches me in his eloquent way for not making a clear distinction between the 'witch' and the 'magician' (the first unequivocally evil, the second only capable of using his/her special powers in a more positive way).[18] John Hund (now at the University of the North, South Africa) attacks me even more forcefully by quoting me as an outstanding example that academic writers are 'unfortunately some of the worst perpetrators of confusion'. He is clearly shocked that I repeat my informants' view of the *nganga* ('traditional healer') being a kind of 'super-witch' since (s)he can only heal by using the same powers as witches tend to do. For Hund this is an 'overwhelming misunderstanding').[19] He insists instead that healers (for him especially the *sangoma* of South Africa) should be radically kept apart from the witches.

Of course, the whole witchcraft conundrum would be a lot easier to solve if such a separation could be applied so easily. The problem is, again, the subversive character of witchcraft discourse that so easily erodes all such nice conceptual distinctions—in Africa, just as elsewhere in the world.[20] It is clear

---

[17] For most historians of witchcraft in early-modern Europe it is self-evident that it had to be seen as an evil force—after all they mainly based themselves on the files of the courts condemning witches. However some studies offer glimpses that for certain parts of Europe as well, those who could control these dangerous forces were locally not seen as unequivocally evil. See, e.g., C. Ginzburg, *I Benandanti—Stregoneria e Culti Agrari tra Cinquecento e Seicento*, (Einaudi, 1966) on the Benandanti in the Friuli; or W. de Blécourt, *Termen van Toverij—De Veranderende betekenis van Toverij in Noordoost-Nederland tussen de 16e en 20ste eeuw* (Nijmegen, 1990) on 'healers' in the Netherlands; see also Favret-Saada, *Les mots* on 20th-century Normandy).

[18] C. Toulabor, 'Sacrifices humains et politique: quelques exemples contemporains en Afrique', in Piet Konings, Wim van Binsbergen, and Gerti Hesseling (eds), *Trajectoires de libération en Afrique contemporaine—Hommage à Robert Buijtenhuijs* (Paris, 1999), 207–33.

[19] J. Hund, 'Witchcraft and Accusations of Witchcraft in South Africa: Ontological Denial and the Suppression of African Justice,' *Comparative and International Law Journal of Southern Africa*, 33 (2000), 369/70.

[20] See for particularly spectacular examples of such ambiguity Favret-Saada, *Les mots* on Europe and Taussig, *Shamanism* on Colombia.

that there are wide differences as to how African societies view central figures, like the chiefs or the healer, and notably in the ways in which they relate them to the occult powers (or try to separate them from these powers).[21] It is true that in the forest societies in Cameroon where I did my main fieldwork, the central notions (*djambe* among the Maka and *evu* among the Beti) are extremely broad and fluid, covering a wide array of different expressions of the occult, from highly negative to fairly positive ones—*djambe/evu* being potentially lethal but also essential for healing, exercising authority or accumulating wealth. Elsewhere, for instance in the more hierarchical societies of Cameroon's western highlands, there is a determined effort to 'compartmentalize' the sphere of the occult through clear terminological distinctions between more negative and more positive forms. In these societies the chief, though certainly associated with occult powers, is normally rigidly separated from the darker manifestations of these powers. However, it might be important to emphasize that such distinctions are always precarious and never self-evident. It seems to require a constant struggle to maintain them against the inherent fluidity of any discourse on the occult. For instance, recently, when many chiefs from the Cameroonian highlands got into trouble with their subjects for their continued support for the hated regime of President Biya, people were quick to accuse them of being real witches.

There may be good reasons therefore not to take the distinctions that are often emphasized in the literature on South Africa between 'witch' and *sangoma*—or between the *sangoma* as a 'priest-diviner' and the *inyanga* as his disreputable colleague—too easily for granted. Even Hund (373) emphasizes that they all use 'the same occult forces', but he insists that there is an 'ontological' difference. Again, one can sympathize with his effort to separate the *sangoma* as a reliable ally in these dark struggles. But who makes this ontological difference between actors that are so closely involved with the same forces? And how can such a distinction be maintained in practice? It is clear that widely different views of the *sangoma* pertain in daily life. Several spokesmen quoted in the Ralushai report (especially from Vendaland) say quite nasty things about *sangoma* ('with a lust for blood and easy money' 268). Adam Ashforth quotes a *sangoma* (for whom Ashforth clearly had great respect) who mentioned that someone asked him to use his powers to kill another man. This the healer 'of course', refused to do—yet the prospective client clearly had another idea of what *sangoma* do and do not do.[22]

---

[21] Such variations make it a bit disconcerting that Hund still speaks so easily of 'African culture'.

[22] A. Ashforth, *Madumo, A Man Bewitched* (Chicago, 2000).

Rather than taking such terminological distinctions as givens, it might be more urgent to study how exactly—through which struggles and by what means—such compartmentalization is maintained, as for instance Eric de Rosny has done with great subtlety in his studies on Douala.[23] Apparently maintaining such distinctions will always entail a highly precarious struggle against the blurring tenor of discourses on the occult. It might be this subversive charge, undermining any clear-cut distinction between good and evil (or any attempt at a clear definition whether by academics or by lawyers), that can help scholars to understand the impressive resilience of these discourses in the face of modern changes. It is also this blurring tenor—the Comaroffs speak of 'unroutinizable powers'—that makes it so difficult for the state to find reliable allies in its witchcraft struggle.[24]

Subverting the law; the circularity of witchcraft discourse

A basic problem for any legislative intervention in the field of witchcraft is what might be called its 'circular' character. Unequivocal terminology and clear-cut definitions are supposed to be crucial for any law-making (as they are for respectable academic research). It might be all the more important to emphasize that the very ambiguity and the fluidity of core notions are at the heart of the resilience of witchcraft discourse. This seems to be an important reason why changes can be integrated so easily into this discourse and why it is capable of explaining whatever outcome an event has, making it impervious against any Popperian attempt to try and falsify it. It might also be an important reason why both lawyers and academics have such difficulty in making sense of this tricky field.

For me, the first confrontation with the quite alarming circularity of witchcraft talk was when my neighbours in the village in South Cameroon where I had just settled started to gossip about my new friend Mendouga. The latter was a dignified lady of a certain age and with a somewhat enigmatic air who had already honoured me twice with a visit. This was really an honour since, at the time, she was generally seen as the greatest *nganga* (healer) of the area. But after her second visit, my assistant and his friends pointed out to me that 'of course' this meant that she was a great *djindjamb* (lit. someone who has a *djambe*/'witchcraft'). Indeed, for them it was only because she had developed

---

[23] Eric de Rosny, *Les yeux de ma chèvre: Sur les pas des maîtres de la nuit en pays douala* (Paris, 1981); and, E. de Rosny, *L'Afrique des guérisons* (Paris, 1992).

[24] J. L. Comaroff and J. Comaroff, 'Criminal Justice, Cultural Justice: The Limits of Liberalism and the Pragmatics of Difference in the New South Africa,' *American Ethnologist*, 31:2, 188–204.

her *djambe* in an extraordinary way—thanks to the help of her 'professor'—that she could 'see' what the witches were doing[25], fall upon them and force them to lift their spell so that their victim (Mendouga's client) could be healed. Mendouga herself later on assured me, as all *nganga* will do, that her *djambe* was 'different': her professor had bound her with heavy 'interdictions' to use her powers only to heal and never to kill.[26] However, it was clear that my fellow-villagers were not so sure of this: a *djambe* is a *djambe*, and there is always the risk that the basic instinct of the *djindjamb*—that is to deliver your own kin to be devoured by your fellow-witches—will break through. Indeed, *nganga* are always seen as highly ambiguous figures: they are the obvious persons to turn to when one feels attacked; yet they are also terribly dangerous. And, indeed, about all *nganga* there was constant gossip that they had betrayed their own clients, that they worked in league with the witches, and so on. Throughout the forest area of Cameroon, as in others parts of the continent, there is even a basic belief that, in order to become initiated, an aspiring *nganga* has to offer one of his/her own relatives to his/her professor.[27]

There is a basic circularity here: the *nganga* can only heal because (s)he has killed before. Moreover, the main protection against a *djambe* attack is to be found within the realm of the very same *djambe*. But by invoking the help and protection of a *nganga* one already allows oneself to be drawn into *djambe's* vicious circles. No wonder it is so difficult to escape from it.[28] Again, it might

[25] By referring to her ability to 'see' this, Mendouga implied that she had 'the second pair of eyes'. In many parts of Africa—especially in the central and southern areas where Bantu languages are spoken—the acquisition of such a 'second pair' is seen as the first and indispensable step in initiation into the world of witchcraft forces.

[26] Thus, the *nganga* is the best example that witchcraft's evil forces can also be canalized and used in a highly constructive way: it is only because the *nganga* has learnt to control his/her dangerous powers that (s)he can heal. However, this control is always seen as precarious and so is, therefore, any distinction between more constructive and more destructive uses of the *djambe*.

[27] See Eric de Rosny, *Les yeux de ma chèvre* and *L'Afrique des guérisons*, who describes this as a crucial moment in his own initiation as a *nganga* in Douala. De Rosny is a French Jesuit who worked in Douala for more than forty years. After his intiation as a *nganga* he combined local forms of healing with Christian notions and practices in a most sophisticated and at the same time honest way. Luckily in his case the demand of his 'professor' for *une bête sans poil* (an animal without body hair—that is, a human being) could be met by offering a goat as a substitute.

[28] See Geschiere, *Modernity of Witchcraft* for a more detailed analysis of Mendouga's vicissitudes (and those of other *nganga* in East Cameroon). See Ashforth, *Madumo* for a very vivid (and therefore all the more disconcerting) description of how his friend from

be good to emphasize that this example has aspects that may be particular to certain parts of Cameroon (or maybe to the Equatorial forest area). Yet the practical difficulties in keeping witch and healer apart—and the circularity this entails—seem to be much more general.[29] The question is what happens when the state with its judicial apparatus intervenes in such a tricky field?

The Ralushai report is plagued by similar ambiguities when addressing the role of the local 'experts', the *inyanga*. In its recommendations the committee insists on the need for more clarity: it severely criticizes the failure of 'most of the legislation to draw a clear line between the so-called witch, the sorcerer, and the witch-finder' (61). The distinction between witch and sorcerer is not further elaborated in the report. But the aim of setting apart the 'witch-finder' is clear. To Ralushai and his fellow commission members the 'witch-finder' (in other passages the term *inyanga* is used) performed a key role in triggering the popular frenzy that led to the horrible witch-hunts. And, no doubt with good reason, many of the report's recommendations aim to make it possible to undertake legal action against these witch-finders.

Yet, on close reading, it is striking how the report gets entangled in the fluidity and circularity of these local notions. Its own case material shows with much detail how difficult it is, again, to distinguish witch and witch-finder. In many cases, an *inyanga* is furiously accused of being a witch and even physically attacked. And, as said, many of the witches that were killed in the large-scale hunts around 1990 were apparently *inyanga*. The report's appendices spell out in detail how the 'comrades' first forced the accused to display all his/her herbs and pots in front of the house and explain their use. Only after this was (s)he lynched. Often, the victim was explicitly accused of being involved in *muti* murders. Indeed, the *inyanga* figure as some sort of archetype of the witch; yet, as said, they worked also closely together with the comrades as witch-finders. Ramaredi Shaba with her 'African Television' screen in Sekhukuneland[30] may have been a particularly frightening example of what an *inyanga* could do, but she was certainly not exceptional. In nearly all documented cases of witch-hunts by the comrades, the latter explicitly

---

Soweto was sucked ever deeper into witchcraft's circular reasonings on his long quest among all sorts of healers. The overview of court cases in the Ralushai report indicates also that a considerable number of 'witches' killed by the youth gangs around 1990 were *inyanga*. Apparently, to the people, *inyanga* and witch were more or less equivalent (which did not stop them from asking the help of other *inyanga* for 'sniffing out' the witches within the community).

[29] See for exactly the same 'confusion' Favret-Saada *Les Mots* on Normandy in the 1970s.

[30] Above, p. 320. Delius, *A Lion amongst the Cattle.*

sought the help of one or several *inyanga* to help them to expose the witches. Indeed, it is quite clear that the *inyanga* were often in some sort of catch-22 situation: if they refused to collaborate with the comrades they were in grave danger of being exposed themselves as witches to be lynched. After all, any *inyanga* is a self-evident suspect. There seems to be the same circularity here as in the Cameroonian examples above: apparently the very capacity of the *inyanga* to 'see' witches indicates that they are involved with the same occult powers.

Ralushai's simple recommendation to 'draw a clear line' between witch and witch-finder might, therefore, be quite naive. Yet, at the same time, it touches upon a central issue in the whole conundrum: how are judicial interventions in the field of witchcraft to deal with the *nganga*?

Cameroon: the *nganga* as a Trojan horse?

In earlier publications on the witch-trials in East Cameroon, we compared the central role of the *nganga* in the judiciary offensive against witches to that of the Trojan horse that helped the Greeks to finally break the resistance of the proud city of Troy.[31] As said, the Cameroonian judges feel that the 'expertise' of the *nganga* is crucial for establishing 'proof'. How else can they prove 'beyond reasonable doubt' that the accused did 'go out'—that is, left their bodies at night to attack their fellow men? However, as emphasized before, to the Maka—as to other groups in the forest—the *nganga* is the most conspicuous representative of the world of *djambe* (or *evu*, or *sorcellerie*, or whatever term people use). The newly enhanced prestige of these local experts—who, instead of being persecuted by the courts, now play a central role during its sessions—seems therefore to confirm the popular belief in these powers.

This official recognition of their expertise seems to coincide with new aspects in the performance of these *nganga*. Especially after 1980, a novel, more modern type of *nganga* emerged. The *nganga* I knew in the Maka region during the 1970s—for instance our friend Mendouga, referred to above - were true villagers. They hardly spoke French and their knowledge of the exterior world was limited. Some were considered to be rich, but people would always comment that the wealth of witches, the *nganga* included, is based upon 'delight without sweat'—which seems to mean that it is easily acquired but does not last long. Most of the *nganga* lived in simple *poto-poto* houses (mud walls with a frame of poles), often situated slightly outside the village, not far from the bush. In everyday life they remained in the background: they were supposed to operate in secret.

---

[31] Fisiy and Geschiere, 'Judges and Witches'; Geschiere, *The Modernity of Witchcraft*.

However, the *nganga* who figure in the court files as expert witnesses against the 'witches' exhibit quite a different profile. They present themselves emphatically as modern figures. Often, they worked for some time elsewhere, sometimes in public service. They speak French fluently and use, with certain ostentation, French (or even English) books on occultism, 'Eastern magic', and other forms of secret knowledge. They brag about their modern education. One *nganga* (thirty-five years old) told me, for instance, that he had been admitted to a Swiss medical school when his ancestor 'took' him. He remained paralyzed for six months. Then he started as a 'traditional healer'. But he still called himself 'doctor'. These modern *nganga* often emphasize that they work with the government, as members of the new association of traditional healers. Their membership card is used as a sort of licence and, more generally, as a symbol of their modern prestige.[32]

Baba Denis, a *nganga* who played a central role in several of the court cases we could follow, can serve as an example here. Baba established himself as 'traditional healer' in a village, close to the one where I lived, in the early 1980s. But his compound was very different from that of, for instance, our former friend Mendouga (who had died in the meantime; people said she had 'lost her power' already several years earlier). When I visited Baba in 1988, he lived in the middle of the village on the main crossroads. His house was adorned with several large signboards: not only 'Traditional Healer' but also '*Astrologue*' and '*Rose-Croix*' (Rosicrucian). The last sign, especially, underscored the modernity of this healer: the Rosicrucians are supposed to be highly present among the new state elite (President Paul Biya is the most prominent acolyte). Indeed, Baba often spoke of his brother who would have an important position in the President's office in the capital. He himself had the authoritarian air of a *fonctionnaire*, which was hardly surprising since he served in the army for a long period. According to the villagers, he was sent home because of 'problems'. It was said that he even spent some time in prison. But this rumour only served to enhance his renown as a specialist, since—as noted—people generally believe that in prison one meets the really dangerous sorcerers. Baba himself, however, emphasized the scientific nature of his expertise: before the tribunal he would explain how he applied 'his science'. Like his colleague referred to above, he called himself a doctor and talked about his compound as his 'hospital'.[33]

The high profile of such *nganga*, reinforced by the official recognition of their expertise, automatically enhances the popular idea that the *djambe*

---

[32] In Cameroon, this association is still not officially recognized, in contrast to other countries (Ghana, Zimbabwe—see below). Yet it has some sort of semi-official status.

[33] It is also characteristic that he referred to his clients as *les coupables* (the guilty ones).

is everywhere. Of special importance in this context is, moreover, that these modern *nganga* exhibit much more aggressive behaviour in recruiting clients and in unmasking suspects. In the 1970s, most *nganga* were still fairly discreet. They appeared in public only on special occasions, such as when the village notables invited them to perform a purifying ritual or an oracle. They were often hesitant to advance specific accusations, no doubt for fear of difficulties with the authorities, but also because vague allusions seemed more useful to their forms of therapy. The treatments of a 'healer' like for instance Ms. Mendouga were, indeed, mostly aimed at repairing family relations.

A *nganga* like Baba intervenes in a very different manner. In several of the court cases on which we could read the files, it was he who took the initiative to 'purify' a village, since he had 'seen' that it was invaded by the witches (in one of these villages he even claimed to have destroyed a 'nocturnal airstrip' where the witches 'landed their planes'). During such purifying actions, it was he who pointed out the witches and had them arrested by the villagers. Moreover, it was Baba who insisted that they should be handed over to the *gendarmes*. Other modern *nganga* as well have little scruple in launching direct accusations against persons they often do not know. And they are constantly trying to attract new clients by warning them that they are victim to occult attacks and that they urgently need protection against evil-doers from within their close surroundings.

One reason for such aggressive behaviour is clearly that these *nganga* hope to make quick money: the world of the *nganga* is becoming ever more monetized and people often pay significant sums of money for protection or purification. But they are also inspired by the new possibility of gaining some sort of official recognition as a witch-finder. As said, it is quite clear that the high profile of these new *nganga*, as expert witnesses before the tribunals and allies of the government, hardly contributes to putting an end to *la sorcellerie*. [34] On the contrary it strengthens a general sense of 'metaphysical disorder' among the people, since the omnipresence of these *nganga* seems to confirm that witchcraft is, indeed, proliferating.

---

[34] At stake here is not only the impact of the *nganga* on the courts but also, vice versa, the effect of their performance before the courts on their role as healers. In our earlier publications (Fisiy and Geschiere, 'Judges and Witches'; Geschiere, *The Modernity of Witchcraft*) we emphasized that the association of the *nganga* with the courts and the *gendarmes* in their offensive against *la sorcellerie* seems to turn them into disciplinary figures (some sort of outgrowth of the authoritarian State). It remains to be seen how this will affect their performance as healers.

The Ralushai report: 'drawing a clear line'

The patterns that emerge from the ways in which the South African courts try to deal with witchcraft, and from the Ralushai report, may differ in many respects from developments in Cameroon. Yet, there are also many similarities as far as the daily context is concerned. For instance, in everyday life in South Africa, *inyanga* are certainly as present as the *nganga* in the Cameroonian context. The Ralushai report (48) quotes an article by Mihalik and Cassim:

> By 1985 there were some 10,000 sangomas and inyangas practising in greater Johannesburg. These traditional healers were consulted at least occasionally by 85 per cent of all black households and were supported by a national network of approximately 40,000 traders in healing and magical herbs. The African Traditional Healers Association claimed a membership of 179,000 outnumbering western doctors by 8 to 1."[35]

These figures are quite convincing for anyone who has visited the Durban *muti* market, serving as a magical hub for the whole of South Africa (and beyond). Moreover, as said, it is clear that these specialists played a key role in the outbreak of the shocking witch-hunts of the 'comrades' in the Northern Province towards the end of apartheid. Delius' story about Rameredi Shoba with her fearsome 'African Television' screen is paralleled by many similar reports in the rich case-material collected in the Ralushai report (cf. also Niehaus, *Witchcraft, Power and Politics*). As in the judicial offensive against witchcraft in Cameroon, these local specialists were indispensable to the comrades' action against similar dangers: who else could 'sniff out' the witches?

However, the eagerness with which the comrades—apparently encouraged by the changing political context—took matters in their own hands, and the violent consequences of this, gave the whole issue of witchcraft a somewhat different twist than in Cameroon (and many other Sub-Saharan countries). In Cameroon, witchcraft as such became increasingly defined by politicians as the ultimate form of subversion of the state, sabotaging *le développement* and undermining the position of the state elite. Indeed, while I was living in the village in East Cameroon, I regularly witnessed officials haranguing the villagers that they should stop sabotaging the government's development projects with their eternal witchcraft, or else . . . The judicial offensive against

[35] J. Mihalik and Y. Cassim, 'Ritual Murder and Witchcraft: A Political Weapon,' *South African Legal Journal*, (1992), 138. It is striking, that these authors seem to take it for granted that only black households make use of the services of such specialists.

witchcraft after 1980 seemed to be as much inspired by such worries among the Cameroonian authorities as by pressures 'from below' (from the people) on the state to do something about the proliferation of occult attacks. In South Africa, at least in the former Northern Province, it was the proliferation of violent witch-hunts—the summary executions of 'witches' by the comrades—rather than supposed conspiracies by the witches that posed an urgent threat to the state. As several observers noted, the witch-hunts seemed to highlight that the state was no longer in control in the area—which was highly problematic both for the apartheid regime and for the subsequent ANC government (see also Ralushai report 231). The vital question became, therefore, what the state courts had done—and could do—to contain these hunts. It is notably on this point that Ralushai and his co-authors evaluate the rich array of cases in the annexes of their report.

The authors note with clear dismay that in several cases the courts did not intervene at all. This seems to have occurred notably in those cases where chiefs were actively involved in the witch-hunts. The report sees this refusal of at least some courts to act as a crucial failure, since it must have encouraged further witch-hunts (Ralushai 236, 270). It notes also that in several cases, where the courts did condemn the perpetrators of witch-killings, they imposed punishments that were purely nominal, which again meant encouraging the further spread of the hunts (40, 245). Only in a few cases were proper punishments imposed on the main culprits of the lynchings.[36] Moreover, the report notes that in none of these cases was judicial action undertaken against the *inyanga* who had been involved in 'sniffing out' the witches; it clearly sees this as another failure of the judiciary apparatus (187, 269).

Indeed, Ralushai and his co-authors seem to recognize—and rightly so— that the *inyanga* were at the heart of the whole problem. Several of their most stringent recommendations are directed against the *inyanga* and the problematic implications of their role as witch-finders. It is striking, for instance, that the new 'Witchcraft Control Act' (which the commission proposes as replacement for the Witchcraft Suppression Act of 1957/70) retains the article from the older law that declares guilty and 'liable on conviction' anybody who 'employs or solicits any witch-doctor, witch-finder or any other person to name or indicate any person as a wizard or a witch' (art. 1c, Ralushai 1996:55). Since it is central to the expertise of any *inyanga* (or any healer in general) that (s)he is able to 'see' from where the occult aggression comes that is supposed to undermine the client's wellbeing, this article would mean that anybody

---

[36] 247; cf. also 270: 'The harsh sentences imposed by the courts in the Venda Supreme Court have also played a significant role in curbing these killings. Venda is quiet now except for the case at Mutale...'.

who consults a local healer risks being prosecuted. How is a client to stop the healer from exercising the gift that is supposed to be the secret to his/her powers? Not only the impressive figures quoted above, but also the rich case material in the report's Annexes vividly illustrate the omnipresence of the *inyanga* in everyday life. So how is this article ever to be applied with some degree of success?

The report's draconian recommendations against *inyanga*, understandable as they may be, are also difficult to reconcile with the emphasis in its opening pages on the need to take the popular concern about witchcraft seriously. For instance, after a few preliminary pages about the composition and the procedures of the committee, the report with eloquent simplicity raises right away what might be considered as the crucial issue:

> The question may be asked whether a community that still strongly believes in witchcraft can be blamed for insisting that the old man, who had made the threat [of witchcraft—PG], should not be removed from the area. (13)[37]

The next question that automatically seems to follow from this is whether it is possible to take such concerns seriously without involving in one way or another a local expert? Indeed, the commission seems to highlight both how

---

[37] The quoted passage sums up the basic dilemma of any official who has to deal with a witchcraft case. Cyprian Fisiy and I came upon exactly the same proposition in various parts of Cameroon. For instance, during an interview we had in 1992 with the new Prosecutor at Kribi (in the South Province), this official complained to us that right after his installation he had been caught in the same dilemma. Just before his arrival at Kribi, his predecessor had been confronted with a gang of young men from the village of Ntdoua who had dragged an old man to his office, demanding that he should be locked up since he was a witch. His predecessor refused to do so. A few months later the young men set fire to the old man's house and he perished in the flames. Now the new Prosecutor was stuck with the young men in his jail. 'What can I do? If I will have them accused of murder, the people will say the state is protecting witches. If I let them go, people might start murdering witches throughout the region.' Our Prosecutor tended to accept the proposition that if a community wanted to expel a 'witch', the state had to accept this (if only for the protection of the accused—see Geschiere, *The Modernity of Witchcraft*, 185). The catch in such an apparently convincing statement is of course the notion of 'community'. Only in very exceptional cases will a whole community agree about a witchcraft accusation—it rather seems to be in the nature of witchcraft that there is always disagreement over it. These quotes from the Ralushai report and from the Kribi Prosecutor may show, therefore, that there is some urgency for anthropologists in debunking the notion of 'community'.

indispensable the *inyanga* are for reassuring the population; and, at the same time, what dangerous and unreliable partners they are in any attempt by the government to intervene.

The report seems to look for a way out from this dilemma in the institution of a National Traditional Healers Association. No less than 23 pages of the report (64–87) concern a 'Proposed Draft Legislation to Control the Practice of Traditional Healers'. This draft is strongly influenced by the example of Zimbabwe where such an association has been functioning since the 1980s. Professor Ralushai himself and Mr. Ndou, another commission member, visited Harare and had a long interview with Prof. Chavunduka, Vice-Chancellor of the University of Zimbabwe and President of the Zimbabwe National Traditional Healers Association. They talked also to other members of the Executive Committee of this association. The law text they proposed on the basis of these interviews has a strikingly disciplinary character. It mainly consists of a long enumeration of all sorts of controlling instances and possible disciplinary measures against 'improper or disgraceful conduct' by members. The text itself does not spell out what such conduct might be. But the rest of the report (notably the proposed text for the Witchcraft Control Act) makes it quite clear that this would especially be 'to name or indicate any person as wizard or witch'. As a consequence the heavily disciplinary tenor of the proposed Traditional Medical Practitioners Act seems to leave it completely open what 'traditional healing' is: if the whole aspect of 'seeing' is cut out, what is left of this 'healing'?

The basic problem is, again, the highly fluid character of notions of healing and healing power. The proposed Act on traditional healers for South Africa reminded me strongly of long debates in Cameroon on how to distinguish 'bona fide' and 'mala fide' *nganga*. In Cameroon as well, some people advocate official recognition for a national association of traditional healers (which has existed for some time but still has a somewhat shadowy form). Here also the idea is that it would help to separate charlatans—and in this context people often mention Nigerian 'specialists'—from real *nganga*. Some insist that the line should be drawn between healers working with herbal medicine and other forms of 'local knowledge' on the one hand, and those dabbling in 'witchcraft' on the other. However, to the people in general such distinctions are never convincing: at least the capacity to 'see'—to have 'the second pair of eyes'—is seen as crucial to any form of local knowledge. In this respect again, any distinction in the field of occult knowledge seems to be precarious and constantly shifting. There may be good reasons to doubt whether Ralushai's disciplinary Act on Traditional Practitioners can ever relate to ambivalences of popular perceptions on healing and protection against occult aggression.

Conclusions: anthropologists, historians and 'superstition'

Despite considerable differences, the two examples above exhibit similar trends: in both cases the state became, through its interventions against witchcraft, caught in the ambivalences of the local discourses on occult forces. In both contexts the local 'healers' turn out to be both indispensable and highly ambiguous allies. Especially because of this collaboration, the offensive of the state and its officials risked becoming counterproductive: it served to strengthen, rather than weaken, the popular panic about a supposed proliferation of ever new forms of witchcraft against which the older sanctions would no longer suffice.

The obvious question is, of course, whether there is a solution? The above might suggest that the state would do better to stay out of this conundrum. After all, its sanctions (jail, fines) are strikingly inept in this tricky field. Moreover, there are alternatives. Chiefs do still retain some of their 'traditional' authority. There are also novel recourses. One of the reasons for the spectacular spread of Pentecostalism in many parts of Africa over the last decades is that it boasts of its ability to tackle witchcraft head-on.[38] Maybe it is better to leave the struggle against witchcraft to such agents.

However, such reservations about the state getting involved reflect very much the view of an outsider. A recent conference in Yaoundé on *Justice and Sorcellerie* at the Catholic University of Central Africa (Yaoundé) offered a graphic illustration of how heavy the pressure on the State is to do something about witchcraft running wild. Probably a pragmatic approach is more promising than the kind of 'paradigmatic change' of the law proposed by several authors who are looking for solutions at an 'ontological level'.[39] Such principled approaches might only prove that the spirit of the law is indeed impossible to reconcile with local discourses, while practical compromises do seem possible.[40]

For our discussions in this volume it might be more relevant to return to the notion of 'superstition' and its relevance for these kind of issues. I am

[38] Instead of denying its reality as the estbalished churches do (who seem therefore unable to deal with it in the eyes of the population). See B. Meyer, *Translating the Devil—Religion and Modernity among the Ewe in Ghana* (Edinburgh, 1999). One may wonder to what extent Pentecostals will be able to stay out of the vicious circles of witchcraft discourse. E.g. in Nigeria, there seems to be a rapid increase of rumours about the involvement of the more successful preachers in pacts with witches or Satan himself to get rich.

[39] See Hund, 'Witchcraft and Witchcraft Accusations in South Africa'; and also H. Ludsin, 'Cultural Denial: What South Africa's Treatment of Witchcraft Says for the Future of Its Customary Law', *Berkeley Journal of International Law* 21:1, 62–111.

[40] See Comaroff and Comaroff, 'Criminal Justice, Cultural Justice'.

afraid that the above suggests that in this context especially the problematic aspects of this notion come to the fore. It is, for instance, not a very helpful concept if one wants to discuss these popular anxieties with the people involved. My more educated Cameroonian friends will invariably protest that they do not understand why witchcraft is labelled 'superstition' while believing in angels or Zen Buddhism are not. As indicated already in my Introduction, anthropologists have increasingly accepted that in order to understand the power of such beliefs, one has at least to take them seriously, rather than categorically declassify them as superstition—that is, as not real. The postmodern relativization of the notion of reality seems to offer some help here. An obvious answer to the question—constantly posed to the researcher in the field—as to whether (s)he 'believes' in the reality of witchcraft, is that there are more realities than just one and that, after all, each discourse creates its own reality.

However, in practice, this solution works only to a limited extent. In practice, anthropological fieldwork constantly confronts researchers with the fact that some realities are at least more pressing than others. To put it simply: when a good friend seems to be in danger of being lynched because some hotheads got the idea that (s)he is a witch, it is not very satisfying to just cling to the viewpoint that all we can do is study the 'reality of discursive practices'. Rather than retreating into such fairly glib formulas, it might be better to accept that the whole issue of the reality of witchcraft raises dilemmas that are not easily solved for an anthropologist.

Historians will be less often confronted with such dilemmas—at least during their research—since they mostly look at things in retrospect. So the term 'superstition' may pose less of a problem to them. Still, I wonder whether this does not reflect an attitude that has its costs for historical research as well. The term is strongly reminiscent of what Diane Purkiss calls the 'rituals of distanciation' that according to her characterize many historical studies of the witchcraft craze in early-modern Europe. In her (polemical) view such rituals help historians to cling to the empiricism that is so dear to most of them, rather than having to face the worrying question as to whether there was something 'real' in these weird 'fantasies', and how they could get such a hold over people.

> Rather than trying to understand how witch-beliefs were structured for and by the believer, historians have often bent their energies towards explaining witch-beliefs away. Assuming witch-beliefs were an abnormality and a pathology, they sought to explain how such ideas could have arisen, rather than what those ideas were . . . . The only serious question to be asked about witchcraft, it seems,

is still 'why, oh why?', perhaps only because this question is distancing.[41]

It is interesting to compare here with anthropologist Michael Taussig's vivid plea that the only way to understand the hold such images can get over people's minds is to 'go along with them'—a principle that made this anthropologist participate in the ecstatic *yagué* sessions of his Amazonian shaman. *Yagué* is a drug that has quite violent effects (through all the bodily openings) and the book Taussig wrote about all this is clearly an attempt to convey this violence in writing—without much patience with academic rules. Still, it remains one of the most influential anthropological monographs of our times. Clearly, we have come some distance away from the notion of 'superstition'.

---

[41] Diane Purkiss, *The Witch in History, Early Modern and Twentieth-Century Presentations* (London, 1996), 61. It is interesting to compare this comment with Briggs' seminal overview of historical work on witchcraft in early-modern Europe (R. Briggs, *Witches and Neighbours, The Social and Cultural Context of European Witchcraft* (London, 1996). Briggs comes to very interesting conclusions on the role of neighbourhood and other topics. But, to an anthropologist, it is striking that the whole book consistently downplays the force of these representations. Briggs starts from an opposition—apparently unproblematic for him—between false and real, and he tries to show that, after all, not that many people believed in these strange convictions, that there was general scepticism. However, it is important not to exaggerate the contrast between anthropology and history on this point. Favret-Saada, *Les mots*, is also ironical about the tendency of many anthropologists to keep a safe distance from the convictions of the people they study. Yet, anthropologists seem to follow different 'rituals of distanciation', notably by emphasizing the 'otherness' of 'their' people (see J. Fabian, *Time and the Other: How Anthropology Makes Its Object* (New York, 1983). More recently, anthropologists tend to emphasize the role of scepticism in African societies vis-à-vis witchcraft rumours (see, e.g., H. West, *Ethnographic Sorcery* [Chicago, 2007]; and Geschiere, *Modernity of Witchcraft*), though for them this emphasis has very different implications from Briggs' interpretation of witchcraft in Europe. For anthropologists the prevalence of scepticism is certainly no ground for doubting the omnipresence and force of witchcraft in the societies they study.

List of Contributors

Michael D. Bailey is Assistant Professor of History, Iowa State University.

T. H. Barrett is Professor of East Asian History at the School of Oriental and African Studies University of London.

Stephen Bowd is Lecturer in European History, University of Edinburgh.

Hugh Bowden is Senior Lecturer in Classics and Ancient History at King's College, London.

Lauren Derby is Assistant Professor of History, University of California at Los Angeles.

Simon Dixon is Professor of Modern History, University of Leeds.

Peter Geschiere is Professor of African Anthropology, University of Amsterdam.

Richard Gordon is Honorary Professor of the History of Religions in Antiquity at the University of Erfurt in Germany.

Alan Knight is Professor of the History of Latin America, University of Oxford.

Basile Ndjio is Visiting Fellow in the African Studies Centre, University of Leiden.

Alison Rowlands is Senior Lecturer in European History, University of Essex.

S. A. Smith is Professor of History at the University of Essex.

Alexandra Walsham is Professor of Reformation History, University of Exeter.

Index